BARGAINING WITH MULTINATIONALS

Bargaining with Multinationals

The Investment of Siemens and Nissan in North-East England

Henry Bernard Loewendahl

palgrave

First published 2001 by
PALGRAVE
Houndmills, Basingstoke, Hampshire RG21 6XS and
175 Fifth Avenue, New York, N.Y. 10010
Companies and representatives throughout the world

PALGRAVE is the new global academic imprint of
St. Martin's Press LLC Scholarly and Reference Division and
Palgrave Publishers Ltd (formerly Macmillan Press Ltd).

ISBN 0–333–94813–0

This book is printed on paper suitable for recycling and made from fully managed and sustained forest sources.

A catalogue record for this book is available from the British Library.

Library of Congress Cataloging-in-Publication Data
Loewendahl, Henry.
   Bargaining with multinationals: the investment of Siemens and Nissan in north-east England / by Henry Bernard Loewendahl.
      p. cm.
   Includes bibliographical references and index.
   ISBN 0–333–94813–0
   1. International business enterprises—Great Britain. 2. International business enterprises—England—Case studies. 3. Investments, Foreign—Great Britain. 4. International business enterprises— Government policy—Great Britain. 5. Globalization—Economic aspects—Great Britain. I. Title.
   HD2845 .L628 2001
   332.67′3′09428—dc21   2001019441

10   9   8   7   6   5   4   3   2   1
10   09 08 07 06 05 04 03 02 01

Printed and bound in Great Britain by
Antony Rowe Ltd, Chippenham, Wiltshire

The views expressed in this publication are the author's and are not necessarily shared by PricewaterhouseCoopers

Contents

List of Tables

List of Figures

xiii

List of Boxes

Preface

This book scrutinises the relationship between multinational corporations (MNCs) and regional economic development, using an international political economy framework of bargaining between governments and multinational companies. The main focus is on examining how governments can link foreign direct investment (FDI) to economic development. The book is divided into three main parts. Part I analyses the globalisation of production, technology and innovation, and concludes that there are increasing opportunities for locations to benefit from FDI as MNCs move towards a network form organisation. Part II examines the relationship between governments and MNCs, and argues that MNCs are able to extract large incentives from governments due to their greater structural power. A political economy model of bargaining is developed, which is used to analyse Nissan's automotive investment and Siemens' semiconductor investment in the UK. Part III of the book analyses in detail FDI in the UK, and finds that while the UK has been highly successful in attracting inward investment, the lack of an industrial strategy to link FDI with indigenous competitiveness has limited the long-term contribution of FDI to economic development. Regions within the UK have lacked the institutional capability to develop alternatives to attracting FDI. A case study of North-East England is used to examine FDI policy at the regional level, which reveals the growing importance of after-care policies in embedding MNCs and the re-focus of resources towards supporting technology and indigenous companies. The book concludes by recommending a framework to integrate endogenous and exogenous approaches to development and proposes a greater role for the region and the European Union (EU) to control investment incentives and monitor multinationals.

HENRY BERNARD LOEWENDAHL

Acknowledgements

First of all I would like to thank Volkswagen and the Institute for German Studies for the scholarship which enabled me to study for the PhD from which this book is the outcome. I would like to thank all the people I interviewed for their insights and valuable time without which this book would not have been possible. I would particularly like to thank the Northern Development Company for inviting me into their organisation to conduct research and for their full support and co-operation.

HENRY BERNARD LOEWENDAHL

List of Abbreviations

ABB	Asea Brown Boveri
ACEA	Association des Constructeurs Européens d'Automobiles
ASEAN	Association of South East Asian Nations
ASIC	Application Specific Integrated Circuit
CCMC	The Committee of Common Market Automobile Constructors
DM	Deutschemark
DRam	Dynamic Random Access Memory Chip
DTI	Department of Trade and Industry
EC	European Community
ECU	European Currency Unit
EEC	European Economic Community
ESPRIT	European Strategic Programme for R&D in Information Technologies
EU	European Union
FDI	Foreign Direct Investment
G-5	Group of Five (France, Germany, Japan, UK, US)
GATT	General Agreement of Tariffs and Trade
GDP	Gross Domestic Product
GM	General Motors
GNP	Gross National Product
GO–NE	Government Office–North-East
IBB	Invest in Britain Bureau
IBM	International Business Machines
IC	Integrated Circuit
ICI	Imperial Chemical Industries
ICTs	Information and Communications Technology
IDA	Irish Development Agency
IDU	Industrial Development Unit
IFA	Invest in Frame Agency
IMF	International Monetary Fund
IPE	International Political Economy
IT	Information Technology
IT&T	Information Technology and Telecommunications
JESSI	Joint European Submicron Silicon Initiative
JETRO	Japanese External Trade Organisation
JIT	Just-in-Time

LG	Lucky Goldstar
M&A	Mergers and Acquisitions
MAI	Multilateral Agreement on Investment
M-form	Multidivisional-Form
MIT	Massachusetts Institute of Technology
MITI	Ministry of International Trade and Industry
MNC	Multinational Corporation
MNE	Multinational Enterprise
NAFTA	North American Free Trade Agreement
NDC	Northern Development Company
N-form	Network-form
NMUK	Nissan Motor Manufacturing UK
NTB	Non-Tariff-Barrier
OECD	Organisation for Economic Co-operation and Development
OEMs	Ordered-Export Manufacturers
OLI	Ownership-Location-Internalisation
ONS	Office of National Statistics
OPEC	Organisation of Petroleum Exporting Countries
PMT	Project Management Team
PROBE	Promotion of Business Excellence
R&D	Research and Development
RDA	Regional Development Agency
RDG	Regional Development Grant
RDO	Regional Development Organisation
RED	Regional Economic Development
RSA	Regional Selective Assistance
RSO	Regional Supply Office
SCAT	Supply-Chain Assessment Tool
SDA	Scottish Development Agency
SEL	Standard Elektrik Lorenz
SEM	Single European Market
SEMATECH	Semiconductor Manufacturing Technology (Consortium)
SMEs	Small and Medium Sized Enterprises
SWOT	Strengths, Weaknesses, Opportunities, Threats
TCEs	Transaction Cost Economics
TEC	Training and Enterprise Council
TI	Texas Instruments
TNC	Transnational Corporation
TOP	Time-Optimised Processes
VER	Voluntary Expect Restraint

1 Introduction

Governments across the world have removed restrictions on FDI in order to improve their ability to attract the investment of MNCs. Inward investment is increasingly seen as vital for economic development and growth, and to further encourage companies to invest in their country or region a wide range of investment incentives are offered to MNCs by governments. The incentives on offer to multinationals are increasingly 'negotiatable'. The amount of incentives awarded to companies is therefore determined to a large extent by a bargaining process between the government agency with reponsibility for incentives and the multinational company.

Bargaining is a power relationship, and governments face on the one hand intensifying competition to attract inward investment from other countries and on the other hand increasingly global MNCs that can locate their investment in any one of a number of countries. The incentives offered to MNCs may therefore represent not only attempts to encourage greater inward investment due to the positive impact on economic development but also the greater bargaining power of MNCs.

The aim of this book is to examine the role of inward investment in economic development, and explore how the bargaining relationship between governments and MNCs affects the location of inward investment and the economic benefits to the host country.

1.1 THE STUDY

The interest in examining the role of MNCs in economic development and their relationship with governments stems from two sources. First, prior to starting the PhD from which this study is the outcome,[1] this author studied a Masters degree in international political economy, where the key research focus was Japanese FDI in Asia-Pacific and its contribution to the region's rapid industrialisation. The main finding was that although state policies in the host countries linked inward investment to an economic development strategy, a degree of technological dependency on Japan was emerging, symbolised by persistent and growing bilateral trade deficits (Loewendahl, 1996). Inward FDI was not sufficient for technological advance, which has been identified as the major determinant of economic growth in developed countries (Pianta, 1995), of firm competitiveness (OECD, 1996), and the most dynamic force for change in the international system (Strange, 1988; Lawton, 1997).

In this study we shift the focus to the UK, an industrialised country, with the key objective of examining the role of inward FDI in public policy and economic development. Important research questions are:

(1) What is the role of government inward investment policy in attracting FDI?
(2) How, if at all, has inward investment policy and incentives been linked to an overall industrial strategy to maximise the benefits of FDI?
(3) How do foreign companies contribute to the development of the national technology base?
(4) What are the policy options for linking inward investment to economic development?

Secondly, this author has identified a gap in the existing literature relating to bargaining between MNCs and governments over inward investment, which this study hopes to fill. Key research questions are:

(1) What factors influence the bargaining relationship between governments and MNCs?
(2) What are the implications of bargaining for inward investment and economic development policy?

Inward investment in the United Kingdom is selected as a country case study, with the UK the second largest host for FDI in the world – the most penetrated of the major economies by inward FDI. At the sub-national level, the exposure to inward FDI is even more pronounced with regions like Wales, Scotland and North-East England highly dependent on foreign MNCs for employment and investment. The attraction of inward investment has arguably been *the* major component of the UK government's industrial policy and there is ample ground for investigating the impact of FDI on the economy and the relationship between governments and MNCs at the central and sub-national levels.

Furthermore, examining FDI in the UK is particularly interesting in the European context, as the country remains the biggest host for inward investment in Europe and other European countries are also converging towards the UK's 'open' FDI policy. In addition, many of the pressures facing the UK government and inwardly investing MNCs are intimately connected to changes at the Europe-wide level.

A company case study of Nissan's automotive investment in North-East England is examined in more detail as:

- Nissan succeeded in its demands for a single union plant, which was highly controversial, unprecedented in the UK motor indus-try, and set the stage for the future investment of Honda and Toyota. The new work practices introduced were widely perceived as best-practice and seen as a challenge to British and European producers.
- It was the single largest investment in the UK at a time of severe industrial decline and the investment represented a turning point for the North-East region.
- The lengthy negotiations between Nissan and the UK government were at the centre of academic and media debate, providing many sources from which to examine the bargaining relationship between governments and MNCs.
- The investment signalled the revival of the UK car industry, the emergence of Japan as a major new investor in the UK and, after a period of nearly 15 years, the impact of the investment over time can be assessed.

The negotiations surrounding Siemens' semiconductor investment in North-East England are also examined which highlight the response of German MNCs to intensifying global competition and the conver-gence towards Anglo-Saxon corporate governance. This case study is also particularly significant as:

- Like Nissan before, the project was the biggest greenfield manu-facturing investment in the UK.
- Siemens' investment was in semiconductors, one of fastest growing and technologically complex industries in the world, which has led other industries in the growth of new forms of co-operative FDI.
- The electronics sector as a whole is the world's biggest multi-national industry accounting for 17 of the top 100 MNCs with assets of US$1.1 trillion (UNCTAD, 1995b; 1998).

- The case-study would complement the study of Nissan, with the project taking place 10 years later, revealing changes in the bargaining between the UK government and MNCs.
- Siemens' plant was subsequently closed in 1998, with important implications for inward investment and economic development policy.

Through examining Nissan and Siemens' investment, the North-East is adopted as a regional case study. The North-East is of particular interest as:

- Structural changes in international business and public policy are increasing the importance of the sub-national level of analysis.
- Since Nissan's investment, the North-East has been the most successful region in England in terms of attracting inward FDI but, at the same time, is the poorest region in England and has the highest unemployment in the UK.
- The present crisis in the North-East, following the collapse of many foreign investment projects in 1998, reflects wider global debate about approaches to economic development in peripheral regions and the role of MNCs.
- British research on MNCs and regional development has focused more on Scotland and Wales, with less research on the English regions.
- With the formation in April 1999 of Regional Development Agencies in England, a study of the North-East offers the opportunity to explore the possible implications for the role of inward investment in regional economic development.

1.2   RESEARCH CAVEATS

In examining the role of MNCs in regional economic development (RED) and their relations with governments, a plethora of different bodies of research from various academic disciplines are encountered, each embodying different methodologies, ideologies and balance between theoretical constructs and empirical analysis. Three groups of research have been identified: the first focusing solely on the existence, organisation and management of the MNC (international business studies); the second exploring industrial organisation, spatial location and regional development (economic geography), and the third examining the interaction of governments and firms (government-business relations). However, there has been until very recently little overlap between the groups.

Each strand provides valuable insights into the issues explored by other disciplines and, as will be seen in Chapter 2, there is both a convergence in the key issues being researched and gradually in the theoretical frameworks adopted. A combination or cross-fertilisation of approaches has therefore become crucial not only to capture theoretically and empirically the multi-faceted dimensions of the relationship between MNCs, governments and RED but also to reflect changes taking place within the different bodies of thought.

An important research caveat has, however, been identified by several academics working within the different disciplines; central to understanding the role of MNCs in RED is the bargaining relationship between MNCs and governments (e.g. Stopford and Strange, 1991; Dicken, 1994), and between MNCs and labour (e.g. Mueller and Purcell, 1992; Ietto-Gillies, 1997a). While Ruigrok and van Tulder's excellent 1995 study looked at the impact of bargaining relations in the home country on core firms' internationalisation and various researchers are analysing bargaining between MNCs and labour (e.g. Mueller, 1996; Ferner, 1997), there is little conceptual or empirical work looking at bargaining between MNCs and host country governments. This study will therefore contribute to the third strand of research, government-business relations, building new conceptual and analytical tools and using empirical examples to understand bargaining between MNCs and host country governments.

The approach taken in this study, based on combining different strands of research, often encounters criticism on account of its eclecticism. A counter-argument is that there are problems, difficulties and dangers in 'adopting an overly dogmatic and ideologically pure approach' (Dicken, 1990b: 236). Furthermore, it is necessary to differentiate between two forms of 'eclectic' approach: First, a multi-disciplinary approach, which utilises the approaches of various academic disciplines to find multi-directional explanations to research problems. Secondly, an inter-disciplinary approach which, rather than adopting the 'theoretical baggage' of each discipline, involves 'the selection of a methodology which *transcends rather than reproduces* the boundaries set by academic disciplines' (Cawson *et al.*, 1990: 10–11). An international political economy (IPE) framework will be used in this study to underpin the second, inter-disciplinary approach.

1.3   AN IPE APPROACH

In IPE, the work of Susan Strange has been profoundly influential. Strange argues that economics cannot be separated from politics and that the international level of analysis cannot be separated from the domestic level (Strange, 1988). The processes linking these spheres 'have to be studied and analysed together, and the structures analysed within which the processes takes place' (Strange, 1995: 169).

Structures are a key analytical concept in IPE. They set the agendas and determine the range of options within which states and other groups and individuals contest the central issue of politics; who gets what?, both within the state and in the world economy (Strange, 1991a: 34).[2] Strange (1988) identifies four interdependent structures: finance, production, knowledge and security. The knowledge structure is argued to be of over-arching importance, affecting change in each of the other structures. Central to knowledge is technological advance, which drives structural change (Stopford and Strange, 1991; Lawton, 1997: 231).

Building on the starting point that economic processes involve politics and therefore power (Strange, 1988) and that these processes are interacting with changing structures, Strange differentiates between the exercise of two types of power: *Relational* power – the ability to persuade someone to do something that they would not have done otherwise, and *structural* power – the power to influence structural change and general policy. Strange argues that structural power is often more decisive in influencing outcomes and defines it as a situation:

> in which one actor determines how the game is played, under what rules and conventions... they are able to affect the range of options within which others can choose what to do (1997: 136).

Structural power translates into relational power (Lawton, 1997: 2) and the exercise of structural power is argued in this study to be crucial for understanding the bargaining relationship between states and firms.

In conclusion, IPE is the study of how the total system works and of the social consequences of its functioning (Strange, 1997: 133), which:

> inevitably reunite domestic politics and economics with international politics and economics. Moreover, it cannot realistically be done without locating both governments and enterprises within

the ever-changing structures of power that make up the international political economy at any one time (Strange, 1991a: 48–9).

International political economy as an area of investigation, a particular range of questions asked and a series of assumptions (Murphy and Tooze, 1991), offers several advantages for examining the intersection of MNCs, governments and RED:

- Recent developments in IPE offer a critical framework or method of analysis, pointing out that as there can be no all-embracing theory (Cox, 1981; Strange, 1988), carefully combining and selecting from various approaches, based on context specificity and the underlying questions of who gets what, how and why?, is crucial in order to understand the complex world.
- IPE argues that theory must examine the interaction between the international and domestic levels and the importance of structural changes in influencing the outcomes of these interactions. IPE therefore reflects the emphasis on the multi-level and dynamic relationship between MNCs, governments and regional economies in this study. Only through analysing structural changes can we understand how this relationship has changed over time.
- IPE breaks down the distinction between 'politics' and 'economics'. The fusion of economics and politics facilitates an understanding of the internal organisation and strategy of MNCs and their relationship with the external environment.
- Central to IPE is the exercise of power, an analysis of which is crucial to understanding bargaining – in our case primarily between MNCs and governments, but also between MNCs and labour.

The perspective of IPE will therefore act as the general framework for this study, a critical lens through which the complex relationship between MNCs, governments and regional economic development can be analysed.

IPE directs research towards examining the two-way relationship between structural changes and international and domestic processes, with the exercise of power and role of the state central. IPE helps us define four levels of analysis pivotal to this study:

- *Structural changes*: to understand the organisation and strategies of MNCs we must examine the dynamics of the broader system within which they operate. These dynamics are pervasively influenced by the knowledge structure, in particular through technological change.

- *Multinational companies*: transformations in the production and knowledge structure and related changes in corporate organisation and strategy coincide with changes in the spatial distribution of production and in part determine the economic position and scope for action of regions.
- *The local level*: the performance of MNCs and national economies depends on the local milieu (Belussi, 1996; Maskell *et al.*, 1998), especially for the exchange of tacit knowledge and for innovation (Tödtling, 1994; Braczyk and Heidenreich, 1998).
- *The state*: concrete spatial outcomes reflect state policy and bargaining within and between MNCs and states – necessarily a power relationship.

The analytical framework of this study is based, therefore, on the hypothesis that the organisation and strategy of MNCs is conditioned by forces operating at two levels, structural and local, with the state the key mediating force operating between these two levels. The interaction of these forces plays the major role in determining the prospects and path of economic development.

1.4   OVERVIEW

Through the use of IPE as a framework, this study can be divided into three parts:

- The globalisation of production, technology and innovation, which examines the impact of structural changes on multinational companies, FDI and economic development (Chapters 2–4).
- The bargaining relationship between governments and MNCs, with case studies of Nissan and Siemens (Chapters 5–8).
- Inward investment policy and the impact of FDI on economic development (Chapters 9–11).

The key theoretical approaches are discussed in Chapter 2. The contribution of each approach to understanding the relationship between MNCs, governments and RED is highlighted. Three broad groups of approaches are identified – economic geography, international business studies, and government–business relations – each of which points to globalisation and the importance of innovation and network relations for the competitiveness of MNCs, countries and regions. Conceptually, MNCs are recognised to be diverse, political institutions.

These insights are used to understand globalisation, which is argued to be driven by three key structural changes: intensifying competition, technological advance and regional economic integration. The main argument is that globalisation comprises both internationalisation and interdependence and that the structural changes driving globalisation do not indicate stateless firms or the end of the nation state, but rather point to globalisation as a differentiated process, which will lead to opportunities for some localities but not for others.

In Chapter 3 the investment location decision-making process in MNCs is examined and the key factors determining investment location are analysed. Existing theories of MNCs do not explain why one country is selected in preference to another and a new model of investment location is developed based on understanding the conditions which enable firms to become multinational, the strategy of the firm, and the project-specific location requirements. The role of incentives in investment decision-making are examined and it is argued that they can and do influence the location of investment.

In Chapter 4, trends in FDI over the last century are analysed, and it is seen how FDI has shifted from developing to developed countries reflecting the evolution of MNC investment strategies from resource-seeking to efficiency and especially market-seeking FDI. Using empirical data, the globalisation of technology, which reflects the emergence of asset-seeking MNC strategies is examined. Asset-seeking FDI, and FDI in general, is dominated by merger and acquisition (M&A) activity and cross-border collaboration between MNCs. One of the major motivations for these new forms of investment is to exploit, access and co-operate in the development of technology, indicating intensifying globalisation of technology. Data on research and development (R&D) and patents also suggests that there is a steady internationalisation of technology and innovation.

We argue that countries and localities with a strong technological base can attract the R&D activities of MNCs, especially with the emergence of the network-form (N-form) as the ideal type MNC to respond to globalisation. The N-form develops networking relations globally to leverage firm capabilities and exploit opportunities and, after giving a brief overview of the evolving organisation of MNCs, we use the example of the multinational ABB to illustrate empirically the

N-form MNC. Drawing on Bartlett and Ghoshal (1989), the differentiated roles of subsidiaries in the N-form are outlined, pointing-to the impact of multinational strategies and organisation on regional development.

In Chapter 5 the changing relationship between governments and MNCs is discussed and the impact of structural changes on governments inward investment policy is examined. The greater cross-border mobility of MNCs, their increasing control over core technologies, and the increasing importance of FDI in national economies, has led to MNCs having asymmetrical structural power. Empirical evidence is presented indicating that MNCs are bargaining for ever higher government investment incentives, despite government and academic rhetoric suggesting that governments have shifted away from direct subsidisation of industry and discrimination between firms. Regional integration is identified as a key structural change increasing the ability of MNCs to bargain for incentives.

Drawing on the political economy and the bargaining literature, in Chapter 6 a bargaining model is developed to analyse negotiations between MNCs and host country governments. We argue that the key factors determining the bargaining process and outcome are the alternatives and commitment of each actor to the resources controlled by the other. However, to interpret a bargaining relationship the institutional structure and interest structure of each actor are crucial in determining negotiating ability and the conversion of potential bargaining power into actual power and control over outcomes.

The bargaining model is used to examine in detail Nissan's investment in the UK and negotiations with the UK government in Chapter 7. The importance of conceptualising the political economy of bargaining is revealed, with the negotiations infused by interest group pressures. The impact of Nissan on the UK economy is examined, and it is argued that the impact has been very positive in terms of exports, production, and the supply industry, although there are doubts over the quality of the jobs created. Nissan also encouraged the investment of Honda and Toyota, and combined the Japanese producers appear to have reversed the decline of the UK automobile industry. It is concluded, though, that the future of Nissan and other Japanese manufacturing FDI in the UK may depend on the UK remaining at the centre of European economic and political integration.

Siemens' investment in the North-East is analysed in Chapter 8, and the bargaining model is used to examine the negotiations with the UK government. Strong mutual dependence and few political constraints allowed the negotiations to proceed much more smoothly than in the case of Nissan. The negotiations also highlighted how the professional facilitation services provided by an inward investment agency (the Invest in Britain Bureau and NDC) can increase the probability of winning a major investment project.

Siemens' investment, it is argued, must be seen as part of the company's 'Anglo-Saxon' globalisation strategy, as much as trends in the semiconductor industry and the project specific location advantages of the UK. The Tyneside investment was intended to send a message to the managers in Germany that Siemens was now a global firm, whose key objective is share-holder value. It is therefore important to understand the corporate strategy of the firm when examining the location of FDI. The investment, though, collapsed in 1998, in part due to the classic 'silicon cycle' and the corporate restructuring that Siemens would initiate to achieve share-holder value. The example of Daimler Benz is used to illustrate further the globalisation of German multinationals and the shift towards Anglo-Saxon governance, which Siemens is now following.

The collapse of the Tyneside investment reveals the contradictions in UK industrial policy. While the government saw Siemens' 'high-tech' 'flagship' investment as an indication of the competitiveness of the UK economy, the case of Siemens shows the inherent problems of an inward investment policy that has no strategic or sectoral component. There is no collaboration between central and regional government to build-up centres of research and manufacturing expertise, or ensure linkages between FDI and local industry. Siemens would not depend on an existing supply or research infrastructure in the North-East and there were limited possibilities for integration into the regional economy. Siemens only sunk cost was its capital outlay, leaving the region vulnerable to changes in corporate strategy and market forces.

In Chapter 9, trends in FDI in the UK are analysed and the inward investment policy of the British government is examined. Although the high level of outward FDI has reduced the willingness of the government to regulate inward FDI, the UK's historically open FDI policy and reliance on inward investment as the principal component of industrial policy reflected the Conservative government's non-intervention ideology and the weakness of the domestic manufacturing base. The negative influence of the City and the role of the military have weakened the UK's national system of innovation, leaving fewer alternatives to attracting inward FDI as well as reducing the quality of inward investment. FDI in the UK is both less research intensive and has lower value added than FDI in other countries and foreign MNCs in the UK are also less research intensive than indigenous industry. The emphasis of recent industrial policy on technology and small and medium-sized enterprises (SMEs) is discussed, and it is concluded that the effectiveness of these policies depends on the ability to integrate industrial, technology, education and regional policy.

Regional policy is discussed in more detail in Chapter 10, when FDI in the UK regions and development policy at the regional level is analysed, and regional investment incentives are looked at in particular detail. Control by central government and the transfer of power to centrally controlled quangos has left little policy autonomy at the regional and local levels. Regional policy has therefore followed the emphasis of central government on attracting inward investment, and peripheral regions have used the key instrument of investment incentives to attract FDI. These incentives have been based on job creation and, in combination with the bargaining power of MNCs, incentives have favoured labour-intensive inward investment over higher value added activities or SMEs. This is a key reason for the high vulnerability to closure of FDI in peripheral regions. While the new Regional Development Agencies, set-up in 1999, will go some way towards facilitating a more endogenously driven development policy, the English regions need greater political autonomy if they are to have the legitimacy to develop and implement economic development strategies.

In Chapter 11, inward investment in North-East England is analysed. Japanese FDI has made a larger contribution in terms of job creation and capital investment than either German or US FDI, but the region is dependent on the performance of Nissan, especially with the collapse of Siemens and Fujitsu. The vulnerability to plant closure led the Northern Development Company to re-direct its emphasis from luring inward investment to supporting existing investors through after-care and supply-chain initiatives. However, with the failure of FDI to improve the relative competitiveness of the region and with increasing emphasis on innovation, in the second half of the 1990s the NDC began to favour supporting SMEs and R&D over inward investors. This policy shift is reinforced by the new regional development agencies (RDAs). However, technology policy in the region is fragmented, with little support for SMEs or raising the R&D of multinationals. RDAs must integrate inward investment and technology policy with a regional economic strategy and link this strategy to the financial incentives allocated to companies. Partnership in the region is a necessity, which may favour the establishment of a legitimate tier of democratically elected regional government to whom the RDAs would be accountable.

In the conclusion in Chapter 12 the findings relating to the role of inward investment in regional development and bargaining with multinationals are summarised. Policy recommendations are provided for linking FDI to an endogenous approach for regional development. It is recommended that a new strategic framework is put in place involving five integrated policy dimensions: technology, SMEs and training, after-care, a targeted FDI strategy, a new incentive system, and a new institutional structure for FDI at the national and EU levels to balance the bargaining power of MNCs. Some theoretical reflections are also outlined, and our main contributions to original research and several topics for further research are suggested.

Part I

Globalisation of Production, Technology and Innovation

2 Theoretical Approaches and Structural Changes

In recent years many commentators have emphasised the need for an inter-disciplinary understanding of the multi-faceted nature and impact of MNCs[1] that combines insights from different bodies of thought. In this chapter several theoretical approaches are drawn on and three structural changes (international competition, technological change, and regional integration) are identified, which are argued to be the key drivers of change in international business and are central to understanding the implications of MNCs for economic development.

These structural changes underpin the changing relationship between MNCs, governments and economic development, and are integral to transformations in corporate strategy and public policy. It is argued that MNCs are moving towards network-based relations as the ideal-type organisational structure for responding to and benefiting from globalisation. Governments, in particular in sub-national regions – the key spatial unit for economic growth (Porter, 1990a; Ohmae, 1995; Maskell *et al.*, 1998) – are also moving towards fostering network based relations.

2.1 THEORETICAL APPROACHES

Three distinct groups of theoretical approaches have been identified, which make it easier to understand the different levels of analysis (structural changes, MNCs, the local level, and the state) explored in this study. The first group is defined here broadly as *economic geography*. Approaches in this group include:

- regulation theory;
- flexible specialisation;
- japan school;
- agglomeration/cluster theory;
- evolutionary/innovation theory.

The second group is concerned with the organisation and strategy of the MNC per se. This group is defined as *international business studies*, and includes:

- transaction cost economics;
- management theory of the MNC;
- labour theory of the MNC.

The final group includes approaches concerned with *government–business relations*:

- government–industry relations;
- government–MNC relations.

The approaches in the first group are outlined in Table 2.1 and Table 2.2 outlines the approaches of the other two groups. The tables indicate some of the main contributors to each body of thought, the core propositions of each approach and the organisational and economic development implications.

There is considerable over-lap between the approaches, particularly *within* each of the three groups. The objective of this chapter is to explain why a cross-fertilisation *between* the groups is crucial in order to explain the activities of MNCs and their relationship with governments and economic development. Only by combining the contributions of each approach can a theoretical and empirical understanding of the four levels of analysis that underpin this study be developed.

2.1.1   Economic geography

The economic geography approaches in Table 2.1 are broadly concerned with the spatial impact of changing industrial processes. Regulation theory, flexible specialisation and the Japan school argue that since the 1970s there has been a transformation in industrial organisation based on production flexibility (Lung, 1992; Morris and Wilkinson, 1995).

Each approach focuses on different aspects of industrial organisation and different spatial levels. While the regulation school concentrates on system-wide transformations and the implications for state policy and sub-national regions, flexible specialisation is concerned with networks operating at the industrial district level, and the role of institutions in economic development. Both see flexible technologies as central to new forms of industrial organisation, whereas the Japan school, who are

Table 2.1 Approaches to economic geography

Approach	Core propositions	Organisation	Spatial implications
Regulation school Aglietta (1976); Lipietz (1986a,b); Moulaert *et al.* (1988); Schoenberger (1988); Boyer (1990); Stoker (1990); Moulaert and Swyngedouw (1991); Altvater (1992); Jessop (1992, 1994, 1995); Goodwin and Painter (1995); Hay (1995); Peck and Tickell (1995); DiGiovanna (1996)	Focus is on capitalism and the transition between institutionally co-ordinated modes of social regulation (MSR) involving concrete struggles, underpinned by the state. From the 1970s, the end of US hegemony, deflationary state policy, globalisation, a defence of real wages, and reaching the technical limits of the labour process led to crisis in the Fordist MSR. The restructuring disciplines labour	Fordism-post Fordism dichotomy. Crisis of mass production, with inflation, falling profits, productivity and high unemployment, is giving way to a new regime of flexible accumulation. Adaptability and sensitivity to volatility and rise in competition require flexible technologies, organisations and labour practices. Also need stability and regulation, achieved at all levels, and compatible with the wage relation	Fordist over-accumulation led to FDI to access new markets and cheap labour, heightening competition. Post Fordism's new flexibility increases inter-firm links, and leads to vertical dis-integration. A tighter, more specialised spatial organisation results. The old MSR was national, the emerging MSR is local, with greater role for sub- and supra-national levels. But MNCs may limit local autonomy
Flexible specialisation Piore and Sabel (1984); Sabel (1989); Streeck (1989); King (1990); Sabel *et al.* (1991); Hirst and Zeitlin (1992); Jessop (1992); Saxenian (1992); Herrigel (1993)	Distinction between mass and flexible or craft production. Saturated markets for standardised goods favour SMEs, industrial districts and networks. Non-market, trust-based exchanges, and a 'public sphere' of institutionalised co-operation blur economy and society	SMEs operating through horizontal networks can offer high quality, innovative, customised goods, and have the flexibility to respond to volatile markets. Flexible technologies and high skills facilitate the dis-integration of hierarchies and network-based organisation	Firms and territories increase flexibility and specialisation in heterarchical industrial districts. Regions face opportunities with technological advance, but need for access to external innovation milieus, may change nature of districts. MNCs functionally decentralise

Japan school Womack *et al.* (1990); Lung (1992); Morris (1992b); Mair (1993); Cooke and Morgan (1994); Tomaney (1994b); Humphrey (1995); MacDuffie (1995); Dyer (1996a); Streeck (1996); Masayuki (1998)	Success of Japanese firms is premised on lean production, or flexible mass production, based on the integration of design and manufacture, and of suppliers and workers into JIT and TQC systems, led by the auto industry. Flexible, high productivity, high quality, low cost output results. Incremental innovation is facilitated	Production flexibility is achieved through dis-integration with segmented vertical supplier networks. Relations with suppliers are trust-based and involve co-operation, joint learning, devolving of design activities, and access to cheaper labour. Team-based work practices are at heart of production flexibility and innovation	Interdependence within the firm and externally, with tightly-knit logistic and innovation systems, favours proximity. New supplier relations may allow transfer of JIT and TQC globally, but heterogeneous institutions and cultures limit transfer of work practices. Core firms keep control of network, limiting regional autonomy
Agglomeration/cluster Marshall (1890); Vernon (1966); Porter (1990a, 1996, 1998); Storper (1995); Asheim (1996); Markusen (1996); Oughton and Whittam (1997); Pyke (1997b); Maskell *et al.* (1998)	Spatial clustering of similar or related activities leads to economies of proximity – specialised skills, inputs and services and knowledge spill-overs. Proximity reduces transaction costs, increases efficiency, effectiveness and flexibility. Urban and dynamic economies arise, the latter based on learning and innovation	Non-market, vertical and horizontal social networks link firms, infrastructure and supporting institutions, compensating for market failure in knowledge transfer. Clusters are in-between market and hierarchy. Industrial districts are favoured by SMEs, reducing opportunistic behaviour and pooling capabilities	Leads to national and regional specialisation. Flows of information and goods are greatly facilitated by reciprocity and trust, fostered by proximity. Clusters emerge, often by chance, and became major centres through self-reinforcement. MNCs diffuse functions and product lines to these centres but not to others

Table 2.1 (*continued*)

Approach	Core propositions	Organisation	Spatial implications
Evolution/innovation Nelson and Winter (1982); Lundvall (1992); Nelson (1994); ed., (1993); Freeman (1995); Belussi (1996); Hassink (1996); Varaldo and Ferucci (1996); Braczyk *et al.* (1998); Cooke and Morgan (1998)	Firms are dynamic, learning entities, with heterogeneous histories, routines and strategies reflecting responses to uncertainty and external influences. Innovation and knowledge are key to competitiveness, achieved through the non-linear processes of learning by doing, using, interacting and learning by learning	Innovation involves interdependence with other firms and institutions. The creation and diffusion of (tacit) knowledge favours cohesive heterarchical, networked and trust relations for SMEs and MNCs. Both benefit from industrial districts, but complexity of innovation may lead to path dependence and lock-in	Evolutionary firms and institutions lead to spatial diversity of innovation systems. Innovation is highly concentrated, in the MNCs home base. But move to heterarchical forms, with faster technological advance and competition, leads to simultaneous innovation and diffusion to certain centres of excellence

Table 2.2 Approaches to international business studies and government–business relations

Approach	Core propositions	Organisation	Spatial implications
Transaction cost economics Coase (1937, 1960); Hymer (1959); Williamson (1975); Buckley and Casson (1976, 1985); Dunning (1977); Caves (1982); Hennart (1989, 1991)	Focus on firm ownership and FDI. Multi-activity is explained through transaction costs. Firms are atomistic, rational and grow as they reduce transaction costs, internalising factor and product market imperfections. All actors and constraints are given. The firm is ahistorical	The firm is analysed in a vacuum, independent of other actors. Choice is between the market or hierarchy. New technology, innovation processes, volatility and need for flexibility may increase internal governance costs, leading to de-internalisation and network relations	If the benefits of internalisation outweigh the costs, and advantages of intangible specific assets offset costs of FDI, MNCs emerge. No differentiation between parent and affiliates, with perfect diffusion of specific advantages. Implies that host countries benefit from FDI
Management Chandler (1962); Hofstede (1980); Porter (1986); Prahalad and Doz (1987); Bartlett and Ghoshal (1989, 1993a); Ohmae (1990); Ghoshal and Westney (1993); Edwards et al. (1996); Edwards (1998a, 1998b); Goold and Campbell (1998); Martin and Beaumont (1998)	MNCs face choices in co-ordinating the centre and affiliates and demands for global efficiency and local responsiveness. Growth of MNCs is evolutionary and heterogeneous. Transnational or heterarchical, federal, network-based forms are emerging using new technologies with advantages in scale, scope, flexibility, innovation and learning. MNCs become more interdependent internally and externally	Competition, mass customisation, technology, and volatility favours a back-to- basics strategy, delayering of management, subcontracting and co-operation for innovation. Forward diffusion (FD), reverse diffusion (RD) and tacit knowledge flow best in heterarchical networks. Cohesion through normative integration is facilitated by bench-marking, socialisation and new global personnel structures	Four forms: 1. Multinational – local autonomy; 2. Global – global integration, minimal local autonomy; 3. International – federal, central control of FD; 4. Transnational – global linking and leverage of innovation, learning, FD and RD from differentiated affiliates through integrated cross-border networks. Specialisation in centres of excellence. External relationships crucial for flexibility, efficiency, and innovation

Labour Cowling and Sugden (1987); Dohse (1987); Mueller and Purcell (1992); Walton *et al.* (1994); Armstrong *et al.* (1995); Ietto-Gillies (1996, 1997a); Marginson and Sisson (1996); Mueller (1996); Ferner (1997)	MNCs are distinguished not by formal ownership but by the control and co-ordination of activities across borders. With liberalisation, regional integration and new technology the flexibility of MNCs increases and together with their control over resources, MNCs have advantages over firms, governments and labour	Multiplant firms increase their bargaining power and fragment unions through divide and rule and punish and reward strategies. Labour problems are externalised by subcontracting and resistance to new working practices is eroded through benchmarking and the mobility of capital. Fostering labour is by socialisation	MNCs have advantages over national firms in flexibility and the diffusion of labour practices. Heterarchical MNCs enhance diffusion. Areas with 'permissive' environments attract new plants and affiliates can play a role in diffusion. But regions and countries face less autonomy, and MNCs maintain centralised control
Government–industry Grant (1982, 1989, 1990); Cawson *et al.* (1987, 1990); Wilks and Wright (1987); Atkinson and Coleman (1989); Hart (1992); Bennet and Krebs (1994); Peterson (1995); Van Ruigrok and Tulder (1995); Lawton (1997)	Industrial policies influence firm decisions to promote policy objectives. Success depends on corporatist consensus and policy communities. Networks link actors to establish and implement coherent objectives. Firms ensure their interest is provided for, but networks involve power relations and must mediate interest pressures	An autonomous agency with a clearly defined, functional responsibility and value system and independent access to expertise and information maximises bargaining power in networks. Collaboration with firms is critical to industrial politics, but EU integration, globalisation, and technical change increase the power of firms	Complex plurality of actors and issues favours networks at the sub-national level with a shared common focus and ability to support individual projects, especially important for declining regions. Industrial policy networks are increasingly supra-national. Key influence on FDI is home networks and bargaining sphere

Table 2.2 (*continued*)

Approach	Core propositions	Organisation	Spatial implications
Government–MNC Moran (1974, 1993, 1996); Julius (1990); Reich (1990); Sugden (1990a,b); Dunning (1992a, 1993b); Safarian (1993); Boddewyn and Brewer (1994); Heintz (1994); Lenway and Murtha (1994a,b); Sally (1994); Kozul-Wright (1995)	Nations and MNCs are not monolithic or unified actors. Interplay of interest groups, networks and external environment determine state and MNC policy. Global MNC strategies increase their influence on direction, content and outcome of public policy. Negotiation process is integral to outcomes. Bargaining premised on asymmetry of intensifying mutual interdependence	Economic perspective helps elucidate path of government–MNC bargaining, but outcomes reflect perceptions, relative autonomy and political constraints. State perceptions have become more open to MNCs with structural changes. Centralised organisations increase bargaining ability, but the influence of interest groups depends on corporatist policy networks	At the regional level, the supply-side infrastructure, incentive package and after-care are often crucial for the MNCs' investment decision. At the national, or ultimately supra-national level a centralised agency, negotiating with MNCs improves the states bargaining position. Increasing competition from other localities and countries also affects negotiations

also interested in explaining a new hegemonic method of production (lean production), focus more on flexible work practices and the integration of functions within and between large firms and suppliers.

The three approaches argue that horizontal and vertical networks linking SMEs to each other and to large firms, production and market flexibility, the development and diffusion of innovations and flows of knowledge increase the importance of the local level. However, to explain economic development at the local level, they draw on agglomeration/cluster theory and evolutionary/innovation theory.

These latter two approaches argue that the local level is crucial for learning and innovation, but also that economic activity is likely to be specialised and unevenly distributed. Cluster theory focuses more on sectors and industries, and emphasises the importance of competitive rivalry, spatial proximity and clusters of suppliers and customers,[2] while evolutionary innovation theory concentrates on firm dynamics and the interdependence between the firm and other firms and institutions. Like flexible specialisation, industrial districts are argued to be the key spatial level for learning and innovation.

As research has demonstrated (Powell and Smith-Doerr, 1994; Storper, 1995; Cooke, 1997), the insights of each approach need to be incorporated to understand the changing industrial organisation of MNCs and the spatial implications for economic development. Economic geography broadly argues that:

- Economic development in the late 1980s and 1990s was driven by productivity improvements and flexible production, and the most successful locations were those that could benefit from re-engineering and the lean production techniques demonstrated by Japanese firms in particular. Through large-scale rationalisation of industry and attracting Japanese companies, the UK was able to reverse previous economic decline relative to mainland Europe. Emerging economies in East Asia achieved rapid economic growth based on high quality, high productivity export-based production.

- At the same time, sub-national regions in countries like Italy and Germany achieved economic development based on a strong SME sector, with extensive links between small firms, large firms and other institutions, in particular research establishments, with a strong co-ordinating or broker role for state bodies. However, regions traditionally based on indigenous SMEs and large companies are placing increasing emphasis on attracting foreign

MNCs, and the challenge for economic development in these regions is to support the continued success of the SME sector through integrating SMEs into the networks of MNCs.

- The key spatial unit for economic development is at the regional, local or cluster level. The most successful examples of cluster-based development, such as the Silicon Valley in the US and the high-tech cluster in Cambridge, UK, revolve around a world-class research infrastructure. Cluster development depends crucially on the research infrastructure, competitive environment, and institutions supporting the flows of information and knowledge. However, clusters have initially developed by chance, rather than by a pro-active government policy.

- In the late 1990s and into the 21st century, the key driver of economic development, especially in developed countries, is shifting from efficiency based productivity increases to innovation driven productivity growth. Vital to innovation is access to and combination of R&D in centres of excellence around the world and an environment that supports entreprenuership, risk-taking and access to venture capital – as embodied in institutions supporting innovation and cultural attitudes.

2.1.2 International business studies

Turning to the second broad group, international business studies, Dicken *et al.* (1994: 29) observe that while the international business literature do not use the same terms as the economic geography approaches discussed above, they have the same strong emphasis. They incorporate rather than explain structural changes such as the growth of competition, market volatility, mass customisation, and the importance of flexibility, learning and innovation. The explanatory emphasis is narrowly focused on the internal organisation and strategies of MNCs.

Transaction cost economics (TCEs) has spawned an enormous amount of literature relating to the ownership of multi-plant firms, and the trade-off between hierarchies and markets, of which Dunning's OLI (*ownership, location and internalisation*) paradigm is perhaps the most well-known. The OLI paradigm has been adopted as the main explanatory framework for FDI by both the European Community (EC) (1998) and UNCTAD (1993). Transaction costs help to explain why firms internalise certain activities across borders rather than licensing or exporting (I-advantages), and point to the importance of analysing the firm-specific advantages of MNCs

(O-advantages) and the location advantages of the host country (L-advantages) in order to understand different types of FDI and favoured locations (see Dunning, 1977; 1981; 1988). Drawing on Hymer (1959), TCEs argue that product and factor-market imperfections open the door to FDI. However, TCEs is limited in terms of explaining the diversity and complexity of firm organisation and strategy, power and network relations between firms and other actors, as well as learning and innovation (Cooke, 1998b; Mucchielli, 1991).

Although the management approach to MNCs has been quite distinct from TCEs, focusing on the international strategies and co-ordination processes within heterogeneous MNCs, managerial theories counter some of the main weaknesses of TCEs. In particular, they explore how changes in the external environment influence firm strategy and examine relations between corporate headquarters, subsidiaries and labour. The MNC is analysed as a political actor, by necessity rather than as part of an intentional conceptualisation, involved in internal and external power relations.

During the 1990s there has been some convergence, with both TCEs and managerial theory emphasising the importance for firm competitiveness of flexibility, learning, innovation and the utilisation of new technologies in the context of international liberalisation and regional integration. While TCEs argue that these new sources of competitive advantage increase the costs of hierarchies and managerial theory argues that heterarchical MNCs are more responsive, facilitate the diffusion of knowledge, and that MNCs with multi-plant activities and subcontracting relations increase their bargaining ability, the outcome is the same: the dis-integration of MNC activities, globalisation and the growth of networking relationships.

Approaches to international business have not explicitly considered the implications of their theories and empirical research for economic development. However, the implications of each approach are very different. Traditional approaches to the MNC, as represented by Dunning's OLI paradigm, do not differentiate between the subsidiaries of MNCs domestically or internationally. They see the MNC as a homogenous, autonomous actor that makes calculated decisions based on transaction costs and business fundamentals. The MNC does not interact with non-firm actors, and there is no role for government policy to pro-actively influence the diffusion of activities between parts of the MNC. The implication is that the impact of MNCs on host countries is also homogenous and in general is perceived to be highly beneficial. Host countries benefit from the transfer of the same ownership advantages (such as new technologies, access to markets, and better management practices), that allow the company to internationalise in the first place.

At the other extreme, labour approaches see the MNC as a political actor, using its power advantages over governments and workers to exploit their multinationality. These approaches are most explicit in the implications for economic development. They argue that MNCs influence government policy to serve their interests, with investment subsidies a key example, and at the same time lower labour standards and the quality of work life for employees working in MNCs and in particular in host country subsidiaries and subcontracting firms.

Management approaches to the MNC have totally disregarded the implications of their research for economic development. However, we can infer from their research several powerful implications for economic development. The work spear-headed by Bartlett and Ghoshal (1989) argues that MNCs are evolving from global, multi-national and international organisation types to the transnational organisational form. It can be inferred that:

- *The global form* offers minimal scope for economic development, except in countries providing conditions for the centralisation of activities. This organisation form concentrates production in a few regional centres with high value added decision-making and R&D activities staying in the home country.
- *The multinational form* offers many opportunities for attracting the activities of MNCs, as the operations of the MNC are dispersed. However, while host countries can capture production and higher value added R&D activities, the activities of subsidiaries are likely to be aimed at the local market rather than for export, as the multinational form does not integrate the activities of its subsidiaries across borders.
- *The international form* offers less autonomy for subsidiaries and host countries than the multinational form, and controls the diffusion of activities, but there are greater prospects of host countries developing as an export base.
- *The transnational form* is based on a network-based organisational structure that leverages the competitive advantages of different locations and develops differentiated roles for subsidiaries. The implication for economic development is that host countries and regions with specialised competitive advantages have the opportunity to attract strategic and high value added MNC activities and

can also assist MNC subsidiaries to evolve to higher value added functions over time. However, locations that do not offer high quality location advantages will miss out the opportunities for MNC-led economic development.

In conclusion, approaches to international business suggest that:

- Host locations for investment can benefit from the ownership advantages of MNCs.
- MNCs may have a negative impact on economic development through rent-seeking behaviour and exploitation of the power relationship with labour.
- The contribution of MNC subsidiaries to their host location can depend on their organisational form. As companies move to the transnational form, host locations have new opportunities for attracting high value added functions, but will increasingly have to demonstrate competitive location-specific advantages.

2.1.3 Government–business relations

The final group is perhaps the most isolated. Theories of government–industry relations have remained distinct from both approaches to government–MNC relations and from international business studies and economic geography more generally. Government–industry relations has in general focused narrowly on how to make and implement coherent industrial policies domestically, while government–MNC relations is concerned more with the bargaining negotiations that determine the relative gains from these policies for MNCs and states. Both approaches argue that the exercise of power determines outcomes, and that power is influenced by institutional structures and interest groups. There is, then, a potential for fruitful cross-fertilisation between the two approaches, as can be seen in chapter 6.

The key implications of government–business relations for economic development are:

- Industrial policy and strategy plays a major role in the economic development process, with almost all government actions influencing corporate business decisions and competitiveness. It is therefore essential that there is a coherent industrial strategy and policies to achieve this strategy with cohesive networks linking firms and government.

- Increasingly, industrial strategy and policies are shifting from the national to sub-national levels. The regional state best understands the needs of business and can most appropriately design and execute strategies that integrate the needs of business with the wider economic development needs of their location

2.1.4   A synthesis

While cross-fertilisation within and between the different groups is minimal, several commentators are beginning to incorporate the insights from different perspectives into their own disciplines and are acknowledging the important contributions that different approaches can make to each other:

- Economic geographers are using the insights of regulation theory, flexible specialisation and the Japan school in order to understand the impact of new production systems on economic development. At the same time, they are drawing on managerial theories of the MNC to examine the relationship between the subsidiaries and headquarters of MNCs and prospects for regional development (e.g. Dicken *et al.*, 1994; Birkinshaw and Hood, 1998).
- Economic development theorists have integrated the insights of agglomeration/cluster and evolutionary/innovation theories with regulation theory, flexible specialisation, and the Japan school to examine RED (Cooke and Morgan, 1994; Storper, 1995; Scott, 1996; Maskell *et al.*, 1998).
- Both economic geographers (Dicken, 1997) and international business theorists (Dunning, 1992a, 1993b; Rugman and Verbeke, 1998) have started to analyse the relationship between governments and MNCs, drawing on the IPE research agenda.
- Lawton (1997) has used the insights of Porter's (1990a) cluster model of competitive advantage to emphasise the importance of competitive rivalry for the success of MNCs in the semiconductor industry, but also explicitly compensates for the limitations of the model through analysing how structural changes influence government policy, corporate competitiveness and bargaining between states and firms.
- Buckley and Casson (1998), key figures in the development of internalisation theory, have broken away from TCEs, arguing that models of the MNC must focus on rationalisation and restructuring, flexibility, uncertainty, volatility, competition, environmental

impacts on strategy, decentralisation of R&D, networks, culture, and trust – factors central to economic geography and managerial approaches.

- Dunning (1998) has broadened considerably the OLI paradigm, arguing that knowledge, alliance capitalism, agglomeration and government institutions are crucial in location as are idiosyncratic firm strategies.
- The process of innovation is becoming central to all of the approaches.

However, there is still a lack of integration between approaches across several key dimensions. For example, while Bartlett and Ghoshal (1990) define the type of MNC most suitable for innovation, they do not draw on the extensive innovation literature. Ostry (1998) also argues that while traditional TCEs and Porterian approaches emphasise the importance of networks, drawing on the innovation literature, both ignore the importance of government in the policy process and ignore the capabilities of MNCs derived from global scope. They do not draw on dimensions that are central to regulation theory (the role of government in economic development) and management and labour approaches to international business (the advantages of multinationality for accessing and developing new technologies and for exerting bargaining power over governments and labour).

A cross-fertilisation of approaches is crucial to interpret the interdependence between the four levels of analysis of this study – structural changes, MNCs, the local level and the role of the state. The insights of economic geography, international business studies and government–business relations point to converging pressures, converging issues and converging theories:

- *Converging pressures*: market volatility and uncertainty, overcapacity, technological change, global competition, internationalisation, and regional integration are influencing the organisation and strategies of both MNCs and states.
- *Converging issues*: in response to the above pressures, a premium is being placed on efficiency, flexibility, innovation, R&D, knowledge, learning, co-operation with other actors, supplier relations, new work practices, and the importance of the local level for both MNCs and states. The balance between competition and co-operation and force or foster strategies in developing and sustaining competitive advantage are key issues facing MNC managers and

public policy makers. The implications of e-business are also becoming a top priority for firms and governments.

- *Converging theories*: MNCs and sub-national regions are recognised to be political institutions, subject to diverse, evolutionary learning processes. Technological and organisational change is path-dependent/subject to administrative heritage and context specificity mediates the diffusion of practices in MNCs and regions.

Technological advance, innovation and the associated internationalisation of economic activity have become central. Each approach argues that the emergence of differentiated and specialised networks involving regions, MNCs and SMEs is the organisational form most adept at responding to global pressures and exploiting opportunities for innovation and learning (Bartlett and Ghoshal, 1989; Storper, 1995; Capello, 1996). A decentralised, network-based organisation is emerging as the new paradigmatic model, facilitated by advances in information and telecommunications technology (IT&T).

The three groups of theories help to explain the relationship between MNCs, governments and RED through their contribution to understanding:

- Structural changes and their impact on MNC and state organisation and strategies.
- The impact of new forms of competition, new sources of competitive advantage and new industrial organisation on FDI and the prospects for economic development.
- The role of bargaining power in managing interdependence between and within states and firms.

A cross-fertilisation of approaches underpins the theoretical and empirical analysis in the following chapters. First, in order to outline in more detail the main pressures facing states and firms, it is important to define globalisation and the key structural changes influencing the relationship between MNCs, states and RED.

2.2 Globalisation

A study examining multinationals inevitably confronts the term 'globalisation'. Globalisation is the catch-word used by most of the authors cited in Tables 2.1 and 2.2, among many others, to indicate that the international political economy is changing, creating new pressures, opportunities and constraints for the actors within. This section clarifies what globalisation means for this study.

Globalisation has different meanings for different people. As Gill (1995: 405) argues, globalisation is:

> not amenable to reductionist forms of explanation, because it is many-faceted and multidimensional and involves ideas, images, symbols, music, fashions, and a variety of tastes and representations of identity and community. Nevertheless, in its present mythic and ideological representations, the concept serves to reify a global economic system dominated by large institutional investors and transnational firms which control the bulk of the world's productive assets and are the principle influences in world trade and financial markets.

If we equate globalisation with changes in the world economy, then the growth of MNCs and the associated internationalisation of production and finance are the key forms of globalisation (Strange, 1991b; Cox, 1994; Gray, 1995; Ostry, 1998). Identifying the major structural changes driving internationalisation becomes crucial to explain globalisation.

The usefulness of the term globalisation is not only in revealing underlying structural changes but also in characterising the nature of the present world economy. Chesnais (1993: 13) considers the process of globalisation to refer to the loss of economic and political sovereignty of countries, and Cox (1996) and Gill (1996) also see the key differentiation between a world and global economy as the loss of regulatory control of the state. Reich (1990) and Ohmae (1990) therefore argue that the globalisation of the world economy is leading to stateless firms, implying for Miller (1991) that states have no autonomy. However, we have seen that economic geography approaches identify an important and growing role for state institutions in economic development processes and, as Box 2.1 illustrates, we are far from stateless firms.

If the world economy is still overwhelmingly based on nation states and companies dependent on their home base for competitiveness (Hirst and Thompson, 1995; Ruigrok and van Tulder, 1995), how can globalisation be a useful term? Globalisation should be defined not as stateless firms and the end of the nation state, but as intensifying

Box 2.1   The myth of the stateless firm

Studies by Hu (1992); Ruigrok and van Tulder (1995); Patel (1995) and Wade (1996) have persuasively established that in terms of geographic spread and scope, R&D, ownership and control, management and workforce, legal nationality, and tax domicile, MNCs are not stateless. Estimates show that FDI represented 9% of world output in 1913, more than in the 1990s. In terms of R&D, a study of 569 of world's major MNCs found that over 40% did less than 1% of patenting activities outside their home countries between 1969–1990. In the second half of 1990s, 89% of US patents taken out by 600 of world's largest firms listed the inventor as a resident of home base. Philips has only 15% of its assets in its home country, but still does 40% of its R&D at home. The workforce of MNCs also remains concentrated at home, but even so the internationalisation of workers, as well as of sales and assets, far exceeds the internationalisation of shares; only a few firms maintain over 10% of their shares abroad. In Japan, around 70% of the shares of core companies on the Tokyo stock exchange are held by 'stable' shareholders. Only 5 of 30 US core firms have had a foreigner as a member of their executive board – in 1991 only 2% of board members of big American companies were foreigners – with the percentage even less in Japan, Germany and France. Even for Nestlé, one the most internationalised of firms, with only 5% of assets and employees in Switzerland, non-Swiss voting rights are limited to 3% of the total. Furthermore, the vast majority of global employment is in SMEs, not MNCs. While increasing number of SMEs are becoming global (as UNCTAD World Investment Reports indicate), facilitated by advances in IT&T, most of the world's companies are operating in the national or sub-national economy, rather than the global economy. Their competitiveness depends significantly on state policies at the national and sub-national level.

internationalisation *and* interdependence linking and integrating states, regions, firms and functions on a global scale. Increasing inter-penetration is driven by MNCs, but globalisation as increasing interdependence is also a dialectical, contested process, uneven and differentiated in its impact (McGrew, 1992; Hurrell and Woods, 1995; Cox, 1996; Scott, 1996). Globalisation may even reinforce the importance of the nation state (Cantwell, 1995), and is fully compatible with the growing importance of the local level, as identified by economic geography and managerial theories.

Globalisation is a varied and spatially uneven process – the growth of European, American and Japanese MNCs is differentiated, each moulded by their home base. MNCs concentrate high value added activities in some regions but not in others, and this differentiated specialisation increases as globalisation intensifies (de Vet, 1993; OECD, 1996: 17; Scott, 1996). As Markusen (1996) describes, globalisation may lead to 'sticky places within slippery space'.

The major carrier of globalisation is no longer identified solely to be the *growth* of MNCs, but rather the *integration* of their activities on a world-wide scale. Internationalisation is the increasing geographical spread of activities across national boundaries, while globalisation is the intensified degree of purposeful functional integration between internationally dispersed economic activities (de Vet, 1993: 90–1; Dicken, 1994: 106; Peck and Stone, 1996: 62). While Bartlett and Ghoshal (1989) define a 'global' industry as one where there are no national differences, which favours the centralisation of strategic control, assets, resources and decision-making, their conceptualisation of a transnational firm is closest to our definition of globalisation. Bartlett and Ghoshal (1989) argue that MNCs are moving towards a transnational form, with an integrated network of operations characterised by interdependence and linkages among dispersed units. Central to the transnational firm is the specialisation of subsidiaries, with each playing different strategic roles. Globalisation therefore leads to spatial differentiation.

The ideal-type global firm is functionally integrated world-wide, capturing linkages across borders, and organised along global product lines with a single world-wide strategy. The strategy MNCs are moving towards at present appears to be glocalisation (Ruigrok and Tulder, 1995), as found in a 1993 study of 131 MNC executives (Leong and Tan, 1993). In the words of the President of Honda, firms must 'act locally, think globally' (cited in Harukiyo, 1998: 46), with innovation locally leveraged and globally linked (Bartlett and Ghoshal, 1989). While many MNCs may emphasise regional or triadic strategies more than global strategies (Stubbs and Underhill, 1994; Ruigrok and Tulder, 1995; Oman, 2000), globally co-ordinated networks with interdependent regional activities is the ideal-type to which many MNCs are moving towards.

2.3   STRUCTURAL CHANGES

In explaining changes in the level and structure of FDI and the relationship between governments and MNCs (Dunning, 1992a), the strategy, structure and management of MNCs (Bartlett and Ghoshal, 1993a), and pressures on MNCs relating to the local level (Amin and Malmberg, 1992; Dicken *et al.*, 1994), three key structural changes have been highlighted:

- intensifying global competition;
- accelerating technological change;
- regional integration.

Globalisation, as increasing internationalisation and interdependence, is underpinned by these inter-linked structural changes. Building on the insights of the above approaches, each structural change is discussed.

2.3.1   Intensifying global competition

Competition is intensifying and changing in nature. This is driving transformations in the organisation and strategy of MNCs. Intensified global competition is an outcome of six major factors:

- *Over-capacity and a slow-down of growth in the West* has led to greater competition for market share (the growth of the US economy since the early 1990s is the major, albeit significant, exception).
- *New competition* – in capital and innovation intensive mature sectors such as in the semiconductor, computer, and electronics industries (from Japan, Taiwan, South Korea, and Singapore), in new sectors such as software (for example, from India and Israel), and in manufacturing and heavy industries (from China, Brazil, Mexico, South East Asia, and Eastern Europe–Turkey).
- *Homogenising consumer preferences* – internationalisation and the opening up of markets, combined with increasing incomes in emerging economies and new information and advertising mediums, especially satellite communications and the internet, is leading to a standardisation of tastes and products for established goods (such as consumer electronics, computers, and clothing) and for new technology products (such as mobile phones) across countries.

- *The growth of new and more flexible MNCs* – from 1992 to 1998 the number of MNCs has increased by nearly two-thirds, the number of foreign affiliates of companies and their global sales has almost tripled and the global FDI stock has more than doubled (see Table 4.1). More and more companies are facing direct competition in their own home country.
- *Market access* – liberalisation is opening up markets and leading to a rapid growth in FDI, most strikingly seen in the case of China since the 1980s and Eastern Europe since the 1990s, but also countries like Mexico, Argentina and Brazil (Thomsen, 2000: 13)
- *New technologies* – advances in IT&T's, falling transportation costs, and the growth of the internet and e-business is facilitating new market entrants and intensified competition both nationally and internationally.

The rapid integration of world markets has heightened competition between firms and the different institutional systems within which firms are embedded (Hollingsworth *et al.*, 1994: 10). At the same time, the nature of competition is in constant flux, as Porter, paraphrasing Schumpeter, states 'competition is a constantly changing landscape in which new products, new ways of marketing, new production processes, and whole new market segments emerge' (1990, cited in Lawton, 1997: 25). Bartlett and Ghoshal, (1989: 29) argue that changing competition is leading to a situation where 'more and more businesses are being driven by *simultaneous* demands for global efficiency, national responsiveness, and worldwide leveraging of innovations and learning'.

To remain competitive, MNCs increasingly must combine innovation, efficiency and flexibility. In particular, it is argued that knowledge, learning[3] and innovation[4] have become the new competitive resource (Bartlett and Ghoshal, 1989; Stopford and Strange, 1991; Cooke, 1998b). The key driver is increased international competition and the associated search for higher productivity, which stimulates innovation (Bartlett and Ghoshal, 1990; Nelson, 1992; Stopford, 1993; Porter, 1998). Competition has increased with the catch-up of more nations in capital and knowledge-intensive industries. International rivalry is shifting from access to capital, important in the era of rapidly growing markets, to investments in intangible capital, especially specialised knowledge and expertise which enhances technological capabilities (Bartlett and Ghoshal, 1993a: 32; Chandler and Hikino, 1997: 54).

Learning and innovation are transforming from linear processes in vertically integrated research laboratories to interactive processes involving the combination of diversified bodies of knowledge and the social embedding of new technologies (Asheim, 1996: 385; Cooke, 1997: 358; Braczyk and Heidenreich, 1998: 432). Innovation and learning becomes dependent on securing co-operation within the firm and between the firm and other firms, especially suppliers and customers, and institutions at the local, national and international levels (de Vet, 1993: 99; Cooke and Morgan, 1998: 9).

As codified knowledge is disseminated faster, tacit knowledge becomes increasingly important as a basis for sustained competitive advantage (HMSO, 1998a). However, the more tacit the knowledge involved, the more important is spatial proximity between the actors taking part in the exchange (Maskell *et al.*, 1998: 62–3). The capacity to share knowledge requires robust communication channels and a high degree of trust and commitment (Cooke and Morgan, 1998: 16).

Networks based on long term co-operative relations become the key response to international competition based on tacit knowledge and innovation (Ostry, 1998: 89; Braczyk and Heidenreich, 1998: 432). Networks spread risks, combine resources and assets, and share know-how and experience (Tödtling, 1994: 79). For MNCs:

> By creating flexible linkages that allow the efforts of multiple units to be combined, a company can create synergies that significantly leverage its innovation process (Bartlett and Ghoshal, 1989: 120).

However, to keep abreast of relevant innovations, the firm must have access to multiple channels of information and diverse methods of learning (Cooke and Morgan, 1998: 33). Global expansion can provide global scanning capabilities (Vernon, 1979) and listening posts (Patel, 1995) to tap into new sources of innovation and learning for the company.

It is also argued that we have entered a period of 'new competition' (Best, 1990). The new competition combines efficiency and flexibility, with the key innovation developments in the organisation and technology of production processes. Major factors in the new competition include:

- flexibility and lean production;
- focus on core competencies;
- shift to external sourcing.

The importance of flexibility in production processes, product development and labour relations is heightened by increased competition, volatility and uncertainty in exchange rates, markets, technologies and tastes. Flexibility, quality and price competitiveness are embodied in the Japanese challenge. Lean production involves continuous improvement in product quality, flexible work practices and flexible manufacturing technologies, rapid innovation, and close supplier relations (Loewendahl, 1998). As large firms become more flexible, competition also increases for SMEs (Garmise, 1995: 154; Belussi, 1996: 16; Heidenreich, 1996), and massive capital costs and intense world-wide competition create pressures for convergence to lean production.[5]

At the same time, intensified global competition, volatile world markets, mass customisation, product destandardisation, higher quality, shorter product cycles, and the demands of flexibility are putting enormous pressures on firms to become as lean and efficient as possible. This favours a back-to-basic strategy, with specialisation on a limited number of core activities, and a shift towards external sourcing of non-core activities and long-term technical partnerships with other firms (see Moulaert and Swyngedouw, 1991; Sabel, 1995; Scott, 1996).

MNCs are vertically disintegrating and emphasising external relations with both other firms and non-firm institutions, including public sector research centres, technology transfer bodies and universities. Vertical disintegration and lean production has reinforced the emphasis placed on developing and managing new supplier relations. New supplier relations involve co-operation as well as competition (Powell and Smith-Doerr, 1994: 384) and allow greater flexibility, customised products, improved quality, continuous information exchange, and the sourcing of new ideas and technologies (Dyer *et al.*, 1998; Mascarenhas *et al.*, 1998: 129–30). With the focus on innovation and pressures of the new competition, external relationships become crucial to firm competitiveness.

2.3.2 Accelerating technological change

Lawton (1997: 5) argues that, 'Technology, and the rapid pace of innovation, is one of the most dynamic forces for change in the international system', and the third scientific revolution, with new IT&Ts and flexible manufacturing technologies, is intimately connected to globalisation.[6] Technological advance[7] has encouraged new forms of FDI and is facilitating the global integration of economic activity.

Accelerating technological advance is increasing rapidly the R&D costs and risks of remaining at the leading edge of rapidly transforming and complex technologies, and shortening product life cycles have placed a premium on the time span it takes to commercialise technological innovations. Firms are forced to exploit investments in technology more rapidly in overseas markets (Holtbrügge and Welge, 1997: 348), and the global context provides more opportunities for developing and leveraging technology and more possibilities of transferring technologies and know-how from one product to another and one market to another (Dunford and Perrons, 1992: 390; Mascarenhas *et al.*, 1998: 121).

To penetrate foreign markets, overseas production, with the MNC internalising and keeping control of technological capability, may be favoured (Gomes-Casseres, 1990: 221). For accessing and scanning for new technologies, establishing small R&D labs or acquisitions of local firms is encouraged. To develop and share the risks of new technologies, co-operative agreements may be preferred. Technological advance can therefore encourage different types of FDI.

Cross-border, inter-firm collaborative arrangements are particularly important for highly research and capital intensive activities. They are crucial for gaining market access to generate a stronger revenue flow, amortise large fixed costs, obtain intangible and tangible assets, exploit complementary resources and capabilities, share risks, reduce the time taken for innovation, and increase flexibility. Since the 1980s, high technology collaboration has become crucial for MNCs to develop, sustain and remain at the leading edge of technology. Collaboration is becoming a precondition for competitive success.

Change in the technology structure encourages the introduction of networking arrangements to allow the firm to recombine various components to exploit opportunities better (Powell and Smith-Doerr, 1994: 381), and the rapid decentralisation of production, with specialisation and focus on core competencies, subcontracting and alliances, is a response to technological complexity. As Lawton (1997: 137) explains:

> Changes – such as shortening product life cycles and the increasing integration of previously separate industries – increased the value of production flexibility and monitoring the new technologies. This rapid change and constant uncertainty...weakened the

business reasoning behind vertical integration and... increased the corporate rationale for moving towards strategic collaboration for R&D.

The costs, risks, complexity and pace of technological advance have therefore encouraged FDI, inter-firm co-operation and new organisational structures, facilitated by rapidly falling costs and advances in transport and communications. Information and telecommunications technologies were a necessary condition, if not cause, of the rapid growth of MNCs and integration of economic activity (Dicken, 1992a: 97; Chesnais, 1993: 13–14; Chan, 1996: 2). They have increased the transparency of assets at different locations (de Vet, 1993: 101; Lipsey, 1997: 81) and communication, monitoring, networks and control can be extended efficiently across borders (UNCTAD, 1998: 111–13). With the latest advances in e-business,[8] MNCs can integrate their activities globally and the barriers to internationalisation for SMEs, such as lack of information and difficulty in finding cross-border partners and in co-ordinating international operations, are likely to be reduced dramatically.

2.3.3 Regional integration

Regional integration and the related liberalisation and deregulation of markets have facilitated the growth of MNCs, global competition and the integration and specialisation of economic activity. Regional integration is the third major driver of globalisation. Key examples are the Single Market in the EU, which will include 13 new countries when EU enlargement is completed, the North American Free Trade Area (NAFTA), and the Association of South East Asian Nations (ASEAN), which is considering expansion to other Asia-Pacific countries including Australia and New Zealand. There are also increasing links between regional integration areas, such as the free trade agreement signed between the EU and Mexico in 2000.

The reduction or removal of barriers to trade and factor flows associated with regional integration and trade and capital market liberalisation on an international scale has underpinned the growth of FDI (Dunning, 1998: 47–8; Karl, 1996: 1–2; Peck and Stone, 1996: 62). Liberalisation of FDI facilitates production for differentiated markets, allowing firms to have a local presence in overseas markets, take advantage of scale economies in production, marketing, distribution, and R&D, and exploit their comparative advantage globally. At the same time, as well as offensive FDI to expand market share, the emergence of regional trading blocs stimulates defensive tariff-leaping FDI with 'insiders' in a regionally integrated market enjoying advantages over 'outsiders'.

The gradual reduction in protectionism and move towards a unified single market associated with liberalising trade and capital flows, deregulation and levelling the playing-field, encourages the growth of FDI and intensifies international competition (Gill, 1991: 63; Capello, 1996: 489; Lawton, 1997: 92). Firms are put under increasing pressure to adopt new technologies and work practices (Humphrey, 1995), and the complex integration strategies of MNCs are facilitated on a regional or global scale (Dunning, 1992a: 316–17; UNCTAD, 1998: 111–13).

A single regional market with increased competition encourages large firms in particular to pursue efficiency seeking investments along the lines of a regional division of labour with a strategy of regional production, marketing, distribution and innovation to protect or advance their competitive positions (Dunning, 1993b: 60; Peck and Stone, 1996: 62–3). Falling internal barriers to trade and substitution of regional for national frameworks has therefore raised the possibility of economies of specialisation with the servicing of a regional market from a smaller number of locations, gaining economies of scale and agglomeration, and at the same time has facilitated product and market rationalisation to reduce costs (Krugman, 1991; Weiermair, 1991; Sadler, 1992b; Venables, 1995).

2.3.4 Summary

Globalisation, argues Mittelman (1996a: 3), 'is a market-induced, not a policy-led, process'. However, intensifying competition, accelerating technological change and regional integration are driven by the interaction of states and firms. Strange (1991a: 42–3) points out that in terms of computers, IT&Ts, and the growth of competition, US policy played a key role through financial and communications deregulation, and satellite development. This has put pressure on other countries to imitate US policies (Cawson *et al.*, 1990; Cerny, ed., 1993).

In terms of regional integration, the example of the EU shows how policies were the outcome of negotiations between governments and core firms. Large firms were active proponents of regional integration, with MNCs benefiting greatly through increased mobility, specialisation and integration and accruing the most financial benefits from regional initiatives (Ruigrok and van Tulder, 1995: 108; Scott, 1996: 407; Bailey, 1997: 1; Lawton, 1997). The idea of 'Europe 1992' can be traced to Volvo and Philips who, together with other large companies like Siemens, were at the core of lobbying their national governments for completion of the Single Market (Sally, 1995: 116; Anderson, 1996: 202–03; Bellak, 1997: 20; Cowling *et al.*, 1997: 8). Technology initiatives at the Europe-wide level have also resulted from a bargaining process between MNCs and the European Commission, often bypassing national state involvement (*Management Accounting*, 1992: 43; Stubbs and Saviotti, 1994: 155).

Globalisation, then, is mediated by the interaction of states (national or supra-national) and firms, and is transforming international business. Intensifying competition, technological change and regional integration are globalising the international political economy, accelerating the internationalisation and interdependence of firms and states. In responding to new competitive pressures, new technologies and new institutional environments, MNCs are integrating functions both within the firm and across borders, focusing on the knowledge, learning and innovation necessary to strengthen their core competencies. MNCs are forging deeper external relations to increase flexibility, cost and quality competitiveness and reduce product life cycles. With vertical disintegration and specialisation within the MNC and spatially, competitive advantage is further premised upon relationships with other firms and institutions.

Central to our discussion on the cross-fertilisation of approaches, globalisation and structural changes is the emergence of the integrated network as the ideal-type organisational form. While structural changes and new organisational forms are encourage MNCs to disperse their strategic assets, only subsidiaries operating in locations which offer the conditions for high value added activities and innovation will have the opportunity to attract higher order functions and regional or global product mandates. MNCs specialise in clusters with pre-existing multiple linkages and synergies, reinforcing the strength of existing centres of excellence in advanced regions while limiting the possibilities for attracting strategic functions to others. The network-form or N-form MNC is also characterised by vertical disintegration, with the multinational co-ordinating a network of suppliers. To benefit from the opportunities of the N-form regions must themselves move towards a network-form of organisation and concentrate on innovation, which is at the heart of the transition to the N-form multinational.

3 FDI and Location Decision-Making

FDI is the focal point of this study. It is therefore important to define what we mean by FDI. In the first section of this chapter we outline different types of FDI and the limitations of official FDI data. We adopt a holistic definition of FDI, which takes into account FDI that does not involve a cross-border capital flow.

In the second part of this chapter, we evaluate theoretical explanations for FDI and develop a new model of FDI to act as a framework for understanding in particular why one location is favoured in preference to another. We compensate for the limitation of existing theories of FDI, by integrating into our FDI model strategic and project specific dimensions. Building on our discussion of the MNC location decision-making process, in the final section of this chapter we examine the role of government incentives in FDI location.

3.1 METHODOLOGY OF FDI

The OECD defines FDI 'as capital invested for the purpose of acquiring a lasting interest in an enterprise and of exerting a degree of influence on that enterprise's operations' (OECD, 1998b: 6) and identifies three main types of FDI:

- the creation or extension of a wholly owned enterprise, subsidiary or branch, or the acquisition of full ownership of an existing enterprise;
- participation in a new or existing enterprise;
- a long-term loan over five years (cited in Tokunaga, 1992: 13).

FDI therefore refers to the cross-border transfer of managerial resources (Alvstan, 1993: 64), with FDI involving the acquisition of a lasting interest and effective voice in the management of an enterprise in a host country (Fong, 1992: 193). FDI therefore does not necessarily involve the transfer of physical capital – the defining feature of the multinational company is the cross-border *control* and *management* of activities outside of its home country.

44

We can expand the OECD typology of FDI and identify five key types of FDI:

- M&As;
- privatisation-related investment;
- new forms of investment (joint ventures, strategic alliances, licensing and other partnership agreements);
- greenfield investment (a new operation);
- brownfield investment (expansions or re-investment in existing foreign affiliates).

Only greenfield investment reflects the traditional view of FDI, and most types of FDI do not necessarily involve cross-border capital investment and hence may not be recorded in balance of payments data as aggregated by international organisations.[1] Measuring FDI is particularly complex when New Forms of Investment (NFI) are included in the definition of FDI. New forms normally involve a non-capital contribution such as technology, skills and market access provided by foreign investors (Lim and Fong, 1991: 13). The potential benefits of FDI for economic development therefore derive not only from new capital investment but also from non-capital contributions.[2]

Official data records only physical capital – externally financed investment by overseas companies in their branches, subsidiaries or associated companies of a host country. Investment that is not registered in the balance of payments is left unrecorded, for example in the cases of:

- new forms of investment;
- capital that is recorded as portfolio investment but is actually intended for direct investment;
- a parent enterprise which raises debt and equity finance in the host country to finance a new greenfield, brownfield or M&A project;[3]
- capital whose origin is attributed to one country but which is intended for direct investment under the control of companies originating in another country (Nicolaides, 1993c: 110; Jones, 1996b: 6).[4]

Furthermore, in the case of a cross-border acquisition, capital from inward foreign *direct* investment accruing to share-holders or owners of the acquired firm, may leave the host country as outward foreign *portfolio* investment. Even though official data will show an increase in FDI, there may therefore be no net addition to capital in the host economy (see Hausmann and Fernandez-Arias, 2000).

For statistical purposes the IMF defines foreign investment as direct when the investor holds 10% or more of the equity of an enterprise – usually enough to give the investor some say in its management. However, there are problems in the reliability and comparability of FDI data:

- The percentage that constitutes control varies across countries. For example, in the UK the threshold to be considered FDI changed in 1997 from 20% to 10%, while in Germany it remains 20%.
- Different definitions of FDI are used. For example, the Ministry of Finance in Japan has no minimum threshold and, unlike most countries, excludes re-invested earnings.
- Exchange rate changes affect the measurement of FDI.
- Timing of flows may reflect fluctuations in intra-company trans-actions and in the case of M&As actual cross-border capital flows are often spread over several years, so that announced deals do not normally correspond to actual FDI flows in the same year.
- Stock data relates to the historical value of an investment, not updated at market prices.
- Comparing FDI in developing countries is particularly difficult as the FDI data often gives an indication of the stage and extent of each country's privatisation process.[5]

We therefore adopt a holistic interpretation of FDI, defining FDI as the acquisition of a lasting interest and effective voice in the manage-ment of an enterprise located in a foreign country. Our definition differs from that of the OECD and national statistical bodies, as FDI does not necessarily have to involve the transfer of physical capital.

3.2   FDI AND THE LOCATION DECISION-MAKING PROCESS

The emphasis of most international business theories is on explaining the conditions that allow firms to engage in FDI rather than the decision making process determining *why* firms expand across borders and *where* they locate international investment. In this section we develop a new model of FDI based on three key dimensions of FDI and the location decision making process:

- conditions for firms to become multinational;
- strategic determinants of FDI;
- project determinants of FDI.

3.2.1 Conditions for firms to become multinational

There are four major groups of theories explaining multinational firms:

- Hymer (1959) develops a *specific-advantages theory*, which states that firms need to have internal-specific advantages over domestic rivals, in particular economies of scale and superior product technology, in order to invest in that country.
- Knickerblocker (1973) and Graham (1991) emphasise *oligopolistic rivalry* as an explanation for FDI, with firms investing in each other's home markets to gain first mover advantages, leading to a follow-the-leader pattern of international investment to reduce risks in an uncertain oligopolistic environment.
- Vernon's (1966; 1979) *product life-cycle theory* explains the shift from exports to direct investment in developed and developing countries. Rivalistic firm behaviour drives firms in developed countries to locate lower value added or mature activities in low cost developing countries so that the firm can move up the product cycle and focus on developing new products. An international division of labour is created between developed (core) countries and developing (periphery) countries.
- Williamson (1975) and Buckley and Casson (1976), building on the work of Coase (1937; 1960), develop *internalisation theory* in order to understand why firms invest abroad instead of exporting or licensing to domestic firms. They argue that high transaction costs, such as enforcing contracts, maintaining quality, and keeping proprietary rights over technical and marketing knowledge, may justify direct ownership (internalisation) of overseas activities. This theory has been expanded to include the transaction costs of political intervention and trade barriers (Jacobson *et al.*, 1993).

Dunning (1977; 1988) has brought together the main tenets of these theories and developed the OLI paradigm, which clearly identifies three conditions for direct investment to take place:

- *Ownership advantages* – the firm must have some firm-specific or intangible assets such as proprietary technology or managerial or marketing expertise that allows it to compete with local firms in each market (based on Hymer, 1959).

- *Location advantages* – the firm must have a reason for wanting to use this asset abroad rather than at home (building on Vernon 1966; 1979).
- *Internalisation advantages* – the firm must decide that control over production is better than simply licensing the technology or intangible asset or exporting (based on Buckley and Casson, 1976).

Box 3.1 shows how international business theory can be used to explain FDI in the semiconductor industry. However, as Box 3.1 discusses, these theories do not explicitly consider how the firm decides where to locate its investment. They are also limited in explaining the internationalisation strategy of the firm. To explain investment location we need to understand the motivation driving firms to invest overseas and why one location is selected in preference to another, as well as the underlying conditions that allow companies to become multinational.

Box 3.1 Theories of international investment and FDI in the semiconductor industry

Vernon suggests that firms will shift mature activities to low cost locations as they move up the product cycle. We would therefore expect firms with rapid product life cycles to be very active in international investment in developing countries. The semiconductor industry is a good example as the industry has experienced exponential technological advance – in 1995 the latest 1 gigabite memory chip was 1,000 times more powerful than the leading chip in 1985. At the same time, the semiconductor industry has from its very beginning established an international division of labour. Just four years after Texas Instruments patented the integrated circuit (microchip) in 1959, US companies set-up offshore assembly of chips in Hong Kong. By 1974, 26 US semiconductor firms had established 56 offshore assembly facilities, driven by domestic and international rivalry. Through shifting low value added mature parts of the value chain to developing countries they could free-up resources for semiconductor fabrication and R&D, which was costing each firm US$2 billion for each new generation of microchip by the end of the 1990s. In the 1990s, semiconductor firms also internationalised capital-intensive semiconductor fabrication, to access markets protected by trade barriers. Prior to 1990 there was no Japanese semiconductor investment in Europe, but a 14% EC tariff on imports, 50% minimum local content requirements, and 169 anti-dumping investigations between 1987 and 1991 provided incentives for FDI. Direct presence in Europe was also a requirement if the semiconductor firms were to win lucrative defence contracts due to political pressure from host governments. By 1990, 10 new Japanese semiconductor facilities were planned for Europe and 7 of the 10 largest US producers were planning to establish plants in Europe. FDI in Europe was primarily to overcome the transaction costs of trade barriers and political intervention. In the vast majority of cases semiconductor facilities have been wholly-owned, due to concern over quality, speed in setting-up the operation, and control over proprietary process technology. Internalisation theory can therefore explain the costs leading Japanese and US firms to invest in Europe and the modality of overseas investment. Hymer's specific advantage theory points to the ownership advantages of the semiconductor firms (economies of scale and access to technology and capital), that enables them to compete with indigenous companies in host locations. The observed clustering of semiconductor overseas investment with over two thirds of Japanese semiconductor plants in the EU located in the UK can be explained by Knickerblocker, who points to the follow-the-leader pattern of FDI. International business theories therefore provide us with an understanding of why and how semiconductor firms internationalised their operations, and also point to investment in locations with low labour costs, tariff protection and large contracts. However, they do not explain why certain low cost locations were favoured over others or why Japanese and US firms invested in the UK market in the first place instead of other locations in Europe. They also do not explain the recent rapid growth and location of overseas semiconductor R&D investment. These are crucial questions from both an academic and policy making point of view that remain unanswered.

Source: Derived from Dicken (1992a: 335); *The Economist* (1992b); Brainard (1993: 223); Yoffie (1993: 211–12); Millward (1995); Jones (1996b: 141–2); Lawton (1997); Hamill *et al.* (1998); Moran (1999: 107–8).

3.2.2   Strategic determinants of FDI

Traditional theories of FDI have tended to neglect considerations of corporate strategy in investment location decisions (Mucchielli, 1991; European Commission, 1998). This is a major short-coming as a country's attractiveness for inward investment cannot be defined without reference to company strategies (Michalet, 1997: 23).

There are two key elements to company strategy:

- *Corporate strategy*: the long-term strategy of the company;
- *FDI strategy*: the specific internationalisation strategy.

Corporate strategy is firm specific and depends on the particular industry and history of the firm, the embeddedness of the firm in its home country, and the influence of structural changes in the firm's environment (Chandler, 1962; Ruigrok and van Tulder, 1995). As we discussed in Chapter 2, a key structural change is regional integration, which is encouraging companies to develop triadic corporate strategies based on each of three main regions in the world. The home country context is also particularly significant for the firm's development and overall internationalisation strategy. Key impacts of the home country upon the firm are the production factors, institutional support, industry structure, demand patterns, policy framework and human and technological capabilities Corporate strategy conditions the degree of internationalisation of the firm and the organisation and geographic location of international operations.[6]

Given an overall corporate strategy that favours internationalisation, Dunning (1998) has identified four generic types of specific strategic motives for international investment, which we expand upon below:

- *Market seeking or horizontal investment strategy*: according to Thomsen (2000: 17) 'Market size is the primary determinant of the global distribution of FDI flows'. Empirical studies have also demonstrated that the size of a country's GDP has a major impact on FDI (Mody and Wheeler, 1992; Bende-Nabende, 1999; Di Mauro, 1999; UNCTAD, 1998). Firm surveys have also demonstrated that market seeking is the most important motive for foreign investment (IBB, 1991; NEI, 1992; HMSO, 1996; Michalet, 1997). Thomsen and Woolcock (1993) define market-seeking FDI in terms of *distance costs*, which are described as 'the penalties imposed on an exporter by being far removed from the final market for its products'. Examples include the requirement for greater flexibility and increased awareness of how local tastes differ in each market (e.g. Geroski, 1990; Lung, 1992; Phelps, 1997, 52–3) as well as industrial customers demanding local presence for Just-in-Time production (Thomsen and Woolcock, 1993: 37–8). Similarly, Di Mauro (1999) defines market-seeking FDI in terms of *proximity*, which highlights the observed preference of MNCs to locate not only in large markets but also in geographically and psychologically proximate markets.[7] Both definitions of market seeking strategies ultimately explain FDI in terms of better access to markets.

- *Efficiency seeking or vertical investment strategy*: this strategy emphasises differences in unit costs between locations. While efficiency-seeking FDI is argued to be most appropriate for analysing FDI between developed and developing countries (Di Mauro, 1999: 6), many studies have shown that FDI in developing countries is primarily market seeking (e.g. Yeung, 1996; Agarwal, 1997; Estrin *et al.*, 1997). Efficiency seeking FDI driven by cost differences is only likely to play a critical role in determining investment location when the investor needs to choose between countries 'short-listed' as possible FDI locations – which are likely to be part of the same regional market.[8] The relevant market for many investors is at the regional or often sub-regional level (see Loewendahl and Ertugal-Loewendahl, 2000). The scope for efficiency seeking FDI increases with the deepening and widening of regional integration areas and as flexible technologies facilitate production of differentiated and individualised products at one location. Di Mauro defines efficiency seeking investment in terms of *concentration*, which highlights the cost advantages of 'plant level' economies of scale that make it profitable to concentrate production in one location and export to the wider regional zone. Competition for FDI is therefore primarily at the regional or sub-regional level.
- *Resource seeking investment strategy*: companies expand internationally to access raw materials availability in a host country.
- *Asset seeking investment strategy*: this strategy is the most recent motive for FDI to be identified. It refers to a strategy that aims to exploit technological assets in overseas countries. Following Serapio *et al.* (2000) we can identify two motives for asset-seeking FDI: (1) meeting host country customer needs and supporting the

parent's local manufacturing facilities (demand side); and (2) gaining access to science and technology and enhancing the company's global capabilities for technology development and innovation and an opportunity for learning (supply side). Serapio *et al.* find supply side motivations for asset-seeking FDI to be increasing in importance.

The location of FDI is therefore influenced by overall corporate strategy and the specific motives for internationalisation:

- *Corporate strategy*: this is likely to determine the broad location of FDI. For example, our discussion in Chapter 2 argued that multinationals are moving towards a glocalisation strategy, which requires FDI in all of the main regions in the world. The particular stage in a company's glocalisation strategy determines which region will be considered for current international projects.
- *Market seeking strategy*: the size of the economy and population and growth potential of the host country are likely to be key locations factors, together with the level of per capita incomes.
- *Efficiency seeking FDI*: labour costs, productivity and work relations, and access to a regional integration area are the main location factors determining FDI location. Political and economic stability and policy certainty are likely to be pre-requisites if the location is to serve as a major export centre for regional markets.
- *Resource seeking FDI*: natural resource availability and costs of extraction and transportation are key location factors. A strong legal framework is likely to be a prerequisite if substantial capital investment in required. Markets with excess demand (such as China, India, Brazil and Turkey) may also attract resource seeking FDI.
- *Asset seeking FDI*: labour skills, education, training and availability are essential location factors. The technological infrastructure and clusters in the host country are key location factors for R&D and innovation-related activities.

These generic strategies cannot be taken in isolation from one another. There is a constant trade-off in MNC location decision-making between proximity and concentration (Di Mauro, 1999: 5), revenues and costs (Haigh *et al.* cited in Thomsen and Woolcock, 1993: 38), and exports and selling locally (OECD, 1998c: 20). With regional integration, intensified competition and technological advance, MNCs are now pursuing both market and efficiency seeking FDI strategies *at the same time* (Michalet, 1997), increasing the potential contribution that FDI can make to economic development in host countries. Rather than purely substituting imports and indigenous output for production by foreign subsidiaries, FDI increasingly provides opportunities for export-based growth.

The transition towards the N-form MNC also provides opportunities for attracting asset-seeking FDI, but heightens the importance of the technological infrastructure of the host country. Our case study in Chapter 8 shows that Siemens is assessing alternative investment locations on the basis of market seeking, efficiency seeking *and* asset seeking motives as the company globalises and moves towards the N-form. To compete for FDI, locations increasingly need to offer the combination of access to markets, a competitive production base and a strong technological and innovation infrastructure.

3.2.3 Project determinants of FDI

FDI varies not only according to firm strategy but also according to project type (Ernst and Young, 1992; Tatoglu and Glaister, 2000). As PricewaterhouseCoopers (1999) states: 'The company needs to find business environments that reliably match a complex array of success factors unique to the competitive strategy and specific project of the enterprise.'

The project determinants depend on the type of project and the stage in the decision-making process. Academic and consultancy research points to six generic project types, each with specific key location factors:[9]

- *Information technology and software* (IT & Software): telecommunications infrastructure, educated and skilled labour, high numbers of university graduates, labour costs, high quality of life.
- *R&D and high technology*: high-tech clusters, entrepreneurial and risk-taking culture, protection of intellectual property rights, telecommunications infrastructure, educated and skilled labour, high numbers of university graduates, and access to regional markets and government financial incentives for high tech manufacturing. R&D is a critical part of a company's business strategy and high technology manufacturing very costly. Stable and sophisticated markets are therefore a pre-condition for attracting R&D and high tech investment.

- *Front and back office activities* (such as call centres and shared service centres): Labour regulations, telecommunications infrastructure, labour costs, high numbers of university graduates, multi-lingual skills.
- *Manufacturing and assembly*: labour regulations, access to regional markets, domestic market size for some projects, transport infrastructure, proximity to customers and suppliers, labour costs, property and site costs and availability.
- *Headquarters*: access to regional markets, high quality of life, transport infrastructure, telecommunications infrastructure, finance clusters, prestige location, educated and skilled labour, taxation policy, property availability.
- *Distribution and logistics*: access to regional markets, transport infrastructure, telecommunications infrastructure, logistics costs, site and property availability.

For half of the project types, traditional market and efficiency seeking location factors are not key location factors. For example, IT & Software and R&D projects are most likely to locate where they can access available people skills rather than large markets or low costs. If we are to understand investment location we must analyse not only the investment strategy of the firm but also the requirements of different project types.

The importance of different location factors also varies according the stage in the decision making process. Drawing on our previous analysis, Table 3.1. illustrates the four stages of a typical location decision. The first stage involves determining the regional geographical focus of the company. As we suggested above, this is likely to depend on the overall corporate strategy of the firm. A 'long list' of countries is drawn up that meet a broad location criteria. The criterion reflects the importance of market seeking motives in the initial decision to invest internationally.

In stage two the investor reduces the long list to a 'short list' of countries which meet a more focused criteria. The location criteria in stage two emphasises efficiency seeking motives in selecting between countries. It also focuses on the labour skills and quality in each country, which are often key criteria for many project types. After stage two the investor focuses on the sub-national level in the short listed countries, and in stage three assesses localities according to a project-specific location criteria which emphasises factors (often labour costs and availability) that determine the feasibility of the

Table 3.1 The typical MNC decision-making process

Stage	Geographical focus	Decision stage	Location criteria
One	Regions	Long list of countries	• Market size • Market access and proximity • Policy environment for FDI
Two	Countries	Short list of countries	• Operational costs • Proximity to markets • Labour skills and quality
Three	Localities	Regional decision inside country	• Financial incentives • Labour availability • Labour costs
Four	Sites	Sub-regional decisions	• Size and availability of premises • Property costs • Infrastructure

project. Financial incentives on offer in different locations also come into play in this stage (Oman, 2000), and it is in this stage that the host government is likely to be contacted by the investor and the policy inputs into the investment decision-making process start to become most discernible.

In stage four the investor will usually visit the remaining localities, focusing on site availability and suitability, property costs and infrastructure. The service offered by the host country government in facilitating the viewing of sites and generally supporting the investor can be critical in the final location decision.

3.2.4 A model of FDI location

To understand FDI and the location of international investment we need to consider the conditions that allow firms to become multinational, the strategy of the firm, and the project requirements. Figure 3.1 shows the relationship between these three dimensions of FDI.

FDI will take place by firms with ownership advantages and when there are transaction costs in other methods of penetrating international markets. The overall corporate strategy is also often central

Figure 3.1   The determinants of FDI location

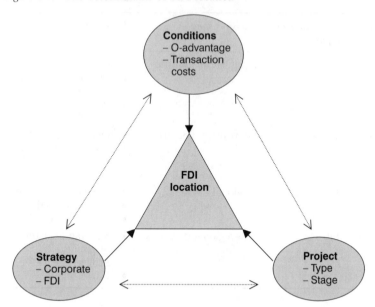

in the decision to expand across borders. The location decision-making process is based on the corporate and FDI strategy of the firm, the type of project and particular stage in the location appraisal. Figure 3.1 indicates that while the conditions for multinationality, firm strategy, and project requirements each have an independent impact on FDI location, they are also interdependent.

3.3   THE ROLE OF INCENTIVES IN THE LOCATION DECISION-MAKING PROCESS

The role of government incentives in MNC location decision-making is important to this study for three main reasons:

- Incentives can play a key role in determining the location of FDI, as Table 3.1. indicates, and were a major aspect of the negotiations between the UK government and Nissan and Siemens, as we discuss in Chapters 7 and 8.
- In Chapter 6 a bargaining model is developed which explicitly examines *how* MNCs can extract incentives and other concessions

from governments, and it is therefore important to understand *why* incentives are important for MNCs.

• In later chapters industrial and regional policy in the UK is examined, which to a significant degree has been based on using incentives to attract and influence the location of multinationals.

Brewer and Young (1995: 48) note that at the aggregate level FDI is market or oligopoly driven, but at the sectoral, firm, or project-level the policy inputs are most discernible. Incentives are a key part of policy inputs at the project level (Table 3.1). The UK government argues that its regional policy, which has been largely based on incentives, is vital in channelling and attracting investment (HMSO, 1995c: xliii). The Northern Ireland Economic Council also argues that:

Policies undertaken by development agencies and governments, through the use of financial and other incentives to attract investment from outside a region or country, can and do have significant impacts (NIEC, 1992: 5).

The view of the UK government has been supported by several empirical studies:

• Hill and Munday (1992; 1994) from 90 observations over 1980–89 found that the regional share of national preferential assistance divided by the regional share of employment accounted for 57% of new jobs generated by FDI and 64% of projects.
• Taylor (1993, cited in Phelps, 1997) found government assistance to be the main determining factor in attracting FDI.
• Sheehan (1993), in an empirical study of manufacturing FDI in Northern Ireland, found that over half of firms would have shifted production if incentives were not forthcoming.

Incentives therefore appear to play a major role in determining the location of investment at the *sub-national level*. Several commentators, however, argue that government incentives do not play a significant role in attracting FDI at the *national level* (Gold, 1991; Stopford, 1994: 66–67; Yeung, 1996), with incentives no more than 'icing on the cake' (Buxton, 1995a; Barnett, 1996). Lenway and Murtha (1994a) find that MNC managers generally discount locational incentives as the new location must retain its strategic, long-term viability with or without the government's help. Managers also perceive that the government is more likely to intervene in their operations at a later date if incentives are accepted.

On the other hand, several studies have found that firms incorporate government incentives into their financial appraisal. One of the earliest studies on incentives was a UK government study in 1983, which found from a survey of 140 foreign companies that 90% incorporated Regional Development Grants in their investment appraisal (cited in Hamilton, 1987: 188). Similar results were found by Begg and McDowall (1987) in an extensive overview of previous studies, and a more recent study on manufacturing investment in Northern Ireland, found that 75% of non-indigenous firms incorporated selective government grants into their investment appraisal (Sheehan, 1993).

In explanation, Dunning (1986) notes that incentives, while not affecting the 'locational fundamentals,' do allow a quicker rate of replacement of machinery and equipment thus influencing the amount, timing and location of FDI. With plant, equipment and information technology ever more expensive, incentives allow faster project completion and also a quicker response to market needs.

This argument is supported by Allen *et al.*, who in 1986, found that 50% of companies which failed to obtain RSA abandoned or changed the size and timing of the project (cited in Amin *et al.*, 1994: 46). Sheehan (1993) also found that 59% of respondents from Northern Ireland said investment expenditure would be delayed and 44% said that the quality of investment would have been reduced without automatic assistance. A more recent 1996 study by the Scottish Electronics Forum of manufacturing FDI in Ireland, Canada and Australia, concluded that financial incentives played a key part in helping companies to upgrade plants.

In conclusion, at the long listing stage incentives do not play a major role, with the location fundamentals of a country the key factors influencing company decision-making. At the short listing stage, if the company is appraising several locations across countries incentives may 'tip the balance' in favour of a particular country if all the locations fit the key strategic and project specific requirements. The influence of incentives is strongest in influencing the allocation of investment at the sub-national level. Incentives therefore play a significant role in the location decision making process. While they influence the *allocation* rather than *quantity* of FDI (Oman, 2000), there is detailed empirical evidence indicating that incentives can influence the location of FDI.

4 Globalisation and Economic Development

FDI is central to the relationship between MNCs and economic development. MNCs, by definition, are firms that engage in FDI (Dunning, 1981), and the level and structure of FDI in countries and localities influences the scope for economic development. The objective of this chapter is to examine international trends in FDI over time to understand the significance of FDI for economic development. Given the importance of technology and innovation to structural change and the competitiveness of firms and states (Chapter 2), we assess the extent to which the growth of FDI involves the transfer of technological activities to host countries.

The discussion of globalisation in chapter two suggests that internationalisation is nothing new. As historical studies of the MNC have shown (Dunning, 1983; Jones and Schröter, 1993; Jones, 1996a; Chandler *et al.*, 1997), FDI played an important role in the world economy even in the late nineteenth century. This chapter will illustrate, though, that the speed of internationalisation has accelerated in the post-war era and that the location and structure of FDI has changed considerably. The analysis of new forms of FDI will detail the growth of interdependence as well as internationalisation – indicating the globalisation of economic activity. However, we find that while overseas R&D and innovation by multinationals is increasing, leading to opportunities for government's to attract high value FDI, the rapid globalisation of technology and innovation is associated more with mergers and acquisitions (M&As) and cross-border alliances than greenfield investment.

4.1 MULTINATIONALS AND THE GROWTH OF FDI IN HISTORICAL PERSPECTIVE

This section will overview the growth, structure and location of FDI in historical perspective and examine the increasing role of FDI in the economic activity of states. As Table 4.1 shows, the growth of MNCs has been rapid.

Between 1967 and 1998 the accumulated FDI stock has increased by over 40 times, and on average over 1,600 new MNCs have been

Table 4.1   The growth of multinational companies, 1967–98

Year	No. of MNCs	No. of affiliates	Accumulated FDI stock (US$ trillion)	Global sales of foreign affiliates (US$ trillion)
1967	7,000	–	0.1	–
1992	37,000	170,000	2.0	4.0
1995	40,000	250,000	2.6	5.5
1997	53,000	450,000	3.4	9.7
1998	59,902	508,239	4.1	11.4

Source: Gill (1995: 405); Mittelman (1996b: 231); UNCTAD (1999, 1998, 1995b).

established annually, with almost 5,000 created each year since 1995. The number of affiliates doubled from 1995 to 1998 and the global sales of foreign affiliates in 1998 at US$11.4 trillion exceed the gross domestic product (GDP) of Japan, China, Germany, France and the UK combined. The first year that the sales of foreign affiliates exceeded world exports was in 1989, and in 1997 their sales were 44% higher. It is estimated that one-third of world trade is among the affiliates of MNCs, with more goods sold through their foreign subsidiaries than exported from their home countries (Kaminski and Riboud, 1999). Overall, the pattern is clear; the expansion of MNCs and FDI has accelerated since the 1990s, leading to a rapid inter-nationalisation of the world economy in which MNCs are playing an ever more pervasive role.

Table 4.2 shows that as the growth of FDI has accelerated, its global location has transformed, indicating changing motivations behind foreign investment. Before the Second World War developing countries accounted for about three-quarters of inward FDI, in 1967 they accounted for less than half and by the end of 1998 only around one-third of all inward investment was concentrated in developing countries.

The US and Western Europe emerged as the major locations for inward investment, and Asia replaced Latin America as the main host region for developing countries. By the end of the 1990s developed countries accounted for about two-thirds of inward FDI and over 90% of the outward FDI stock (UNCTAD, 1999). Since the 1990s Asia-Pacific countries have emerged as both important hosts and homes for FDI, with Japan and the four tigers becoming major outward investors and China attracting the third largest FDI inflows in the world in the

Table 4.2 Percentage share of the global inward FDI stock by host region, 1914–98

Region	1914	1938	1967	1980	1993	1997	1998
USA	10	7	9	16	21	21	21
Canada	6	10	18	10	6	4	3.5
Western Europe	8	7	30	36	43	37	38
Eastern Europe	10	2	–	–	–	2	2
Latin America	33	31	18	12	8	11	10
Asia	21	25	5	7	13	17	18
Africa	6	7	5	3	2	2	2
Rest of World	6	11	15	16	7	6	5
Total (US$)	18.2bn	26.4bn	106bn	480bn	2,222bn	3,456bn	4,088bn

Source: Jones (1996b); OECD (1996); UNCTAD (1998, 1999).

1990s. Three major three regions of the world economy have come to dominate FDI; Western Europe, North America, and Asia-Pacific (Japan plus South, East and South East Asia) accounted for over 80% of the inward FDI stock and nearly 100% of outward FDI in 1998.

The historic shift in the location of FDI from developing to developed countries, and to Asia-Pacific since the 1990s, reflects the change from resource seeking to market and efficiency seeking investment. The shift away from natural resources can be seen in Table 4.3. In 1914, 55% of FDI was in natural resources – by 1992 just over one-tenth was in this sector. Manufacturing FDI grew rapidly from 15% of total FDI in 1914 to 52% in 1978. However, by the 1990s FDI in the service sector exceeded manufacturing FDI.

Data collected by Ernst & Young, provides a more detailed breakdown of FDI by type and sector. Table 4.4 shows FDI *projects* in Europe from 1997 to mid-1999. The data avoids many of the measurement problems we identified in Chapter 3, as only actual greenfield and

Table 4.3 Distribution of accumulated world FDI by sector, 1914–92

Sector	1914	1978	1992
Natural Resources	55	22	11
Manufacturing	15	52	39
Services	30	26	50

Source: data from Jones (1996b: 32–55).

Table 4.4   FDI projects by type and sector, January 1997–June 1999

Total projects (6,075)		Manufacturing projects (3,016)	
Type	% of total	Sector	% of total
Manufacturing	49	Chemicals	21
Sales & marketing	22	Automotive	17
Distribution	9	Machinery	10
R&D	8	Electronics	8
Headquarters	8	Food	7
Other	6	Pharmaceuticals	5
		Computers	3
		Medical	3
		Other	27

Source: Ernst & Young's *European Investment Monitor*, cited in *Corporate Location* (2000a).

brown field projects are recorded and it gives the most accurate breakdown available of the key sectors of actual FDI projects.

Table 4.4 indicates that there were over 6,000 FDI projects in Europe over the two-and-a-half year period, with approximately half of all projects in manufacturing. The next most important project type was sales and marketing, which accounted for 22% of total projects. This demonstrates the importance of market seeking FDI, as the establishment of a sales and marketing subsidiary or office is a clear indication that the multinational will serve the domestic or regional market. Of the 3,000 manufacturing projects, 38% were in the chemicals and automotive sectors – two of the most internationalised industries in the world. The chemicals and automotive sectors accounted for the highest number of total FDI projects, followed by IT & Software projects in the service sector.

The key importance of market seeking FDI and role of efficiency seeking investment was revealed an extensive study of 900 MNCs, commissioned by the UK government. The study concluded that the prime motivation for foreign investment:

is to gain new customers or achieve market entry. Improving services to existing customers and establishing a regional hub are other [significant] objectives.... Very few companies were driven primarily by the desire to reduce costs, although cost may be one factor determining the selection of a location of a hub within a particular geographical market (HMSO, 1996).

Intensifying competition, technological advance and regional integration encouraged the shift away from resource to efficiency and market seeking investment, with different implications for MNC's strategic choice of investment location (Thomsen and Woolcock, 1993: ch.3). Regional integration in Europe stimulated efficiency-seeking FDI within the single market (Barrell and Pain, 1997a: 52; Landsbury and Pain, 1997: 96), and intensifying global competition and rapidly rising domestic costs increased the pressure on firms to shift low cost production abroad, in particular in high cost developed countries and in several Asian economies.[1] The new competition, symbolised by lean production, favours locations with low costs and flexible labour (Loewendahl, 1998), and technological advance stimulates new forms of investment cross-cutting the most technologically advanced countries to gain access to markets and complementary assets.

The growth of market-seeking investment is pulled by regional trading blocs and pushed by saturated markets at home and the need to access new markets to amortise the costs of technological advance (Caves, 1982). Increased competition and new flexible technologies also stimulate FDI to meet differentiated tastes (Barrell and Pain, 1997c: 1773–4; Phelps, 1997: 52–3), calling for presence in each of the major markets. The rapid economic growth in East Asia and

Table 4.5   Country distribution of 500 largest industrial firms, 1962–98

Country	1962	1993	1998
US	298	160	175
Britain	55	43	39
Germany	36	32	35
France	27	26	30
Japan	31	135	121
South Korea	0	11	11
Canada	13	7	13
Italy	7	7	11
Switzerland	6	9	11
Sweden	8	12	9

Source: derived from Chandler and Hikino (1997: 53) and *Industry Week* (1999).

from the 1990s the opening up of the former communists countries, has further stimulated market-seeking FDI.

With developed country MNCs investing in each other's markets, and with certain developing countries emerging as major foreign investors, the number of 'multinational' countries is increasing, as indicated in Table 4.5. The US and the UK accounted for 71% of the top 500 MNCs in 1962, but in 1998 this percentage had fallen to 43%. Japan has rapidly emerged as the second major source of MNCs, and large rapidly industrialising developing countries like South Korea are also important home countries. During the 1990s, France, Germany, Italy, Switzerland and, most notably, Canada all increased their presence as homes for the top 500 industrial MNCs. The home base of MNCs is therefore widening.

The rapid growth of MNCs is increasing the role of FDI in national economies, as Table 4.6 shows. Although FDI flows account for less than 3% of GDP in both developing and developed countries, the stock of FDI as a proportion of GDP has doubled in developed countries between 1980 and 1996 and quadrupled in developing countries, accounting for roughly one-fifth of GDP in both groups. As a proportion of GDP, FDI now has a greater weight in developing countries, despite the majority of FDI flows taking place between developed countries.

The same pattern is found with trade flows. From 1970–72 exports and imports and inward and outward FDI flows were more significant for developed countries, but from 1994–96 they accounted for a higher proportion of GDP in developing countries.

While FDI flows have been growing three times faster than trade flows since the early 1980s, exports and imports account for over 40% of GDP, still nearly twice that of FDI. However, about 40% of world trade is intra-firm trade within the 350 largest MNCs (Nicolaides, 1993c: 108), and in the US nearly half of manufacturing exports and over 60% of imports flow within MNCs (Ostry, 1998: 87). MNCs therefore control a large part of the world's trade as well as FDI.

In terms of employment, in 1995 73 million people were employed in MNCs – 10% of the world's non-agricultural employment and 5% of the world work-force (Gill, 1995: 405; Dunning and Sauvant, 1996: xi). According to UNCTAD (1994), if we include the impact on indirect employment, then at least 40% of employment in the developed countries depends on MNCs. Through the growth of FDI, MNCs play a significant and growing role in the GDP, exports and employment of developed and developing countries.

Table 4.6 Internationalisation in FDI and trade, 1970–96

Country	FDI inflows & outflows as % GDP			FDI inward & outward stock as % GDP			Exports & imports as % GDP		
	1970–72	1980–82	1994–96	1980	1990	1996	1970–72	1980–82	1994–96
Developed countries	0.3	1.1	2.1	11.2	18.0	22.1	8.2	39.2	37.0
Developing countries	0.1	0.9	2.9	5.0	10.3	20.5	7.1	51.5	56.6
World	0.3	1.0	2.2	9.5	15.8	21.4	8.0	42.4	41.2

Source: derived from UNCTAD (1998).

4.2   MULTINATIONALS AND THE GLOBALISATION OF TECHNOLOGY AND INNOVATION

In examining the extent of globalisation and implications for economic development, FDI data is of limited use. While section 4.1 examined the rapid growth of FDI, indicating the *internationalisation* of the world economy, alternative data is needed to capture the extent of *interdependence* and understand the implications of multinationals' control over knowledge and innovation[2] for economic development prospects. In particular, asset-seeking strategies of MNCs need to be examined and the extent to which multinationals are adopting a complex integration strategy that increases their interdependence on foreign locations needs to be assessed.

Data on patenting and R&D is used to examine the innovation and technology-based strategies of MNCs and the implications of globalisation for economic development. Patenting data is particularly useful for analysing the globalisation of technology as the data refers to both the company and country of origin and long-run time-series data has been collected in several studies, providing detailed comparisons over time. There is further utility in inspecting patenting data as patents are a measure of innovation, not just R&D (Cantwell, 1995: 157), and therefore indicate trends in the commercialisation rather than simply generation of technology. R&D expenditure accounts for part of the costs and efforts of developing and commercialising new goods and services (OECD, 1996: 58) – in the case of German manufacturing industry, about one-quarter of total innovation expenditure at the end of the 1980s (Keck, 1993: 150).

R&D expenditure also gives firms and countries the capacity to generate, absorb, and diffuse technology and, for large firms, R&D is the most important source of new knowledge and skills (Cantwell, 1995: 157; Cooke and Morgan, 1998: 25, 137). R&D is therefore a good proxy indicator of innovative behaviour and is central to economic development, with empirical studies finding that R&D expenditure is an important determinant of growth, especially in developed countries (Gittleman and Wolff, 1995; Pianta, 1995). The increasing importance of R&D expenditure and technology flows to states and firms suggests, according to the OECD (1996: 17), 'that policy must take greater account of the national knowledge base and how globalised firms contribute to the development of this base'.

4.2.1 Globalisation of patenting and R&D

Accelerating technological advance, as Chapter 2 discussed, has increased R&D costs and complexity and shortened product life cycles, encouraging FDI:

- to access new markets and increase market share in existing markets in order to increase revenues so that R&D expenditures can be more quickly recouped;
- to access new sources of technology;
- to make new products more responsive to local consumer requirements.

At the same time, R&D is a key ownership advantage for the firm, and in accordance with international business theory, studies have found that R&D and patents are correlated with FDI (Grubaugh, 1987; Kogut and Chang, August 1991; Wheeler and Mody, 1992; Hennart and Park, 1994; Landsbury and Pain, 1997). In other words, firms need intangible assets to be able to expand abroad. FDI through direct production abroad is encouraged due to market imperfections in the transfer of intangible knowledge and desire for control over proprietary technology, as also argued by international business theory (Buckley and Casson, 1976: 45; Schienstock, 1992: 462–3).[3] The trend for new products to become component parts of broader systems and the growth of systems solutions in industries like automotive components, machine tools and electrical engineering demands close co-operation with customers (HMSO, 1998a; Lane, 1998: 478), which is facilitated by direct market presence.

We should therefore expect technology to be closely connected to globalisation. Following Archibugi and Michie (1995), globalisation of technology and innovation is manifested as three main trends:

- global exploitation of technological/innovation activities;
- global technological collaboration;
- global generation of technology/innovation.

In terms of the exploitation of technological activities, the growth of patents extended in foreign markets in the OECD was 6% annually in the 1980s and, as shown in Table 4.7, by 1990 the foreign exploitation of technological activities in the G5 was intense. From 1990 to 1997 in the US and Japan – the world's two largest economies and most

Table 4.7   Domestic and foreign patents, 1990–97

Country	Domestic patents (%)		Foreign Patents (%)	
	1990	1997	1990	1997
USA	55.1	53.1	44.9	46.9
Japan	88.5	84.0	11.5	16.0
Germany	32.6	35.3	67.4	64.7
France	16.2	16.6	83.9	83.4
UK	21.5	18.0	78.5	82.0

Source: derived from Archibugi and Michie (1995) and World Bank (2000a).

prolific innovators – the proportion of foreign patents in total patents increased, most dramatically in Japan by almost 40%. By 1997, foreign patents accounted for the majority of patents in the UK, France and Germany, and overwhelming proportions in most other developed and developing countries (see World Bank, 2000a).

Data on the share of foreign affiliates in manufacturing R&D in host countries also indicates the vital role of FDI for many countries. The extreme case is Singapore, with over 90% of manufacturing R&D accounted for by foreign affiliates, while in Japan the figure is only 2%. The share of foreign affiliates R&D in total R&D (Figure 4.1)

Figure 4.1   Share of foreign affiliates in total manufacturing R&D expenditures in 1994 (or nearest year)

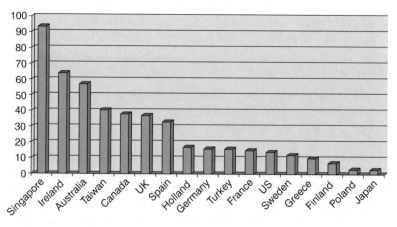

Source: UNCTAD (1999) and OECD (1999b).

Table 4.8 Share of United States patents registered by the world's largest
firms attributable to research in foreign locations, 1969–95 (%)

Nationality of parent firm	1969–72	1973–77	1978–82	1983–86	1987–90	1991–95
US	5.0	5.9	6.4	7.5	7.9	8.6
Germany	12.8	11.1	12.1	14.5	17.1	20.7
UK	43.1	41.2	40.5	47.1	50.4	55.8
Italy	13.4	16.0	13.9	12.6	11.1	16.5
France	8.2	7.7	7.2	9.2	18.2	33.2
Japan	2.6	1.9	1.2	1.3	0.9	1.1
Netherlands	50.4	47.4	47.7	54.0	54.0	55.7
Belgium-Lux	50.4	51.1	49.3	58.2	47.5	53.3
Switzerland	44.4	43.6	43.8	41.6	43.0	52.5
Sweden	17.8	19.9	26.2	28.9	30.6	42.4
Austria	5.1	16.8	19.8	11.8	8.0	–
Norway	20.0	1.7	12.3	32.5	37.1	20.2
Finland	18.9	27.1	26.9	18.7	27.9	39.5
Canada	41.2	39.3	39.5	35.8	40.1	44.0
Others	28.2	22.2	26.4	30.3	7.5	3.9
Total	10.0	10.5	10.5	11.0	11.3	11.3
Total excluding Japan	10.5	11.6	12.3	13.9	15.8	16.5
Total European countries	28.0	25.2	24.5	27.0	30.0	34.8

Source: Cantwell and Janne (1998) cited in UNCTAD (1999).

is much lower than the share of foreign patents in total patents
(Table 4.7) suggesting that FDI plays a greater role in the commercialisation rather than the generation of technology in host countries.

In terms of the global generation of innovation, at first glance
activity appears to be highly concentrated in the home countries of
multinationals. Table 4.8 shows that for the US, the world's major
source of technology,[4] over a 26-year period the proportion of patenting accounted for by foreign subsidiaries increased from 5.0% to only
8.6%. In Japan the proportion of US patenting accounted for by
overseas research actually fell from 2.6% to only 1.1%. Globally,
there was only an 11% increase in the share of US patenting from
foreign research locations, from 10.0% to 11.3%.

In Europe though, overseas patenting increased by almost one-
quarter in the 1991–95 period. Over one-third of US patenting of the
largest European companies was conducted overseas. For many European countries this figure is over 50% and for Canada it is also very high.

Table 4.9   R&D per employee in the US and overseas of US multinationals, 1990–95

Affiliate	1990 (US$)	1995 (US$)	% change
Foreign affiliates of US MNCs	1,900	2,200	14
US parent companies in US	3,500	5,200	33
Foreign-based MNCs in US	2,400	3,600	33

Source: adapted from UNCTAD (1998).

The global generation of technology is therefore vital to companies from most countries. The US, and to a lesser extent Japan, are likely to be exceptions given the size of their economies. The US economy is roughly the same size as Europe and therefore should be compared with Europe taken as a region rather than with individual countries. In fact, the proportion of US patenting accounted for by foreign subsidiaries of US firms increased by over 70% over the 26-year period, demonstrating a steady growth in global innovation. If we exclude Japan, over the period overseas patenting increased by 57 per cent.

If we look at R&D data, Table 4.9 shows that from 1990 to 1995 the growth of R&D per employee in the foreign subsidiaries of US MNCs was 14% – less than half of the increase experienced by the parent companies in the US. However, foreign MNCs in the US increased their R&D per employee by one-third over the period and conducted nearly two-thirds more R&D per employee in the US that the foreign affiliates of US firms. US affiliates of foreign companies spent US$19.7 billion on R&D in 1997 compared to US$6.5 billion in 1987. The overseas R&D expenditure of US MNCs increased from US$5.2 billion in 1987 to US$14.1 billion in 1997 – accounting for 11% of all US R&D (Serapio *et al.*, 2000). While R&D has inter-nationalised rapidly since the late 1980s, the US is clearly more attractive for R&D activities that other countries.

Ernst & Young's European Investment Monitor also shows that in Europe R&D is concentrated in advanced developed countries. Table 4.10 compares the top 10 locations for manufacturing FDI projects in Europe in 1999 with the top 10 locations for R&D projects. There are three developing countries in the top five manufacturing locations, whereas the top five R&D locations are all in advanced developed countries. The small, technologically advanced countries of Sweden, Austria and Switzerland are in the top 10 R&D locations, but are not present in the main manufacturing locations. The main exception to

Table 4.10   Manufacturing and R&D projects in Europe in 1999

New manufacturing projects			R&D projects		
Rank	*Country*	*Projects*	*Rank*	*Country*	*Projects*
1	United Kingdom	57	1	United Kingdom	55
2	France	44	2	France	21
3	Poland	42	3	Ireland	17
4	Hungary	38	4	Germany	14
5	Czech Republic	30	5	Spain	11
6	Germany	23	6	Sweden	8
7	Spain	23	7	Austria	6
8	Belgium	21	8	Hungary	6
9	Ireland	20	9	Italy	6
10	Netherlands	12	10	Netherlands	5
			10	Switzerland	5

Source: Ernst & Young, cited in Site Selection (2000).

the concentration of R&D in developed countries is Hungary, which is the only developing country to be in the top 10 R&D locations.

In explaining why R&D is concentrated in particular countries, we can draw on research by Patel (1990) and Porter (1998) who argue that economies of scale and association in innovation favour agglomeration and co-location of R&D and other activities such as component fabrication, assembly, marketing and customer support. This leads to internal efficiencies in sourcing and sharing technology and information. New product development needs close interaction between R&D, design and production, and decision centres (Patel, 1995; Belderbos, 1997: 95) and the integration of functions allows R&D to become more commercially rather than technologically driven (Cooke and Morgan, 1998: 42).

R&D is therefore likely to gravitate towards existing centres and the advantages of centralising R&D in the home country may outweigh the costs of not exploiting fully overseas R&D potential. Similar to Vernon's (1966) product cycle model, products are developed at home and adapted overseas, with minimal overseas R&D to exploit the technological base of host countries – a hypothesis which has empirical support from Papanastassiou (1995), Papanastassiou and Pearce (1995), and Patel (1995). The OECD (1999b: 16) also argues that: 'Economies of scale, the complexity and cost of managing geographically dispersed research centres, impediments to the diffusion of technology, the importance of proximity between production and research, and even weaknesses in foreign systems of innovation, counter act incentives to globalise research.' The transfer of R&D-intensive activities to overseas subsidiaries of multinationals may therefore be limited in geographical scope.

However, while technological activity continues to be concentrated, the steady growth in overseas patenting and R&D by MNCs and the significance of R&D by foreign affiliates in host countries indicates the internationalisation of technology and innovation. There are also increasing opportunities for attracting the R&D activities of multi-nationals, despite the advantages of centralisation, with rapid growth in overseas R&D projects by MNCs in recent years. In the US, by the mid-1990s there were at least 635 foreign-owned and free-standing R&D centres – over half established after 1986. In Europe, in 1995 there were over 300 Japanese R&D facilities, double the number of 1989 (OECD, 1999b: 13). Of all Japanese manufacturing companies 42.2% had R&D centres in Europe (Harukiyo, 1998: 51), each gen-erally employing between 10 and 40 personnel (Belderbos, 1997: 97). Of the 71 independent (rather than attached) R&D facilities, 39.4% conducted basic research and over two-thirds of both the attached and independent facilities were engaged in product development (JETRO cited in Harukiyo, 1998).

For US MNCs, in the first half of the 1990s the growth of R&D in subsidiaries was faster than that of either sales or employment (Table 4.11), indicated increasing R&D intensity of FDI. Table 4.4. also shows that 8% of total FDI projects in Europe from 1997 to mid-1999 were classified by Ernst & Young as R&D projects – in just two and half years there were nearly 500 R&D projects in Europe.

Motivated by accelerating technological advance and the movement towards the N-form, the growth in overseas patenting and R&D projects indicates that MNCs are acting more and more as global

Table 4.11   Activities of US foreign
affiliates, 1991–95

Activity	Increase (%)
R&D	340
Sales	250
Employment	170

Source: adapted from UNCTAD (1998).

scanners for new technology, increasingly developing, linking and leveraging innovation world-wide.

Vernon's product cycle model, while pointing to the concentration of innovation at home, does not capture the formation of R&D networks in MNCs, and therefore the possibility that the overseas subsidiaries of MNCs may play a vital role in the firm's R&D activities. In fact, this was recognised in the late 1970s by Vernon (1979), who argued that MNCs engage in almost simultaneous innovations in several markets due to highly compressed product cycle in some industries. More recent research has shown that:

> Previously, companies expanded their R&D operations overseas primarily to support local manufacturing and marketing operations. But now companies are making overseas investments to complement their domestic research, technology and product strengths. Overseas R&D operations are thus becoming important sources of new science and technology for the entire global corporation (Serapio *et al.*, 2000).

However, only countries with a deep technological supply-base (Belderbos, 1997: 95) and sub-national regions which form strong links between business and major research universities (Mowery and Oxley, 1995: 90; Bass, 1998) can draw technological activities to host base clusters. The globalisation of R&D and technological activity therefore becomes concentrated at three levels:

- *In specific (developed) countries*: the G7 account for close to 85% of total R&D expenditures in the OECD and only 15 developing countries can be said to be doing any notable R&D (OECD, 1999b: 16). Of the total foreign R&D of US MNCs 91% was in developed countries in 1994 compared with 79% of their total foreign sales (Dunning, 1998: 51).
- *In specific, cluster-based localities*: the foremost example is the Silicon Valley in the US which attracts one-third of the world's high-tech venture capital and where there are estimated to be over 1,000 MIT-related companies with world-wide sales of US$53 billion (HMSO, 1998a; *The Economist*, 1999d). In Texas, Austin alone has 25,000 high-tech firms and over 75 semiconductor plants (Millward, 1995: 28). In the UK, there is a cluster of high-tech industry around Cambridge University, which established its first industrial park in 1970, an Innovation Centre in 1987 for start-ups,

and a Small Business Research Centre in 1992. In proximity to the university there are now over 1,000 innovation-based companies employing over 27,000. In 1997, Microsoft announced that it would establish its first R&D centre outside the US in Cambridge and in 1999 AT&T acquired a Cambridge-based research laboratory, injecting £30 million into a leading centre for communications research. The proportion of business value added invested in R&D in 1997 in the Cambridge region (East England) was nearly 19% – nearly three times higher than the UK average (derived from DTI, 1999). Another example, is Ile-de-France, which by the 1990s accounted for 51% of France's R&D employment, 55% of R&D expenditure, and 58.9% of the civil R&D budget (Dunford, 1995: 184).

- *In specific (multinational) firms*: at the firm level, in-house R&D capability is crucial if firms are to be able to monitor, evaluate and learn about research done elsewhere and assimilate and further develop externally acquired technology (Nelson, 1994: 130; Powell and Smith-Doerr, 1994: 387; Hassink, 1996: 173). However, developing in-house technological capability is a long term learning process. Chandler (1997) finds that long-established large firms with learned R&D capabilities have huge benefits in exploiting new technologies, with the result that R&D remains concentrated in several core firms. For example, of the 200 largest US corporations in 1988, 40 were in chemicals and all but one had pre-war roots. Of the 86 high-tech firms, other than in electronics, all were established before 1941 (Chandler, 1997: 83–4). In the UK, 95% of manufacturing R&D is carried out by 100 firms (Cooke and Morgan, 1998: 137). In Germany, Siemens, Daimler-Benz, Bayer, Hoechst, VW and BASF account for nearly one-third of domestic industrial R&D capability (Keck, 1993: 138), and the OECD (1992) estimates that MNCs account for 75% of all industrial R&D in the OECD.

4.2.2   M&As and cross-border collaboration

M&As have become the major component of official FDI statistics. Table 4.12 indicates the scale and growth of FDI and M&As from 1985 to 1997. In the second half of the 1980s, the growth of FDI inflows exceeded that of M&As, however in the first half of the 1990s the growth of M&As was 50% higher than that of FDI inflows, and M&As were roughly 40% of FDI inflows. By the end of 1998, the

Table 4.12   The role of M&As in FDI, 1985–98 (US$ billion)

FDI type and annual growth rate	1985–90 annual average	1991–95 annual average	1996	1997	1998
FDI inflows	159	225	359	464	644
FDI inward stock	1,736 (1990)	2,865 (1995)	3,086	3,437	4,088
Cross-border M&As*	–	88	163	236	411
Growth FDI inflows	23.6	19.6	9.1	29.4	38.7
Growth FDI inward stock	18.2	9.6	10.6	11.4	19.0
Growth M&As	21.0 (1987–90)	30.2	15.5	45.2	73.9

Source: UNCTAD (1999).

growth of M&As was almost double that of total FDI inflows – accounting for 64% of FDI. In fact, almost all of the growth in FDI from 1996 to 1998 can be accounted for by M&As. For example, from 1997 to 1998, if we subtract M&As then FDI would have grown by only 2% – a fraction of the 38.7% growth in total FDI recorded in 1998.[5]

For FDI in the US, the role of acquisitions is even more intense, increasing from 82% of inward FDI in 1990 to 90% in 1997 (UNCTAD, 1998). The growing importance of M&As, particularly in advanced markets like the US, represents structural changes taking place in the world economy. With accelerating technological advance and the growing importance of knowledge in competitiveness, acquisitions are multiplying. At the same time, with a back-to-basics strategy, non-core activities are being divested and core activities strengthened through M&A activity, made possible due to world liberalisation and deregulation (UNCTAD, 1998). M&As are concentrated in knowledge and information-intensive sectors (UNCTAD, 1997), and international acquisitions are often aimed at technology capture (OECD, 1996: 41). It is no coincidence that the patenting data (Table 4.8) show British MNCs to be the most globalised in terms of innovation activities out of all the world's major economies and at the same time, as *The Economist* (1999a) shows, British companies now lead the world in international acquisitions. Serapio *et al.* (2000) also argue that foreign acquisitions of US companies have had a significant impact on foreign R&D spending and investment in R&D in the

United States and Belderbos (1997) found that Japanese acquisitions of European firms are motivated by technology acquisition. Cross-border M&As are a key driver for the globalisation of technology and innovation.

The surge in M&As since the 1990s has been mirrored by the rapid growth of inter-firm collaborative agreements – or new forms of investment. These agreements can involve joint ventures, licences, strategic alliances, sales and R&D co-operation and also supply agreements and common distribution systems in foreign markets (Capello, 1996). They are motivated by the increased importance of knowledge-intensive production, which has led to soaring R&D costs and risks (UNCTAD, 1998; Ham *et al.*, 1998: 140), and are of particular importance for accessing and developing technology.

Prior to the 1980s, strategic alliances were relatively uncommon. However in many industries they are now favoured over M&As and the internalisation of knowledge (Lawton, 1997: 30). In the second half of the 1980s international joint ventures increased by 6% per annum (Archibugi and Michie, 1995), and a statistical study by Kogut and Chang (1991) found joint ventures to be motivated by the sourcing of technology. In fact, the growth of science and technology alliances has been even faster – from 1980 to 1994 the total number of grew at 10.8% per annum. Furthermore, about 65% involved partners from different countries (OECD, 1999b: 13), indicating that new technologies and innovative concepts are not only increasingly found outside company walls but also outside national borders (OECD, 1999b: 7). The growth in licensing, shown in Table 4.13, also points to the importance of technology access in the formation of co-operative arrangements and indicates the significance of innovation networks in MNCs with the majority of receipts intra-firm.

The total number of new cross-border alliances (including M&As) has amplified to an estimated 15,000 in 1995 and 1996 (Allen and

Table 4.13   Receipts from patents, royalties and license fees, 1986–96

Year	United States		Japan		Germany	
	US$ million	*% intra-firm*	*US$ million*	*% intra-firm*	*US$ million*	*% intra-firm*
1986	7,927	76	1,230	58	778	92
1996	29,974	79	6,443	52	2,453	95

Source: UNCTAD (1998).

Hamilton, 1997, cited in Dunning, 1998: 61), reflecting changes in the technology structure. New IT&Ts facilitate cross-border communication and technological complexity is leading to products and processes that increasingly involve the combination or re-combination and exploitation of synergies of a wider range of existing and new technologies on a global scale (Cooke, 1997: 358; Braczyk and Heidenreich, 1998: 433–38; *The Economist*, 1999d). For example, sectoral specificity has broken down in the computing, consumer electronics and telecommunications sectors, with the functions of each sector merging (Cawson *et al.*, 1990: 363–4; *The Economist*, 1992b).

Similarly, in the financial sector the rapidly growing importance of the Internet and customer relationship management is likely to lead to growing alliances between traditional financial institutions and telecommunications and software firms. For example, in February 2000 the Spanish bank BBVA and telecommunications company Telfonica established a joint venture internet bank (Uno-e) – one of first examples of vertical integration in the banking industry. BBVA provides the product, customers and security, while Telefonica brings distribution and technology skills. Another significant example is the recently established Mobey Forum with the world's leading financial service and mobile technology firms co-operating to establish a new global technology standard and overcome technical obstacles to mobile financial services. Strategic alliances are therefore crucial for merging separate technologies and for creating new technology standards. They are heavily concentrated in the most advanced and fastest growing industries.

While faster access to and exchange of complementary technologies are major motives behind the formation of strategic alliances, other key motives include:

- sharing the costs and risks of rising R&D expenditures (Hamill, 1992; Ham *et al.*, 1998: 140);
- facilitating market and geographical expansion (Buckley and Glaister, 1996);
- providing greater flexibility and leverage of R&D investments (Capello, 1996: 491–2; UNCTAD, 1998).

The trend towards R&D co-operation can be seen from the latest statistics from UNCTAD, in Table 4.14. While the overall growth in inter-firm technology agreements is rapid, with the number more than doubling from the early 1980s to the early 1990s and the total reaching

Table 4.14   Inter-firm technology agreements, 1980–96

Year	Average each year	One-way	Two-way
1980–83	280	–	–
1984–87	493	–	–
1988–91	502	223	279
1992–95	626	158	569
1996 (total)	650 (8,260)	109	541

Source: adapted from UNCTAD (1998).

8,260 by the end of 1996, of particular interest is the growth in two-way agreements. This type of co-operation represents the growing importance of joint R&D and development, rather than one-way access to technology.

UNCTAD records that from 1980 to 1996 37% of inter-firm technology agreements were in information technology and 27% in pharmaceuticals – two of the most research-intensive industries. In research-intensive sectors MNCs are rapidly integrating their technological and innovation activities, and are accessing, developing and marketing their technology globally through new forms of FDI. The growth of M&As is one side of the globalisation of technology and is favoured if technology is easily appropriable, but the exponential growth in inter-firm, cross-border co-operative agreements is the key driver behind the globalisation of technology and innovation. In the next section we look at how the organisational form of MNCs has changed, in part a response to changes in the technology structure.

4.3   TOWARDS THE N-FORM

Three structural changes were identified in Chapter 2 as fundamental to globalisation: intensifying global competition, technological change and regional integration. This chapter has focused on FDI, and we have seen how structural changes have led to market and efficiency seeking FDI and, in particular, how technological change has led to new forms of FDI and asset-seeking investment. Changes in the knowledge structure therefore have a perpetual influence on MNC corporate strategy, but the purpose of this section is to examine the impact of structural change on the *organisation* of MNC activities.

4.3.1 The importance of organisation

In much international business research, the organisation of multi-national operations is not a high priority research agenda. In particular, perspectives on the MNC derived from transaction costs economics see the firm as a unitary, homogenous actor, as out-lined in Table 2.2. Dunning (1981), for example, defines MNCs as simply 'firms that engage in FDI'. What is important is FDI per se, not the organisation making FDI strategies and locating and managing foreign direct investment projects.

However, if we are to understand the impact of MNCs on economic development the organisation of multinational activities is significant. We argue that the organisation of MNCs has changed over time in response to structural pressures, creating more opportunities for locations to attract FDI.

Multinational companies are heterogeneous actors, characterised by significant differences in organisational structure according to industry and country. The idiosyncratic evolution of MNCs is context specific. Nonaka (1990), Ruigrok and Tulder (1995), Pauly and Reich (1997) and Edwards (1998b) and show that the internationalisation strategy of companies varies according to their home country. We can generalise and say that:

- Multinationals from the US have been among the first to integrate their operations on a regional or global basis and move towards international product divisions. The operations of US MNCs are also characterised by sophisticated monitoring and control mechanisms.
- European MNCs have favoured more decentralised operations and the overseas subsidiaries of European MNCs with historically dispersed operations have developed a significant degree of independence as they became embedded in the host country. The interests of subsidiaries lay firmly in ensuring that the institutional structure remained decentralised (see Bartlett and Ghoshal, 1989; 1993b), according to Reich (1996). European MNCs are therefore characterised by the highest degree of dispersal of high value added assets.
- Japanese MNCs have been most centralised in terms of core capabilities and subsidiary relations, which is perhaps not surprising given the relatively recent germination of Japanese MNCs and therefore the limited time scale for subsidiaries to become embedded in host countries.

- Multinationals from small home countries, like Sweden or Switzerland, are among the most internationalised, as in the example of ABB below.

Supporting this picture is Table 4.8, which showed that European MNCs have internationalised innovation to the highest degree and Japanese MNCs the least. Studies have also found that European MNCs produce mainly for their host markets, supporting the hypothesis that they have decentralised operations, while Japanese subsidiaries are the most export oriented, indicating centralised operations (see Papanastassiou and Pearce, 1995). This pattern also reflects the sectoral focus of multinationals from different countries. European MNCs have a greater presence in pharmaceuticals and telecommunications, which require a high degree of national responsiveness, while Japanese MNCs are stronger in electronics and semiconductors, which are more standardised and dependent on economies of scale and access to regional rather than national markets.

A central argument of this study is, however, that intensifying global competition, accelerating technological change and regional integration are creating converging pressures for the emergence of the network-form MNC. As international competition is based more on innovation and as technological change and complexity increase, networks facilitate the flow of knowledge, access to synergies, increased flexibility and improved collaboration in order to exploit opportunities. The importance of innovation and the new competition promotes vertical disintegration and focus on external relations, while regional integration facilitates regional or global corporate strategies for differentiated markets.

4.3.2   From U-form to N-form

Chandler's renowned 1962 study, *Strategy and Structure*, argued that the organisation of MNCs has evolved from a centralised (U-form) to a decentralised multi-divisional (M-form) structure. From a study of 50 of the largest companies in the US, Chandler concluded that market growth and technological change were driving changes in MNC structure, with companies seeking greater diversity in their products and markets.

Companies at the end of the nineteenth century have been characterised variously as uni-dimensional (Chandler, 1962), monocentric (Wilkins, 1974) or ethnocentric (Perlmutter, 1969). Essentially, home country patterns were dominant, with products manufactured and sold abroad by foreign subsidiaries normally identical to those produced by the parent. However, as MNCs sought greater diversity and expanded horizontally (widening their geographical scope), and vertically (increasing their product range), the centralised U-form structure proved inept at co-ordinating complex and dispersed operations. As Chandler and Hikino (1997: 35) note, the headquarters:

> did not have the time or the competence to co-ordinate and monitor – or to devise and implement – long term strategies for their units operating in different geographical and product markets

MNCs were able to manage their new strategies efficiently only if they adopted a multi-divisional, M-form (Chandler, 1962; Williamson, 1975), polycentric (Wilkins, 1974; Perlmutter, 1969) or multidomestic (Porter, 1990a) structure. The M-form was used by Chandler to explain the development of MNCs in capital-intensive manufacturing from the end of the nineteenth to mid-twentieth century.

Integral to the M-form is a decentralisation of responsibility to operating divisions, with national subsidiaries gaining a high degree of autonomy to sell differentiated products in local markets. In many cases, affiliates became almost fully autonomous and local patterns came to dominate, although it should be noted that the M-form is a hierarchical structure. While it is characterised by the decentralisation of management, production, accountancy and marketing to divisions, the central headquarters continues to plan, co-ordinate and control activities, determine long term strategies for the entire firm, and allocate resources (Kocka, 1978; Ghoshal and Westney, 1993: 15). Decision-making is concentrated at the top of the hierarchy, in the home countries.

During the post-war period, multinationals in Europe were replacing the personal control which characterised family-run companies with a bureaucratic model of systematic management (Kocka, 1978) as they adopted the M-form organisational structure. However, already in the 1960s, several US MNCs were moving towards co-ordinating production world-wide, facilitated by regional integration (the European Economic Community, EEC), falling world tariffs, reduced transportation costs and convergence of consumer demand in some sectors (Jones, 1996b: 136). The autonomous, multi-divisional structure acted as a constraint to co-ordinating production (Jones, 1996b: 136), and M-form structures were slowly abandoned.

With intensifying competitive pressures, by the 1990s Amercian and increasing numbers of European multinationals had abandoned their corporate-wide international area divisions and globalised their product divisions (Lane, 1998), especially in technology-driven firms (Kogut, 1993: 149). Multinationals started to co-ordinate more tightly divisions, and have increasingly focused on their core competencies, selling off non-essential divisions, in part motivated by excessive product diversification (Jones, 1997: 129). With regional integration and the opening up of world markets, competition within spatially bounded markets is being replaced by competition for one product globally (de Smidt and Wever, 1990: 4–5).

Multinational companies are under increasing pressure to achieve both global efficiency and to localise their products and value adding activities (Westney, 1993: 68). This is leading to market, efficiency and asset seeking FDI and to MNCs integrating their functions on a global basis through the establishment of international product divisions[6] and powerful regional operations as part of an overall global strategy. Recent examples include:

- In 1967, Ford Europe was formed as a wholly owned subsidiary of the US parent, developing models specific to Europe. In 1993 the Mondeo was launched as Ford's first world car. Ford closely integrated design and production world-wide and in 1995 merged its North American and European units into a single global operating unit designed to achieve common governance of product, manufacturing, supplier and sales activities along global product lines (Jones, 1996b: 143).
- ICI aims to have 33% of their business in each of the triad regions by 2005, as the core element of its globalisation strategy.
- BASF has recently established a new regional headquarters in Singapore for Asia-Pacific, as a core part of its globalisation strategy.
- Honda started regional operations in 1994 as part of a globalisation strategy, dividing the world market into four (Nonaka, 1990; Harukiyo, 1998: 54), and established a large R&D centre in Ohio (Jones, 1996b: 269).
- Hakanson (1990) found that regional integration led to units in Swedish MNCs being given continental or global responsibility for production, marketing and R&D in their particular area of specialisation – global product mandates.

- Daimler-Benz acquired Chrysler in 1998, gaining presence in each of the three regions.
- Toyota has began a globalisation programme, producing the Avensis as a world car.
- In 1999 Renault took a major stake in Nissan giving the combined company global market presence due to Nissan's strength in Japan, Asia and North America, and Renault's strength in Europe and Latin America.

The key difference between the 'global' firm and the M-form, according to Porter (1986), is that the global firm captures linkages across borders, whereas the M-form makes little or no attempt to link its cross-border operations strategically. As with Ferner and Quintanilla (1998), Porter argues that the organisational structure characterising global firms are international product divisions, but Porter (1990a) and de Smidt and Wever (1990) also add that the global firm has a unified strategy, achieved through co-ordinating the various national operations and generating synergies. The case of ABB, which can be seen as an ideal-type for the new N-form organisation, is discussed in Box 4.1. ABB's matrix organisation illustrates how MNCs can achieve global co-ordination, global integration and local responsiveness.

The case of ABB also shows that the shift to knowledge and innovation are key factors in competitiveness and are putting pressure on MNCs to abandon the M-form structure and establish integrated networks between subsidiaries and headquarters. As Dosi (1997: 125), drawing on Pavitt, argues:

the archetypal M-form corporation while solving a complex co-ordination problem makes intrinsically more difficult the accumulation of cross-divisional competencies for technological innovation.

A new organisational form is therefore emerging:

In a context where uncertainty is high, where the environment is unstable, and where the emphasis is on the creation and diffusion of knowledge, the most effective form of organization appears to be *not* the hierarchical M-form but the heterarchical N-form (Cooke and Morgan, 1998: 40).

Box 4.1   N-Form organisation in ABB

Asea Brown Boveri (ABB) is a Swiss/Swedish MNC specialising in electronic equipment, and is the world's second most multinational firm. In 1996, of US$34 billion sales over 97% were foreign and of ABB's 215,000 employees almost 95% were employed overseas. The strategy of ABB is 'being local world-wide' and to achieve global integration and national responsiveness ABB has developed a matrix structure with separate operating units reporting to both their global product-market business area organisation and to their country or regional management. The matrix structure was hoped to facilitate local responsiveness, foster internal competition and identify and diffuse best practice. ABB is a federation, with 7 business divisions and, at the start of the 1990s, 65 business areas and 1,300 operating units, further fragmented into over 3,500 profit centres, reaching 5,000 centres by the late 1990s. Product groupings are intended to allow local responsiveness, with strategies reflecting market, technological and other differences between products, while units across product groups also have an area head, with responsibility for reducing the costs of scanning for each unit. Area heads facilitate horizontal information flows, pass on best-practice ideas, network managers, and publish financial and operating information about each business to encourage learning and competition. The primary concern of corporate head-quarters, which consists of only 100 executives, is to provide a frame-work or common philosophy (the 'policy bible') which passes objectives, behaviour standards, and decision-making rules down to operating units, through the division managers, acting to integrate the MNC. Unlike the M-form, the units are the entrepreneurs and they receive 90% of R&D allocation for their centres of excellence, which is then leveraged across the MNC. They can also retain one third of profits. Division managers also transmit the business needs and oppor-tunities of units up to corporate level managers. A fully automated financial reporting system (ABACUS) aids communication, monitor-ing and evaluation. The overall aim of ABB, through promoting intensive formal and informal communication processes and transfer of knowledge, is to become 'a continuous learning organisation.' In every year since 1994, ABB has been ranked by the Financial Times as Europe's most respected company.

Source: Bartlett and Ghoshal (1993a); English Partnerships (1997a); Goold and Campbell (1998); Martin and Beaumont (1998); UNCTAD (1998); Simonian (1999).

4.3.3 The N-form multinational company

Multinationals have been driven by demands for global efficiency, national responsiveness and world-wide leveraging of innovations (Bartlett and Ghoshal, 1989: 29). To meet these simultaneous demands a new organisational form is emerging, described as geo-centric (Perlmutter, 1969), transnational (Bartlett and Ghoshal, 1989), heterarchical (Hedlund, 1986, 1993), multifocal (Prahalad and Doz, 1987) or, as we describe, network.

There are three major organisational differences between the M-form and N-form:

● the relationship between subsidiaries and headquarters;
● the relationship between suppliers and the MNC;
● the emphasis on intensive socialisation.

As discussed in our example of ABB, the N-form MNC develops the flexibility to specialise products and R&D in different subsidiaries and diffuse best-practice innovations (widely defined) and new or improved technologies across the organisation, made possible by advances in IT&Ts and regional integration. Subsidiaries co-operate and compete with each other and play differentiated roles. According to Bartlett and Ghoshal (1989: 105–10), subsidiaries can play four generic roles:

● *Strategic leader*: in a strategic market with high level of resources and capabilities;
● *Contributor*: in a non-strategic market but has high level of resources and capabilities;
● *Implementer*: important for efficiency and revenues, but not for strategic knowledge;
● *Black hole*: in a strategic market, with little capabilities.

To achieve efficiency, responsiveness, and innovation, each subsidiary is linked in an integrated network of operations (Bartlett and Ghoshal, 1989: 89). The relationship between units of the MNC is therefore based on interdependence, which intensifies as activities become more specialised in particular subsidiaries. Implementer subsidiary units, if highly efficient, may be converted into international production centres, exporting around the world. Contributor subsidiaries may be designated as 'world-wide centres of excellence', and strategic leaders can be transformed into a regional node or hub of the MNC network. The hub is nearer to each market than the home location, reducing transport costs and improving information capture and avoids exclusive commitment to any one market (Buckley and Casson, 1998: 40). Examples of subsidiary roles include:

- Nissan and Honda have concentrated European production at their UK 'implementer' plants, which are central to the companies' global operations and expansion plans.
- Ford and TRW have designated Germany as a 'strategic leader' and 'regional node' in their European automobile activities, with production, R&D and regional headquarters based in Germany.
- Ford's operations in Turkey appear to be in the process of evolving from a 'black hole' status, with Ford and its joint venture partner Koc establishing in 2000–2001 a 'strategic leader' plant in Turkey. The plant has a global product mandate and capabilities to design, produce and export new models for the world market.
- Black and Decker's manufacturing operations in North-East England have evolved into its largest in the world – an 'implementer' plant.
- Philips has specialised teletext design and production in its UK 'strategic leader' subsidiary.
- Ericsson has specialised digital switch technology at its Australian 'contributor' centre of excellence with resultant innovations adopted and implemented globally.
- Renault's operations in Turkey are evolving towards an implemented status. Turkey is Renault's biggest market outside of Western Europe and in 1999 Renault awarded a global product mandate to their Turkish joint-venture plant – Renualt's first ever plant outside of France to gain this status.

Another aspect of the N-form is vertical disintegration. As Porter (1998: 81) argues, 'a fast-changing environment can render vertical integration inefficient, ineffective, and inflexible'. The organisational response is to shift away from the M-form towards forming an integrated network with suppliers. Japanese automotive companies were among the first to develop extensive networks with suppliers (Cusumano, 1985). For example, Toyota's supplier system is so tightly integrated that the entire production network can almost fit inside the distance between GM's two closest car plants (Dyer, 1996a: 287) and 85% of Toyota's value added was subcontracted in 1996 (Cooke and Morgan, 1998: 54). Tightly

Box 4.2   Chrysler's new network relations with suppliers

In the 1990s, Chrysler has transformed its supplier relations through extensive outsourcing. Chrysler reduced its number of first tier suppliers from 3,000 in 1989 to 1,200 in 1994 and to just 150 in 1996. Long term relationships were formed, with implicit guarantees of future business. By reducing the number of suppliers, those remaining could increase their economies of scale and plant specific investment and improve their responsiveness to Chrysler's needs. Through subcontracting more activity, Chrysler concentrates on its core activities of vehicle design and development (R&D in the auto industry increased from 2.4% to 3.3% of production costs from 1973 to 1992), sheet metal stamping, car assembly and developing engines, transmissions and electronics. Closer collaboration with suppliers is intended to replicate the advantages accrued by the Japanese *keiretsu*, including just-in-time production, greater flexibility, lower costs, higher quality and reduced product life cycles. Chrysler has called its approach an 'extended enterprise,' and has taken the form of a de-integrated strategic centre co-ordinating a network of suppliers.

Source: Dyer (1996b); D'Cruz and Rugman (1997); Pyke (1997a); Cooke and Morgan (1998); Dyer *et al.* (1998).

knit supplier relations gives Toyota advantages of lower labour costs, lower stocks and faster delivery to the customer through just-in-time (Dyer, 1996a; Pilkington, 1998: 35). Other companies have followed the experience of the Japanese automotive companies and are adopting integrated network with suppliers. Box 4.2 gives the example of Chrysler.

The N-form MNC faces greater pressure than the M-form to balance the interests of the host and home country subsidiaries, with firm specific advantages developed outside the home base. As the example of ABB's 'policy bible' suggests, the N-form MNC counters home and host pulls through extensive socialisation. The objective is to integrate activities throughout the MNC by ensuring that the allegiance of subsidiary managers is to the company and not the country. Commonalties are developed across the MNC's operations to build a shared vision ('bible') and cultivate individual commitment. A culture-based form of control replaces hierarchical control (see van Maanen and Laurent, 1993; Westney, 1993; Martin and Beaumont, 1998). At the same time, as with Japanese automotive companies, the N-form forges closer, trust-based relations with its key suppliers to gain their commitment to share risks and product development.

Structural changes in the world economy are forcing MNCs to collaborate in order to compete. Accelerating technological advance and increased global competition are putting pressure on MNCs to engage in new forms of FDI and adopt new organisational structures in order to access and exploit complementary technologies and markets, share the risks and costs of R&D, shorten product cycles, and increase flexibility to respond more effectively to user and consumer needs.

4.4 IMPLICATIONS FOR ECONOMIC DEVELOPMENT

FDI has become a major source of investment and employment in countries across the world. In the four decades or so after the Second World War, developed countries were the main recipients of FDI. But since the 1980s, FDI has increased dramatically in developing countries, especially in East Asia. FDI now plays a more significant role in investment, employment and trade in the developing world than in developed countries.

This chapter has focused on the technological activities of MNCs. The analysis shows that the overseas technological activities of the world's leading companies are concentrated in their home markets (see the case of the US and Japan in Table 4.8). However, it was argued that this is more a reflection of the size and sophistication of their home economies, rather than the lack of globalisation of technology and innovation.

As multinational companies move towards the N-form, driven by technological advance, regional integration, intensifying competition and the heightened emphasis on innovation, MNCs are globalising their technological and innovative activities. Countries have increased opportunities to attract R&D and subsidiaries have the potential to develop roles and responsibilities that are crucial to the MNC as a whole (also see Birkinshaw and Hood, 1998). The shift towards the N-form also presents suppliers with greater opportunities to play a strategic role in the activities of MNCs.

Empirical evidence was found for the internationalisation of R&D and patenting, underpinned by the growth of M&As and technology partnerships. It was also found that the number of FDI projects in R&D is increasing. Through M&As and new FDI projects foreign companies have become a vital component of the technology base in many countries, particularly pronounced in locations like Singapore, Ireland, Australia, Taiwan, Canada and the UK.

However, while some argue that localities now have more opportunities to attract high value added FDI that can contribute more to economic development (Ohmae, 1995), the analysis pointed to high value added and innovation-intensive activities congregating in localities which enable the subsidiary to reap economies of scale, scope and agglomeration.

The move towards the network form is therefore unlikely to result in more opportunities for a wider range of localities (Markusen, 1996). Globalisation and regional integration mutually reinforce the specialisation and clustering of advanced activities in centres of excellence. Similarly, the new supplier relations associated with JIT and the N-form MNCs, are premised on building long-term, trust-based relations which, according to Wade (1996: 81), may actually reduce the mobility of production.

The continued concentration of technological activities in the home bases and overseas centres of excellence of MNCs may minimise the technological integration of subsidiaries into their host economies. While advanced regions can benefit from the globalisation of technology and innovation, peripheral regions face heightened dependency on externally determined investment flows, and enhanced vulnerability to the rapid switching of capital investment (Sadler, 1992a; 1992b; Phelps, 1997: 44).

To compete for the technological activities of MNCs, countries and localities need to develop their technological and innovation infrastructure, emulating the success of regional economies revolving around MIT in Massachusetts, the University of Cambridge in East England or the highly developed innovation and technology transfer system in Baden Württemburg, Germany. For example, Porter (1999) argues that countries must create innovative capacity through nurturing the supply side of the economy (for example, science and education, the supply of capital, and an innovative climate) and the demand side (sophisticated needs). The most successful locations are those that link the supply and demand sides through clusters.

Through focusing on developing their supply side technological and innovation infrastructure and creating sophisticated needs through attracting manufacturing and service sector FDI, several previously peripheral locations have emerged as successful in adjusting to the new opportunities of globalisation. Key examples include Ireland,

Singapore, and Taiwan, which have all successfully attracted R&D investment (see Figure 4.1 and Table 4.10) and, have dramatically increased their per capita incomes.[7] Their success has been premised on:

- availability of high quality engineering and R&D personnel;
- proximity to companies specialising in the manufacture, design and development of certain products (information technology and life sciences in Ireland, semiconductors and computers in Taiwan and electronics and life sciences in Singapore);
- availability of world-class R&D institutions;
- government incentives;[8]
- policies to upgrade subsidiaries over time and link MNCs with domestic SMEs and the local innovation infrastructure (Lall, 1997; Serapio *et al.*, 2000; Loewendahl, 2001).

This chapter has demonstrated that multinational companies are increasingly making investment location decisions based on a regional or global strategy that integrates market, efficiency, and asset-seeking motives. To benefit from the globalisation of economic activities, the ideal location should offer access to markets, an efficient production base, and at the same time the technological assets that can contribute to the company's network of critical capabilities across the world.

Part II

The Bargaining Relationship between Governments and MNCs

5 Government–MNC Relations

In this chapter the structural changes influencing the relationship between MNCs and governments are examined and it is argued that bargaining between host country governments and multinational companies is becoming more important as interdependence intensifies. Structural changes are leading to inter-state competition for the attraction of inward investment, particularly as companies are increasing both their locational flexibility and control over core technologies. Interdependence is therefore asymmetrical, with MNCs having increased structural power over governments. The key implication is that while many commentators argue that government industrial policy is shifting from protecting 'national' champions to upgrading the location-specific advantages of the economy for *all* investors, the structural power of multinationals has led to the continued subsidisation of their activities. Hence, companies that have global mobility and control over core technologies, such as in the semiconductor industry, are benefiting from large government R&D subsidies and, most significant for this study, have been able to bargain for investment incentives when making a new investment.

5.1 COMPETITIVENESS, GOVERNMENT POLICY AND MULTINATIONAL COMPANIES

Porter (1990a), in his celebrated work on the *Competitive Advantage of Nations*, argues that the success of the national economy in industries will depend on the four elements of his 'diamond' model of competitive advantage:

- *Factor conditions*: the nation's position in factors of production, such as skilled labour or infrastructure, necessary to compete in a given industry.
- *Demand conditions*: the nature of home demand for the industry's product or service.

- *Related and supporting industries*: the presence or absence in the nation of supplier industries and related industries that are internationally competitive.
- *Firm strategy, structure and rivalry*: the conditions in the nation governing how companies are created, organised and managed, and the nature of domestic rivalry.

For Porter, government plays an important, if secondary, role in influencing the four determinants of competitiveness through developing the skill base, encouraging change, promoting domestic rivalry, and stimulating innovation (Porter, 1990b: 87). The importance of government action for creating a high skill and innovation intensive economy has been emphasised by regulation, flexible specialisation and innovation theorists (Chapter 2). Recent studies have also argued that the role of public policy in promoting competition has been under-emphasised by government, but is equally as important, especially in stimulating innovation and the transfer of technology by multi-national companies (Nelson, 1992; Odagiri and Goto, 1993; Lawton, 1997; Lovegrove *et al.*, 1998). Furthermore, as Balasubramanyam *et al.* (1996) show in a theoretical and empirical study, countries with market-oriented, pro-competition policies will reduce some of the costs associated with inward investment, such as multinationals' exploiting a protected market or weak domestic competition.

Porter goes on to argue that the continued role for government questions the end of the nation state thesis. In particular, Porter draws on cluster theory to emphasise the importance of the home country to MNCs and states:

> Competitive advantage is created and sustained through a highly localised process. Differences in national economic structures, values, cultures, institutions, and histories contribute profoundly to competitive success. The role of the home nation seems to be as strong or stronger than ever. While globalisation of competition might appear to make the nation less important, instead it seems to make it more so. With fewer impediments to trade to shelter uncompetitive firms and industries, the home nation takes on growing significance because it is the source of the skills and technology that underpin competitive advantage (Porter, 1990a: 19).

Host country conditions, especially the skill and innovation base and competition policy, are therefore likely to be crucial to the quality of inward FDI and contribution to economic development in the host country (Brunskill, 1992; Mowery and Oxley, 1995; Thiran and Yamawaki, 1995; Hood and Young, 1997; Lall, 1997; OECD, 1998c). The skills base, innovation infrastructure, and competition in a country are intimately influenced by government policy. There may also be a two-way relationship between host country conditions and policy and inward investment, as foreign MNCs can act as a powerful promoter of greater competition and innovation in the host country (Dunning, 1986; UNCTAD, 1995b), and encourage governments to adopt pro-business policies.

Porter's model, though, has two main drawbacks limiting its usefulness as a framework for analysing and explaining the interaction of governments and MNCs, in particular multinationals investing in a host country:

- The emphasis of Porter's model is on the home country, not host countries.
- Firms and governments are conceptualised as monolithic actors.

In terms of the competitive advantages of MNCs, we have seen in previous chapters that companies are moving towards the N-form structure, whereas Porter's diamond model implies the M-form or multidomestic (Porter, 1990a) organisation. A key difference, as noted in chapter's two and four, is that subsidiaries in the N-form can play specialised roles as part of an integrated network. In particular, 'strategic leader' and 'contributor' subsidiaries question whether innovation and strategic value-adding activities can be conceptualised as a process distinctive to home countries. We need the concept of a 'double diamond' in order to embrace the host countries environment as well (Ostry, 1998: 90).

However, it is the lack of conceptualisation of relations between MNCs and host country governments which is of primary interest in this chapter. As Strange (1991a: 46) notes, much of the literature on international business 'is focused on activity within the hierarchy, rather than how the hierarchy interacts with other hierarchies, including governments.' This is a major omission because, as Sally (1995: 215) explains:

Inevitably, governments and MNEs have to deal with each other: MNEs are important contributors to national wealth and offer the advantages of being global in terms of world-wide market

access and leverage of cutting-edge technologies; just as governments modify the strategic options available to MNEs, both
in their external environments and with respect to their internal
co-ordination.

There is, then, a two-way relationship between MNCs and governments. On the one hand:

> through tariffs, import quotas, technical standards, policies on
> inward investment and the transfer of technology, support for
> domestic producers and for R&D, regional policy and government
> procurement policies, national governments can influence the
> internationalisation of capital, and of course other economic
> variables specific to individual countries, such as company
> taxation and currency exchange rates, are very important (Sayer,
> 1986: 108).

While on the other hand:

> The global strategies of individual MNEs play an ever more crucial
> role in economic development, in shaping the world economy and
> in significantly influencing the direction, content and outcome of
> public policy choices (Sally, 1995: 2–3).

State actions may be endogenous to the value-adding activities of
multinationals and MNCs in turn may be crucial to the industrial
policies of governments. As Dunning (1993a: 545) argues:

> To the extent that MNEs are a key influence both in the ways in
> which resources are located across national boundaries and in
> which these activities are organised, they directly affect, and are
> affected by, domestic government policies.

The relationship is one of interdependence, which, as Cowling and
Sugden (1987: 65–6) note, implies bargaining between states and
firms. The nature of this interdependence has, however, changed
over time. Structural changes in the international political economy
are intensifying the interdependence between states and MNCs,
amplifying the bargaining negotiations. We argue that MNCs have
increased their structural power. Two key features of the changing
relationship between states and MNCs are:

- converging FDI policies and industrial structures;
- the shift away from direct government intervention in the economy.

5.1.1   Converging FDI policy and industrial structures

With MNCs searching for investment opportunities but with the ease and attractiveness of access to such opportunities controlled by host country governments (Doz and Prahalad, 1980: 153), bargaining is central to government–MNC relations. However, the bargaining relationship is not static. As Dunning (1993a: 549) notes, 'The interaction between governments and MNEs needs to be studied in the context of a constantly changing world economic and political landscape.' For MNCs and governments the post-war experience and learning process has led to both a more accommodating and sensitive stance by MNCs (Strange, 1991a: 46–7; Dunning, 1993a: 557), a stance more responsive to host country hopes and fears, and to a greater willingness by government to accept foreign MNCs.

Three phases of policy towards MNCs can be identified. First, the pre-1930s period, which had minimal regulations. Second, from the 1930s to the 1970s when monitoring and restrictions characterised policy, particularly extensive in developing countries (e.g. see Mardon, 1990 for South Korea) and in certain developed countries. In developing countries neo-Marxist *dependencia* theory, which argued that MNCs exploit the periphery, commanded high political support, especially in Latin America (Frank, 1969; Barone, 1985; Roxborough, 1987; Larrain, 1989). The success of OPEC in the 1970s also led many developing countries to perceive that their bargaining power

Table 5.1   Regulatory changes to investment regimes, 1991–98

Item	1991	1992	1993	1994	1995	1996	1997	1998
No. of countries that introduced changes in their investment regimes	35	43	57	49	64	65	76	60
No. of regulatory changes, of which:	82	79	102	110	112	114	151	145
More favourable to FDI	80	79	101	108	106	98	135	136
Less favourable to FDI	2	–	1	2	6	16	16	9

Source: UNCTAD (1999).

vis-à-vis MNCs had increased in a new era (Vernon, 1993: 20–1). In developed countries, the German government protected core firms like Daimler Benz from foreign take-over (Karl, 1996) and the French government was particularly restrictive, as discussed in Box 5.1.

In the third period, since the 1980s, restrictions have fallen in most countries, with the US the most open of the major economies (Jones, 1996b: 270–9). As Table 5.1 shows, on average 56 countries per annum from 1991 to 1998 introduced changes to their investment regimes. In total there were almost 900 regulatory changes, of which 94% made investment regimes more favourable to FDI. By the end of 1994 only three developed countries maintained (limited) restrictions on outward FDI (UNCTAD, 1995b: 157). The incentives offered by developed and developing countries designed to attract foreign companies (see Safarian, 1993; Yeung, 1996) are most explicit of the shift in policy.

More positive government attitudes are an outcome of wider changes in the international political economy. For developing countries, the debt crisis in the 1970s and 1980s led to bank loans drying-up and FDI was seen as an essential source of new funds (Wells, 1998: 107–9). The debt crisis also involved multilateral institutions, in particular the World Bank and IMF, imposing structural adjustment programmes on the debtor countries. These took the form of austerity measures and a shift from state intervention to market-oriented policies (Onimode, 1989; Corbridge, 1993; Riley, 1993). The globalisation of financial markets further undermined national controls over banking and finance for all countries and over the ability of governments to influence the borrowing and other financial strategies of MNCs (Jones, 1996b: 280–1). In France, the economic strategies of the new Socialist President in 1982 had to be reversed under financial market pressure (Strange, 1995a: 162) and in the 1990s a transformation in policy took place, with the government aggressively promoting France as a location for inward FDI, as discussed in Box 5.1. Since the 1980s, both developing and developed countries have been on a converging trend towards liberal, market-oriented economic policies, which favour FDI.

In developed countries, a major force influencing government perceptions of MNCs has been the convergence of industrial structures and reduced effective economic distance between states (Fukao, 1995: xiv). The two-fold impact of this convergence is, first, greater cross-country competition, leading to heightened stress placed on enhancing national competitiveness (Dunning, 1993b). As Dunning and Narula (1996: 7) note:

because of the increasing competition between countries with similar structures of resources and capabilities Direct intervention is likely to be replaced by measures designed to aid the upgrading of domestic resources and capabilities, and to curb the market distorting behaviour of private economic agents.

Box 5.1   French inward investment policy: from national protection to FDI promotion

In 1965, France banned all foreign take-overs of French firms and for a time blocked all new FDI applications. France was particularly hostile to the spread of 'American imperialism,' and a strongly endogenous path to economic development was favoured, built on national, state-owned champions. Even in the 1980s, as other countries shifted towards an open inward investment policy, a system of domestic 'core investors' designed to protect privatised companies from foreign take-overs was introduced in 1986, and the French remained openly hostile to foreign MNCs. For example, as the President of powerful Association des Constructeurs Européens d'Automobiles (ACEA) argued, 'all EC states should act together, and not run after the Japanese and beg them to set up factories.' The government remained committed to supporting national champions, with the EC (1990) documenting government debt write-off and assistance for Renault. Even in 1999, the government had a 44.2% stake in the carmaker. However, in the early 1990s a U-turn in policy took place. Four key factors forced the change in policy:

- Globalisation was blurring the nationality of enterprises and providing new opportunities. From 1985 to 1990 French outward FDI increased by 3.5 times, a growth rate exceeded only by Japan in the G-5. With high levels of outward FDI, the French government came under more pressure to reciprocate the open FDI policy of other countries, as the interests of French companies increasingly depended on their acceptability abroad. The government also realised that it was losing out on opportunities to attract high value added inward investment, particularly R&D.
- France was influenced by the more non-interventionist industrial policy agenda of the EU, which was opening-up member state's markets.

Box 5.1   (continued)

- Attracting FDI was central to the success of the UK economy in reducing unemployment below the EU average and was probably influencing French attitudes, especially as the French government was under increasing pressure to reduce record levels of unemployment.
- The conditions to meet the Maastricht criteria for European Monetary Union waned the ability of the government to use public money to support national champions.

The major change in French MNC policy was symbolised in 1992, when the Invest in France network was created to attract investment from other countries and to give investors better help on arrival. In 1995, the legal requirement for all foreign take-overs to be registered with and formally approved by the government was abolished and a series of measures reducing red tape and making it easier to gain work permits were implemented. The Invest in France Agency (IFA) was established, which has offices in French embassies throughout the world to attract foreign investment and The Invest in France Mission (IFM) was also set up as a complement to the IFA, with the specific purpose of attracting major multinational companies to France. It reports directly to the office of the Prime Minister and the Ministry of the Economy where it has its headquarters. The IFM markets France as a whole, whereas the IFA and IFN promote the regions of France. This policy change has met with huge success. Each year since the early 1990s FDI in France has grown rapidly. In 1999 a new record number of jobs (31,200) was created by FDI and according to Ernst & Young, France experienced the fastest increase in FDI projects in Europe in 1999. The new 'open' inward investment policy was followed in 1997 with the French government succeeding in attracting Toyota to invest £1 billion in a small car plant in North France, with the offer of large government subsidies. A key factor in the government's U-turn regarding the desirability of Japanese FDI was the EU's commitment to opening-up the EU market to Japanese competition by the year 2000; having Toyota produce inside France was infinitely more desirable than Toyota exporting from Japan or the UK instead.

Source: EC (1990); Sadler (1992b); Jack (1996, 1995); Jones (1996b); Burt and Kampfner (1997); Burt and Nakamoto (1997); *The Economist* (1997b).

With the growing quantitative importance of MNCs (Chapter 4), governments are also more aware of the need to maintain the attractiveness of their economies to internationally mobile created assets (Gray, 1995: 50), leading to greater policy openness to foreign MNCs.

Secondly, convergence has meant that the US and the UK are no longer the only significant sources of foreign direct investment, with developed and developing countries increasingly homes as well as hosts for the operations of MNCs, as discussed in Chapter 4. In this context, governments are more aware of the possible consequences of regulation of foreign MNCs for the (retaliatory) treatment of their own (national) MNCs by foreign governments. Hence, Rugman and Verbeke (1998) argue that with symmetry between outward and inward FDI national treatment of FDI is often the appropriate policy.

Eden (1991) argues that convergence is one of the major manifestations of globalisation, and Julius (1990) and Safarian (1993) have documented in detail the convergence not just of industrial structures but also of the deregulatory and liberalising policies of governments. Most recently, the European integration process, the World Trade Organisation, and OECD's Multilateral Agreement on Investment (MAI) are aiming to make domestic markets internationally contestable through the principle of national treatment, with no discrimination against foreign MNCs (Brewer and Young, 1995: 39–43; Fatouros, 1995; Graham, 1996; Hood *et al.*, 1996). This is facilitating the entry of MNCs into foreign states, intensifying internationalisation and interdependence.

As governments become more open to inward investment and as MNCs come to play a more significant role in the economy of host countries, policies on multinational firms have tended to converge into industrial policies (Safarian, 1993: 201). This represents a definite shift in government industrial policy away from national champions.

5.1.2 The changing nature of government intervention

The second main factor influencing the changing relationship between governments and MNCs has been the shift in the interventionary function of government. It is argued that government policy is shifting from protecting national industries to encouraging firms (domestic and foreign) to locate within their territory and engage in high value-adding activities and hence to an industrial policy stressing access to markets

(Nicolaides, 1993b: 2). The shift to market facilitating government strategies is explained by Dunning and Sauvant (1996: xvi):

> On the one hand, the renaissance of the market economy reduces the role of governments in affecting the allocation of resources, capabilities and markets; on the other hand, technological advances and the increasing interdependence between the core assets of firms and the quality of the physical, technological and commercial environment of which they are a part, require national governments to be more systematic and pro-active in their market-facilitating strategies.

Government's role, according to Dunning, is to provide the most favourable economic environment for national firms and foreign MNCs to produce in order to:

> optimise the modality by which resources and capabilities within their jurisdictions are created, upgraded and allocated among different users, and the efficiency at which these are displayed for any given use (Dunning, 1992c: 8).

Direct intervention in particular markets or in the operations of firms is rejected, with competitiveness referring to the domestic economy, not necessarily to domestic firms. Globalisation is seen as the major factor behind this shift in government industrial policy, with Milner (1988: 290–1) commenting that:

> As firms and industries become dependent on exports, imports, multinational production, and global intra-firm trade, state policies that favoured protectionism would hurt many of their most competitive industries, usually the most internationally oriented ones.

The shift away from protectionism is not only a result of the internationalisation of production, which puts pressure upon states to engage themselves fully into the world economy and adjust their national policies to the demands of international production (Cox, 1987: 253; 1994: 49), but is also an outcome of cross-border interdependence between MNCs. As Nicolaides (1993c: 107) contends:

> Globalisation of production, growing foreign direct investment and the expanding web of corporate alliances are increasingly blurring the national origin of both products and processes. For

governments this blurring of national origin critically influences the effectiveness of public policies towards industry.

The growth of cross-border strategic alliances, M&As, consortia and other collaborative ventures, as discussed in chapter four, are major forces behind the blurring of corporate nationality, multiplying the difficulty that national governments have in fostering the competitiveness of 'their' firms. Ruggie (1996) gives the example of an anti-dumping case brought by a Japanese firm producing typewriters in the US against a US firm importing typewriters into the US from off-shore facilities in Singapore and Indonesia and, similarly, Kline (1991) documents the complex policy dilemmas created by cross-ownership of Japanese producers by US companies.

Building on the above arguments, Reich (1990; 1991) vigorously maintains that when companies operate globally it is the capacity of the US domestic economy to add value rather than the competitiveness of solely US firms which is crucial. In support of Reich, Miller (1991) states that globalisation entails much greater integration, co-ordination and equality between the different parts of the MNC, and gives the example of Honda's investment in the US to illustrate the benefits of inward FDI. The logical conclusion is that the attraction of foreign MNCs may be a more important industrial policy objective for governments than supporting the operations of national champions. The work of Reich and others has been influential in the US, with the Clinton administration establishing a new order of priorities for government protection which emphasises the interests of foreign companies operating in the US over US MNCs in third countries (Schwab and Smadja, 1994). However, the first priority is the protection of US corporations operating in US, indicating that the US government still perceives that indigenous companies contribute more to the national economy than foreign investors.

Dunning, Nicolaides and Reich argue that globalisation is leading to states introducing non-discriminatory, market-oriented industrial policies. As Nicolaides (1993a: xii) states:

public policy should primarily aim to make markets function more efficiently rather than support a few select firms at the expense of others, even if the others are of a different nationality.

Subsidisation and protection is no longer seen as a viable or effective policy option:

Nations can no longer substantially enhance the wealth of their citizens by subsidising, protecting, or otherwise increasing the profitability of 'their corporations, (Reich, 1991: 153).

The implication of these arguments is that the most effective policy to promote internationally competitive firms are micro and macro policies setting the environment in which indigenous and foreign firms operate and the subsidisation of location-specific training or research activities instead of national firms or footloose capital. This is very much the policy prescription advocated by Porter (1990a: 6–11), a major reason being that underlying the debate of each of these commentators is their contention that national competitiveness is basically a proxy for productivity, with the idea of government intervention to support strategic industries rejected.

The relationship between governments and MNCs therefore becomes one of collaboration rather than confrontation (Dunning, 1991; 1992b) and one of interdependence rather than dependence. As Stopford argues, collaboration and interdependence implies bargaining between MNCs and governments:

Interdependence within the advanced Triad economies between governments and MNEs is increasing: MNEs are more dependent on infrastructure facilities and the knowledge base of national economies, very much a function of government industrial, technological and other policies to create and enhance factors; governments are competing more in an industrial and technological race for the resources and capabilities of MNEs, in the process losing the power to pursue nationally isolated policies that do not take MNEs into account ... this represents a shift from an agenda of regulation, of MNEs by governments, to one of negotiation, in which a recognition of relative bargaining power is more sharply impressed on multiple agendas of interaction (1994: 177–8).

5.2 STRUCTURAL CHANGES AND BARGAINING FOR INCENTIVES

Converging policies and industrial structures and the shift in government intervention from protectionism to market-facilitation have increased interdependence between MNCs and governments. However, the nature of this interdependence is asymmetric, with MNCs increasing their structural power over governments. This is leading to government subsidies shifting from indigenous to multinational firms, rather than exclusively to the development of location specific assets.

With growing interdependence between MNCs and governments and the heightened structural power of MNCs, the basis of the relationship between governments and MNCs is inter-state or inter-locality competition for the value-adding activities of multinationals and competition between states and MNCs for bargaining power. Strange argues that the bargaining relationship between governments and MNCs is as important as inter-state relations because it is the MNCs that have 'control over the technology, the privileged access to capital, and to the established entry to rich markets that states need, and must have' (Strange, 1994b: 211).

Furthermore, as national economies become embedded into the global economy through the twin processes of internationalisation and interdependence, and as states shift away from 'national champion' industrial policies, the perceived lack of viable alternative development strategies for many governments may mean that the 'best strategy, therefore, is to bargain with MNCs over the terms of FDI' (Grunberg, 1996: 352).

Fundamentally, the terms of the bargaining relationship are created and shaped by the cross-border flexibility of MNCs (Cowling, 1990: 170; Julius, 1990: 94; Cowling and Sugden, 1996: 143–4) – their unique ability to shift production from one geographical location to another to avoid, or to draw upon and make use of, host and home countries policies and diamonds of competitive advantage (Dunning, 1992b: 144). As Blomstrom and Lipsey (1993: 141) argue, 'The more flexible multinationals are ... the more likely it is that governments will compete for the establishment of production facilities by multinationals.'

International capital mobility is, therefore, at the heart of the relationship between MNCs and governments. National governments fear that any attempt to control the activities of mobile multinational capital could cause its withdrawal and thus further divestment (Amin and Pywell, 1989: 476; Bailey, 1997: 4), and as globalisation advances most national and sub-national economies depend more on inward investment (Dunford and Perrons, 1992: 403). The pressures to attract inward FDI, and therefore to bargain with MNCs, are further heightened by the increasing control of value-adding activities by MNCs (Strange, 1994a: 108) and the long-term decline in manufacturing employment in many localities (King, 1990: 269–70). Multinational companies have asymmetrical structural power, heightened by three key systemic changes: accelerating technological advance, globalisation of MNC activities, and regional integration.

A key pressure stimulating the international expansion is accelerating technological change. The scale of fixed costs and R&D expenditures and the complexity of technological innovation expand the boundaries of the firm globally, placing MNCs beyond the control of any one state. And with the concentration of technology, managerial knowledge, advertising and export intensity, capital and access to world markets in MNCs, many governments have often followed the strategies of dominant firms. As Lawton (1997), in relation to the semiconductor industry, notes, in the 1960s and 1970s government created policy and firms operated within its parameters but since the 1980s firms have gone from policy outsiders to policy insiders. Multinationals not only have structural power enabling them to bargain over the terms of investment but they also influence the policies adopted by government which affect the diamond of competitive advantage.

Information asymmetry and bargaining power is particularly weighted towards MNCs pursuing global or regional strategies (Dunning, 1992a: 320) with operations in global industries that control core, fast changing and complex technologies. Core technologies, like semiconductors, facilitate globalisation (Lawton, 1997: 41) and are highly desirable firm-specific assets which governments hope to attract (Brech and Sharp, 1984: 19), increasing MNC bargaining power. Companies with integrated regional or global strategies circumvent state authority, with the output from one location only having value if combined with that from other location units in the value-adding chain. This constrains any host country restrictions imposed on such MNCs (Kobrin, 1987: 618; Tarzi, 1991: 161–62).

Regional integration has also been instrumental to the increased bargaining power of MNCs. In the first place, as argued by Defraigne (1984: 376) for the European context, 'Community industrial strategy would no doubt be more liberal within the Common Market than the continued juxtaposition of several national industrial policies.' In other words, regional integration inhibits national governments from attempting to privilege the interests of firms on the basis of national ownership (Cawson *et al.*, 1990: 377; Sadler, 1992b), increasing the substitutability of localities and mobility of MNCs (Guisinger, 1985).

Of major significance in Europe is the Single Market Programme, announced in 1986. Through reducing internal barriers to trade and gradually homogenising policies, moves to create a Single Market raised the possibility of economies of specialisation, encouraging efficiency-seeking investments along the lines of a regional division of labour. Hence the Cecchini Report (1988) forecast job losses of up to 500,000 in the first year following the implementation of the Single European Market (cited in Hart and Roberts, 1995: 97). Scott (1996: 407) therefore argues that MNCs 'are among the most important private beneficiaries of the global regional mosaic'. Multinationals have greater flexibility within a Single Market and through a regional division of labour can increase competitiveness. The single European currency, introduced in 1999, further enhances the ability of MNCs to operate regionally integrated strategies by increasing the transparency of different countries and localities, improving the monitoring capacity of MNCs. According to economists at the Department of Trade and Industry, the single currency may put pressure on governments and labour to converge to the lowest standard.

Changes in the international political economy are therefore leading to many locations becoming more dependent on inward investment just as MNCs have reduced their dependence on them. Demand by localities within a Single Market for the value-adding activities of MNCs has intensified, and MNCs have increased structural power. The investment incentives offered to MNCs are a manifestation of this greater bargaining power, as Hood *et al.* (1996: 239–40) argue:

> Despite formal adherence to the principles of 'national treatment,' the incentives offered at state and local level in the USA and at regional level in the EU are widely believed to discriminate in favour of inward investors, if only because incentives are targeted towards the latter and MNEs possess greater bargaining power.

A detailed study by Thomas (1996) has highlighted the link between regional integration, bargaining and the subsidies offered to MNCs. According to Thomas, in the 1960s no incentives were provided by Canadian authorities for automobile investment, but following the US–Canada Auto Pact of 1965 the creation of a regional market led to bidding between US states and Canadian provinces. As Thomas (1996: 7) puts it:

> In this new environment, the bargaining power of the Canadian government fell relative to that of Ford and General Motors (GM) because of the new cross-border mobility of production and investment competition among states and provinces.

Table 5.2 Estimated incentives for automotive, electronics, chemicals and semiconductor FDI projects, 1980–2000

Date of package	Country of project	Investor	Amount per job (US$)	New jobs/investment
Automotive – USA				
1980	United States	Honda	4,000	–
Early 1980s	United States	Nissan	17,000	–
Mid-1980s	United States	Mazda-Ford	14,000	–
Mid-1980s	United States	GM Saturn	27,000	–
Mid-1980s	United States	Mitsubishi-Chrysler	35,000	–
Mid-1980s	United States	Toyota	50,000	3,000 jobs
Mid-1980s	United States	Fuji-Isuzu	51,000	
1993	United States	Mercedes-Benz	170,000	1,500 jobs/US$300m
1994	United States	BMW	79,000	1,900 jobs/US$800m
1997	United States	DaimlerChrysler	100,000	3,500 jobs/US$750m
1998	United States	Toyota	69,000	2,300 jobs/US$1.2bn
1999	United States	General Motors	60,000	3,800 jobs/US$500m
2000	United States	Honda	105,000	1,500 jobs/US$400m
Automotive – Other				
1985	United Kingdom	Nissan	54,000	2,700 jobs
1992	Portugal	Ford-Volkswagen	265,000	1,900 jobs/US$484m
1993	Hungary	GM	300,000	213 jobs/US$64m
1995	Brazil	Volkswagen	54,000–94,000	–
1996	Brazil	Renault	133,000	–
1996	Brazil	Mercedes-Benz	340,000	–
1997	Germany	Volkswagen	180,000	–
1997	India	Ford	420,000	–
1998	United Kingdom	Ford	138,000	500 jobs

Electronics, chemicals and
  semiconductors

1993	United States	Intel	120,000	2,400 jobs
1994	United Kingdom	Samsung	30,000	3,000 jobs/US$89m
1995	United Kingdom	Siemens	51,000–190,000	1,500 jobs/US$1.1bn
1996	United Kingdom	Hyundai	190,000	–
1996	United Kingdom	LG	48,000	6,100 jobs/US$320m
1996	Israel	Intel	300,000	2,000 jobs/US$1.8bn
1996	Germany	Dow	3,400,000	2,000 jobs/US$6.8m
1997	United States	Shintech	500,000	250 jobs/US$125m
1998	United Kingdom	IMR	63,400	50 jobs/US$3.17m
1998	United Kingdom	Dupont	201,000	100 jobs/US$128m
2000*	Canada	Mosel Vitelic	450,000	1,500 jobs/US$1.5bn
2000*	Israel	Intel	350,000	2,000 jobs/US$2bn

*Planned.
Source: Moran (1999); EUBIR (2000); Oman (2000). Agency sources.

From the late 1970s through to the 1980s Thomas illustrates cases in which the incentives offered increased from about 10% to over 40% of the value of inward investment. The key factor was not so much government authorities subsidising the creation of jobs in high unemployment provinces but the greater mobility of capital in an environment of free-trade, which led to competitive bidding. US auto manufacturers used divide and rule tactics to play-off different locations.

Therefore, while we have seen a shift in policy away from protectionism, the increased structural power of MNCs has shifted direct subsidisation of industry from indigenous to multinational firms. This questions the assumptions of Porter and company who argue that governments are adopting non-discriminatory policies, as government aid and resources are being diverted from initiatives to support overall competitiveness towards attracting mobile inward investment projects.

Table 5.2 indicates that the scale of financial incentives given to over 30 large FDI projects in the most global industries (automotive, electronics, chemicals and semiconductors) has increased rapidly over time. The table is an indication of the scale of incentives that are generally being awarded, albeit for high profile projects. In the automotive industry, incentives per job created have increased from US$4,000 in 1980 to around US$30,000 in the mid-1980s and too over US$100,000 in the 1990s. In the electronics industry incentives have been around US$40,000 per job in the mid-1990s, while in the semiconductor industry incentives hovered around US$300,000 per job created in the 1990s. In the chemical industry, incentives have reached a massive US$3.4 million per job. Oman (2000), in a detailed study of incentives in Brazil, Argentina, Malaysia, Singapore, China, India, United States, Western Europe and Canada, also found that incentives have increased over time in response to the growing mobility of MNCs and competition for inward investment.[1]

Globalisation, regional integration and the technological and commercial expertise of MNCs have changed the relationship between MNCs and governments from one of confrontation to one of openness, heightening bargaining over investment. Multinationals have asymmetrical structural power in this relationship, which has led to increasing incentives being 'offered' to large inward investors. It will be seen in Chapter 6 that another asymmetry in favour of the MNC is that conferred by the relative cohesiveness of the MNC *vis-à-vis* host country governments.

6 A Model of Government–MNC Bargaining

Building on the discussion of government–MNC relations in Chapter 5, in this chapter the project-level negotiations between governments and MNCs over inward investment are examined. It is argued that the key factor in negotiations are perceptions of bargaining power, and a differentiation is made between potential and actual power. Derived from political economy and dependency bargaining theory, potential power is argued to depend on the alternatives and commitment of each bargaining actor while actual power depends on the ability and willingness to implement potential power. Alternatives indicate the degree of mobility of the MNC and alternative economic development options for the government, while commitment is a function of the strategy of each actor. Ability is a function of the political constraints and institutional structure of each actor, while willingness to exercise power depends on implicit assumptions, in particular government perceptions relating to the benefits and costs of inward investment. A formal bargaining model is developed, conceptualising potential power and its implementation, and it is argued that the model can be used as heuristic tool to analyse government–MNC bargaining and other bargaining relationships.

6.1 POLITICISING GOVERNMENTS AND MULTINATIONAL COMPANIES

Chapter 5 explored the impact of the changing structural context on the relationship between MNCs and governments, and analysis at the structural level helps us to understand *why* bargaining between MNCs and governments has become more important in the international political economy. It was argued that structural changes are increasing the asymmetrical structural power of MNCs, which is leading to increasing incentives being channelled to multinationals. In this chapter we focus on *how* MNCs and governments bargain with each other over the terms of a potential investment project. Central to the explanation of the bargaining process is the exercise of relative power and the degree of mutual dependence. However, relative power is influenced by structural power and throughout the following analysis we highlight how the changing structural context conditions the bargaining negotiations between MNCs and governments.

In order to examine the bargaining relations between the MNC and the original multi-divisional, political institution – national government – the MNC must be explicitly conceptualised as a global political actor. In Chapters 2 and 4 the MNC was defined as a heterogeneous organisation and, with the notable exception of transaction cost economics, many of the approaches discussed in Chapter 2 draw attention to the political dimension of MNC behaviour that heterogeneity invokes. For example, Bartlett and Ghoshal (1990: 266) note that networking linkages within Matsushita Electric:

> reflect the company's open acknowledgement that the parent company is not one homogenous entity, but a collectivity of different constituencies and interests, each of which is legitimate and necessary. Collectively, these multiple linkages enhance the subsidiary's ability to influence key headquarters decisions.

More specifically, in an excellent in-depth study of the interaction of firms and governments in the electronics industry, Cawson *et al.* (1990: 8) immediately draw attention to the fact that 'firms are themselves systems of power, with constituent groups (e.g. of engineers, managers, workers, R&D staff) challenging each other's power'. This is particularly the case for multinational firms, which face the competing demands of subsidiaries with each bargaining for more resources and decision-making autonomy. Edwards *et al.* (1996) give the example of bargaining between the managers of a French subsidiary and their UK headquarters and cite Forsgren's 1990 evidence when arguing that MNCs are 'loosely coupled political systems rather than tightly bounded, homogenous, hierarchically controlled systems'.

There is, then, a political bargaining process taking place within the MNC, which leads Schienstock (1992: 471) to state that it is much more realistic to regard the management of a multinational corporation as a political system. At the same time there is a bargaining relationship not only among the constituent parts of the MNC but also between the MNC and other actors. However, research relating to the external political bargaining relations of MNC activity, especially in connection with the interaction of MNCs and governments, is relatively sparse. As Dicken (1990b: 242) argues:

What determines the outcome of this interaction is the nature of the bargaining process and, especially, the relative bargaining power of the two sides.... So far, there has been little empirical work on the bargaining process between firms and nation-states.

Bargaining is central to the relationship between MNCs and governments, and underpinning bargaining is the exercise power, which is inherently a political as well as economic phenomenon. Therefore, while we have argued that the relationship between MNCs and governments is one of *economic* interdependence, the bargaining that is engendered by this very interdependence introduces a *political* dimension into their interaction. As discussed in chapter one, we cannot separate economics from politics or the international level of analysis from the domestic level; MNCs and governments are political actors interacting at the local, national, and global levels.

In the next sections, approaches to government–industry relations are integrated with approaches to government–MNC relations allowing us conceptualise the plurilateral relations and institutional context influencing the bargaining process. Political economy provides the theoretical basis for the formal bargaining model developed later in the chapter.

6.2   THE POLITICAL ECONOMY OF BARGAINING

Two fundamental sources of *relative* bargaining power were identified in Chapter 5: the cross-border flexibility of MNCs and their control of resources. We argued that structural changes have increased the flexibility of MNCs and heightened their control over resources, in particular over core technologies. The more flexible MNCs are and the more alternatives they have available the greater is their capacity substitute between locations, which is a key source of bargaining power and their ability to gain government incentives. The power of multinationals also increases when government's demand for the resources controlled by MNCs is higher, which is manifested as intensified competitive bidding between locations for projects. In this context, countries and localities have higher commitment to the value adding activities of MNCs and due to the multinational's greater cross-border flexibility and alternative investment locations, they compete to attract MNCs. Multinationals have greater bargaining power.

This latter dimension of bargaining power, demand for resources, is most comprehensively researched, and is described in the government–MNC relations literature by Moran (1974) as a 'balance of power model' premised on bilateral monopoly bargaining. The bargaining resources of the two actors are divided, with MNCs controlling the technology, skills, expertise, access to markets, and finance that the host country needs to develop its resource base, while the host country has the natural resources, labour force, and the control of taxation attractive to the investor. As Poynter (1985: 41) suggests:

> Overall bargaining power is determined by who has control over, or access to, factors which are perceived to influence the continued success of the subsidiary in question. . . . The amount of bargaining power in the hands of the interventionists and their government is determined by the amount and significance of their contribution to . . . technology, resources and markets.

Bilateral balance of power models (e.g. Kindleberger, 1969; Behrman and Grosse, 1990) are methodologically very similar to Dunning's OLI paradigm. In both cases, a never-ending list of situation and historically specific ownership and location advantages can be produced in an attempt to weigh-up the relative power position of MNCs and governments. Such an approach can be seen in the study of MNC-host country bargaining by Doz and Prahalad (1980). There is no conceptualisation of the exercise of structural power. Furthermore, there is no conceptualisation of *how* bargaining takes place.

In relation to the discussion of IPE in Chapter 1, MNCs and governments are examined in the above models as black boxes that mechanically produce outcomes. They are treated in bilateral terms, divorced from other actors, and hence external, plurilateral bargaining processes. Furthermore, they are conceptualised as unitary, internally homogenous actors, ignoring internal bargaining processes. The relationship between MNCs and governments is abstracted from politics.

In order to develop a holistic conceptualisation of MNC–government bargaining relations, it is crucial to avoid these reifications so that the policy-making processes surrounding the implementation of bargaining power in a particular MNC–government negotiation can be interpreted. The MNC and host country government must be conceptualised as *arenas of politics*, with individuals and groups vying support for or against the wills of others in order to make *contested* decisions in an investment negotiation (Stopford and

Strange, 1991; Strange, 1997: 135–6). A political economy analysis is needed.

From a political economy perspective it is critical to distinguish between potential power and its implementation (Keohane and Nye, 1975; Kobrin, 1987) and perceived versus actual bargaining power (Poynter, 1985; Tarzi, 1991). The implementation of potential bargaining power depends on the influence of interest groups and negotiating competence, while actual power is both the *ability* and *willingness* to exercise bargaining power to exert more favourable terms.

Two key insights of political economy for understanding the bargaining process are:

- Actual power, in other words the conversion of potential power into control over outcomes, requires an exercise of government or MNC autonomy that may not be possible because of political constraints (Moran, 1993: 7).
- The bargaining strategies of government are typically based on policy maker's implicit assumptions about the effects of foreign investment on economic development (Encarnation and Wells, 1986a: 285).

With the convergence of FDI policies and industrial structures and the shift in the interventionist function of government, the establishment of favourable assumptions towards MNCs and the formation of an endogenous community of interests (Poulantzas, 1975; Pitelis, 1993) has become more likely.

We can conclude, therefore, that structural changes in the international political economy influence the bargaining power of MNCs and governments across three key dimensions:

- *Alternatives*: the relative location flexibility of MNCs and the alternative economic development options for governments to attracting inward investment.
- *Commitment*: the relative demand for and control of resources.
- *Potential versus actual power*: the ability and willingness to exercise potential power.

6.3 THE INFLUENCE OF POLITICAL CONSTRAINTS ON BARGAINING

The ability to exercise potential power depends on the influence of political constraints. The influence of political constraints is a function of the interest and institutional structure of each bargaining actor. The interest structure indicates interest group pressures and political constraints to the exercise of bargaining power and to agreement while, drawing on the government–industry relations literature, the institutional structure determines negotiating autonomy and competence of each actor. Each is discussed below.

The main point made in the political economy literature is that:

> Neither host countries nor governments are coherent or monolithic actors; various societal groups and governmental agencies have different objectives with respect to foreign investment and the domestic political process may affect the translation of potential bargaining power to control over outcomes. Business firms are also a political organisation made up of coalitions competing for power and intra-firm conflict over objectives may constrain the firms ability to fully exploit its potential power (Kobrin, 1987: 617–18).

Furthermore, from an analysis of MNCs in developing countries, Lall and Streeten (1977) argue not only that interest groups within government affect outcomes but also that external interest groups may impinge on policy making autonomy. Thus, government policy:

> may correspond to the interests of particular sectors of the dominant classes rather than those of the majority of the population... [and] policy may be strongly influenced or conditioned by external forces (1977: 221–2).

Therefore, to understand how actual policy towards MNCs is determined:

> it is necessary to discard the state-centric abstraction called the 'host country' and to look at policy as the outcome of the interplay of domestic [and international] forces trying to maximise their own particular interests as well as the larger national interest (Moran, 1974: 154–5).

Crucially, policies in any organisation are determined by the interplay of the major interest groups and their environment. This argument is supported by several studies utilising a political economy approach. Jenkins (1986), in a study of US MNCs in the Canadian oil industry, draws attention to the importance of analysing economics and politics and the international and domestic levels in order to explain bargaining between the MNC and host country government:

> Domestic politics, the international economy, home government pressure, and the bargaining tactics of MNCs all acted as intervening variables between the 'inevitable' trend of the obsolescing bargain and the execution of government control.

Similarly, Weiss (1990), in a comprehensive analysis of the mid-1980s negotiations between IBM and the Mexican government, found that 'IBM' and 'government' were shorthand labels as many actors were involved in the various stages of the negotiation, each bargaining with one another. This particular study even went so far to point to the prominent role of specific individual representatives although, as Ruigrok and van Tulder (1995: 65) note, if bargaining is analysed in such detail personal rivalries are often more important than the matter itself, and one risks losing the overall picture.

Another detailed study, this time examining a US company investing in Chilean copper at the turn of the twentieth century, also concluded that interest group pressures play a major role in bargaining relations. The study also noted that FDI itself can stimulate the creation of new pressure groups: 'The state's actions were significantly influenced by social groups who had in part been spawned, and were directly influenced by, foreign direct investment' (O'Brien, 1989: 332).

Multinational companies and governments are permeated by political rivalries among coalitions of interests both within and between their organisation and other groups. They are therefore unlikely to have a unified position on issues and face many obstacles in formulating coherent strategies (Nixson, 1988: 380–1; Boddewyn and Brewer, 1994: 137). Negotiations become particularly complex when many issues are involved and if each actor takes different positions on each issue (Brewer, 1992). In the case of inward FDI, investment projects in sectors like energy, construction and manufacturing are often of significant interest to many government departments and interest groups. For example, an inward investment project may have environmental implications, and hence involve government environmental departments and lobby groups. There may be security implications if, for example, the project involves the acquisition of an indigenous firm supplying strategic technologies to the defence ministry. A project may also lead to the closure of domestic firms, import substitution and to the offer of government aid, each affecting different departments and interest groups.

Inward investment is therefore likely to involve national, regional, and local government, trade unions and even supra-national bodies like the EU. Inward investment potentially affects many government departments and interest groups, which can lead to conflicts over how the project should be handled. The government may not be able to formulate a coherent inward investment strategy, implement agreed policies, or negotiate with inward investors quickly, effectively, and consistency. Even in supposedly more cohesive and centralised states, like Japan, there are difficulties in formulating coherent policies when actors take different positions on issues (Krauss, 1992: 52–3). Similarly, in the more centralised MNC, internal differences within the firm, competing demands of subsidiaries, and the pressure from the MNC's home government and trade unions may impinge upon decision-making autonomy.

The penetration of the state and MNC by interest group pressures is therefore central to understanding the translation of potential into actual bargaining power. The interest structure in states may lobby for or against government intervention in the activities of inwardly investing MNCs, and influence the bargaining relations between MNCs and governments. The interest structure can exert a powerful influence even when lobbying over a different issue. For example, MNC bargaining power has been particularly strong in situations where governments, as an outcome of interest intermediation, have set performance objectives, such as the competitive enhancement of the domestic electronics industry (Lawton, 1997: 120). As Cawson *et al.* (1990: 361–2) argue:

> Where governments are committed to specific political objectives, such as job creation and preservation, or regional development, it is commonplace to observe that firms may more easily extract subsidies or preferential policies.

However, the mediation of interest pressures depends on the institutional structure of each actor. Research on government–industry relations has examined the network relations between actors, which influences the determination and implementation of policy. Contrasts have been found between countries, with Germany, for example, developing cohesive corporatist networks while fragmented interest groups in Britain have limited consensus and facilitated control of policy strategy by central government and the City of London (Grant,

1990; Walker, 1993). Different states therefore vary in their capacity to implement a coherent, autonomous policy:

> States differ widely in the capacity of private interest groups to affect policy, in the need to reconcile the interests of central and regional governments, in the degree of consensus on the roles of private and state-owned firms and of government intervention, in the quality and influence of their government bureaucracies; and in the public acceptance and mode of operation of their political processes (Safarian, 1993: 53).

The major point emphasised in the government–industry relations literature is that a network will only function successfully if the state is strong and autonomous and not open to capture (Atkinson and Coleman 1985: 25). The strength of the network is determined by the 'extent of power and autonomy granted to or gained by the state agency' while autonomy is influenced by 'the degree of monopoly closure in the relationship between the state and firms and private interest organisations' (Cawson *et al.*, 1987: 30).

Following Atkinson and Coleman (1985), state autonomy depends on four conditions:

- The agency has a clearly defined role and a value system that supports it, which is more likely where the agency has a functional mandate rather than one which obliges it to represent the interests of a particular clientele.
- State autonomy will be greater where the legal and regulatory framework provides barriers between the agency and the sector.
- State autonomy will be greater where functional responsibilities for a given sector are clearly assigned to a single agency.
- The state agency requires independent access to expertise and information in order to act autonomously from firms and sectoral associations.

Atkinson and Coleman (1989: 79–80) therefore argue that a centralised, autonomous and single agency or bureau in a given sector will have greatest capacity to make and implement policy. Government's may then be expected to establish an agency to handle MNC policy. A single, centralised and autonomous Atkinson and Coleman type agency should increase the government's negotiating capacity through reducing inter-governmental conflicts and a single body should be able to attract and co-ordinate enquiries and negotiate with MNCs more effectively. A centralised agency would also be in a better position to diffuse interest group pressure. The establishment of such an agency is particularly important given the institutional advantages of MNCs. As Cawson *et al.* (1990: 361) point out:

> Although many large firms... have a conglomerate structure, they nevertheless tend to be less fragmented than governments. Relations between firms and governments thus often take the form of a relatively centralised organisation confronting and negotiating with a number of different departments with various and often conflicting objectives. In such circumstances firms have considerable structural advantages.

Table 6.1 highlights the key strategic and operational aspects to institutional strengthening of a national inward investment agency. Investment promotion and project handling is of particular importance for negotiating with MNCs. Successful investment promotion increases alternative projects for the government, reducing dependence on a particular project, and effective project handling and negotiation increases both the attractiveness of the host country[1] and improves the government's bargaining capability. Both factors increase the government's bargaining power.

The strategic aspects of institutional strengthening are particularly important for ensuring that inward investment meets economic development needs. Attracting FDI that 'fits' with domestic economic development objectives and location conditions in turn is likely to increase the success of FDI projects, increasing future investment. However, effective co-ordination and co-operation between departments at the national, sub-national and inter-national level may be crucial for bargaining with multinationals. Studies have shown that the localities often consider themselves their main competitors (Dicken and Tickell, 1992) and in Chapter 10 it is shown that UK regions are competing with each other. This has ratcheted up the incentives awarded to MNCs, and effective co-ordination between national and sub-national government and investment agencies is therefore essential if competition between regions is to be based on location fundamentals rather than on incentives.

For example, the French government, as we saw in Chapter 5, has established a centrally controlled Invest in France Mission to promote France as a whole and the Invest in France Agency (IFA) and Invest in France Mission (IFM) to promote and facilitate FDI in the regions

Table 6.1 Aspects of institutional strengthening in an inward investment agency

Strategic	Operational
• Definition of clear, coherent objectives • Development of a focused strategy • Identification of policy actions to meet strategic objectives • Effective co-ordination and co-operation across government departments and between the national and sub-national levels • Effective co-ordination and co-operation between national governments • Sufficient status and visibility nationally and internationally • Control over strategic and executive functions	*Organisational* • A single, autonomous co-ordinating and promotion agency • Effective business planning • Appropriate resource allocation • Recruitment of relevant skills • Agile and flexible *Investment promotion* • An active search to attract FDI in carefully targeted sectors and from carefully targeted companies • Development and delivery of consistent marketing and promotional programmes and information provision • Visibility and commitment of senior government officials to FDI • Strong commercial focus • Fully empowered to take decisions *Project handling and negotiation* • Efficient project handling (information, site visits, red tape, etc) • Ability to negotiate incentives • Cohesive, centralised and autonomous negotiating teams • Speedy and predictable approvals • Clear accountability

Source: Encarnation and Wells (1986b); Wells and Wint (1991); Moran (1993); Wint (1993); (1998).

of France. The IFA is part of DATAR, France's regional economic development network. This institutional arrangement helps limit the negative aspects of competition between regions for FDI and supports the development of strategic objectives and policies that meet the needs and gain the commitment of different regions.

6.4   A BARGAINING MODEL OF MNC–GOVERNMENT RELATIONS

The objective of this section is to develop a model, a conceptual tool which can be used to clarify, structure and interpret the basic elements of a particular FDI project negotiation, with the primary objective to derive bargaining power, and hence the outcome of negotiations. The utility of the model depends on its ability to accommodate the changing facets of the MNC–host government relationship when different investment negotiations are examined, while still having a basic, underlying structure conceptualising the fundamental dimensions of MNC–host government bargaining.

From the above sections we can derive two key dimensions of the bargaining relationship:

- *Potential path of bargaining*: the ability and willingness of the MNC to substitute between different locations and the government between different investment sources, determined by *alternatives* and the resource demand (*commitment*).
- *Implementation of potential bargaining power*: the ability and willingness to implement potential power and translate perceived into actual power – crucial for control over outcomes and dependent on *political constraints* and *institutional structure*.

The following analysis will build a formal model conceptualising these two dimensions, drawing on political economy and the insights of existing bargaining models. The bargaining theory developed by Bacharach and Lawler (1981) is discussed in particular detail, as the theory allows us to move beyond the narrow focus on *relative* power, which characterises traditional economic and political economy models of bargaining. Bacharach and Lawler's dependency theory of bargaining helps indicate not only which party has greater bargaining strength but also when agreement is most likely to be reached, and is therefore of greater relevance to policy makers than models which only focus on revealing relative bargaining power.

6.4.1   Dependency theory of bargaining

The political economy analysis of government–MNC relations utilises the concept of power as central to understanding bargaining and, as

Bacharach and Lawler (1981: 200) argue, 'Power is not simply a part of bargaining, it is the essence of it.'

But power has so far been treated exclusively in relative terms. Relative power captures relative dependence between actors but a complete analysis of power requires separate consideration of absolute, total and relative power. As Bacharach and Lawler (1981: 66) argue:

> If the parties are bargaining over the division of a fixed quantity of a single resource, then it may be appropriate to concentrate on relative power, but if the amount of resources to be committed in the bargain is either ambiguous or variable, or if the parties are bargaining over the exchange of qualitatively different resources, then concentrating on relative power will obscure issues that are at the heart of the bargaining process.

Crucially, the degree of mutual dependence or interdependence between bargaining actors is pivotal to understanding the process and outcome of bargaining. An analysis of bargaining power in terms of dependency theory (not political economy) is discussed in this section, based on Bacharach and Lawler (1981).

According to Bacharach and Lawler, bargaining is about dependence, defined as the degree that the parties have a stake in the bargaining relationship. The stake in the relationship will depend on the degree to which parties have alternative outcome sources and the degree of commitment to the outcomes at issue. Alternatives can be seen as a proxy for the locational flexibility of MNCs – their substitution capacity – and commitment for the demand by governments and MNCs for each other's resources. Bacharach and Lawler, through theorising bargaining power as a function of alternatives and commitment, help elucidate the bargaining processes surrounding our first dimension of the MNC–government bargaining relationship – the potential path of bargaining.

In a two-actor model, the crucial variables for the analysis of bargaining power become:

- A's alternatives (to the resources controlled by B and to agreement);
- B's alternatives (to the resources controlled by A and to agreement);
- A's commitment (demand for and perceived value of B's resources);
- B's commitment (demand for and perceived value of A's resources).

Three dimensions of power can be explained in terms of these variables:

- *Absolute power*: the power of A irrespective of B's power. The absolute power of A is determined by B's alternatives and commitment, regardless of A's alternatives and commitment.
- *Total power*: the sum of A and B's dependence on one another – mutual dependence.
- *Relative power*: the dependence of one party compared to the dependence of the other party. Relative power is hence the ratio of B's dependence on A to A's dependence on B.

An increase in A's dependence (reduced alternatives, increased commitment) on B increases the perception of B's absolute power, but does not affect the perception of A's power. The absolute bargaining power of a party is based upon the other's dependence. So if B wishes to increase its absolute bargaining power it must reduce A's perception of its alternatives or enhance A's commitment. This increase in perceived dependence of A on B increases B's absolute power, which will make B tougher in negotiations, with B attempting to extract greater concessions from A.

Party A is more likely to try tactical action to extract concessions from B if they can:

- increase their absolute power by B becoming more dependent on A (B has fewer alternatives / higher commitment to A's resources);
- decrease B's absolute power by A becoming less dependent on B (A has more alternatives / lower commitment to B's resources.

From the above analysis it is possible to hypothesise not only which actor has the most bargaining power but also when agreement is most likely. The higher mutual dependence (total power) generally the more likely agreement, as an increase in total power within the bargaining relationship decreases mutual toughness. Total power or mutual dependence is maximised when the bargainers' decrease their alternatives or increase their commitment, and the likelihood of agreement is greatest when the power positions are equal on both the alternatives and commitment dimensions.

Bacharach and Lawler note, however, that high commitment does not necessarily imply reduced bargaining power. The reason is that if one party is highly committed, despite apparently increasing their concessions, it would also compel them increase their effort in the negotiations and improve the image projected to the bargaining partner. The negative power implications of high commitment might even be overcome, especially if the other party has less commitment and has little to lose from acquiescing.

Hence, high power on the alternative dimension is a definite advantage, while high power on the commitment dimension can be a disadvantage. To reach agreement, bargaining parties should increase their absolute (rather than relative) power, through reducing the alternatives and increasing the commitment of the other party, and convey high commitment. If both parties aim to increase their relative power by decreasing their dependence on the other, there is a decrease in total power / mutual dependence and agreement is less likely.

6.4.2 Existing bargaining models

We have identified six important approaches to government–MNC relations that provide important insights, as shown in our overview in Table 6.2. The table shows the key parameters and main contributions and limitations of each approach. In combination, they indicate that a new political economy bargaining model needs to address:

- how policy formation takes place – the implementation of bargaining power;
- the conceptualisation of governments *and* MNCs as political actors;
- relative stakes – the dependence of each actor, determined by alternatives and commitment;
- structural changes – forces changing commitment and alternatives over time;
- the development of an analytical model that can be used to determine relative bargaining power (with implications for concessions) and mutual power (with implications for the likelihood that the investment will take place).

6.4.3 A political economy bargaining model of MNC–government relations

From an analysis of structural changes and political economy, it was argued that there are two key dimensions to the bargaining relationship between MNCs and government: the potential path of bargaining

Table 6.2 Six major approaches to MNC–host country bargaining

Model	Key parameters	Contribution	Limitations
Moran (1974)	• The target of domestic concern (implicit assumptions of host countries regarding FDI) • The setting (balance of power – costs and benefits of ownership and location advantages) • Policy formation (impact of interest pressure on government policy)	Most comprehensive bargaining model in terms of including both a balance of power element and a political economy perspective	• No differentiation between types of power • No analytical framework to analyse different bargaining situations and when FDI is most likely to take place • No structural context – the three parameters of the model are discussed in static terms
Bacharach and Lawler (1981)	• Relative stakes (dependence) of the actors determines bargaining • Alternatives and commitment determine relative stakes in a negotiation	Model to determine bargaining power of each actor, how likely negotiations are to succeed, and which actor will bargain for the most concessions	• The model was developed for bargaining between individuals, not institutions • Bargaining is treated in bilateral terms – with no conceptualisation of external relations
Kobrin (1987)	• Focuses on relative bargaining power determined by: • Relative demand for resources (balance of power) • Constraints to the implementation of potential power (interest pressures and institutional autonomy)	Identifies the distinction between potential power (determined by relative demand for resources) and its implementation, and recognises the role of negotiation skills	• No differentiation between actual power and potential power • Focus is on the host country as a political actor, not the MNC • Does not differentiate between relative and absolute power, and therefore cannot determine the conditions when agreement is most likely • There is no structural context

Behrman and Grosse (1990; 1992)	• Negotiation skills (trained and experienced negotiators) • Relative power of the government (demand for the MNC's O-advantages and perception of their contribution to the national economy) • Relative stakes of the firm (significance of the host country to the MNC's global business, the importance of the specific negotiation to the MNC, and of alternative locations) • Congruence of interest (likelihood of government restrictions and regulations)	The first attempt to develop a formal analytical model of the bargaining relationship between MNCs and government. Identifies the importance of mutual dependence to the bargaining relationship and the role of alternatives and commitment	• No analytical framework is developed to examine bargaining • The alternatives dimension of government power is ignored • Treat congruence of interest in purely bilateral terms – plurality within and between the MNC, government and interest groups is disregarded • Do not integrate a political economy dimension into their model – although the authors note that this needed • No mention of the importance of implementing relative power into actual power
Dunning (1993a)	• OLI paradigm is central • Relative power (O-advantages of MNC and L-advantages of host country determine bargaining relations) • Dependence (interdependence)	Envisages a complex matrix of bargaining situations. Focus on information asymmetries	• Alternatives are left out of the equation • No political economy dimension • Not an explicit consideration of bargaining nor an attempt to develop a model of bargaining
Rugman and Verbeke (1998)	• Goal consistency, congruence and conflict • Dispersal of firm specific assets • Symmetry between inward and outward investment of countries	Focus on the determinants of FDI policy (dispersal of MNC assets and FDI symmetry)	• Bargaining is not central • Political economy and the exercise of power are excluded from the analysis

and the implementation of potential power. In this section, the two dimensions are integrated into a conceptual framework for analysing MNC–host government bargaining. Drawing on the models of bargaining and MNC–government negotiations discussed previously, a holistic, political economy model of bargaining is presented.

The political economy bargaining model is constructed in three stages:

- First, the bilateral relationship between MNCs and government is conceptualised, which involves developing ideal-types of the potential path of bargaining. Alternatives and commitment are adopted as key parameters, using the model of Bacharach and Lawler (1981) as a basis.
- Secondly, the political economy dimension is introduced, and ideal-types of the implementation of potential power are described. This initial separation between bilateral and plurilateral relations will aid clarity in understanding the derivation of the model and how the model is to be used as a heuristic tool for analysing bargaining.
- The final stage integrates the two interdependent dimensions into a formal, graphical bargaining model.

Conceptualising the potential path of bargaining is central to most of the bargaining models discussed in Table 6.2. The path is determined by perceived bargaining power. The bargaining models described in the last section define the parameters determining bargaining power in different ways. For example, Moran (1974) focuses on the setting (costs and benefits) of the negotiations, Kobrin (1987) on the relative demand for resources, and Behrman and Grosse (1990; 1992) on the relative stakes – the demand for resources and alternatives. Through-out this study, we have also argued that structural changes are increasing the cross-border alternatives and flexibility of MNCs and their control over core technologies.

However defined, the potential path of bargaining is determined in large part by two key variables: alternatives and commitment. Alternatives refer to alternative sources open to the two bargaining actors, while commitment refers to the demand and value attached to the resources controlled by the other actor. Government alternatives in a particular inward investment case will depend on perceptions of the firm specific assets that the MNC will transfer relative to the perceived assets of other potentially investing MNCs and indigenous firms. Government commitment reflects not only demand for the assets controlled by the MNC but also implicit assumptions about the overall value of FDI and symmetry of FDI flows. Assumptions and symmetry are represented by overall government inward investment policy, which forms part of the bargaining setting. For an extreme example, whether or not inward investment will take place at all is ultimately determined by government policy.

For the MNC, the degree of alternatives is a function of alternative hosts locations which offer similar location advantages to the host location under consideration. The commitment of the MNC reflects its demand for the resources controlled by the host country and the overall strategy of the firm – in other words commitment is a function of the corporate and FDI strategy and project specific determinants of FDI location discussed in Chapter 3.

Alternatives and commitment delineate the relative stakes of the bargaining actors, in this case governments and MNCs. Through differentiating between absolute, total and relative power we can interpret the potential bargaining path in a negotiation. Figure 6.1 illustrates the derivation of absolute power.

Points G and M illustrate the example of Intel's negotiations with Costa Rica during 1996. Intel, a US$20 billion MNC and the world's principle manufacturer of microprocessors, was looking for a location for a US$500 million semiconductor assembly plant for its Intel II processor. The government of Costa Rica, with an economy less than

Figure 6.1 Potential bargaining path: derivation of absolute power for Intel and Costa Rica

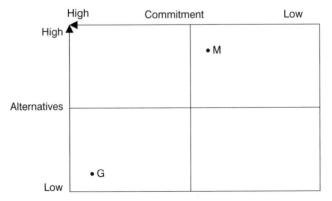

half the size of Intel's turnover, was hoping to diversify its economy and attract electronics investment.[2]

Point M indicates that the MNC is mobile with a number of alternative investment locations and a medium level of commitment. Distance costs, defined as costs associated with being located away from the market that is being served (see Thomsen and Woolcock, 1993), were low and Intel could have established the plant anywhere in the world.

However, Intel's corporate strategy was globalisation through regional diversification, with the company aiming for not more than 30% of revenues or production at any one site or in any one geographical region. In particular, as part of a globalisation strategy Intel wanted to establish a strong manufacturing presence in emerging markets for the low-tech end of a very technology-intensive business. Intel hoped to map-out microprocessor assembly and testing functions across the former Soviet Union, China and Latin America.

A location in Latin America was therefore favoured as part of the company's globalisation strategy, increasing Intel's commitment to this particular project and to Latin America. At the regional level, the FDI strategy was both market and especially efficiency seeking, but within Latin America Intel had minimal commitment to any one country and many alternatives to investing in Costa Rica.

The location advantages of Costa Rica were, though, very favourable when compared to other potential locations in meeting the project-specific requirements.

- While microprocessor assembly and testing is only about one-third as capital intensive as fabrication, the planned investment would be substantial. With high sunk costs, Intel was looking for stable economic and political conditions. In this respect Cost Rica stood out in Latin America. The country had the best credit rating in the region, a strong democratic tradition with a reliable political system and a transparent operating and legal environment. Economic conditions were positive with a pro-business environment.
- Compared to fabrication, assembly and testing is labour-intensive (the plant would create over 2,000 jobs) and employee compensation accounts for 25–30% of total operating costs. Costa Rica could offer a relatively inexpensive workforce, with per capita incomes among the lowest in the region at less than US$3,000. Free trade zones gave benefits of tax, tariff and custom fees exemptions and eased capital repatriation.

• The investment would, though, be dependent on a trainable work-force, as while the plant would be at the low end of the value-added chain in the microprocessor business, it still required quite high levels of technical competence. The 'excellent educational system' was praised by Intel's vice president, and with 12,000 engineering students, 2,000 computer systems designers graduating per year and a 95% literacy rate Costa Rica was well-placed to compete for the investment. In fact, the competition was narrowed down to a short list of Costa Rica, Brazil, Chile, and Mexico.

Point G indicates that the government has few alternatives, but high commitment. Since the 1980s the Costa Rican government had been attempting to shift exports towards high tech sectors and the government therefore attached the highest commitment to attracting Intel. The government had minimal alternatives. Intel was a leading firm in one of the most high tech industries and Costa Rica, given its small size and weak location advantages relative to small developed economies like Ireland, Singapore and Israel, was unlikely to attract more than one major high-tech project. The subsequent collapse in the world semiconductor market and the Asian crisis further reduced the probability of attracting a similar project. In addition, Costa Rica lacked an export-oriented domestic manufacturing sector. Given the objective to attract high tech investment and diversify exports the government had almost no alternatives to Intel's investment.

From dependency bargaining theory, the MNC (Intel) has high absolute bargaining power because the host country has few alternatives and high commitment. The host country government has quite low absolute power, with the MNC having many alternatives and a medium level of commitment. We would expect the firm to be able to bargain competitively for concessions. Overall, total power or mutual dependence is quite high, and agreement is therefore quite likely. The main obstacle to agreement is the high number of alternatives of Intel. However, with high government commitment it is possible that the host government will increase their effort in the negotiations, and the MNC has little to lose from acquiescing given the strategy of investing in Latin America and the favourable location advantages of Costa Rica. Agreement is more likely than not, although given higher relative power it will be made on the terms of the MNC.

This example illustrates one particular outcome from the matrix of potential bargaining power possibilities. Table 6.3 completes the matrix for all ideal-type combinations of perceived alternatives and

Table 6.3 Bargaining matrix of potential power possibilities

Government		MNC		Potential Bargaining Path		
Alternatives	Commitment	Alternatives	Commitment	Total power	Relative power	Agreement
High	High	High	High	Medium	Equal	Ambiguous
High	High	High	Low	Low	MNC	Unlikely
High	High	Low	High	High	Government	Likely
High	High	Low	Low	Medium	Government	Ambiguous
High	Low	High	High	Low	Government	Unlikely
High	Low	High	Low	Very low	Equal	Very unliKely
High	Low	Low	High	Medium	Government	Ambiguous
High	Low	Low	Low	Low	Government	Unlikely
Low	High	High	High	High	MNC	Likely
Low	High	High	Low	Medium	MNC	Ambiguous
Low	High	Low	High	Very high	Equal	Very likely
Low	High	Low	Low	High	MNC	Likely
Low	Low	High	High	Medium	MNC	Ambiguous
Low	Low	High	Low	Low	MNC	Unlikely
Low	Low	Low	High	High	Government	Likely
Low	Low	Low	Low	Medium	Equal	Ambiguous

commitments for the government and MNC. Total power determines the potential bargaining outcome, and building on the analysis in section 6.4.1, we can differentiate between degrees of total power:

- *High*: agreement is likely if the absolute power of each actor is high (both actors have few alternatives and high commitment) or if one actor has a medium level of absolute power and the other a high level.
- *Medium*: agreement is ambiguous if the absolute power one actor is high and the other is low, or if both actors convey medium levels of absolute power (e.g. low commitment / low alternatives).
- *Low*: agreement is unlikely if the absolute power of each actor is low or if one actor has a medium level of absolute power and the other a low level.

Table 6.3 also derives relative power, to indicate which actor will be tougher in the negotiations. The actor with higher absolute power will have greater relative power, although, as noted in section 6.4.1, high commitment may also be a source of negotiating strength. Therefore an actor with high alternatives / high commitment will have greater bargaining ability than an actor with low alternatives / low commitment.

From Table 6.3 we can derive four main bargaining hypotheses:

- If the absolute power of the government is *more* pronounced than that of the MNC then the government will have greater potential relative bargaining power.
- If the absolute power of the government is *less* pronounced than that of the MNC then the firm will have greater potential relative bargaining power.
- If the combined absolute power of both the government and the MNC is *high* then the bargaining matrix is one of high total power and mutual gain, with agreement likely.
- If the combined absolute power of both the government and the MNC is *low*, total power / mutual dependence is low and agreement is unlikely.

The second stage in developing a bargaining model is conceptualising the political economy dimension of the bargaining relationship between MNCs and governments. This dimension involves the implementation of potential bargaining power. We identified two key variables influencing the translation of perceived into actual power: the interest structure and the institutional structure. The interest structure introduces the possibility of plurilateral relations within and between MNCs, governments and third party interest groups. The negotiating actors may therefore face political constraints to implementing potential power.

Institutional structure determines the influence of political lobbying on negotiating strategies and also negotiating competence. For example, for the host country government, a well-directed, autonomous inward investment agency can speed up investment decisions, reduce intra-governmental conflicts and generally increase the attractiveness of the country *vis-à-vis* other countries competing for the investment (Encar-nation and Wells, 1985). We also noted in our discussion of the political economy of bargaining that MNCs are likely to have a more autonomous decision-making structure.

Figure 6.2 shows the implementation of potential power. 'Interest pressure' refers to the degree of lobbying by the interest structure, with 'high' representing many political constraints to reaching agree-ment. 'Institutional strength' refers to how autonomous the institu-tional structure for decision-making of the bargaining actors are to the interest structure and indicates their negotiating capability. A central-ised, co-ordinated and experienced agency with clearly identified objectives is most effective in terms of translating potential power into actual power (see Table 6.2), and a high level of institutional strength is represented by 'high' in Figure 6.2.

The implementation matrix of Intel's microprocessor assembly pro-ject in Costa Rica is illustrated by points M and G. Point M indicates

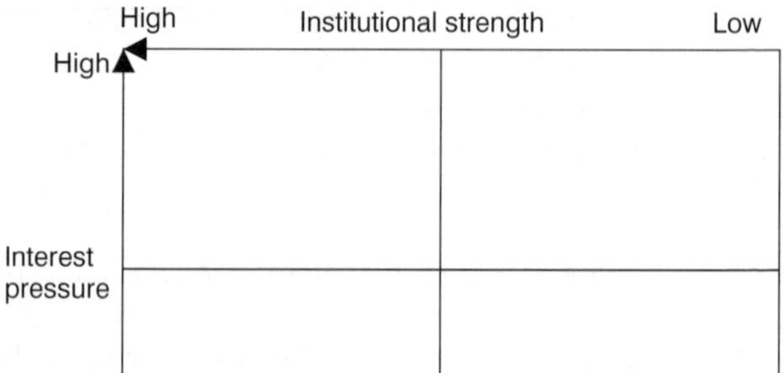

Figure 6.2 Implementation of potential power: the influence of political constraints for Intel and Costa Rica

that the MNC has a very autonomous institutional structure and faces minimal interest group pressures. The proposed assembly plant was not a crucial component in Intel's strategy or core capabilities and met with little opposition within the firm. The scale of the project was also small relative to Intel's fabrication projects and the resources of the company.

In Intel's home country there was also little opposition. The relatively labour intensive plant would not displace employment in the developed US market, and the US workforce did not lobby against the investment. Similarly, the home country government, potentially a major interest group affecting both the negotiating strategies of the home MNC (Ruigrok and Tulder, 1995) and host government policy (Jones, 1996b: 273), had no interest in the project. The potential power of the MNC is likely to equate with actual power.

For the host government, point G illustrates that there are also few political constraints to agreement. The proposed FDI project met with little opposition as there are no domestic competitors to lose market share and with the government's commitment to economic deregulation, the unions were in a weak position to bargain for recognition and worker's rights. Point G also indicates that the government has a well-directed, centralised system of FDI decision-making.

Costa Rica has a private-sector based investment promotion agency (called CINDE) actively targeting potential electronic investors. CINDE had a cohesive, motivated team, trained in project handling, and able to facilitate Intel's enquiries. CINDE conducted detailed research on Intel and the semiconductor industry so that it would better understand and be able to meet Intel's needs. Intel also obtained a quick, efficient service and easy and timely access to Costa Rica's key decision-makers, more difficult in the larger more bureaucratised countries competing for the investment.

The bargaining path described in Figure 6.2 is likely to be implemented, and agreement is more likely given the effectiveness of Costa Rica's FDI institutions (from 1994 to 1998 CINDE attracted 25 high-tech inward investment projects).

Table 6.4 shows the bargaining matrix of ideal types for implementing potential bargaining power, from which we can derive two further bargaining hypotheses:

• The greater the potential political constraints the greater the impediments to translating potential power into actual power and the more complex the negotiation process.

Table 6.4 Bargaining matrix for the implementation of potential power

Government		MNC		Implementation of potential power		
Interest structure	Institutional structure	Interest structure	Institutional structure	Bargaining ability		Implementation
				Government	MNC	
High	High	High	High	Medium	Medium	Uncertain
High	High	High	Low	Medium	Very low	MNC unlikely
High	High	Low	High	Medium	Very high	Likely
High	High	Low	Low	Medium	Medium	Likely
High	Low	High	High	Very low	Medium	Gov. unlikely
High	Low	High	Low	Very low	Very low	Very unlikely
High	Low	Low	High	Very low	Very high	Gov. unlikely
High	Low	Low	Low	Very low	Medium	Gov. unlikely
Low	High	High	High	Very high	Medium	Likely
Low	High	High	Low	Very high	Very low	MNC unlikely
Low	High	Low	High	Very high	Very high	Very likely
Low	High	Low	Low	Very high	Medium	Likely
Low	Low	High	High	Medium	Medium	Likely
Low	Low	High	Low	Medium	Very low	MNC unlikely
Low	Low	Low	High	Medium	Very high	Likely
Low	Low	Low	Low	Medium	Medium	Uncertain

- The greater the autonomy of decision-making structure from potential political constraints and negotiating capability the greater the bargaining ability of the key actors.

The final stage of developing a formal analytical political economy bargaining model is to integrate the two dimensions of alternatives/commitment and interest/institutional structure in order to explicate the potential path of bargaining and the implementation of potential bargaining power. We have argued that the potential path of bargaining involves how likely agreement is and which actor is most likely to bargain for concessions. Agreement is determined by the degree of total power and bargaining tactics are determined by absolute power. Relative bargaining ability is determined by relative power (the ratio of the absolute power of the bargaining actors). Figure 6.3 integrates and structures the analysis of bargaining extended in Figures 6.1 and 6.2.

We have referred to total power as mutual dependence, which is the relative stakes of the two actors. Figure 6.3 illustrates mutual dependence on the Y-axis. The higher mutual dependence, the more likely that agreement is the outcome.

Figure 6.3 Political economy bargaining model

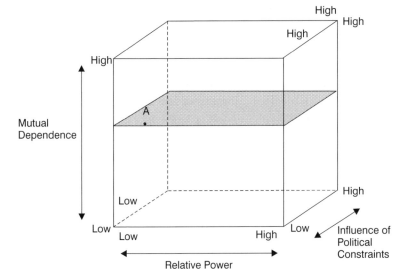

Relative power defines the relative stakes of each actor in the outcome of the negotiation. The X-axis in Figure 6.3 gives the relative power of the government. The higher the relative power of the government, the lower is the relative power of the MNC. If the government has high relative power it has greater bargaining ability.

The implementation of perceptions of potential power depends on the degree of political constraints (interest structure) and the autonomy and negotiating capability of the actors (institutional structure). The Z-axis in Figure 6.3 illustrates the influence of political constraints in a negotiation. A high degree of influence represents situations of strong interest pressures and lack of institutional autonomy to these pressures. Negotiations will not necessarily follow the potential bargaining path as indicated by various permutations of alternatives/commitment. One drawback of the final model is that it does not illustrate the implementation of potential power separately for the government and the MNC. We need to refer back to Figure 6.2 to gain this information. The model also does not reveal the *willingness* to implement potential power, which will depend on the overall strategy and ethos of the MNC and host country government.

Point A illustrates the example of the microchip assembly plant. TheCosta Rican government has weaker relative bargaining power while the degree of mutual dependence indicates that agreement is quite likely, though by no means assured. The influence of political constraints is minimal. In terms of actual events, the project went ahead and Intel received a package of training, tax and tariff incentives.

In conclusion, to interpret a bargaining relationship we must analyse the potential path of bargaining (alternatives and commitment) and the implementation of potential power (interest and institutional structure), which together inform us of how likely agreement is and on whose terms the agreement is likely to be made.

6.5   BARGAINING WITH MULTINATIONALS: THE UTILITY OF THE MODEL

According to Heintz (1994: 224), there is an underlying bargaining matrix intrinsic to MNC investment. We have attempted to outline the key factors influencing this matrix and derive the possible outcomes through developing a political economy model of bargaining. Central to the bargaining model is the exercise of power, and the model builds on previous bilateral economic models through using dependency bargaining theory to conceptualise the use of power in negotiations and by integrating a political economy dimension into the analytical framework.

The model can be used not only as a heuristic tool for analysing a specific MNC–government negotiation over an inward investment project, but also as a general framework for interpreting government–MNC relations for a particular country. The model also allows us to understand the impact of structural changes on government–MNC bargaining. For example, if we use the bargaining model to compare government policy in the UK and France we gain insights into why the UK has historically attracted more FDI than France and how structural changes in the 1990s increased inward FDI into France.

Inward investment has been central to UK industrial policy, as we analyse in detail in Chapter 9, with the British government displaying very high commitment to attracting inward investment. At the same time, the poor performance of indigenous industry and a non-intervention philosophy have reduced the industrial policy alternatives to attracting inward investment available to the government. According to the bargaining model, MNCs have very high absolute power when negotiating with the UK government, increasing the intensity of their concessionary bargaining tactics. However, mutual power is also increased, which improves the likelihood of agreement, i.e. increasing FDI into the UK.

In contrast, the French government has had a low commitment to attracting inward investment and many industrial policy alternatives, with the government willing to support indigenous enterprises and with a strong indigenous manufacturing base. The absolute power of MNCs wishing to invest in France is low and mutual power is lower than in the UK case, reducing FDI in France. However, with the changing industrial policy philosophy of the French government in the 1990s, representing structural changes including the growth of long-term unemployment, globalisation and constraints at the EU level, commitment to attracting inward investment has increased. At the same time, alternatives to inward investment decreased as the government came under pressure, especially from the EU, to reduce support for national champions. The government was more willing to attract FDI, mutual power increased and, with the increased relative power of foreign MNCs, they are able to bargain for government investment incentives. The bargaining model helps to understand how structural changes and government policy influence the bargaining relationship between MNCs and governments.[3]

Our example of Intel and Costa Rica showed that, as well as government commitment and alternatives, in order to understand an investment decision the commitment of the MNC and alternative investment locations plays a crucial role. Using the model of FDI location in Chapter 3, alternative locations are a function of the congruence between the requirements of the MNC's specific FDI strategy and project and ownership advantages, and the location advantages of the country. In the case of Intel, while Costa Rica was in a strong position to meet the location criteria of the assembly plant, other countries could also meet the criteria.

The commitment of the MNC also plays an important role in investment decisions. Commitment to an investment project reflects the strategy of the MNC. The example of Intel highlighted the company's globalisation strategy as an important factor in Intel's investment within the Latin America regional market. Structural changes in the international political economy affect the strategy of MNCs as well as governments. Intel's globalisation strategy reflects the growth of international investment and shift toward triadic investment strategies of international business as a whole, as we discussed in previous chapters.

The bargaining model also introduces a political economy dimension into the investment decision. The case of Intel and Costa Rica showed how the interest and institutional structure potentially influence investment negotiations. In this particular example, there were minimal interest group pressures interceding in the potential path of bargaining and the institutional structure of Costa Rica's FDI apparatus further facilitated Intel's investment.

The primary motivation for developing the political economy bargaining model is to analyse MNC–government bargaining over inward investment decisions. However, this is not its only use; the theoretical basis of the model is not specific to inward investment, but can be used for interpreting bargaining relationships between other institutions. In particular, the model provides insights into the changing bargaining relationship between MNCs and labour. As MNCs become more global they have more alternative sites for investment and as MNCs move towards regional and global strategies they become less dependent on their home base for production and the N-form MNC specialises R&D in world centres of excellence – not necessarily at home. Through structural changes, MNCs have more alternatives and are reducing their commitment to activities in their home base, increasing their relative power over trade unions. Multinational companies are able to bargain for more concessions, such as flexible work practices in the automotive industry. In our conclusion in Chapter 12, we draw on the bargaining model analysis to examine how governments and labour can address the asymmetrical structural power advantages of MNCs.

7 Nissan's Investment in the UK

More than any other greenfield investment in the UK, Nissan has had the greatest impact. In political terms, Nissan vindicated for the Conservative government Mrs Thatcher's ideological struggle against the trade unions. In economic terms, Nissan and the follow-on investment of Honda and Toyota have prevented the collapse of the British car industry and Nissan is propping-up the North-East manufacturing economy. In global terms, Nissan symbolised the new production practices and philosophies that were causing a sea-change in the world automobile industry. In social terms, the costs and benefits of Nissan's manufacturing system for workers is a hotly debated subject. But of interest in the first part of this chapter are the lengthy negotiations that clouded Nissan's investment in the UK. We argue that only through conceptualising the political economy of bargaining relations can we understand the negotiations surrounding Nissan's decision to invest in the UK.

In the second part of this chapter we analyse the economic impact of Nissan. We argue that while Nissan has boosted the British car industry and is the lynch-pin of the North-East's manufacturing economy, the future contribution of Nissan will depend on the competitiveness of the UK supply industry and the UK remaining a core member of the European Union. Inward investment is not a substitute for a strong domestic industry – the long-term success of inward investment depends on it.

7.1 COMPANY HISTORY AND INTERNATIONAL EXPANSION

The history of Nissan's corporate evolution and international expansion can be divided into two phases. In the first phase from 1930 to the early 1990s Nissan rapidly went from a position of technological dependency to becoming one of the world's leading automotive manufacturers, with extensive operations in Asia-Pacific, North America and Europe. In the second phase from 1990 to 2000 Nissan experienced financial crisis and was forced to make major cuts in production and costs. However, this did not solve the crisis and, almost unheard of in Japanese corporate history, a foreign company (Renault) bought a major stake in Nissan, giving the combined company the global scope it needed to compete.

7.1.1 From technological dependency to global player: 1930 to early 1990s

Nissan originated during the 1930s as the abbreviation used for the holding company that owned it – Nippon Sangyo, founded in 1928 and run by Aikawa Yoshisuke (Cusumano, 1985: 28). Francks (1992) describes the formation of Nissan in three stages:

- In 1931 Aikawa acquired shares in DAT Motors, which had been licensed by the army to produce subsidised trucks and was experimenting with designs for a small passenger car.
- In 1933 DAT Motors entered into a merger which was to create Isuzu and as it was to concentrate on truck production it gave Aikawa the Osaka factory producing the Datsun in return for his shares in the company.
- In 1934 Aikawa merged his new factory with the auto-parts section of his original company to form a new subsidiary, the Nissan Motor Company.

Nissan sought a tie-up with GM, employed American engineers to design and direct production operations, and even purchased an entire US plant to re-assemble in Japan (Francks, 1992: 77, 194). In 1936, Nissan purchased a conveyor system from the Graham Page Corporation in US and started mass production of the Datsun (Takeuchi, 1990: 168). The purchase of the 70-metre conveyer from the US allowed Nissan to be first Japanese company to produce parts and finished cars on a machine-paced assembly line, and Nissan was the leader in assembly-line technology in Japan (Cusumano, 1985: 40–1; Francks, 1992: 195). After the Second World War, Nissan continued to depend for its incremental development on foreign technology, and in a technical tie-up with Austin in 1952 Nissan assembled Austin A40's at first from kits and then gradually from domestically made parts (Francks, 1992: 195).

This lay the ground for domestic production and the development of advanced technology (Takeuchi, 1990: 170), most of which was concentrated in Tokyo. The clustering of Japan's machinery industries in the Tokyo region developed into a technological complex combining the plants and research institutes of southern Tokyo, and 65% of Nissan's subcontractors were located in southern Tokyo in the late 1980s (Takeuchi, 1990: 177). Nissan's vertically disintegrated subcontracting network was integral to its productivity and cost advantage (Cusumano, 1985: 383).

Although Nissan led in terms of automated technology (Cusumano, 1985: 342) and was the market leader in Japan in the pre-war period, after the war Toyota caught-up and took the lead. Toyota's automobile division became an independent corporation in 1937 (Takeuchi, 1990: 169) and, unlike Nissan, Toyota took the endogenous path to technological catch-up (Odagiri and Goto, 1993: 100). A new modern technical centre was built in 1954, and Nissan's investment in research facilities only began to approximate Toyota's in the 1960s (Cusumano, 1985: 71). Furthermore, Nissan had management problems from the mid-1960s, which started when the firm merged with Prince in 1966. The merger created antagonism between the employees of the two companies, with Prince employees under-valued, and R&D continued carried out independently by the two groups of former Nissan and Prince (Takeuchi, 1990: 171–8).

Nevertheless, by the end of the 1960s Nissan's productivity surpassed US levels (Cusumano, 1985: 374) and with unions weakened from 1949, culminating in federations of co-operative enterprise unions being founded in 1969 (Yutaka, 1998), Japanese firms like Nissan were able to introduce team-based work organisation. These involved practices such as *kaizen* and quality circles and productivity and quality increased dramatically. In the 1980s, total quality control was refined through the introduction of various methods of 'flexible automation', including flexible manufacturing systems, industrial robots, direct numerical control, and computer integrated manufacturing (Masayuki, 1998: 189).

The success of Japanese auto manufacturers was compounded by the oil crises in the 1970s, which led to demand for small cars (Takeuchi, 1990: 172), of which Japan was the lowest cost and most efficient producer (Moore, 1994: 317). Japan's share of world car production increased from just 1% in 1960 to 27% in 1985 (Sadler, 1992a: 221) and in 1996 Nissan's share of the world passenger car production, at 5.8%, was the sixth highest in the world and exceeded that of Renault, Rover and Alfa Romeo combined.

With rapid growth at home and abroad, Nissan began overseas production as early as 1962, setting-up in Thailand – the first overseas investment by a Japanese automobile company (Shoichi, 1998: 70). By 1990, Nissan had 11 overseas production bases, with output of its foreign subsidiaries increasing by over 10% per year. Nissan started production in Mexico in 1966, established fully fledged manufacturing operations in the US in 1980, with production beginning in 1983, and Nissan UK was established in 1984. Nissan also set-up smaller operations in Spain, Greece, Portugal and the Netherlands in Europe and Australia in Asia-Pacific (Takeuchi, 1990: 179–80).

Table 7.1 shows the foreign and total assets, sales and employment of 12 Japanese MNCs and gives their world rank. A comparison is made between 1990 and 1996 (or the nearest years for which data is available) and an index of multinationality is calculated, based on UNCTAD.

Electrical and transport machinery accounts for half of Japanese manufacturing FDI in the EU (EC, 1998), and from Table 6.1, we can see that the leading Japanese industrial MNCs are concentrated in these two sectors. By 1990, over one-third of Nissan's sales and employment was overseas, with Nissan's foreign subsidiaries employing over 30,000 workers. From 1990 to 1996 Nissan's foreign sales nearly doubled the company's overseas employment reached almost 35,000. By the mid-1990s, Nissan was the second largest Japanese industrial MNC in the world when ranked by foreign assets, being eclipsed by Toyota. But in terms of multinationality, Nissan (and Honda, Sony, Canon and Bridgestone) had a higher proportion of its activities located overseas.

7.1.2 Financial crisis and loss of independence: early 1990s to 2000

Nissan's expansion since the late 1980s was over-ambitious and, in combination with a sharp decline in domestic vehicle sales with the Japanese recession and the precipitous drops in regional Asian demand in 1997 and 1998, Nissan faced severe financial problems, leaving the company chronically unprofitable (see Pilkington, 1998: 34). In the six years to 1998, Nissan only once reported a profit, and Nissan's dealers alone have debts of 1 trillion Yen and are turning to Nissan as a lender of last resort. Only in Europe is Nissan profitable (Abrahams *et al.*, 1998).

In response, Nissan unveiled a new pricing system in 1994 and put together the Vehicle Innovation Programme which embraces 12 principal component manufacturers and aims to achieve a 40% cut in prices through standardising models and components (Masayoshi,

Table 7.1 Multinationality of Japanese industrial multinational companies, 1990–96

Company	Industry	Year	Assets (US$ billion)		Sales (US$ billion)		Employment		Rank/Index (%)**
			Foreign	Total	Foreign	Total	Foreign	Total	
Toyota	automotive	1996	39.2	113.4	51.7	109.3	34,837	150,736	7 / 35
		1990	12.8	55.1	24.8	60.1	11,326	96,849	29 / 24
Nissan	automotive	1996	27.0	58.1	29.2	53.8	34,464[1]	143,310[1]	16 / 42
		1990	–	36.4	16.8	35.7	30,050	129,546	46 / 35
Sony	electronics	1996	23.5	45.8	32.8	45.7	95,000	163,000	24 / 61
		1990	–	32.6	12.7	20.9	62,100	112,900	15 / 58
Honda	automotive	1996	17.8	33.5	26.4	42.3	19,668[1]	92,800[1]	36 / 45
		1990	6.7	18.0	16.1	26.9	23,760[2]	79,200[2]	13 / 42
Matsu-Shita	electronics	1996	12.3	67.8	23.8	62.0	112,314[1]	265,397[1]	53 / 33
		1990	–	62.0	21.0	46.8	67,000	210,848	12 / 38
Hitachi	electronics	1996	11.4	80.4	19.8	68.7	56,400	330,100	60 / 20
		1992*	–	66.6	13.9	58.4	80,000[1]	331,852[1]	5 / 24
Fujitsu	electronics	1996	8.9	38.1	10.8	36.3	53,000	167,000	7 / 28
		1993*	9.1	35.0	7.9	30.6	65,000	163,000	51 / 33
Nippon	metal	1996	–	36.3	5.8	24.7	15,000[1]	50,438[1]	78 / 27
		1993*	–	42.3	5.0	26.8	15,000	50,438	55 / 24
Canon	electronics	1996	8.3	22.6	14.9	22.1	38,197	75,628	81 / 52
		1992*	5.6	17.4	9.5	13.6	27,800[3]	64,500[3]	82 / 56
Mitsubishi Motors	automotive	1996	8.0	26.1	8.5	29.6	18,900	74,700	84 / 28
		1993*	22.5	77.2	31.7	64.3	98,639	254,059	14 / 56
Bridge-Stone	rubber and plastic	1996	7.8	15.2	10.0	18.0	52,000[1]	89,711[1]	87 / 55
		1990	–	13.0	7.6	13.2	56,000	87,234	79 / 44
Toshiba	electronics	1996	7.6	46.8	14.0	44.0	38,000[1]	190,000	91 / 23
		1990	–	39.2	10.3	33.3	27,000	162,000	64 / 20

Source: Derived from UNCTAD (1993; 1994; 1995a; 1996; 1997; 1998); **index of multinationality is calculated as the average of 3 ratios: foreign to total assets; foreign to total sales and foreign to total employment. Rank compares a company's multinationality with the world's top 100 industrial MNCs; [1]1994 figures; [2]1992 figures; [3]1993 figures; *Year first in top 100.

1998: 110). However, in 1998 Nissan still produced over 50 models on more than 20 platforms – about the same as the whole of Europe (*Financial Times*, 1999). With continuing losses, Nissan closed 25% of foreign production in 1998 and cut production to 1.62 million cars in Japan in 1998 compared with peak capacity of 2.3 million in 1989 (Nakamoto, 1999).

However, Nissan's financial crisis and global consolidation in the automotive industry, most recently seen in the merger of Daimler and Chysler and the acquisition of Volvo cars by Ford, pre-empted a strategic partnership between Nissan and Renault in March 1999. The partnership was short of a full merger, with Renault taking a 36.8% stake in Nissan for US$5.9 billion and a 22.5% stake in Nissan Diesel. The partnership allows a maximum 44% share in Nissan, and therefore appears to prevent an ultimate merger.

The rationale for the partnership is the strategic fit between the two companies:

- *Geographic fit*: Nissan has a strong presence in Asia-Pacific and North America while Renault is strong in Western Europe, Eastern Europe (in particular Turkey) and has plants in Latin America. The only over lap is in Western Europe, but Nissan is stronger in Northern Europe and Renault in Southern Europe.
- *Business strengths*: Nissan is strong in manufacturing capability, product technology, and its supplier technology base, while Renault is strong in management, product planning and product design capabilities. Nissan needed a partner to provide funds and to enable the company to have the economies of scale to amortise its technology.
- *Product range*: Nissan is strong in light trucks and sports utility vehicles (although Nissan's product portfolio covers nearly all segments), while Renault is strong in passenger cars.

In the longer term the partnership has the potential to develop economies of scale and scope, but this will require co-operation in platform development and purchasing. The new Nissan Micra and Renault Clio will use the same vehicle platform. The implication for Nissan and Renault's global ambitions is that they can benefit from each other's presence in different regions of the world. Already, in 2000, Nissan announced that it will build Renault cars at its plant in South Africa and Nissan is investing US$300 million at Renault's plants in Latin America to build sports utility vehicles. However,

Renault-Nissan will have to confront global excess capacity in the automotive industry, especially in Western Europe.

7.2   NISSAN IN THE UK: A BARGAINING MODEL APPROACH

In Chapter 6 we built a political economy bargaining model in order to conceptualise government–MNC relations and develop a heuristic tool for analysing the bargaining relations in a specific inward investment project. We will use the model to analyse Nissan's investment in the UK – which remains the single biggest Japanese investment in Europe.

The bargaining model is based on understanding two sets of relationships:

- *The potential path of bargaining*: determined by the commitment and alternatives of the actors.
- *The implementation of potential bargaining power into actual power*: determined by the institutional structure of the actors and political constraints to agreement.

We suggested that in order to facilitate the use of the model as an analytical tool, we need to first analyse the potential path of bilateral bargaining, and then analyse the implementation of potential power. Interpreting a particular bargaining relationship will require a consideration of both potential and actual power, which is facilitated by this initial separation.

7.2.1   Potential bath of bargaining for Nissan and the UK government

The potential path of bargaining negotiations between Nissan and the UK government is determined by the absolute power of each actor, which in turn is a function of commitment and alternatives. The level of commitment and alternatives reflect the dependency relations in a bargaining relationship. Let us first examine Nissan's commitment and alternatives (the UK government's absolute power).

In 1980, internationalisation was a major corporate objective of Nissan's then President Mr Ishihara (Goto: 1987: 73). Nissan's internationalisation strategy was focused on the US and Europe. Nissan needed manufacturing operations in the US market, in part due to emerging trade tensions between the US and Japan, but also to strengthen its position in the world's biggest market and Nissan increasingly felt that it was also essential to establish a production base within the EEC market. The reason was three-fold:

- *Nissan's market share was threatened by protective barriers*: For example, the threat of protectionist measures by the UK government on Japanese cars in 1978 led Japanese manufacturers to restrict exports to below 11% of the market, and by 1986 a voluntary export restraint (VER) was instituted on EC-wide basis.
- *Global competition*: Already in the early 1980s competition was compelling the major car manufacturers to form alliances, which Nissan sought to avoid by establishing an independent future through rapid expansion.
- *Strategy to increase market share*: This demanded local presence, in order to be more sensitive to local market conditions and consumer tastes and overcome trade barriers.

Nissan's commitment to investing in the UK was therefore influenced by structural changes (regional trade blocs and intensifying global competition) and Nissan's strategic response to these changes. Any potential investment in the UK would be dependent on Nissan's commitment to investing in the EEC as a whole, with Nissan's commitment to the UK basically a function of its commitment to Europe. Nissan's major FDI strategy for setting-up production in the EEC was market-seeking, and the UK was Nissan's largest market in Europe, accounting for one-third of Nissan's EEC sales in 1982. The UK market was also characterised by relatively high selling prices. Nissan was strongly committed to investing in the EEC as part of its internationalisation and expansionary strategy, and the UK market was the most highly valued within Europe.

However, in the early 1980s Nissan was facing intensifying competition in its home market, with the success of Honda (*The Economist*, 1983a), and Nissan's US project was of higher priority. Nissan was therefore faced with competing demands at home and abroad. We can posit that investing in the EEC was of high strategic importance in the medium to long term, but that in the short-term Nissan had more pressing agendas. Overall, in the first half of the 1980s, Nissan manifested a medium level of commitment to investing in the UK as part of the company's EEC market-seeking FDI strategy. While the UK could meet the requirements of Nissan's market seeking FDI strategy, investing in the EEC was not the main priority of the company's overall corporate strategy in the early 1980s, especially as none of its competitors were yet planning investment in Europe.

In terms of alternatives, the search for optimum labour market conditions would play a vital role in Nissan's location appraisal in Europe. As, Okama, then Executive Vice President for overseas operations, said in January 1982:

> The only problem is how we will be able to manage the workforce well, avoiding disputes. If we can succeed, we shall have an edge over the established car manufacturers (cited in Dohse, 1987: 139).

The importance of choosing a country and plant site with the right workforce was heightened for Nissan due to three main factors:

- First, Nissan's central corporate philosophy and goal was, and is, quality above everything else (Wickens, 1987: Ch.5). According to Nissan (1995): 'Quality is not something left to quality control staff – it is the responsibility of every single person in the organisation from the receptionists to employees working on the production line and all administrative staff including the Managing Director.' Total quality control at all stages of production is central to Nissan's lean production manufacturing system and labour flexibility is seen as crucial (see Loewendahl, 1998). As Nissan's Personnel Director, Peter Wickens, states: 'What we are after are people who are totally flexible in working practices and attitudes. We want to have no demarcations and as few job titles as possible' (cited in Sadler, 1992a: 299).
- Secondly, Nissan's experience in Japan during the 1950s was one of being badly disrupted by union militancy, causing the company to strongly favour the establishment of only one negotiating body, preferably along the lines of the right wing, company centred union model in Japan (*The Economist*, 1983b). Nissan was fundamentally opposed to union power, and Nissan demanded a single union deal to ensure the industrial relations flexibility and stability necessary for its manufacturing system (Oliver and Wilkinson, 1988: 63). The stability achieved in Japan can be seen by the fact that Nissan's major plant at Oppama has never had a strike since it opened in 1962 (Sadler, 1992a: 301).
- Third, the transferral of Nissan's 'lean' system to its Tennessee plant in the US had led to socio-technical problems, in particular

relating to racial problems (Rehder and Thompson, 1994: 94–5), which Nissan sought to avoid in Europe.

Within the EEC, the UK stood out as having an incumbent government committed to labour market deregulation and to reducing union power in order to improve labour flexibility. Furthermore, the economic conditions in several UK regions provided an environment suited to Nissan. While industrial relations in the UK in the early 1980s were not good (as far as Nissan was concerned), the Thatcher government promised radical changes. The good labour relations already achieved by Japanese electronics firms in the UK (*The Economist*, 1983c) also increased Nissan's confidence to investing in the UK.

Through investing in a peripheral region, Nissan could implement a divide and rule strategy, split the unions and offer a non-negotiable agreement with a single union legally obliged to act in the interests of the company as well as employees (McCooey, 1991: 71; Crowther and Garrahan: 1988: 56–7). A single union deal would also give Nissan a considerable advantage over the then Austin-Rover which negotiated with 13 unions in five company level bargaining groups (Enderwick, 1993: 19), but most importantly a single union was seen as crucial for the successful transplantation of Nissan's manufacturing system.

Nissan considered conditions in the North-East to be particularly favourable for establishing a single union and introducing new work practices. As with the location of Japanese auto plants in Southern locations in the US, away from the industrial heartland of the auto industry in Detroit, Sunderland would provide an acquiescent workforce, and one with no tradition of automobile production, in a region of high unemployment. Sunderland also had relatively good industrial relations at a time of generally poor labour relations (McRae, 1997). According to *Regional Trends*, the North-East has the most flexible working patterns in the UK (ONS, 1998c). With unemployment peaking in 1986 at 17% and over 60% in inner Sunderland (Crowther and Garrahan, 1988: 52–3), trade unions would meet Nissan's demands as they had few alternatives to job creation.

The industrial history of the North-East was also important, with Nissan's deputy managing director, John Cushnaghan, stating:

We chose Sunderland because it is an area steeped in manufacturing history and the industrial mentality which sees that shift patterns are normal because fathers and sons have worked in them for generations (cited in Thorpe, 1997).

Additionally, the relatively ethnically homogenous populations of the two sites most favoured by Nissan – Wales and Sunderland – promised to reduce the problems of racial discrimination associated with Nissan's US plant. Box 7.1 details the single union agreement forged by Nissan, which covers 40% of the work-force.

Box 7.1. Nissan's single union agreement: negotiating flexibility

Following Dohse (1987) there were four main problems in the UK auto industry facing Nissan:

- First, job demarcation made it difficult to integrate direct and indirect functions to considerably save manpower. The multi-union structure made the lines of job demarcation particularly rigid
- Second, 'scientific' time standards were not as nearly accepted as in Germany or the US. Workload was still in part a matter of informal bargaining on the shop floor
- Third, it was hard to enforce redundancies
- Fourth, minimal central union control meant work sections could withhold their labour, and thus apply pressure to achieve their particular interests.

Flexibility was therefore enshrined in Nissan's single union agreement with the Amalgamated Union of Engineering Workers (AUEW), which was contracted out of the three main unions competing to represent Nissan's workers. Nissan played off the three main unions to ensure its demands for flexibility were met. The AUEW was favoured because the extensive use of robots (over 80% automation levels) would create more engineering jobs but less jobs for the blue-collar workers of the Transport and General Trade Union and the AUEW was perceived to be less aggressive and assertive. For example, the union publishes a booklet in several languages inviting inward investors and offering their full support if they are selected as a single union. Nissan stated that, 'We believed the AEEU was the union that was committed to our philosophy of teamworking, flexibility, single status and an absolute dedication to quality' and the AUEW agreed to a no-strike pendulum, arbitration, common conditions, and complete flexibility. For example, all manual tasks are covered by just two job titles, manufacturing staff and technicians, while Ford UK had 516 job classifications for manual workers in 1985. Wickens (1987) argues that the union agreement was 'one of the bedrocks on which the future success would be built,' and since Nissan invested, no days have been lost to industrial disputes and absenteeism is 2%.

Sources: *The Economist* (1983b); Dohse (1987); Wickens (1987); Sadler (1992a: 256, 299–300); NDC sources.

Given the ability to establish a single union, the UK was favoured on several other grounds. While having a strong supplier infrastructure (Nicolaides and Thomsen, 1991: 131–2), the indigenous car producing sector was weak, especially compared to Germany, France and Italy, the latter two of which had especially strict regulation of Japanese imports, the implications of which can be seen in Table 7.2.[1] As the Chief Executive of the Invest in Britain Bureau (IBB) argues, with the absence of national champions in UK, 'global corporations have faced minimal resistance, either from the government or companies in the market place' (Fraser, 1995: 7).

The domestic environment in the UK was therefore considered less hostile than in the other major EEC countries and Nissan's productivity advantage would be most apparent in the British market. In addition, the English language, competitive production costs and availability of government grants were also important (*The Economist*, 1983c; HMSO, 1994a). Other factors, including Japanese financial

Table 7.2   Market share of Japanese manufacturers in Europe, 1997

Unrestrained markets		*Restricted markets (formal/informal)*	
Country	*Market share (%)*	*Country*	*Market share (%)*
Norway	31	United Kingdom	14
Switzerland	22	Germany	12
Netherlands	21	Portugal	11
Austria	20	Spain	7
Belgium	15	Italy	6
Sweden	14	France	5

Source: Lovegrove *et al.* (1998).

services in London, similar commercial and legal systems, low taxes and cultural proximity, with a shared interest in gardens, rugby, golf and tea, have also been cited as playing in role in the decision-making of Nissan and other Japanese MNCs (Morris, 1988: 34; McCooey, 1991: 71; Buxton, 1995a; Thiran and Yamawaki, 1995).

Nissan's alternatives to investing in the UK were therefore closely related to two key factors: market access and the ability to introduce lean production. For market access, Nissan needed to be inside the EEC to increase its market share due to trade barriers, and presence in the EEC would improve Nissan's market responsiveness. Given a strategy of market expansion, exporting from Japan was ruled out, and Nissan's options were restricted to investing in a member state. Theoretically, Nissan had many alternatives within the EEC, as it could produce in any member state and then export to the rest of the EEC. Furthermore, in terms of accessing a good quality supplier and skills infrastructure, Nissan also had several alternatives, such as the UK, Germany or France. However, in practice many member states were hostile to Japanese investment and the customs union was not perfect. Spain, for example, still protected its car market against EEC competitors (Dohse, 1987: 137). Nissan was aware that antagonism in Europe against Japanese producers could lead to restrictions being placed on its tariff-free exports from one member state to another, and the 'friendly' UK government had the political clout get acceptability for Japanese producers in Europe, which smaller EEC members did not have. In addition, given general hostility towards Japanese companies in the highly politically sensitive automotive industry, investing in its major market within the EEC, the UK, also made most sense in terms of reducing business risk.

While market access favoured the UK over other locations, the institutional environment in the UK was the crucial reason why Britain was the only member-state extensively assessed by Nissan. Labour market policies and the government's commitment to supporting Nissan, plus favourable costs and fewer cultural barriers, left few alternatives to locating in the UK in the first half of the 1980s. Overall, in terms of market access Nissan potentially did have several options, but when combined with the ability to establish work organisation on its terms in the UK, Nissan had few alternatives to investing in the UK. In fact, Nissan's location appraisal involved an incredible 53 sites in the UK over a period of three and half years, which has been described as the 'most exhaustive study in the history of industrial relocation ever undertaken' (NDC, 1998f).

The next stage in analysing the potential path of bargaining negotiations between Nissan and the UK is to examine Nissan's absolute
power – the UK government's commitment and alternatives to Nissan
investing on British soil.

From the 1980s, Conservative administrations promoted market-
facilitating policies and actively encouraged the attraction of inward
FDI through the IBB and regional development organisations. The
government assumed unequivocal benefits deriving from FDI (both
inward and outward) and was highly committed to improving the
attractiveness of the UK as a location for Japanese and other inward
investors. In terms of our bargaining model, the UK government
manifested very high levels of commitment.

The commitment to inward investment was heightened in the case
of Nissan due to four main factors:

- The government coveted Japanese investment in particular
  because of the perceived superiority of its production techniques
  and demonstration effects on domestic firms.
- The potential transformatory impact upon labour relations of
  Japanese investment was highly attractive to a Thatcher administration, determined to curtail union power.
- Nissan's investment would undoubtedly boost the UK car industry,
  which was in crisis due its inability to compete with imports. The
  project would represent a breakthrough for the government in
  terms of attracting a major new foreign car producer to the UK,
  based on full production facilities not just local assembly. The
  Nissan investment would represent the first major Japanese car
  company to invest in the UK and could forebode future Japanese
  investment.
- The collapse of manufacturing and high unemployment in the
  North-East, with 15,000 manufacturing redundancies in 1986,
  was in stark contrast to estimated 10,000 spin-off jobs that Nissan's
  investment would bring (Crowther and Garrahan, 1988: 52–3).
  The Chief Executive of the Northern Development Company
  (which was created as an outcome of Nissan's investment),
  described the instructions from Mrs Thatcher as 'do anything to
  get Nissan' (Bridge, 1998b).

In terms of alternatives, the UK government perceived that it had no
realistic options other than Nissan to lift the UK car industry. No other
major foreign investors were proposing to invest and the government

Figure 7.1   Potential bargaining path: derivation of absolute power for Nissan and the UK government

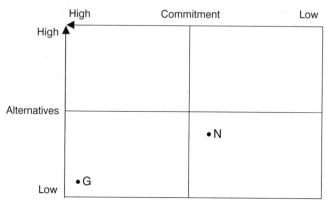

was ideologically against direct intervention to support indigenous industry, especially with past attempts at subsidisation failing to spur the beleaguered UK car producers into international competitiveness. The combination of Nissan's multi-fold impact on car production, exports, jobs, suppliers, other foreign investors, and labour relations was irresistible to the UK government at the national and local levels with no perceived alternatives. The potential path of bargaining between Nissan and the UK government is illustrated in Figure 7.1.

Nissan has a medium level of commitment, and relatively few alternatives to investing in the UK, indicated by point N, while the UK government has a very high level of commitment and very few alternatives, indicated by point G.

If we refer to the bargaining matrix of ideal type potential power possibilities in Table 6.3 (Chapter 6), the Nissan–UK government bargaining relationship would be placed somewhere in the third group of alternative/commitment configurations. The UK government's absolute power would be high if Nissan's commitment to investing in the EEC increases, but at the start of the 1980s the government's absolute power, on a scale from low to high, was at a medium level. Nissan, though, has very high absolute power, given the government's very high commitment and few alternatives. Nissan has greater relative power, and is therefore most likely to bargain for concessions with the balance of perceived costs and benefits from agreement tilted in Nissan's favour. Total power or mutual dependence is high, making agreement likely.

The key factors increasing mutual dependence are the low alternatives of Nissan and the UK government and the high commitment of the latter. Barber and Enderwick (1992: 273) argue that the 'new realism' of countries' changing workplace practices offers the possibility for firms to increase their competitive advantage by increasing flexibility facilitated through decentralisation of labour relations to the plant or company level and reduced labour restrictions. In the Nissan case, the Thatcher government moved first within the EEC towards this 'new realism,' and their anti-unionist ideology was highly compatible with and supportive of Nissan's lean manufacturing system (Garrahan, 1986: 8–9; Ackroyd *et al.*, 1988: 18). In the terminology of the OLI paradigm (integrated into our FDI location model in chapter three), there was a high congruence between the ownership advantages of Nissan and the location advantages of the UK. The UK could also meet the requirements of Nissan's market seeking FDI strategy and project specific requirements and Nissan would meet all the requirements of the UK's inward investment-led industrial and regional policy. This led to high degree of mutual dependence, with the final (bilateral) outcome depending on Nissan overall corporate strategy.

7.2.2 Implementation of potential power

The next stage of the bargaining model approach is to analyse the implementation of potential power, which involves identifying the political constraints and institutional structure of Nissan and the UK government and therefore an examination of the plurilateral relations surrounding the investment negotiations.

Looking first at the implementation of Nissan's absolute power, in terms of political constraints, three main factors were apparent:

- Japanese trade unions opposed the investment, as they feared lost jobs at home.
- Internal disputes within Nissan complicated the decision-making process and Nissan's overall corporate strategy.
- Trade disputes between the Japanese government and the EEC led the Japanese government to favour Nissan's investment in the UK because of the potential to reduce the trade imbalance (by substituting exports for local production) and alleviate to some degree trade tensions.

The influence of these constraints on the bargaining ability of Nissan depends on Nissan's institutional structure. As Nissan is a corporation, not a democratically elected government, the degree of centralisation, co-ordination and coherence within the firm would be expected to be greater than for a government, and Nissan's recent US venture gave it experience in dealing with host governments. Furthermore, Nissan's institutional structure was centralised, with all key activities kept at home, minimising fragmentation across Nissan's international operations. The enterprise-based system of unions in Japan was also relatively weak, especially when compared to the institutionalised systems of union representation in many European countries. Nissan seemed therefore to be in a good negotiating position.

However, within Nissan, as within all large corporations, there are competing interests. Members of the board had different conceptions as to the future of the company, and many of the older and more risk-averse members saw a major investment in the UK as too risky, especially considering a weak financial situation due to loss of market share in Japan. Nissan's President, Takashi Ishihara, strongly supported the UK plan, but the Chairman, Katsuji Kawamata, and the head of Nissan's union, Ichiro Katsuji, wanted to concentrate on the US instead. There was therefore considerable indecision within the firm (Hamill *et al.*, 1988: 224; Sadler, 1992a: 254; Safarian, 1993: 358).

The third major political constraint to the implementation of potential power was the Japanese government, which aimed to increase Nissan's commitment to the proposed UK investment. Ruigrok and Tulder (1995) argue that core companies, like Nissan, with a strong domestic bargaining arena are more dependent on their home country, which affects their internationalisation strategies. The influence of the Japanese government on Nissan was likely to be quite significant, especially because the Japanese government continued to support Nissan through low interest bank loans.

Nissan faced several major constraints to the implementation of potential power. Indecision within Nissan undermined the company's strategic commitment to investing in the EEC and therefore in the UK while, conversely, the Japanese government put pressure on Nissan to go ahead with the investment. These counterpoised pressures complicate the translation of potential into actual power.

The UK government also faced considerable political constraints at the national and international levels, with several powerful interest groups and governments actively lobbying for restrictions on Nissan's investment when negotiations began. Within the UK, the domestic automotive producers were acutely aware of the competitive advantage that Nissan's greenfield, single union plant would have (see Table 7.2 for the high Japanese market share in unprotected markets). They lobbied against government support for Nissan and were in favour of restrictions on Nissan's operations. Similarly, as we touched on in chapter five, Japanese automotive firms have led the way in vertical disintegration, and the local supplier industry in the UK saw the potential for Nissan's manufacturing operations to subcontract out a large proportion of components, especially with just-in-time production. This stimulated the local components industry to form another major pressure group, calling for high local content regulations. British trade unions were also lobbying to ensure union representation but, without centralised co-ordination, Nissan was able to divide and rule between competing unions and pick a union that suited its interests, as we saw in Box 7.1.

At the international level, car manufacturers and governments of other member states in the EEC became politically active, with concerns over the implications of Nissan being able to export behind the tariff barriers of the customs union. They lobbied the European Commission to make sure that Japanese exports from the UK were counted as Japanese, not 'European'. This view was especially voiced by France, who labelled the UK as a 'Trojan horse' – an export platform for the Japanese based on low labour costs. Peugeot's Chairman described Nissan as a 'Japanese aircraft carrier' off the coast of Europe (cited in Moore, 1994: 317). American multinationals in the EEC also lobbied to impose restrictions on Nissan, with Ford claiming that Nissan's new working practices and conditions would save Nissan between £330 and £530 per car (Sadler, 1992a: 256).

However, the impact of these pressure groups depended on the institutional structure of the UK government. There are five key points relating to the UK:

- The UK government is democratically elected and is therefore likely to be penetrated by indigenous business and other interests.
- In chapter nine we will see that the UK lacks a comprehensive (civilian) industrial strategy, with attracting inward investment the main aim of policy. Without a cohesive industrial policy making network and no established co-ordinating structure for making

and implementing policy, business group pressure is more open and harder to reach a compromise on.

- Although the Invest in Britain Bureau acts as a centralised inward investment agency, real power lies with the Secretary for Trade and Industry and ultimately the Prime Minister in major investment cases, especially for awarding incentives. Negotiations with inward investors are therefore potentially based on a political as much as economic rationale. In the early 1980s the IBB was also fairly inexperienced.

- The UK is a member of the EEC and has to acknowledge the importance of other member states and the European Commission within that context.

- The system of mandatory regional development grants, in operation until 1988, left the government in a weak negotiating position, with Nissan virtually guaranteed to receive government financial support if it invested in an Assisted Area.

The UK government therefore faced many political obstacles to reaching agreement with Nissan and translating potential into actual power.

Figure 7.2 illustrates the implementation of potential bargaining power for Nissan and the UK government. Point N shows that in terms of interest structure, Nissan faces a high level of political constraints. In terms of institutional structure, Nissan has a quite high level of institutional strength. Point G shows that UK government

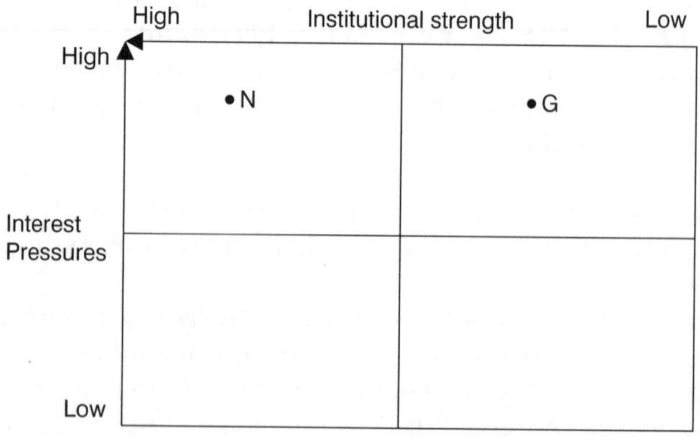

Figure 7.2 Implementation of potential power: the influence of political constraints for Nissan and the UK government

faces a very high degree of political constraints in terms of the interest pressures and that the government has a quite low level of institutional strength.

Looking at the bargaining matrix in Table 6.4, the Nissan–UK government negotiations are located in second group of interest structure/institutional structure permutations. The influence of plurilateral relations constrains the negotiating ability of both Nissan and in particular the UK government. The translation of potential into actual bargaining power is likely to be uncertain.

The final stage of the bargaining model approach is to integrate the two dimensions of potential power and its implementation, which is shown in Figure 7.3.

Point A shows that the level of mutual power is quite high, the UK government has relatively less bargaining power than Nissan and that the influence of political constraints is high. The potential path of bilateral bargaining indicates that agreement is likely, with Nissan bargaining for concessions, but when we introduce plurilateral relations, reaching agreement is likely to be complicated by the influence of the interest structure.

Figure 7.3 Political economy bargaining model of Nissan–UK government negotiations

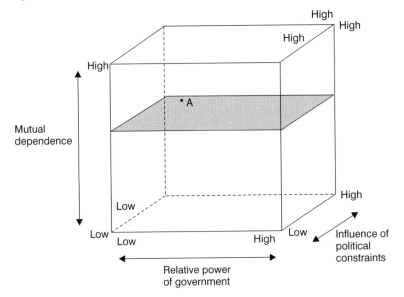

7.3 NISSAN IN THE UK: THE ACTUAL NEGOTIATIONS

In this section we examine the actual negotiations between Nissan and the UK government, which will demonstrate the utility of the bargaining model in identifying the key factors influencing the negotiations and indicating the likely path that the bargaining relations would follow.

When Nissan announced its plans in July 1981, a deal with the unions was crucial and, given Nissan's cash-flow difficulties and differences within the firm, a government-subsidised factory was stated to be a pre-requisite if the investment was to go ahead (*The Economist*, 1981a). Nissan's bargaining tactics with both the trade unions and the UK government were based on its high level of relative power. The trade unions in the high unemployment North-East had few alternatives to Nissan, and the Thatcher government was determined to undermine trade union power, increasing the commitment of the trade unions to any plant where at least they would be recognised. With a lack of perceived alternatives to Nissan's investment and the explicit commitment of the UK government, Nissan therefore had high absolute power *vis-à-vis* the trade unions and the government.

By December 1981, with high mutual power, the investment seemed likely to go ahead, especially with Nissan promising a local content at least that of British Leyland (*The Economist*, 1981b). However, by the following March tensions were rising in the negotiations. The formation of an industrial pressure group by British and EEC car-producers called The Committee of Common Market Automobile Constructors (CCMC) and pressure from EEC governments meant that Nissan's relations with the British Industry Secretary reached an impasse. The CCMC demanded that Nissan's proposed 60% local content was increased to 80% – higher than the local content of many of Europe's national producers.

The idea that Nissan must meet certain restrictions to be considered 'European' was premised on uncertainty because of the vagueness of Community Law. As Dicken (1992b: 18) notes: 'The Treaty of Rome does not specify any quantitative threshold of local content.' However, EEC case law had resulted in an understanding that local content must be 60% for the last substantive manufacturing process to take place in a member state and therefore for a product produced by a foreign company to be considered as 'European' (Dicken, 1992b: 18).

The CCMC were not only lobbying for 80% local content, but demanded that local content be measured in terms of local component value, not just the UK government's definition of ex-works price. This was to further reduce Nissan's competitive advantage and at the same time gain lobbying support from local component suppliers who wanted to ensure they were fully utilised (Sadler, 1992a: 262–4). Car producers in the UK also wanted additional monitoring of Nissan's activities. Nissan, though, argued that if local content exceeded 60% the car would be unprofitable, especially due to the low quality of local suppliers. But once local suppliers were 'educated' Nissan projected local content to rise to 80%.

The bargaining tactics of the CCMC led to what seemed to be an irreconcilable deadlock in the negotiations by summer 1982. The local content issue, combined with financial difficulties at Nissan and strong objections from Japanese trade unions, fuelled the internal struggles within Nissan over the proposed investment (Safarian, 1993: 358; Hamill *et al.*, 1988: 224). As the bargaining model analysis suggested, the influence of the interest structure prevented agreement. *The Economist* (1982b) noted at the time that, 'The interests of the would-be investor and the host country do not always coincide', with the UK government insisting 'on too tough and rigid conditions crafted by the British car industry'.

If Nissan was to invest, the UK government had to ensure that Nissan's UK built cars were not labelled as Japanese and therefore barred from the rest of Europe, and that local content was reasonable to Nissan. The wavering support for the proposed investment in Nissan's Board would also need to be addressed. The importance of Nissan gaining access to the EEC market as a 'European' producer was of added significance, with the UK government calculating that this would appeal to other Japanese investors, particularly Toyota (Strange, 1993: 190).

The newly re-elected Conservative government therefore renewed its commitment to the EEC to show Nissan and other investors that the UK was an ideal location for exporting to the rest of Europe, and Mrs Thatcher directly intervened through private discussions with the Japanese Prime Minister in July 1983. This led to official encouragement for Nissan's project from Japan as a means to get around the 11% VER in the UK market and to subdue trade frictions between Japan and the EEC. After the Prime-Minister's met, there was a concomitant reshuffle in the board of directors at Nissan leading to a more outward looking perspective. Nissan's commitment had effectively been boosted by reducing political constraints. In the following months, the UK government heavily lobbied the EEC and the dispute over the local content was settled at 60% – as Nissan had initially demanded.

When the decision to invest was finally made in February 1984, Nissan announced that the investment would be made in two stages, with the first stage involving only a small investment to appraise the UK production environment. The plant would assemble 24,000 Japanese kit cars from 1986 at a cost of only £50 million and the kits would be counted under the Japanese 11% quota, reducing the political lobbying of the CCMC. This cautious and long term approach (Dohse, 1987: 136) reflected uncertainty due to hostility towards Nissan from the CCMC and fears over local content, the quality of local suppliers and the introduction of new work practices. As Nissan's Vice-President, Kaichi Kanoa, emphasised, 'Whether we have good working relationships with the unions will be a big factor in determining whether we go on to the second stage' (cited in Sadler, 1992a: 297).

The local content would rise in the second phase of production thus dissipating the demands of component makers, the CCMC and member states. Stage two would commence from 1991 with capacity to be expanded to at least 100,000 cars at a cost of £300 million, over one-third provided through UK government regional subsidies. This was still half the size of production planned three years ago (*The Economist*, 1984). However, the employment prospects of 3,000 new jobs continued to moderate trade unionism (*The Economist*, 1985), and Nissan received 11,000 applications for the first 300 jobs in September 1985 (NDC, 1998f). The expansion in stage two would involve the local manufacturer of major components, in particular the engine, to meet guidelines for an 'EEC' built car (*The Economist*, 1986a).

In reality, the rapid appreciation of the Yen, increasing by over 30% *vis-à-vis* the pound in 1985 following the Plaza Accord, brought forward the plans for phase two by two years. In September 1986, the assembly plant was to be transformed to a fully fledged car factory at a cost of almost £300 million plus £100 million in government subsidies, employing a 2,700 work-force. All the major components were to be manufactured locally not only to meet EEC local content rules, but also to be cost-effective with the rise of the Yen (*The Economist*, 1986b).

Although the first car was produced in July 1986, the influence of the interest structure had not been completely eroded. With Nissan's

Sunderland plant exporting to Europe from 1988, in 1990 the French government set a maximum 3% market share of the domestic market for Japanese cars (EC, 1998), and France refused to accept the Nissan Bluebird as a European product unless the imports had an EC content of 80%, to the fury of the British government (Lahiri and Onu, 1998: 445). This was inconsistent with both the Single Market and the definition of local content adopted by the EC. Having just lost a case at GATT to the Japanese government and under sustained pressure from the UK House of Lords Select Committee on European Affairs (Sadler, 1992b: 1721), the Commission eventually persuaded France to accept these cars as being of UK origin (Moore, 1994: 318–19).[2] Nissan and the UK government established a precedent, which it followed with Toyota and Honda. Local content should rise to 60% before the vehicle could be counted as European-produced, and this local content was to be measured on the basis of ex-works price, including a wide range of indirect costs of production.

The negotiations surrounding Nissan's investment were therefore only fully concluded in 1990, nine years after they first began. Despite the apparent endogenous community of interests (Pitelis, 1993) between the incumbent Thatcher administration and Nissan, political constraints prevented a smooth and quick path to agreement. To achieve agreement, the political constraints had to be overcome and increasing Nissan's commitment would help. The bargaining model suggested the mechanisms by which this could be achieved – namely through the intervention of the UK government, given its very high commitment. High commitment increases the probability of agreement, as Nissan's President, Mr Ishihara, said in February 1984 when he signed a memorandum of understanding with Norman Tebitt of the DTI: 'There is no denying that Mrs Thatcher has been a great influence behind this project, inviting us to come here 'to show our example of efficiency' (cited in Goto, 1987: 75).

Once the internal coherency of Nissan was strengthened and the UK government effectively lobbied the Commission on behalf of Nissan, Nissan was able to structure the agreement in such a way to pacify the interest structure. The intensification of trade tensions between Japan and the EEC and the Plaza Accord also increased Nissan's commitment, mutual power and the impetus for agreement. Nissan's high relative power, with the UK government perceiving no alternatives to Nissan's investment and displaying total commitment, gave Nissan a clear idea of its bargaining strength *vis-à-vis* the British government. As Nissan's Chairman, Kawamata, said in February 1984:

When I went to Europe in 1983, the British Secretary of Trade and Industry expressed a wish to see me. I asked him bluntly, 'You are very eagerly inviting Nissan to advance into Britain. This is very strange to me. What is your reason?' He answered in the following way: 'Nissan has acquired very new production. It has good labour-management relations. Everything is an object of envy for us. We want you to set up your operation in Britain to demonstrate not only to our automakers but also to other industries these aspects of Japanese management.' When I heard this I thought in my mind: 'Of all the things, they just want us to be a tutor at their home. If we are to be that ... they should pay us return air fare, our expenses during our stay in Britain and a very big salary' (cited in Dohse, 1987: 138).

Therefore, as well as grants of £125 million, with 22% of total investment costs provided by mandatory RDGs and nearly 12% of costs available as Selective Financial Assistance (Garrahan, 1986: 8), Nissan negotiated a large greenfield site available at low (agricultural) cost. The site offered was Sunderland's old airfield which had a large expanse of flatland allowing new buildings to be built easily and quickly – essential for rapid expansion – and the area had excellent infrastructure and close proximity to a deep water port for Nissan's exports to mainland Europe.

Given changes in Nissan's corporate strategy favouring investment in the EEC and the few feasible alternatives to investing in the UK, it is very likely that the government could have offered less incentives and the investment would still have gone ahead. The key obstacles preventing investment from going ahead sooner was uncertainty in overall corporate strategy and real concerns over market access to the EEC- neither of which would have been removed by the offer of high government incentives.

7.4   JAPANESE FDI AND THE UK CAR INDUSTRY: THE END OF DECLINE?

In the early 1980s, the UK car industry was in a worst state than at any time in its history; output, exports and employment had been falling for the last decade and the UK domestic market was becoming saturated by imports just as the appeal in international markets of British cars collapsed with poor quality, lack-lustre products, and bad management. However, by the mid-1990s exports were increasing rapidly and production was on trend to exceed its post-war high. Japanese investment in the UK lifted the industry out from protracted decline.

Nissan is arguably becoming as important to the British car industry as Rover, with a full product range by 2000–2001 and the UK benefiting from the decentralisation of design activities as part of Nissan's globalisation strategy. However, the UK continues to experience massive trade deficits in vehicles (Loewendahl and Hölscher, 2001) and the future of the industry lies in the ability of the public and private sector to work together to ensure a continuous supply of skilled workers and support technological as well as organisational innovation in supplier firms. There is also a real concern among Japanese companies, who depend on exporting from the UK to the EU market, that the UK should be at the core of a more integrated Europe.

7.4.1 The UK car industry in the post-war period

The post-war history of the UK car industry can be divided into four periods:

- expansion from 1945 until the end of the 1960s;
- decline from the 1970s to the early 1980s;
- recovery from the mid-1980s;
- an uncertain future in the 21st century.

In the post-war era, the comparative history of the UK auto industry has reflected that of its economy as whole. In 1950, the UK was the world's biggest automobile exporter, with three times more car exports than the US and, in 1956, total vehicle production was only 3% less than German production. Output grew throughout the first period, culminating in a post-war peak in 1972 of nearly 2 million cars. At the same time, until the end of the 1960s, the UK was the second biggest and second richest economy in the world.

However, since 1972 UK car production fell in almost every year for the next 10 years, reaching a low of 887,679 in 1982, only one-quarter of German output. The performance of the UK economy as whole also lagged behind every other major economy. From the mid-1980s, UK car production grew faster than in the other G-5 economies and in 1996 UK car output was now almost 45% of the German level. At the same time, the growth gap between the UK economy as whole and the other G-5 economies narrowed.

By 2000, the future of the industry again appears less secure. The UK's biggest producer, Rover, has all but collapsed following the failure of BMW to turn-around the company, Ford is closing car production at its largest plant in the UK (Dagenham), and GM is ending Vectra production in the UK. Toyota recently established a new car plant in France and is encouraging suppliers to set-up in the Euro-zone rather than the UK. In 2000, Honda, Toyota and Nissan have all announced plans to source more components from suppliers in the Euro-zone, and all of Toyota's UK suppliers have been asked to settle bills in the single currency. Toyota, Nissan and Honda are sending powerful signals to the UK government that future investment is under threat if the UK does not join the European single currency.

The first three periods can be easily identified when we look at UK car production relative to the US, Japan, Germany and France. Figure 7.4 shows the turn-around in UK output since the mid-1980s, which has led to the UK replacing Italy as the fourth biggest EU producer, after Germany, France and Spain. However, the most dramatic trend is the massive growth of the Japanese car industry from 1960 to 1990 – a 60-fold increase in output in just 30 years.

Although UK output recovered, the trade deficit in road vehicles expanded with import penetration continuing to rise, as can be seen in Table 7.3. From 1968 to 1996 the UK went from having import penetration of only 8% to having the highest in the G-5. The turning point was during the first half of the 1970s, when import penetration nearly tripled from 14.3% in 1970 to 41.4% in 1976. 1976 was the first

Figure 7.4   Passenger car production in G-5 countries, 1950–96

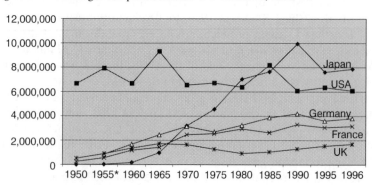

*1956 for Germany.
Sources: AAMA (1998); Pilkington (1998).

Table 7.3   Import penetration for new car registrations, 1968–96 (000s)

Year	UK		Germany		France		Japan	
	Units	Share (%)	Units	Share (%)	Units	Share (%)	Units	Share (%)
1968	91	8	260	20	265	21	15	1
1972	385	24	562	26	338	21	24	1
1976	533	41	500	23	426	23	41	2
1980	858	57	638	26	429	23	45	2
1984	1006	58	639	27	630	36	42	1
1988	1250	56	817	29	817	37	134	4
1992	875	55	1354	35	846	40	181	4
1996	1256	63	1144	33	939	44	393	8

Source: Derived from AAMA (1998).

year when absolute UK imports exceeded those of Germany, which has been the case for every year since 1976. In 1996, import penetration of the UK market reached 63%, a post-war high. Relative to the proportion of imports in new car registrations in the UK, import penetration in Japan was one-eighth, in Germany roughly half and in France about two-thirds of the UK level. In 1999 import penetration had increased even more, accounting for 71.7% of total new car registrations (SMMT, 2000: 26).

The import penetration of the UK market has not been mirrored in the export success of UK car manufacturers. According to Moore (1994: 315–16), out the major 'national champions' in the EU, Rover was dependent on home market sales for 80% of its output compared to only 38% for Volkswagen, 47% for Daimler-Benz, 54% for Renault and Peugeot and 62% for Fiat. In 1984, only 24% of total UK car production was exported, compared to 60% of German output and 56% of Japanese output. In 1990, UK export intensity had increased to only 32% (derived from AAMA, 1998). The poor export performance of UK production symbolised the lack of competitiveness of UK producers. Key decisions regarding the organisation of the UK automobile industry, in particular relating to British Leyland, were major policy failures (Haslam *et al.*, 1987; see Pilkington, 1996, 1998; Jones, 1997; Owen, 1997).

With short-termism and poor performance in the market-place Rover under-invested, and its productivity levels are among the lowest in the EU, when measured in terms of output per employee,

Table 7.4   Relative productivity at European car plants, 1997

Manufacturer	Plant	Country	Productivity	Workforce
Nissan	Sunderland	UK	98	3986
GM	Eisenach	Germany	77	1884
Fiat	Melfi	Italy	70	6006
Volkswagen	Navarra	Spain	70	4877
SEAT	Martorell	Spain	69	7733
GM	Zaragoza	Spain	67	9109
Honda	Swindon	UK	62	2311
Ford	Dagenham	UK	62	4440
Renault	Douai	France	61	6590
Renault	Valladolid	Spain	59	6607
Ford	Saarlouis	Germany	59	5740
Toyota	Burnaston	UK	58	2444
Rover	Longbridge	UK	19.4*	NA
Vauxhall (GM)	Luton	UK	27.2*	NA

*1995a.
Source: EIU cited in IBB (1999).

as Table 7.4 shows. In 1997, Nissan Sunderland had the highest productivity in Europe, and was five times more productive than Rover's Longbridge plant.

With low productivity, poor quality,[3] and generally unattractive products, the lack of competitiveness of British car manufacturers led to huge trade deficits for the economy as a whole. By 1988, the trade imbalance in autos contributed to one-third of the total trade deficit in manufactured goods (Hood and Young, 1997: 263–4) and in 1997 the trade deficit in road vehicles was almost £6 billion, 36% of the total UK trade deficit. This was an increase over the previous two years, a period when the British auto industry was growing at its fastest rate for a quarter of a century (derived from HMSO, 1998b).

However, the arrival of the Japanese producers in the UK massively improved the export performance of the British automobile industry, even if the trade deficit continued to be huge as the domestic market sucked in imports.

7.4.2   The impact of Nissan on the UK economy

Nissan's investment provided the context within which other Japanese auto-manufacturers would invest in the UK, and in fact their investment was partly a response to that of Nissan. Crucially, Nissan demonstrated to Toyota and Honda that favourable industrial relations could be forged in the UK. When examining the impact of Nissan on the UK economy, we must therefore also consider the follow-on investment of the other big two Japanese auto producers.

The UK has accounted for 57% of the investment in vehicle assembly capacity and over one-third of the jobs invested by the Japanese within the EU (UNCTAD, 1995b: 136; Pike, 1996: 70–2). Between 1986 and the end of 1999 Nissan, Toyota and Honda will have invested over £4 billion in the UK. From Table 7.5 we can derive that from 1991 to 1999 total UK car production increased by 549,723 cars, while Japanese car production in the UK increased by 439,630 cars. In other words, 80% of the increase in UK output from 1991 to 1999 was accounted for by Nissan, Toyota and Honda. These three companies accounted for almost one-third of total car production in 1999, and Nissan has replaced Ford as the UK's third major passenger car producer.

The growth of Japanese production in the UK has also coincided with the improved export performance of the British car industry. Total export production more than tripled from 1989 to 1996, reaching nearly one million units in 1996. The export intensity of the UK car industry increased from 32% in 1990 to almost 55% in 1996, with the greatest injection in terms of export production provided by the Japanese producers, who export over 70% of their production (Table 7.6). Rover also increased its export intensity significantly, but this was in part due to loss of sales in the UK market. In 1996, over one-third of total UK car exports were accounted for by Nissan, Toyota and Honda.

Nissan had the highest export intensity out of the major UK manufacturers as well as the highest productivity. In fact, productivity at Nissan UK has increased by 10% per year since 1993 (Godsmark, 1997), and the Sunderland plant has labour productivity equal to Nissan's best plant in Japan (IBB, 1997). Nissan Sunderland is not only the most productive but also among the most flexible and leanest plant in Europe. According to Nissan, the total amount of stock in process in the body assembly plant is less than one hour, and:

> The engine assembly line has the most engine variants on one high volume line in Europe. There are six different engines with a total of 52 variants coming down the single line (Nissan, 1995).

The rapid growth in Nissan's output and exports can be seen in Figure 7.5. An estimate is given for the end of year 2000, based on

Table 7.5 UK passenger car production by manufacturer, 1991–99

	1991	1992	1993	1994	1995	1996	1999
Rover Group	395,624	378,797	406,804	462,614	473,951	473,217	367,718
Ford	339,271	302,146	271,793	269,058	273,896	328,028	255,080
GM	255,733	287,884	232,569	250,439	231,196	268,228	338,984
Peugeot/Talbot	87,983	85,821	72,902	74,440	78,379	85,108	162,554
Honda	0	1,001	32,139	42,805	91,084	105,810	114,479
Nissan	124,666	179,009	246,281	204,944	215,346	231,627	271,157
Toyota	0	0	37,314	85,467	88,440	116,973	178,660
Total	1,236,900	1,291,880	1,375,524	1,466,823	1,532,084	1,686,134	1,786,623

Source: SMMT (2000).

Table 7.6   UK car production by manufacturer, output and exports, 1996

Manufacturer	Production	Exports	Exports (%)
Rover	473,217	257,669	54.5
Nissan	231,627	167,265	72.2
Vauxhall	268,228	152,662	56.9
Ford	328,028	98,060	29.9
Toyota	116,973	76,853	65.7
Honda	105,810	76,853	72.6
Peugeot	85,108	30,506	35.8
Jaguar	38,590	29,969	77.7
Total UK	1,686,134	925,403	54.9

Sources: Eason (1997) and adapted from AAMA (1998).

Figure 7.5   Passenger car production for the domestic and export markets at Nissan UK, 1986–2000 (units)

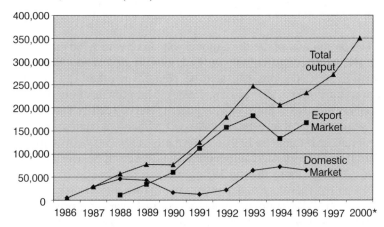

* Estimate.
Sources: Eason (1997); AAMA (1998) and Nissan (1995; 1998a).

Nissan's decision to build a third model at Sunderland. The replacement for the Almera, which is currently imported from Japan, will involve new investment of £215 million, creating 800 direct jobs at the Sunderland plant, and 100,000 cars are expected to be produced when production starts in 2000. The third model will be crucial to Nissan's long term competitiveness, as the company needs a locally produced small family car if it is to reach the volumes already achieved by Ford.

Table 7.7   Investment, employment and suppliers at NMUK, 1986–2000

Year	Total cumulative investment (£m)	Total employees at Sunderland plant	Number of suppliers	Components expenditure (£m)
1986	50	470	46	4
1987	–	1,100	62	28
1988	610	1,800	126	90
1989	–	2,500	126	170
1990	670	2,700	177	220
1991	–	3,000	180	400
1992	900	4,600	195	575
1993	–	4,250	197	790
1994	1,000	4,076	202	670
1995	1,250	4,100	204	745
2000*	1,500	5,000	–	1,095

*Based on Nissan's estimates.
Source: Burt (1996); Tighe (1996b) and Nissan (1995; 1998b; 1998c).

The production of the third model will also create 2,700 jobs at over 100 UK suppliers, with 1,000 of these jobs created at suppliers in the North-East. 1,300 jobs will also be created in other EU suppliers (Cave and Potter, 1997; Nissan, 1998b). The growth of employment, suppliers and expenditure on components can be seen in Table 7.7. By the year 2000 total investment will be £1.5 billion, 30 times more than the initial investment in 1986, employment will be 5,000, over 10 times more than in 1986, and component expenditure will be over £1 billion, over 270 times more than in 1986.

Nissan has therefore had a major quantitative impact on car output, exports and the supplier industry. In fact, with exports of over £1 billion in 1995, Nissan was the eighteenth biggest exporter in the UK (EP, 1997b). In 1996, Nissan had 4.9% market share of the UK car market and 3.5% of the European market. At the regional level, the impact is amplified, with the Chief Executive of the NDC, Dr Bridge, stating that, 'Nissan has played a vital role in the regeneration of the region' (cited in Gales, 1997).

When Nissan started production of the first model, the Bluebird, there were only six suppliers in the North-East, out of a total of 37 suppliers (21 in the rest of the UK and four in continental Europe). Local content was only 20% by value. However, by 1988 local content was 70%, supplied by 126 European companies (see Table 7.7).

When production of Primera began in 1990, it had a 80% local content with 180 suppliers, and the 1992 Nissan Micra had a supply base of 195 companies, of which just 10 were Japanese and 27 were in the North-east. In 1995, Nissan generated £218 million for the region's suppliers. Similarly, at Toyota in 1996 about half of the £450 million spent on materials and components was spent within the UK, with £120 million spent on components, materials and services provided by firms within a 50 mile radius of its Swindon plant. In 1994, Nissan, Honda and Toyota purchased £1.6 billion of components from UK firms.

Of Sunderland's 15 biggest employers, 5 are automotive sector manufacturers, and this sector employs over 9,000 in the Sunderland area. Mr Ian Gibson, Chief Executive of NMUK, estimates the regional figure to be over 15,000 growing to 25,000 by the year 2000, mainly through expansion of suppliers (Nissan, 1998a). At the end of 1996, Nissan Motor Manufacturing UK with a turnover of over £1.5 billion was the joint largest company in the North-East, with Procter and Gamble, and the ninth largest employer and the biggest exporter (EP, 1997a).

As well as a quantitative impact upon the UK and North-East economy there is widespread agreement that this has been accompanied by a qualitative impact. In partnership with local organisations in the North-East, in particular Sunderland TEC and the NDC, Nissan developed an apprenticeship training programme using Wearside College to provide training combining mechanical and electrical skills (Kume and Totsuka, 1993: 48–52; Mair, 1993: 212). This training programme is now supported by 23 companies in the North-East (Lorraine, 1996). As well as spreading a new work-ethic culture across the region (Hall, 1998), it has been widely argued that Japanese producers like Nissan have transferred a package of new technology especially adapted to key Japanese organisational and managerial methods associated with JIT, close supplier links and total quality control (UNCTAD, 1995b: 136).

According to Nicolaides and Thomsen (1991: 111) and Dunning (1988: 234), suppliers of Japanese firms seem unambiguously to have upgraded their quality control, inspection and testing procedures and delivery systems and in some cases re-appraise their production philosophy with help from their Japanese customers. Nissan, Toyota and Honda are establishing 'Japanese-style' close relationships with suppliers, as indicated by the incredibly small number of suppliers – about 200 for Nissan and only 136 for Honda compared to 1,000–2,000 for European and US manufacturers. In 1988, Nissan launched its Supplier Development Team, which ranks suppliers according to quality, cost, delivery, product-development capacity and management calibre (Cooke and Morgan, 1998: 56), which is being followed by other Japanese auto producers. Design capability is becoming especially important with the new Primera Estate and Almera replacement being developed, designed and engineered in the UK and Europe specifically for the EU market.

With closer supplier relations JIT delivery becomes more realistic – the Bluebird was based on monthly orders of parts, the 1990 Primera weekly and in 1993 the target was daily (Sadler, 1994). Quality has also increased dramatically, with proportion of Nissan's suppliers achieving a quality standard of 10 or less defective parts per million increasing from 17% in 1993 to nearly 50% in 1995 (Cooke and Morgan, 1998: 56). The overall number of rejected parts per million fell from 5,000 in 1990 to 150 by 1996 (Lewin, 1996).

According to Phelps (1997: 139), Japanese firms have had been able to improve the local supplier base because of the emphasis on close working relationships with suppliers. By comparison, Phelps argues that US, UK and EU firms may have problems because of their traditionally arm's length, non-collaborative relations with suppliers, based on divide and rule tactics to reduce prices (Lewin, 1996). There is also evidence that Japanese-style management techniques have spread to UK firms as a whole, not only the suppliers to Japanese firms (Julius, 1990: 60; Marsh, 1997b) in part because Japanese subsidiaries have put competitive pressure on other domestic producers and have transferred knowledge of the best practices through normal personnel changes (Rehder and Thompson, 1994: 94).[4]

In terms of exports, suppliers and job creation, Nissan, Toyota, and Honda have made a positive contribution, a conclusion which also applies to Japanese inward investment in other sectors of the economy (Harukiyo, 1998: 41). However, according to a large body of theoretical and empirical research this favourable picture of Japanese investment is tainted when we consider the type of jobs being created. While Nissan has been at the centre of new training initiatives in the North-East, the jobs are not high skilled (Eisenschitz and Gough, 1993; Smith, 1994; Dankbaar, 1997), and are characterised by highly intensive work organisation (Rehder, 1990; *The Economist*, 1992a; Tomaney, 1989, 1990, 1994b; Hoogvelt and Yuasa, 1994; McRae, 1997). The same conclusion is reached by Belderbos (1997) in a study of Japanese inward investors in the electronics industry. Furthermore, Nissan located in a high unemployment region so that they could then attract the best workers from a relatively young workforce i.e., school-leavers. Rehder and Thompson (1994) provide evidence that Nissan's direct employment creation has therefore not significantly reduced unemployment in the North-East.

Despite questions over the quality of the jobs being created, the overall impact of Nissan on the UK has been huge, especially when combined with the follow-on investment of Toyota and Nissan. The Japanese producers are now supporting the whole of the UK car industry. While Ford and Rover announced major cuts in production in 1997 and 1998 respectively, and GM in 2000, the Japanese producers are continuing to expand taking 11.8% of the West European new car registrations in 1998 – exceeded only by Volkswagen (*The Economist*, 1999c). Other than Rover, Nissan will be the only manufacturer in the UK to produce a full product range. The extreme importance of Nissan to the economic wealth of the North-East is widely held by officials at the NDC to actually represent an over-dependence of the region on Nissan's success.

Nissan Motor Manufacturing UK (NMUK) has been highly successful and, unlike Nissan UK or the parent company as a whole, NMUK registered small but growing profits in the mid-1990s. Most importantly for the North-East economy, Nissan is firmly embedded into the region's political economy, a process which Nissan estimated to take 10 years (Lorraine, 1996). In fact, with Sunderland producing three product ranges from the year 2000 and having the status as the most productive plant in Europe, NMUK has established itself as one of Nissan's most important *implementer* subsidiaries. As we discussed in Chapter 4, an implementer subsidiary is crucial to the efficiency and revenues of the MNC as a whole, and Nissan estimates that in the year 2000 Sunderland will produce 90% of Nissan's cars sold in Europe.

With the pressures of regional integration and international competition, Nissan is following the lead of the US car manufacturers, and more recently Honda and Toyota, by regionalising its operations as part of a globalisation strategy. Nissan is attempting to integrate its activities and at the same time achieve greater national responsiveness. Design and development activities are therefore being decentralised to its European operations to cater for the diverging tastes of the European, Japanese and North America mass markets (*Daily Telegraph*, 1997). The new Primera Estate was the first Nissan to be designed and developed in Europe, and Nissan's European Technology Centre in Cranfield, Bedfordshire designed the Almera replacement together with Nissan's technology centre in Germany.

While leading edge technological innovation continues to be concentrated in Japan due to the advantages of keeping the generation of critical technologies at home, as discussed in chapter five, the decentralisation of design, development and engineering represents a competitive advantage for NMUK as the global competitiveness of Nissan becomes more dependent on value-adding activities of its European subsidiaries. The merger with Renault, is likely to hasten this process, as Renault's competence in car styling localises and invigorates Nissan's design activities.

In conclusion, the £125 million in government aid given to Nissan does seem to be money well spent, even if Nissan would have accepted less, and the initial grant offered to Nissan was especially important given the financial problems Nissan was facing in the first half of the 1980s. Furthermore, unlike Ford/Jaguar or BMW/Rover, Nissan did not recourse to government funds during its major re-investment to introduce the new Micra, the new Primera Estate or the Almera replacement. Arguably, the local content saga surrounding Nissan's investment also represented a successful government/ EEC intervention, through the pressure put on Nissan to rapidly localise component production, especially as in the US local sourcing appears to have been diluted by the *keiretsu* procurement policies of Japanese investors (Hood *et al.*, 1996: 235). However, the rise in the value of the Yen and the large, indigenous and independent automotive components sector in the EU were equally important factors behind Japanese assemblers working closely with the existing supply chain. The local content rules were also concerned more with pacifying interest group pressure than embedding Nissan into the local economy.

The ability to develop close relations with suppliers and the work force was crucial in integrating Nissan into the local economy and securing the commitment of Nissan to re-invest in the UK. However, Nissan Sunderland is really a 'super-systems integrator.' NMUK is responsible for supplying the European market and managing its supply-chain, but does not have control over strategic activities including R&D, planning or co-ordinating the global network of operations. These activities remain in Japan, with Nissan's European operations co-ordinated from Brussels.

NMUK is, though, the company's key implementer plant for the whole European market. With trends in the industry requiring first tier suppliers to carry-out more R&D activities, the future of NMUK plant is more dependent now on long term skills availability and the design and development capabilities of the supply-side infrastructure than the balance of power in Nissan's Board.

However, there are two key potential threats for Nissan's UK operations. First, excess capacity of one million cars in the EU forestalls wide-scale rationalisation. Nissan's alliance with Renault has demonstrated their willingness to produce in each other's plants, which is likely to lead to consolidation in their European activities. NMUK will have to demonstrate to Nissan *and* Renault that it can continue to be not only the most productive and cost-efficient plant in Europe but also that it can add value through producing high value cars and by contributing to their strategic capabilities.

Second, the UK's growing isolation from Europe, in particular its reluctance to join the Euro-zone, is seen as particularly worrying to Nissan and other Japanese investors in the UK. In August 2000, Nissan's world-wide President, Carlos Ghosen, met with the British Prime Minister, Tony Blair, outlining Nissan's concerns over the sterling remaining outside of the Euro. Membership of the Euro facilitates the regional integration of activities, through greater cost and price transparency and lower transaction costs, and also substantially reduces currency risk. Japanese companies have invested in the UK to serve the European market, and what matters most are currency fluctuations *within* Europe, not with the dollar and the Yen. With Japanese companies like Nissan concentrating production in one location and exporting to the rest of the European market, the importance of currency stability is heightened. Nissan has also gained substantial benefits from the UK's political clout in Europe, as we saw in our discussion of access to EU markets and local content requirements. A pre-condition for future investment in the UK by Nissan and other Japanese companies in the UK may, therefore, be that the UK remains at the heart of economic and political integration in Europe.

8 Siemens' Investment in the UK

Siemens' 1995 Tyneside investment was the biggest greenfield investment by a foreign company in UK history. The motivations for Siemens' semiconductor project in the UK reveal as much about changing corporate governance in Germany as the location attractiveness of the UK to inward investors. We argue that Siemens invested in the UK as part of a globalisation strategy to improve share-holder value. Central to this strategy is the transition to the N-form MNC. The UK was favoured by Siemens as it would send powerful signals back to Germany and could meet the key project specific location requirements for semiconductor manufacturing. Low costs and flexible labour particularly stood out as key advantages of the UK. Incentives were also important for Siemens, and the multinational played-off different European regions competing for the investment to increase the incentive 'offer'.

The 1998 closure of Siemens' UK semiconductor plant has two major implications: First, it shows the limitations of Siemens' globalisation strategy and associated aspiration to become more Anglo-Saxon in order to improve share-holder value. In response, Siemens initiated a back-to-basic strategy at the end of the 1990s, symbolising the corporate restructuring of German industry. Secondly, the closure exemplifies the problems of regional development in peripheral regions resulting from an industrial policy which is based on the attraction of inward investment without a sectoral industrial strategy to ensure the consistency between inward investment and long term economic development.

8.1 COMPANY HISTORY AND INTERNATIONAL EXPANSION[1]

Siemens is the second largest German firm, and was one of the last core companies in Germany's autarkic industrial order to rapidly expand FDI and restructure in response to a changing domestic and international political economy. In this section we look at the changing organisation and strategy of Siemens, and focus in particular on corporate changes in the 1990s. We argue that Siemens has found it difficult to break-away from its 'German' history, and remained a highly diversified conglomerate driven by technology and engineering more than profit. However, Siemens has attempted to Anglo-Saxonise itself by rapid international expansion and through emphasising the importance of share-holder value above all else. Siemens is presently in the transition from a bureaucratic M-form towards a more flexible, focused, and specialised network-form of multinational organisation.

8.1.1   An 'old fashioned' company: 1847–1992

Siemens was founded in 1847, but at the start of the 20th century the company employed more people in Britain than in Germany reflecting its operations in the UK, which began four years before Siemens was founded in Germany. By the turn of the century the company was expanding into diversified activities, under competition from other German firms but, with the two world wars, Siemens' key overseas operations in Britain and Russia were closed down and the firm was consolidated as a solely 'German' firm. It was not until 1965 that Siemens UK Ltd was re-registered. In the post-war era, Siemens remained dependent on Germany for both markets and competitive advantage, at least up until the 1980s. A key reason was that Siemens enjoyed a virtual monopoly in the German market in rapidly growing and highly profitable sectors like telecommunications. As Sally (1995: 47) explains:

> In telecommunications equipment and particularly in public switching, Siemens has long-standing and privileged relations as the predominant supplier to the German Bundespost in a market in which prices were 100 per cent above the world average by the mid-1980s.

In a study of the relationship between the German telecommunications market and the major national supplying firms, Cawson *et al.* (1990) note four main aspects of government policy which benefited Siemens:

- First, the Bundespost in the early 1980s stated it would give orders only to firms that developed and manufactured their equipment primarily in Germany. The reason was that this would maintain employment and national security in switching technology. Having foreign technology (and jobs) would have been politically insurmountable given the opposition from German firms and their work councils.

- Secondly, with orders predominantly channelled to Siemens and SEL (Standard Elektrik Lorenz) they were able to secure longer production runs and greater economies of scale, facilitating exports. In 1988, for example, Siemens had 43% of the Bundespost's switching orders.

- Thirdly, government subsidies in the form of soft loans to buying states funded by the Development Aid Ministry facilitated the international expansion of Siemens and SEL.

- Fourthly, the very profitable sale of pre-digital exchanges to the Bundespost very likely subsidised the prices offered for digital exchanges to foreign customers.

Wengenroth (1997: 169) therefore argues that:

> Siemens' almost symbiotic relationship with the state-owned telecommunications sector guaranteed the company long-term stability and a basis from which new technologies and their potential on the international markets could be explored.

Through domination of the domestic market with artificially high prices and export earnings, Siemens was able to accumulate huge cash reserves to finance the R&D expenditure needed for rapid innovation. Even before the First World War, 50% of the company's investment was financed from re-invested profits, and by the early 1990s Siemens had accumulated cash of almost DM20 billion in stocks and shares. Over half of pre-tax profit originated from interest payments on these huge reserves. Unlike other German companies, Siemens has therefore had considerable autonomy from the influence of cross share holdings with major banks. In order to reduce its reliance on Deutsche Bank, Siemens became the first German industrial company to found its own investment company (Ruigrok and van Tulder, 1995: 95).

At the same time, Siemens has benefited from a close relationship with Deutsche Bank, with executives sitting on each other's board, lowering the cost of making international sales (Mascarenhas *et al.*, 1998: 124). Ultimately, Siemens' position in the German market gave the firm the ability to meet its aspirations of becoming a global player. This has always been the corporate objective of the company. The company's founding father, Werner Siemens, said in 1861: 'It is my

main concern...to found a lasting firm, which perhaps one day...
could become a world firm' (cited in Kocka, 1978: 531).

Siemens emerged as Europe's largest engineering and electronics
group, a conglomerate with activities spread from telecommunications
to automotive and medical electronics, microelectronics, data processing and nuclear energy (Sally, 1995: 29). Of all business 80% is in the
capital goods sector and Siemens employs one-third of all Germany's
electronics graduates. With financial autonomy, corporate strategy
was to diversify and be a technological leader in every sector of its
operations.

From the 1870s Siemens institutionalised technical and physical
development work within firm laboratories and was committed to
long term research sustained by high levels of investment. Siemens
pioneered the development of the telegraph and cable equipment,
and as scientific activity became more important to the firm, the
academically trained directors of the research departments were integrated into leadership positions, often to the highest managerial levels
(Kocka, 1978: 571–2).

Siemens' business strategy has therefore been technology-driven,
and in 1988 Siemens' R&D expenditure was £2.2 billion, 11.2% of
sales, and a ten-fold increase in 25 years of (Sally, 1995: 168–9, 176).
Siemens accounted for 37% of R&D in the German electrotechnical
industry (Keck, 1993: 139), and by the mid-1990s Siemens' expenditure on R&D was approaching £3 billion per annum (Miller, 1995).
Siemens could be described as a 'high tech bank'.

Siemens was among the world's first multinational companies, with
manufacturing operations in Russia starting in 1855 (Schröter, 1993:
28), and was one of the first companies to move to the M-form
organisational structure. In the early years, Siemens' operations
were co-ordinated by family loyalties, and Siemens' three main
branches in Germany, Britain and Russia operated autonomously.
However, as competition increased in the German market, with
AEG in particular pursuing a policy of aggressive expansion, Siemens
responded by seeking acquisitions at home and foreign investment
abroad. By 1914, Siemens had 10 foreign factories spread over
5 continents, with almost one-fifth of Siemens' total workforce of
80,000 employed outside Germany (Jones, 1996b: 104–7). Market-
seeking motivations were behind Siemens' foreign activities.

The company soon faced the problem of how to co-ordinate diverse
activities and different divisions, and Siemens moved towards a
bureaucratic model of systematic management in the late nineteenth

century. Even before the First World War, the company had a decentralised, multi-divisional structure – 'essentially a non-market organisation' (Kocka, 1978: 554–8). Almost 100 years later, with 18 divisions
and 266 business areas in 1992, Siemens remained a highly diversified
M-form conglomerate.

By end of the 1980s, Siemens was rapidly internationalising reflecting
not only the rising costs of production inside Germany but also the
technological nature of the firm's activities and increased competition.
As we argued in chapter's two and four, technological advance demands
access to foreign markets to recoup the costs of R&D. For Siemens,
intensive R&D and technological sophistication, safeguarded by patents
and trade marks, was best exploited by FDI (Schröter, 1993: 29).

In 1995, two-thirds of Siemens' sales came from products less than
five years old, compared with 50% in the mid-1980s, and in the
Private Communications Systems (PN) group 90% of products were
less than two years old in 1998 (*Business Week*, 1995; Siemens,
1998a). In the semiconductor industry, to amortise the huge costs of
rapid technological advance, firms are forced not only to have *world*
market share but also to form cross-border alliances and research
consortia. In European initiatives, ESPRIT and JESSI, Siemens
played a key role (Sally, 1995), and was a major beneficiary (Ruigrok
and van Tulder, 1995: 108). At the start of the 1990s Siemens also
entered into strategic alliances with Toshiba (Japan) and IBM (USA)
to access technology and reduce costs and risks in the development of
64 mb and 256 mb DRams (Siemens, 1995b). Siemens joined the
international consortia I300I in 1996 and International SEMATECH
in 1998 to collaborate on the latest 300mm technology.

Intensified competitive pressures have also hastened the internationalisation of Siemens' activities. Deregulation in Britain and the US
throughout the 1980s urged German business to change its post-war
strategy of reliance on a protected home market (Woolcock *et al.*, 1991)
and of financing capital investment through a close relationship with
banks rather than via the stock-market (Deeg, 1993, 1996). With
deregulation in the US and UK, in particular in telecommunications,
the costs of business users were reduced rapidly, putting enormous
pressure on continental firms like Siemens with new, often foreign
entrants in the Anglo-Saxon markets (Cawson *et al.*, 1990: 80–114).

Siemens has therefore expanded its presence in the UK and US to
remain competitive. At the same time, since the 1990s Siemens has
favoured deregulation of the German economy as the costs of producing there increased and as Siemens becomes increasingly dependent

on overseas markets and collaboration with foreign firms. With deregulation, privatisation and the opening-up of markets in key countries like the US and UK, the risk of retaliation by foreign governments for the competitiveness of Siemens increased. Siemens in fact maintains its own lobby in Brussels pushing for a level playing field in the EU (Sally, 1995: 116; Anderson, 1996: 202–3).

This is creating the logic of a 'competition state' (Cerny, 1993), where deregulation and privatisation in one country leads to deregulation in others, with the key drivers transnational mobile finance capital and FDI by MNCs. Under pressure from increasing international competition and competitive deregulation, Siemens has therefore shifted its strategy since the late 1980s away from relying on a protected German market towards globalising its operations further and pushing for deregulation of the German telecommunications market (due to begin in 1998) to reduce costs.

Siemens' corporate strategy has been to internationalise production, vertically in terms of lower value-added activities, and horizontally through collaborative alliance networks for accessing new technology and reducing risks. Long term, strategic FDI has been favoured by Siemens with a slow, but steady growth of FDI which gives advantages for the company and employees (Schröter, 1993: 44). By 1992, Siemens had 170 manufacturing sites in 122 countries, employing over 350,000. However, over half of revenues were still generated from inside Germany, reflecting the continuing importance of the home market and overall sales were highly concentrated in Europe. For example, in 1993 information technology sales of Siemens-Nixdorf were the eleventh biggest in the world, but 94% were in Europe compared to 75% of sales by Japanese IT firms in Japan and 50% of sales by American firms in the US (Vickery, 1996: 114).

Overall, in the early 1990s Siemens realised 68% of sales and 77% of employment in Western Europe (Lane, 1998: 477).

With the appointment of Heinrich Von Pierer in 1992 as Chairman, Siemens' strategy began to lean not only towards promoting a deregulated business environment in Germany but to rapidly globalising activities and moving towards the N-form structure in order to embed Anglo-Saxon shareholder values into the firm.

8.1.2   An 'old fashioned' company with new values: 1992–98

When Pierer became Chairman in 1992, Siemens already had listings on the major stock exchanges, but the company was too cash-rich for share-holders to have any influence on strategy. Pierer, the first non-technician to head Siemens, believed that emphasising shareholder value within the firm would encourage a focus on profitability, fostering competition between divisions. Competition was hoped to be analogous to the stock-market pressure exerted on Anglo-Saxon firms, making Siemens more market-oriented, and less bureaucratic and narrow focused. This was seen to be fully compatible with a conglomerate built 'on the firm foundation of technology' (Siemens, 1996) and aiming for expertise in every area. Corporate strategy was to support the emphasis on share-holder value and technology by continuing to globalise activities, reducing dependence on Germany, accessing new markets, and benefiting from synergies across borders. Since 1992 Siemens has had an interdependent three-prong strategy to achieve share holder value:

- changing business culture;
- global efficiency and world-wide learning;
- triadic globalisation.

Changing business culture

A target for return on equity of 15% per annum over the period 1992–96 was set and from 1994 the profits were disclosed for each of Siemens' divisions, making managers answerable for the bottom line. The aim was to increase the pressure for attention to share-holder interests (Goodhart, 1994: 51). Pierer's TOP (time-optimised processes) initiative was introduced to support this aim. The objective of TOP is to re-orient business culture away from a narrow focus on engineering to marketable innovation and customer orientation. Technology is to be driven by commercial expectations to maximise profitability and share-holder return as was re-emphasised in 1998, with Siemens (1998a) stating, 'Siemens can and will no longer tolerate losses in any form ... the overriding challenge is to make a healthy profit.'

Global efficiency and worldwide learning

For most of its history Siemens adopted the M-form organisational structure. The key motivation was to maximise national responsiveness, crucial in sectors such as telecommunications (Bartlett and Ghoshal, 1989: 24). According to Siemens: 'In order to respond quickly and effectively to market needs, the company has a decentralised organisation in which business activities are the responsibility of 18 separate operating units.'

However, under Pierer Siemens appears to be moving away from the M-form to the N-form structure, through creating networking relations across its activities in order to achieve not only national responsiveness but also global competitiveness and world-wide learning. In terms of global competitiveness, Siemens' most recent strategy is to distribute value added according to costs, know-how, capacity and market access. Siemens states that 'we must locate value added in those locations where it can be generated efficiently and cost-effectively. Moreover, these locations must possess an ideal knowledge base and be close to the market' (Siemens, 1998a). Hence, Siemens' location decision making is based on an FDI strategy that combines efficiency, market and asset seeking motives.

Facilitating and benefiting from world-wide learning is seen by Siemens as crucial for competitiveness, with Siemens noting that, 'The challenge is to integrate company resources throughout the world' (cited in Lane, 1998: 480). Creating integrated networks is aimed at exploiting more effectively synergies within the group, especially important for innovation, with Pierer believing that the group is more than the sum of its parts (Bowley and Wagstyl, 1998). However, the ultimate aim of moving to a N-form structure is to improve profitability. As Siemens' notes: 'Organisation must become more flexible and assume the form of a worldwide network with centres located according to a regional and/or competence-based principle. And, naturally, the overriding challenge is to make a healthy profit!' (Siemens, 1998a).

To access the 'synergies of the group', Siemens has adopted a co-operative, internal networking approach, called 'Best Practice Sharing'. The rationale is that through bench-marking ideas a process of learning from the best within the company can become 'second nature to us' (Siemens, 1998a). As we saw in the case of ABB in Chapter 4, the focus on learning is a key feature of the N-form company. For Siemens, in order to increase the 'internal flexibility' of the group and capture linkages across its activities, high significance is attached to developing good relations between workers and management, based on the principle of commitment to each other and consensus (Goodhart, 1994: 22). Pierer has argued that, 'Only well-motivated people can earn good profits' (cited in Bowley and Wagstyl, 1998).

The key reason was pointed out in chapter four, where we argued that in order to introduce a world-wide network of co-operation, MNCs need to socialise employees in the goals or philosophies of the organisation to avoid monitoring costs (Hennart, 1993). Siemens is therefore promoting a corporate culture which reinforces trust and a convergence of common values and objectives throughout the firm. The core principles Siemens is hoping to diffuse throughout the company are: usefulness, innovation, business success, leadership, learning, co-operation and social responsibility (Siemens, 1998a). Siemens has therefore attempted to engender both competition and co-operation within the group, to improve flexibility, synergies and share-holder return.

Globalising business

Writing in 1991 as the Vice President of Corporate Development at Siemens, Anthony Lerner (1991: 58) describes Siemens as 'the epitome of a global company'. However, although the company rapidly internationalised since the 1980s, Siemens in 1998 more realistically notes, 'we are still far from being a global player' (Siemens, 1998a). By the mid-1990s, 40% of business was still in Germany, and two-thirds in Europe. Additionally, over 60% of production and 60% of Siemens shares were concentrated in Germany. A key objective of Pierer's is to reduce Germany's share in group turnover to 25% and Western Europe's share to 50%.

Siemens has already consolidated its presence in North America, and is the biggest German investor in the US (excluding Daimler's acquisition of Chrysler). Siemens' employment in the US increased from around 1,000 at the beginning of the 1970s to 30,000 in the 1990s, with 85% of Siemens' sales derived from production in that country, and local content 70% (Köppen, 1996: 162; Lerner, 1991: 59). In addition, most of Siemens' overseas R&D activities are located in the US. However, Siemens is concerned about its weakness in Asia-Pacific, and local presence through FDI is seen as the key instrument for increasing market share. As Pierer has said, 'Those who want to share in these future markets must be there', and Siemens' turnover in this region increased three-fold from 1990 to 1995 (cited in Lane, 1998: 480).

Siemens hopes that international expansion through FDI would reduce dependence on Germany and balance the business globally. This reflects a shift away from exporting as the dominant strategy to achieve global market share towards FDI and local market presence. High costs of production in Germany and exchange rate risks are major factors behind the increasing importance of direct market presence, with Siemens maintaining that its brand is enough to signal quality, and 'made in Germany' is no longer needed (Lane, 1998: 480).

Globalisation of activities would also support technology and market access, which are crucial for deriving competitive advantage from 'science-based' firm competencies. As we argued in chapter two, globalisation facilitates access to new markets, new synergies and new technologies, generating the firm-specific ownership advantages essential to competitiveness. For Siemens:

> With development and manufacturing activities spread all over the world, the Group benefits from specific local know-how, cost advantages, and proximity to customers or co-operation partners. Moreover for political reasons without local production facilities it would often be virtually impossible to gain a foothold in many markets (Siemens, 1998a).

Vernon (1979) characterised multinational corporations as 'global scanners' and to achieve expertise in every area a 'scatter-gun' approach has been adopted, with Siemens' internationalising its technological activity strategically to take advantage and access new sources of technology, expertise, and learning through market presence and acquisitions in key overseas locations. This is particularly the case in telecommunications and semiconductors. The establishment of 'Centres of Competence' in key technologies around the world is a key component of this globalisation strategy, and represents the formation of 'contributor' and 'strategic leader' subsidiaries associated with the N-form MNC. These centres have world-wide responsibility for the development, manufacturing and marketing of their products and systems (Ferner and Quintanilla, 1998).

A key example is Dresden – Siemens' 'Centre of Competence for the 21st century' in semiconductor development. Other non-German examples include medical systems in Sweden, where Siemens employs 1,000 people in production and 500 in development, and Oxford Magnet Technology in the UK, a joint venture since 1989 which develops and produces magnets for nuclear system and employs 500 people.

The shift towards an N-form organisation has led to a rapid increase in the percentage of R&D carried out abroad, from 0.5% in 1970 to 20% in the 1990s, with one-third of Siemens' 50,000 researchers located outside of Germany (Siemens, 1995b). According to research by National Institute for Economic Research, Siemens has a revealed technological advantage in a total of seven areas of technological activity from research facilities *outside* Germany: electrical equipment, telecommunications, semiconductors, electrical systems, office equipment, professional and scientific instruments and other instruments (NIER, 1998), which indicates the scale of Siemens overseas R&D.

Changes in the technology structure are a major driving force behind Siemens' global strategy. The shift to systems and software solutions in information and communications technology is a key example. In the development of Siemens' latest EWSD digital switching system 80% of costs went into software and its constant improvement, with the emphasis shifting towards services and complex systems solutions. Siemens expects hardware to recede further into the background (Siemens, 1998b), reflecting the importance of knowledge as the key source of competitive advantage. As Siemens' 'products' become more service-based, local market presence is essential.

Under Pierer, Siemens reduced its dependence on Germany, with employment in Germany falling by one-fifth from 250,000 to 200,000 between 1992 and 1996 and, at the same time, the firm expanded globally. From Table 8.1 we can infer that from 1990 to 1996 foreign sales increased by 260% compared to a 60% increase in total sales and overseas employment increased by 33,000, while employment in German fell by 27,000. In 1997, Siemens had 250 manufacturing sites in 190 countries employing 386,000 people world-wide (Ascarrelli, 1996; Siemens, 1998a), a major expansion since Pierer became Chairman.

Becoming a 'global' company was very important for the strategy of moving towards Anglo-Saxon business values. It was hoped that by changing the image of Siemens from a 'German' to 'global' firm, the orientation of managers within the firm would break-away from rooted 'German' business values. However, in Chapters 2 and 4 we emphasised that moves towards the N-form have been associated with vertical disintegration and a 'back-to-basics' strategy.

In Siemens case, a major restructuring was not considered necessary for moving to the N-form structure and achieving share-holder value. Most of Siemens' markets were internal and parts would continue to be sourced internally, blurring the divide between 'making' and 'intellectual property,' and a 'hire and fire' philosophy would not be introduced to streamline the business. Securing technological leadership across each of Siemens' 266 business areas continued to be of utmost priority, and the company was still driven more by technology than profit.

Crucially, while Siemens adopted key elements of the global or N-form MNC, the company did not radically restructure as with the corporate transformations in other major German conglomerates, like

Table 8.1 Multinationality of leading German industrial companies, 1990–96[†]

Company	Industry	Year	Assets		Sales		Employment		Rank/Index* (%)	
			Foreign	Total	Foreign	Total	Foreign	Total		
VW	automotive	1996	–	60.8	41.0	64.4	123,042	260,811	7	55
		1990		42.0	25.5	42.1	95,934	268,744	16	48
Bayer	chemicals	1996	29.1	32.0	25.8	31.4	94,375	142,200	14	80
		1990	14.2	25.4	20.3	25.9	80,000	171,000	24	60
Hoechst	chemicals	1996	28.0	35.5	18.4	33.8	93,708	147,862	15	66
		1990	15.7[1]	26.2[1]	20.7	27.8	82,169	172,890	31	61
Daimler Benz	automotive	1996	15.7[1]	66.5[1]	44.4	70.6	67,208	290,029	19	42
		1990	11.3[2]	52.3[2]	30.2	52.9	73,381	376,785	54	34
Siemens	electronics	1996	24.4	56.3	38.4	62.6	176,000	379,000	22	50
		1990	–	43.1	14.7	39.2	143,000	373,000	14	38
BASF	chemicals	1996	17.9	28.2	23.8	32.4	42,339	103,406	35	59
		1990		24.3	19.1	29.0	46,059	134,647	14	50
BMW**	automotive	1996	–	29.1	25.5	34.8	51,900	116,112	37	59
		1992		17.0	11.6	20.0	10,000	73,600	71	36
Bosch	automotive	1996	–	21.3	16.7	26.7	62,343[1]	172,359[1]	47	52
		1990		15.8	10.0	19.7	62,087	179,636	88	43
Mannes- mann	engineering/ telecomm.	1996	7.3	15.5	8.2	23.0	41,689	119,703	95	39
		1990	4.9	14.3	9.0	14.8	34,021	123,997	87	40

[†]The Table shows that as with Japanese FDI, German FDI has been concentrated in a few sectors where German firms are world export leaders. In pharmaceuticals/chemicals (BASF, Hoechst, Bayer), electrical engineering (Siemens) and motor vehicles (Volkswagen, Daimler-Benz, BMW, Bosch), which together account for around 70% of outward manufacturing FDI from Germany (Barrell *et al.*, 1997: 1).
Sources: UNCTAD (1993; 1994; 1995a; 1996; 1997; 1998); *index of multinationality is calculated as the average of 3 ratios: foreign to total assets; foreign to total sales and foreign to total employment. [1]1994 figures; [2]1993 figures; ** not in the world's top 100 MNCs until 1992.

Daimler Benz and Hoechst. To move towards the Anglo-Saxon philosophy of share-holder value, globalisation has been used to try and lever change in the company's culture in the absence of restructuring. Siemens 1995 semiconductor investment in England is a key example of this strategy.

8.2   SIEMENS IN THE UK: A BARGAINING MODEL APPROACH

In April 1995 Siemens informed the UK government that it would consider the UK for a semiconductor fabrication plant. Whereas Nissan's decision to invest in the UK was only finalised after a turbulent 3 year negotiating process, Siemens confirmed in less than 5 months the decision to invest in Tyneside, North-East England. The announcement, made at the start of August 1995, signalled the biggest ever greenfield FDI project in the UK. Using the political economy bargaining model developed in Chapter 6, we will examine the bargaining relations between Siemens and the UK government. The path of the analysis reveals the motivations for Siemens' investment in the UK and explains why the bargaining process reached its conclusion with far greater speed when compared to Nissan's Sunderland investment.

We argue that while the UK could meet all the location requirements for a semiconductor plant, including the offer of large incentives, underlying Siemens' decision to invest in the UK was the company's Anglo-Saxon strategy to improve share-holder value and lever change inside the corporation.

8.2.1   Potential path of bargaining for Siemens and the UK government

The first stage in examining the bargaining negotiations is to analyse the potential path of bargaining, which involves deriving the absolute power of the UK government and Siemens. We therefore need to identify the commitment and alternatives of both Siemens and the UK government.

Government absolute power is determined by Siemens' commitment and alternatives. Siemens' commitment to investing in the UK reflected its overall corporate globalisation and Anglo-Saxon strategy, its strategy of investing in new semiconductor capacity outside of Germany, and the degree to which the UK could meet project specific location requirements.

Siemens prioritised semiconductor activities in the early 1980s under pressure from international competition (Sally, 1995: 176). To maintain competitiveness and independence in telecommunications meant being able to produce in-house the chips at the heart of rapidly advancing telecommunications industry. Semiconductors are at the basis of the microelectronics revolution, with Siemens (1998a) stating that: 'Information and communications technology is based on intelligent processors and memory chips.' Two major sectors dependent on the development of micro-chip technology especially important for Siemens are digital exchanges and mobile phones.

Siemens was committed to semiconductor capacity, in particular to producing chips application specific to its own digital exchange, computer, mobile phone and auto component activities (*The Economist*, 1994b). Furthermore, in Europe consumer electronics and telecommunications were the two major categories of demand, and Siemens had 7% of the European semiconductor components market in 1994 compared to only 1.9% of the world market. Siemens focused on niche markets, mainly knowledge-intensive Application Specific Integrated Circuits (ASICs) in telecoms, consumer and automobile electronics, and ASICs remain the driving force in Siemens strategy (Lawton, 1997: 75).

The company's overall semiconductor strategy in the 1990s was one of expansion, with the group aiming to enter the top 10 manufacturers, from its present twelfth position (Kehoe *et al.*, 1995; Taylor, 1997b). Industry trends also demanded expansion, with semiconductor chip growth in 1995 of 37%, and Siemens' revenue from semiconductors was increasing by 40% per annum in the first half of the 1990s (*The Economist*, 1996b; Corcoran and Liddle, 1997: 20). In 1995, US$30 billion was spent on new fabrication capacity worldwide, and huge profit margins and growth in demand motivated all companies. Siemens needed to expand to meet current and extrapolated demand:

> The company is aiming to double sales again in the medium term. Even when the new semiconductor plant in Dresden is completed and fully on line, Siemens will need additional production capacity to cover growing market demand (Siemens, 1995b).

By 1994, semiconductors had a high profile in Siemens, with recent fabrication plants in Germany, Austria, France (a joint venture with IBM) and the USA, and activities in Taiwan. Strategic alliances with

Japanese and US multinationals in the early 1990s replaced Siemens' earlier alliances with European companies, reflecting a change in semiconductor strategy from maintaining Siemens' current peripheral position in global terms to catching up with the world leaders.

Siemens saw semiconductors as crucial for the firm and, as part of Pierer's overall global strategy, new semiconductor activities were to be concentrated in each of the world's three major regions. This was to reduce dependence on Germany, have direct presence in key markets, bench-mark between plants, and access best practices and new sources of technology. For semiconductor assembly, plants were established in Malaysia and Portugal, and computers were assembled in China as part of an international division of labour for low value-added activities.

Siemens therefore manifested a high level of commitment to expanding semiconductor activities abroad, particularly with the rise of the DM, but Siemens was less committed to investing in the UK, at least in pure business terms. According to a senior executive at Siemens, 'Extending continental factories would have reduced risk, and have been easier.' A key reason is that economies of scale are vital in the semiconductor industry, with production costs decreasing by over 30% for every doubling of cumulative volume (OECD, 1992: 157). Expansion of Siemens' existing plants would therefore have reduced costs by increasing economies of scale above those of a new facility and, perhaps just as importantly in an area characterised by permanent innovation and short product cycles, would have expanded capacity faster.

Another major factor reducing Siemens potential commitment to investing in the UK, was connected with the nature of the product. Siemens was planning to fabricate Drams, where the relationship between the customer and supplier is weak, and location is internationally mobile with many uses and high global demand. Therefore, while several commentators argued that the UK's rapidly growing £50 billion information and communications technology market – the world's fifth biggest electrical market and the second biggest semiconductor and computer market in the EU – increased Siemens' commitment to investing in the UK (Steinmetz, 1995; Daily Telegraph, 1996b; Corcoran and Liddle, 1997; Wagstyl, 1997 1996a), market-seeking factors were not a crucial motivation for Siemens.

While Siemens did feel that it was under-represented in the UK market, and was aiming for a turnover of £4 billion by the year 2000, a new greenfield memory chip fabrication plant would do little for

Siemens' market presence – Siemens could have put the fab anywhere in the world. To consolidate its position in the UK, Siemens was following a strategy of organic growth of existing operations and acquisitions. Recent acquisitions included Parsons in 1997, a high quality engineering firm, GEC–Plessey in 1989, which is primarily a supplier of chips for military applications, and Mercury Communications private voice communication unit in 1996. As our discussion of technology and M&As in Chapter 4 suggests, Siemens' acquisitions were motivated by accessing new technologies and gaining direct market presence.

In fact, from 1985 to 1995 Siemens' operations in the UK expanded by 25% per annum (Fuchs and Schamp, 1990: 81), and Siemens' employs 10,000 people in 12 manufacturing sites. Turnover increased from £200 million in 1986 to £1.5 billion in 1995, and Siemens is the thirteenth biggest R&D investor in the UK and the third biggest in the electronics sector, with R&D of £134 million (Marsh, 1995; Siemens, 1996). As with German FDI in the UK in general, Siemens' operations in the UK primarily serve the domestic market; in 1995 of Siemens' £1.5 billion UK turnover only £325 million was exported (Siemens, 1996). In contrast, at Nissan Motor Manufacturing UK, turnover is also £1.5 billion but £1.1 billion is exported. Crucially, while Siemens had high commitment to expanding market presence in the UK, this would not be achieved through a new greenfield semiconductor plant.

The key factor increasing Siemens' commitment to the UK was not so much related to Siemens' semiconductor or FDI strategy, but rather to Pierer's strategy of globalising production to re-orientate culture in the firm away from being a 'German' firm with 'German' values to being a 'global' firm. Siemens' commitment to expanding semiconductor production abroad was strengthened as Pierer hoped that it would support the company's image that they were an international company, with the key emphasis on share-holder value. Changing Siemens' culture from a narrow focus on engineering to marketable innovation, customer orientation and above all share holder value favoured expansion in the UK or the US, in order to have a more 'Anglo-Saxon' image. As Heinrich Hamann, a key figure in the investment negotiations from the beginning, said, 'We came to the conclusion to step into the Anglo-Saxon world.' Pierer thought that through investing in an Anglo-Saxon country, Siemens' executives would amplify the signal they were hoping to send back into their own company – that they were now a 'global' company with 'global' values.

Table 8.2   The cost of semiconductor manufacturing,
1970s–1990s

Year	Cost of fabrication plant (US $million)
Early 1970s	2–30
Late 1970s	80
Mid-1980s	100–300
Early 1990s	750
Mid-1990s	1,000–2,000

Sources: *The Economist* (1992b); Yoffie (1993); Chandler (1997) and Ham *et al*. (1998).

Subsequent to Siemens' investment, English became the language of internal communication.

In terms of alternatives, with a US$1.8 billion joint fab with Motorola producing 64mb DRams already planned for North America, the UK was the obvious choice in implementing Siemens' 'Anglo-Saxon' strategy. However, manufacturing semiconductors is a highly costly and sensitive process (see Table 8.2) and the company had a number of acute concerns about the investment process and site.

The UK would also have to meet five key project specific location requirements – skills, people, cost, site and time. Siemens short-listed several sites not just in the UK but also in Austria, Ireland, Germany, Israel, Singapore, Vietnam and the US, demonstrating that the location search was global as is often the case for semiconducor fabrication projects. Austria, though, was the main real alternative to investing in the UK given an existing plant and local supply chain networks and contacts as well as the advantage in terms of lower capital investment costs (Bowman, 1998; Munchau, 1995):

● *Skills*: The availability of skills was a vital consideration in Siemens' location assessment (Siemens, 1995c). The work-force had to be capable of handling technician-level jobs, and two thirds of Siemens' workforce were to be educated to graduate or HNC standard (Bates, 1996). While Germany and Austria had a better training infrastructure, competition for jobs was an important issue for Siemens, as the plant had to be up and running as quickly as possible. The North-East was close enough to Scotland's 'Silicon Glen' to attract trained people to Siemens but not too near, avoiding competition for jobs. The three main universities in the region produce 400 electronics and 560 computing graduates each year, and the NDC provided detailed information to Siemens on graduates, including those who leave the region but would prefer to stay in the North-East if the job opportunities existed. The educational institutions for training offered good support to Siemens, with Tyneside College building its own clean room for training in semiconductor fabrication.

- *People*: Just as important as skills were the qualities and work ethos of the people. As Paul Taylor, Procurement Co-ordinator in the Siemens Project Team Office, argues: 'The most important, most crucial issue was a trained labour force. This was the key local content. The North-East had a good, flexible, educated workforce with a holistic outlook' (Taylor, 1998). Multi-shift, round-the-clock production for memory chips is essential, and was achieved at Siemens' most recent plant in Dresden, East Germany. The North-East, with an industrial background and a history of high unemployment, had a reputation for flexible, adaptable, trainable and committed workers and the institutional environment facilitated the introduction of flexible practices. This was of major importance to Siemens, with the financial controller at Siemens' UK semiconductor plant explaining:

> The UK has no legal restrictions on shifts and the North-East has an industrial background and willingness to work. Germany and Austria since the early 1990s have also allowed continuous shifts but flexibility to negotiate is better in the UK (Hamann, 1998).

- *Costs*: The third major factor in Siemens' location appraisal was costs, as emphasised in a study by Corcoran and Liddle (1997) of the regional partnership in the North-East. The FDI strategy of Siemens was in part efficiency-seeking, and according to Pierer, labour costs were 50% lower in the North-East than in Germany (cited in Bannister, 1996), and labour represented 15% of the projects total costs. At the same time as the investment negotiations a recent engineering wage settlement further contributed to high costs in Germany, by adding 7.6% to wage costs (Hotten, 1995). Labour costs in Ireland and Austria were also more expensive than in the North-East. The importance of relative costs was particularly sensitive to Siemens, with an internal assessment of productivity, as part of Siemens' benchmarking exercise, revealing Siemens to be lagging its international competitors by 20% to 60% in 1994 (Goodhart, 1994: 50). The world leaders were in South

Korea and Taiwan, precisely those countries benefiting from the biggest cost differential. The exchange rate, at the time, was also very favourable for locating in the UK with the DM appreciating against Sterling by 8% in 1995, and the rise of the DM had already cut Siemens global sales by DM3 billion (Hotten, 1995). As a low cost developed country location, the UK had few competitors.

- *Site*: The fourth major consideration in Siemens' appraisal was the site. Semiconductor fabrication is highly sensitive, and Tyneside could offer geological suitability and the enormous quantities of water and guaranteed electricity supply, good infrastructure and access to an airport (NDC, 1996). An abundant supply of high-quality water is critical for successful semiconductor manufacture, with repeated washing and rinsing integral to the fabrication process, and Northumberland's Kielder Water is Northern Europe's largest manmade lake. For semiconductor manufacturing a sound and reliable electricity supply is also a necessity. Another critical requirement is the minimisation of vibration, necessary because the machines that photographically draw electronic circuit patterns on to the silicon wafer are highly sensitive to vibration. The alternative Midlands site in the UK was ruled out due to vibration. A local company, McAlpine, which built the plants of Nissan and Fujitsu in the North-East, was experienced in site construction and the success of Fujitsu's semiconductor plant in the region, recently awarded best plant out of Fujitsu's 400 world-wide (Tighe, 1995c), was a comfort factor. The enormous complexity of the project can be seen in the site's specifications:

> The 200,000 sq m building contains: cables which would stretch around the equator; enough lights to illuminate 50 football pitches; boiler power to heat 3000 homes; chillers equivalent to 150,000 domestic fridges; fans which move half a ton of air every second; over 30 miles of pipes; a 4,000 sq m clean room – 100 times cleaner than a hospital operating theatre; the fab uses water cleaned to one million times purer than tap water (NDC, 1996).

- *Time*: The fifth key location factor was speedy negotiations and a smooth planning process crucial to rapid completion of the project. As Dr Bridge emphasises: 'So suddenly its not necessarily to do with a lot of money or a lot of cheap labour. What it is to do with is how quickly you can get their project into profitability and that is very very important as far as individual companies are concerned' (Bridge, 1998b). The UK government was very experienced in dealing with foreign investors and a centralised investment agency could handle all the enquiries. Red-tape is minimal and sub-national agencies in the North-East were well co-ordinated under the auspices of the Northern Development Company. Siemens notes that one of the reasons the North-East was favoured was due to professional services delivered by local agencies (NDC, 1996) and in Germany the investment process would have taken much longer (Fisher, 1998).

Overall, while Siemens had many potential alternatives, and expansion of the Austrian site was probably less risky, Siemens had few alternatives to investing in the UK given the overall strategy of Pierer was to embed Anglo-Saxon values into the firm through globalisation and Siemens already had plants in Austria, the US and a joint venture with IBM in Paris in 1991 – each part of Siemens' globalisation strategy for semiconductors (Siemens, 1995a). The low labour costs and flexibility of the workforce were also factors balancing the decision in favour of the UK relative to other locations, and the North-East site could meet all the project specific criteria for a fabrication facility, as Fujitsu's plant demonstrated. The UK was certainly not the only alternative to Siemens, but on the other hand there were several key advantages of locating a new fab there. We can say that Siemens had a medium level of alternatives. In terms of commitment, the investment was not crucial to the strategic future of the company, although it would support Pierer's Anglo-Saxon globalisation strategy and meet extrapulated demand. Siemens displayed a medium level of commitment.

Siemens' absolute power is determined by the government's commitment and alternatives. The commitment of the government is reflected in its strategy towards attracting inward investment in general and specifically, in this case, Siemens. We can identify five main influences on the government's commitment to Siemens:

- The UK has a history of actively courting inward investment, assuming unequivocal benefits, as we will see in Chapter 9.
- At the regional level, Fujitsu invested in 1989 and Siemens would consolidate the North-East semiconductor sector and help attract equipment suppliers. The creation of much needed high-skilled jobs was perceived by regional bodies to be of great significance.
- The key UK central government incentive on offer, Regional Selective Assistance, is discretionary and we will see in chapter

ten is based on jobs created, capital expenditure and the mobility of the investment project. The prospect of creating 2,000 direct jobs and another 2,000 indirect jobs in spin-off industries (Hanson, 1995), plus over £1 billion in investment, would undoubtedly increase the commitment of the government to supporting Siemens financially, as would Siemens' global location flexibility.

- Siemens was perceived as a 'flag-ship' investment. Most important for the UK government was that it would be a high tech investment – the world's most advanced semiconductor plant in the most technology-intensive of industries – and by Europe's biggest indigenous electronics firm. It would send a message to other MNCs. As the President of the Board of Trade, Ian Lang, said, 'Siemens' decision is a clear sign that the UK is the most competitive location in Europe... one of the most attractive locations for high-tech, high-quality investments in the world' (cited in IBB, 1995d).
- The UK imports 75% of semiconductors, and the government calculated Siemens' UK plant would provide £200 million import substitution and £700 million exports every year. The balance of trade effect was therefore viewed very positively.

In terms of alternatives:

- The UK economy was in the middle of a recovery and a large job-creating inward investment was not crucial to employment growth.
- Alternative sources of inward FDI were growing rapidly – 1995 was a record year – and, around the same time as Siemens, major semiconductor investments were in the offing by Fujitsu, LG and Hyundai.
- As a 'flag-ship' investment, there were few alternatives to the investment by such a prestigious company.

Overall, the government has high commitment at the central level due to the emphasis on inward investment and flag-ship projects, and at the local level due to the importance of the semiconductor sector and new jobs in the North-East. The extent of job creation was the major factor determining central government commitment to investors, and while Siemens would create many, the economic situation was good, with alternative sources. However, there were no indigenous alternatives to Siemens' high-tech investment, and the 'flag-ship' factor was irresistible to the UK government. The UK government therefore had high commitment and a reasonably low level of alternatives. Notably, neither dimension was as extreme as when Nissan invested.

Figure 8.1 Potential bargaining path: derivation of absolute power for Siemens and the UK government

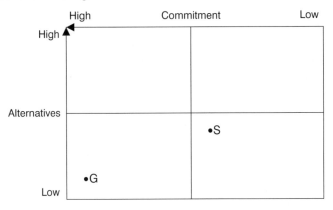

Figure 8.1 illustrates the absolute power of the government and Siemens, based on each actor's alternatives and commitment. Point G shows that Siemens has a high level of absolute power and point S shows that the UK government has medium level of absolute power. The potential path of bargaining can now be derived.

If we refer to the bargaining matrix of ideal type potential power possibilities in Table 6.3, the Siemens–UK government bargaining relationship would be placed somewhere in the third group of alternative-commitment combinations. Total power is quite high, while Siemens has greater relative power, although not as pronounced as in the case of Nissan. According to the hypotheses of the bargaining model, agreement is likely.

8.2.2   Implementation of potential power

The second stage of the bargaining model approach is to examine the implementation of power, which involves examining the political constraints and the institutional structure of Siemens and the UK government.

Siemens faced three main political constraints endogenous and exogenous to the firm:

- Sources indicate that 9 out of 10 commercial people in Siemens favoured expansion of the existing Austrian plant but the board was more open to the UK and hoped to invest in Tyneside as part of their global expansion strategy.

- Siemens' other semiconductor subsidiaries would clearly like to consolidate their operations with a major expansion, securing their long term future and were lobbying for the new investment.
- There was pressure from trade unions to keep the investment in Germany, and other foreign government's also lobbied for the investment.

Siemens therefore faced potentially significant political constraints to the implementation of bargaining power. The impact of these pressure groups depends on Siemens' institutional structure:

- The decentralised structure gave subsidiaries certain autonomy, but also reduced their influence over decision-making in Siemens' Munich headquarters.
- According to Sally (1995: 197), the Siemens group has internal cohesion and integration, reducing conflicts within the firm.
- The institutionalised system of worker representation increased the role of unions in company decision-making in Germany.
- While having a decentralised structure, Siemens was still dependent on Germany for production and R&D and the German government is a major market for Siemens.

The influence of competing demands from subsidiaries within the conglomerate were therefore likely to be minimal due to strong headquarters control over strategic decision-making. The influence of trade unions was dissipated because of rising unemployment in Germany and Siemens was also reducing its dependence on producing in Germany, in part a 'power seeking' FDI strategy to reduce the power of unions through increasing alternative investment locations. In terms of our bargaining model, although Siemens remained committed to its workers in Germany, Siemens' alternatives were increasing *vis-à-vis* IG Metall. Its relative power was rising in the 1990s, and Siemens used a divide and rule strategy to reduce the ability of unions to bargain for concessions, as in the case of OSRAM (see Marsh, 1997a).

In fact, Ferner (1997: 6) argues that Siemens' UK semiconductor investment was a message to the unions and government in Germany – to deregulate – and Mueller (1996: 354) saw the investment as a signal that investment in Germany is not guaranteed. But the investment was not a message in the same way as it was for Daimler Benz, when they openly looked at many sites around Europe for their new small car, to put deliberate pressure on Bonn to relax labour laws. Siemens' investment was primarily about sending a message to managers within the firm rather than to union leaders and politicians outside.

However, leading politicians had a tightly-knit relationship with senior executives in the company; Pierer was very close to Helmut Kohl, visiting his holiday retreat, and a regular tennis partner of Gerhard Schröder (*Financial Times*, 1998a). Siemens could have a say in public policy and conversely the German government had an influence over Siemens' strategy. As a senior executive at the NDC explains from the perspective of an investment agency:

> It is all about getting to the ultimate decision-making people, making friends with decision-makers and nurturing these people. It is all about trust and track record.... Dealing with a national company is obviously easier to influence (Taylor, 1998).

A recent example of the symbiotic relationships between Siemens and the German government can be seen in the case of Siemens' semiconductor fab and research activities in Dresden. According to Mr Hamann, 'Dresden was heavily influenced by political discussions to help Eastern Germany to Re-develop' (Hamann, 1998) and through its investment Siemens ensured that it would continue to derive 'good favour' from the German government; in 1998 the German federal government and Saxony committed up to DM370m, or £124 million, of public funds to support the development of a 'next generation' chip industry in Dresden based on 300mm technology (Norman, 1998).

However, in the case of Siemens' proposed plant in Tyneside, the German government was not a key actor, and was largely supportive of the investment. Like Siemens, the government was aware of the high costs of doing business in Germany, both in terms of labour markets and also government red-tape. In Bonn, the German Economics Minister, Guenther Rexrodt, said he hoped the decision would spur efforts to reduce the cost of doing business in Germany.

Siemens therefore faced few political constraints to the investment, and none that seriously impinged upon its decision-making autonomy. The main political obstacle to the investment were internal squabbles at the top decision-making level, which are likely in most firms when a large investment project is proposed. However, disaggregating decision-making to this level often reveals that personal rivalries are more important than the matter itself (Ruigrok and van Tulder, 1995: 65), and what was at issue was not the overall objectives of the FDI strategy to expand semiconductor activities and globalise, but whether investing in the UK would support this strategy.

The UK also faced minimal political constraints to the implementation of absolute power. In the first place, Siemens is a 'European' firm, removing issues like local content discussions from the negotiations. The British government would not face a hostile reception at home and abroad, as was the case with Japanese firms investing in the UK. In addition, there were no major indigenous semiconductor producers or suppliers in the UK to be spurred into politically motivated action and impinge on the investment negotiations. Finally, at all levels of government there was widespread support for inward investment, increasing the commitment of policy makers to work together and attract the investment, overcoming any minor interest group pressures.

There were therefore no significant political constraints. However, an examination of the government's institutional structure is still important as it influences the government's negotiating ability. Inward investment in the UK is is co-ordinated by the centralised IBB, with the Industrial Development Unit at the Department of Trade and Industry (DTI) taking responsibility in major projects. The IBB presents an inward investor with a single agency to help co-ordinate their appraisal of different locations within the UK, while the IDU acts a single negotiating body.

With a massive increase in inward FDI in the UK since Nissan's investment, both bodies were very experienced in handling investors' enquiries and in meeting their needs. At the regional level, the NDC had developed a reputation as a relatively powerful and cohesive RDO in the North-East region, and has 100% membership from its Local Authorities (Dicken and Tickell, 1993: 204–5). Its effectiveness was one of the rationales behind the RDAs set up by central government in April 1999 (HMSO, 1997: 58). However, while the central and regional agencies have proved to be effective organisations in attracting FDI, we will see in Chapter 10 that co-ordination between the IBB and Regional Development Organisation (RDOs) is far from perfect, with different regions within the UK competing against each other for new investment, bidding-up the incentives offer. A MNC with a mobile investment project, like Siemens, can therefore benefit from weakness in the UK's institutional structure of inward investment decision-making.

Figure 8.2 Implementation of potential power: the influence of political constraints for Siemens and the UK government

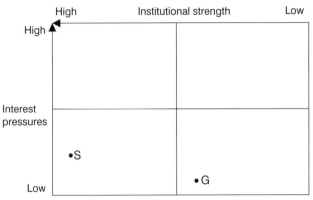

Figure 8.2 shows the interest structure and institutional structure of Siemens and the UK government. Siemens faces greater interest pressures than the UK government, but has a higher degree of institutional strength as shown by points S and G. There are few impediments to translating potential power into actual power, and the bargaining process should be smooth.

Figure 8.2 shows a key change when compared with the Nissan negotiations: the UK's institutional strength has increased from 'low' to 'medium'. By the time of Siemens' investment, the IBB and NDC had established a reputation among investors as among the most professional investment agencies in Europe and the shift from mandatory to discretionary grants also increased the UK's ability to negotiate over incentives. The major factor preventing a 'high' level of institutional strength for the UK government was lack of effective co-ordination between the national investment agency (IBB) and regional agencies in preventing bidding-wars for FDI projects between agencies. Furthermore, we will see when we discuss the actual negotiations that Siemens could exploit weaknesses in co-ordination between the UK and other European goverments.

Figure 8.3 integrates the two dimensions of the bargaining model, showing mutual dependence, the relative power of the government and the influence of political constraints. The bargaining model indicates that the investment would be expected to go ahead as mutual power is high, given a high level of commitment and relatively few alternatives, with the potential path of bargaining translated into

Figure 8.3 Political economy bargaining model of Siemens–UK government negotiations.

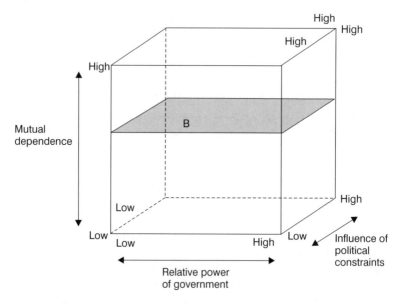

actual outcomes due to the minimal influence of political constraints. Point B shows that the government has lower relative power, representing the government's fewer alternatives and higher commitment to Siemens.

However, the government has greater relative power than when Nissan invested, as at the time the government had no alternatives to Nissan and higher commitment given the crisis in the manufacturing economy, and especially in the North-East. But Siemens was still in an excellent position to bargain for concessions due to its higher relative power, weaknesses in the UK institutional structure, and because Regional selective assistance (RSA) is primarily based on jobs created, capital investment, and the number of alternative investment locations competing for the investment.

8.3   SIEMENS IN THE UK: THE ACTUAL NEGOTIATIONS

Jürgen Gehrels, Chief Executive of Siemens UK from 1986 to 1998, heard about the project in April 1995 by chance. Mr Gehrels was not a member of the main Siemens board, but was receiving the minutes of board meetings and read that a new semiconductor project was being considered. As a staunch Anglophile, winning the Officer's Cross of the Order of Merit for the Federal Republic of Germany for contribution to Anglo-German relations (Elliot, 1995), Gehrels immediately asked the board whether the UK would be considered. Munich gave him three weeks to make a list of options. So Gehrels went straight into the heart of government, contacting Mike Gooch from the IBB and the Deputy Prime-Minister, Michael Heseltine. In the first stage, the key units involved were therefore the arms of central government (Corcoran and Liddle, 1997: 17), with Siemens making it clear to central government that they did not want to be approached by individual regional agencies, as the speed of the nego-tiations and project completion were crucial.

Siemens, therefore, did not choose to play-off different regions in the UK to maximise the incentives forthcoming as time was of the essence and ensuring that the regional authorities would give Siemens full support was more important. Instead, Siemens would later play-off different European countries.

The IBB took responsibility for co-ordinating Siemens' enquiries and contacted English Partnerships, with its £350 million budget, to discuss site possibilities. At Siemens first port-of-call, Heathrow air-port, English Partnerships made a presentation to Siemens, leading to Siemens seeking more information as to site requirements. English Partnerships made a regional analysis, with 10 sites short-listed. These were narrowed down to the West Midlands and the North-East, and on 5 May 1995 the Northern Development Company (NDC) was first contacted and informed that an undisclosed 'German' company (codename 'FABCO') was interested in building a semiconductor plant.

English Partnerships then arranged for Siemens to visit possible sites in England, via English Estates, and brought together other regional agencies. On 16 May 1995, Siemens made one out of what were to be five half-day visits to North Tyneside. Over a three-day period, Siemens visited five sites in England and two in Northern Ireland. The West Midlands was initially the preferred choice, per-ceived by Siemens as the centre of UK industry. However, there were vibration problems at the site due to a nearby railway and others problems of mis-information. The Tyneside option was then taken seriously. The NDC arranged for the general manager of Fujitsu to meet Siemens, presenting a favourable image, especially regarding the availability and quality of labour, which was reported to the IBB by Siemens to be of 'special interest.'

With the regional agencies in the North-East demonstrating their ability to facilitate the rapid construction of the plant, Siemens requested full information on the industrial structure in the North, and made a second visit to the region on 20 June. The NDC gave a presentation to Siemens, in German, on water, electricity and capital costs, and Siemens signalled more clearly its preference for the North-East.

With the North-East now a front-runner for the proposed invest-ment, Siemens still had two major issues to resolve, relating to finance and labour. Siemens began negotiations with central government over the financial package, but was clearly not satisfied with what was on offer and there was confusion among the many regional agencies and central government over who is giving how much of what funds – which, according to internal government documents, were still not resolved at the end of December 1995 – after the investment decision was made. Siemens played on its multinational flexibility as a source of bargaining power. The IBB informed the NDC on 18 July 1995, that:

> The Irish package has advantages compared to what the UK has offered. Siemens is looking for an improvement of the UK pack-age... [especially] in the area of training.... A major concern is as to whether Siemens will be able to run the factory continuously three shifts a day, seven days a week... will it be possible to find personnel willing to work three shifts.

The next day, 19 July, Siemens made a third visit to the NDC, and presentations were given on utilities, labour and universities, empha-sising the cost advantages of UK and flexibility and quality of the local workforce. A professor from Newcastle University, an expert in semiconductor design, gave a presentation to Siemens detailing the graduate and research potential of the University's Department of Computer Science and Department of Electrical Engineering. The NDC, in 24 hours, collected information that would address Siemens' key concerns. Siemens was impressed with the support given by the region, and on 24 July was given a tour of the proposed site and surrounding area. Siemens made it obvious the Dutch, Irish and Austrian government's were offering higher and more transparent grants, based on capital expenditure rather than job creation. English Partnerships therefore offered Siemens direct connection to the national grid – the first time ever for a firm – to increase the value of the package. This was justified to European rules as semiconductor sectoral rather than firm specific help.

Subsequently, the NDC arranged for a highly detailed report on the North-East to be sent to Siemens, which included socio-economic information ranging from league tables on GCSEs, A-levels, truancy rates, universities, quality of life (e.g. sports clubs), plus lists of all students in the region, their grades and subsequent employment, as well as more general economic statistics. This was sent to Siemens on 25 July, just one day after Siemens' site visit.

During the next week a 'package' was agreed by Siemens and the UK government, with the UK government under pressure from Siemens to meet the Austrian offer of £120 million. The final package agreed included:

- RSA £30 million over a 5–7 year period plus £3 million early payment (from DTI Industrial Development Unit, IDU).
- £5 million training – confirmed by Mr Heseltine to Siemens on 1 August, 1995 (from Government Office-North-East and Tyneside TEC).
- £13.5 million in local packages – including 10 years business rate relief at the economic zone and £10 million from City Challenge (from Government Office-North-East, North Tyneside Council, and Tyne and Wear Economic Development Council).
- £12.75 million in infrastructure (from English Partnerships).
- *Total*: £64.26 million, plus 'other' benefits, bringing the total closer to the Austrian offer.

On 2 August, Siemens made a fifth visit, was given another tour of the region and dinner at Lumley Castle. At 11.30am the next day Gehrels said the board had chosen Tyneside 'as part of its global expansion strategy'.

The negotiation process was smooth and quick, as the bargaining model analysis indicated, with the IBB and the NDC and its regional partners providing excellent facilitation for Siemens' investment process. Siemens was able to use its greater number of alternatives to push the government and regional agencies to make more concessions than they otherwise would have given. However, when Fujitsu decided to build a semiconductor fab in the North-East in 1989 it was offered nearly three times more RSA per job created than Siemens.

Central government must have perceived its bargaining position to be better with Siemens and, as the bargaining model analysis suggests, the UK government had a medium level of absolute power. Siemens did, though, receive substantially more RSA per job than the average amount normally given, reflecting the high commitment of central government to Siemens' flag-ship investment, the number of jobs created and level of investment planned. A large 'package' from sub-national authorities in the North-East indicated the bargaining power of Siemens as well as the region's commitment to Siemens in terms of creating high-skilled jobs and consolidating the region's semiconductor industry.

The incentives offered to Siemens were important in attracting the project to the UK, but only in their absence. They were of help to the company, as they would reduce costs (Siemens, 1995c), As Mr Hamann reveals:

> Government incentives are taken into account everywhere... Whether based on job generation or investment related they are of long term help to the firm... They help in the short-term as the project makes losses in the beginning... In the first years the project is not profitable; incentives help to bridge the gap (Hamann, 1998).

However, if other countries were not offering incentives the UK government could still have attracted the investment with a less costly 'package'. Especially for a cash rich firm like Siemens and a huge investment on the scale of Tyneside, the financial incentives are not of major importance, and their impact is more of 'tipping effect' rather than supporting the long term commitment of Siemens to investing the UK. Unlike Nissan, where incentives were important given financial troubles and were mandatory anyway, the UK government offered Siemens financial aid in large part as an outcome of Siemens' alternatives, as well as the government's job-biased RSA system.

The Newcastle investment was planned to be completed in 2 phases. The first phase by mid-1997, initially producing 16mb and 64mb DRam microchips, and after the second phase employment would rise to 2,000. In fact, Siemens' performance in their new plant was ahead of expectations, following a record-breaking factory building schedule and achievement of quality targets months ahead of expectation. The plant was built in a time of 376 days, and commercial production began in May 1997, four months ahead of schedule. The official opening on 23 May 1997, was attended by the Queen and Jürgen Gehrels, like his predecessor William Siemens over 100 years before, received a knighthood.

8.4 WHEN THE 'CHIPS' ARE DOWN, SIEMENS IS NOT SO 'FAB'

The closure of Siemens' semiconductor plant in North-East England signalled a crisis both at Siemens and for the North-East region. The collapse of the Tyneside plant indicates the failure of Siemens' Anglo-Saxon globalisation strategy to meet share-holder expectations, and led to a major corporate restructuring at Siemens. We also argue that the closure of the plant reveals the vulnerability of the North-East region to changing strategies of foreign MNCs, in part an outcome of previous government industrial policy which failed to link inward investment with long term regional competitiveness.

8.4.1 Closure of Tyneside and restructuring of Siemens

In 1997, Siemens delayed phase two of its Tyneside plant and on 31 July 1998, Siemens announced that the plant would close by the end of the year. Just as market trends were behind the company's expansion of semiconductor activities, market trends were behind the rationalisation; the price of memory chips had fallen by 95% since May 1995, and chips selling for more than US$50 in 1995 cost just over US$1 by mid-1998 (Siemens, 1998b). The collapse in the market reversed the company's financial position, from a DM109 million profit in 1996 to a loss of DM1 billion in the year to September 1998 (Atkins, 1998).

According to Ulrich Schumacher, head of Siemens' semiconductor business, the Tyneside plant was closed because it was 'the weakest link in our chain' (cited in Cane and Jones, 1998). Siemens' Tyneside plant was always going to make a loss (DM300–400 million annually) in the start up phase, and with the delay in constructing a second 'clean room' in 1996 the plant would not have the economies of scale to be profitable. The UK plant was only one-third the size of the company's Dresden plant in East Germany and less than half the size of the other plants in Austria and the US. It therefore accounted for 45% of the company's DM1 billion losses from semiconductors in 1998

(*Financial Times*, 1998c). If Siemens had instead expanded existing plants the additional DM1 billion that the firm will incur to close down the plant and repay government aid would have been considerably less.

Tyneside was not only vulnerable due to smaller economies of scale; Dresden was a centre of competence for semiconductor research, and leads much of the group's research and know-how. Siemens' French operations are a joint venture with IBM, complicating the situation (Atkins, 1998), and the US plant is crucial to Siemens' globalisation strategy, with Siemens aiming for presence in each of the three major regions. In addition, the rise in the value of Sterling since 1997 was a significant factor although, in response to the strength of Sterling, Jürgen Gehrels said in January 1997 that, 'There is no question of Siemens going back on its commitment to this wafer fab' (cited in Strong, 1997).

Perhaps prompted by the final decision to close the plant, Gehrels retired in the Summer 1998 and his successor, Alan Wood, was well aware that emphasising factors specific to the UK would only fuel British sensitivity over the closure, with Rita Stringfellow of North Tyneside Council saying, for example, that there had been a 'huge commitment in good faith to get Siemens to come to the North-East. We would have hope that they would honour that commitment' (cited in Jones, 1998). Mr Wood used South Korea as a scape-goat for closing Tyneside:

> Naturally the pound has an influence on competitiveness of companies, but in this case that's just lost in the noise. . . . This is because of extremely aggressive pricing from Korean microchip manufacturers who have a 40% share of the market. It appears the money the International Monetary Fund is pouring into Korea is being pumped into the microchip companies (cited in Groom, 1998a).

However, the collapse of the semiconductor market, whether aggravated or not by the Korean producers, was in line with past movements in the industry and would rebound again as the market recovered. The closure of Tyneside was not only an outcome of market trends and the relative weakness of the UK plant, but was also representative of tensions in Siemens' overall strategy. This led to a fundamental change in strategy in November 1998.

Siemens' investment in Tyneside was far more than a calculated decision to meet market demand and reduce costs; Siemens used the opportunity arising from market growth to invest in Tyneside as an image and culture changing exercise. Siemens was emphasising that it should be seen more as an 'Anglo-Saxon' company rather than a 'German' company. The closure reflects the conflict between the strategy of achieving share-holder value and technological leadership through globalisation, while continuing to maintain a vertically integrated conglomerate structure. Siemens failed to achieve Von Pierer's target of 15% return on equity per annum over the period 1992–96, with Siemens' actual return 10% per annum, 50% below the firm's stated objective, and a fall of nearly 40% against the German stockmarket. In 1997, return on equity was less than 10% (Ascarrelli, 1996; *Financial Times*, 1998a).

The collapse of semiconductor activities brought home the realisation that the present strategy was not sustainable. While the collapse was related to market conditions, the company's Tyneside experience indicated to Siemens that globalising business as a strategy to embed an Anglo-Saxon shareholder philosophy into the firm was, in itself, insufficient. Siemens realised that in order to align Siemens to the stock market, the example of other major German conglomerates, like Daimler Benz, would have to followed. As Box 8.1 shows, only major corporate restructuring and rationalisation would generate high performance.

From now on Siemens would be driven more by commercial design and share-holder expectations than an endeavour to keep the sprawling, technology-based conglomerate alive. In November 1998, Siemens promised to sell DM17 billion (£6 billion), or one-fifth of its business. Semiconductor activities, which had annual sales of DM11 billion, were planned to be floated on the stock market as an independent firm. The remainder of the firm's component operations would also be sold, and Siemens would concentrate on its core competencies in personal computers and mobile phones, although the company would still not have a single core business (Kehoe, 1998).

In February 1999, Siemens announced plans to list in the US in the year 2001, offer share options to 500 top managers and to abolish the voting rights of the Siemens family, clearly aimed to appeal to institutional investors and 'modernise' the company (Harnischefeger, 1999a). A few days later, Siemens stated that all of its 16 divisions must at least cover the cost of capital by the end of the fiscal year 2000 or be divested or merged. 80% of divisions must be number one or two in their fields compared to 60% now, implying streamlining and specialisation (Harnischefeger, 1999b).

Siemens is abandoning its M-form conglomerate and moving towards a N-form organisational structure, emphasising global competitiveness,

Box 8.1   Restructuring Daimler-Benz in the 1990s: a case of 'Anglo-Saxonisation'

Germany's biggest industrial group, Daimler-Benz, exacted a far-reaching change in philosophy and corporate structure in the 1990s to reduce over-engineering and over-bureaucracy within the firm, and meet the challenges of Japanese competition and globalisation:

- First, the conglomerate applied pressure on the 'stake-holders' of the German social market. The key mechanism was a 'punish and reward' strategy, whereby Daimler would apply pressure on German workers to make concessions before locating fresh investment in their home country through a strategy of publicly examining sites in other countries. This was aimed at reducing costs and increasing flexibility. Daimler set up a new plant in Alabama, USA, sending powerful signals back to Germany.
- Second, a major rationalisation of the group began from 1992 to shift the philosophy of the conglomerate towards Anglo-Saxon share-holder values. Daimler stream-lined its business, cutting its workforce by one-quarter – 66,000 employees – and sold 'business areas in which further investment no longer made good economic sense', such as aircraft manufacturing, to concentrate on its core competency – producing cars. Bureaucratic control systems moved towards globalised 'Anglo-Saxon' profit and cost control mechanisms. These shareholder friendly policies were aimed to re-orientate Daimler to the stock-market and reduce bureaucratic inflexibility and costs within the firm. By the end of the 2000, senior management hope to have reduced costs by DM10 billion.
- Third, to support this strategy Daimler adopted transparent US accounting standards, listed its shares on the New York Stock Exchange, and recruited senior managers with an American business background.
- Fourth, in 1998 Daimler entered, as the major partner, into a merger with Chrysler, America's third biggest car manufacturer. Daimler signalled that it was now far more of a 'global' firm, with a strategy of conquering emerging markets. The merger gave access not only to Chrysler's four wheel drive expertise and lower-end cars (facilitating global market penetration), but also to America's 'leanest' car manufacturer. Combined, Chrysler and Daimler-Benz spend an estimated

$60 billion on parts with components accounting for up to two-thirds of the costs of a vehicle. Daimler sourced most of these parts internally while Chrysler had pioneered outsourcing, developing networking relations with suppliers and distributors. Daimler is hoping that Chrysler's 'fit for the market' culture will spill-over; in the new merger responsibility for purchasing will be the remit of Chrysler's chief financial officer.

Daimler Benz's strategy of increasing flexibility, focusing on shareholder value and globalisation seems to have paid off; return on capital invested in 1998 was over 30% – higher than all of the world's major car manufacturers. Other companies like Hoechst and Bosch have followed a similar strategy of re-orientation toward Anglo-Saxon share holder values and restructuring, while continuing to emphasise long term profitability and commitment to employees

Sources: Mueller and Purcell (1992); Ramsay (1995); Mueller (1996); *Business Week* (1998); Ferner and Quintanilla (1998); *Financial Times* (1998d); *The Economist* (1999h).

world-wide learning, multinational flexibility, and a back-to-basics strategy. The key driver is to improve shareholder value.

8.4.2   Crisis in the UK semiconductor industry: a failure of industrial policy

The arrival of Siemens in the North-East was hailed by regional development organisations as signalling the emergence of a major new industrial sector, diversifying the region's industrial base and reducing dependence on the automotive industry. Following Siemens' decision, Fujitsu announced in September 1995 a £816 million expansion of its semiconductor site, boosting Fujitsu's investment to £1.2 billion and increasing employment by 400. The expansion was due to be finished in mid-1997 – the same time as Siemens' new plant (Tighe, 1995a; *Daily Telegraph*, 1996a; Wagstyl, 1997).

Attracted by Siemens and Fujitsu, Applied Materials, the world's biggest manufacturer of semiconductor equipment, made a £15 million investment in Tyne and Wear to supply process equipment to Siemens and Fujitsu – accounting for about 60–70% of the total equipment needed for semiconductor production. Air Liquid Gas from France also followed Siemens' investment. According to the NDC (1997a):

> The investment of Applied Materials was the cornerstone in the development of the Region's support industry for semiconductor companies and will act as a stamp of approval for other suppliers.

Simultaneously, LG and Hyundai were planning major semiconductor investments. LG announced in Summer 1996 a £1.7 billion project in South Wales to create over 6,100 jobs producing cathode ray tubes and semiconductors. Hyundai intended to invest £2.4 billion in two semiconductor plants in Scotland (Barrie and Milner, 1996; Dent and Randerson, 1996).[3] In 1996, the UK accounted for 4% of world capacity and 16% of EU semiconductor production, with a market value of US$5.2 billion. There were 31 fabs in the UK, compared to 27 in Germany, employing 25,000, and Siemens, Fujitsu, LG and Hyundai promised to rapidly increase UK production.

However, just as the Siemens plant signalled a wave of new planned semiconductor projects, Siemens' announcement that it was to close its plant in 1998 was not isolated. In June 1998, Hyundai Semiconductor decided to postpone indefinitely completion of its memory chip plant in Scotland and LG followed suit. LG put on hold its proposed semiconductor activities – producing only television monitors whereas the company had originally envisaged a complete electronics complex. Both announcements reflected the collapse of the semiconductor market and the economic crisis in Korea, which left Hyundai and LG short of cash. A second major blow for the North-East and the semiconductor industry came one year later, in December 1999, when Fujitsu announced that it was putting-up for sale its plant for only US$12 million.

While market trends appear to be the cause of the semiconductor crisis in the UK and North-East (Siemens, 1998b), underlying the plant closures and cancelled investment projects is the weakness of the UK semiconductor infrastructure. Despite the UK having the status as the biggest semiconductor producer in Europe, with Scotland producing 10% of microchips made in Europe, 75% of semiconductors by value were still imported in 1996, most from the US and Germany. Although there are over 300 suppliers in the UK supporting the semiconductor sector, the majority of key, high value-added materials and equipment are imported (*Financial Times*, 1995; Bates, 1996; Taylor, 1997a).

Siemens was a self-contained plant, with a local component, raw material and chemical content of practically zero. Only bulk items such as water, electricity and most of the gasses were from the UK. The strategy of the UK government and regions, based on attracting major semiconductor manufacturers and then hoping suppliers will follow, left the British-based semiconductor industry vulnerable to changes in market conditions and corporate strategy. Most exposed to this vulnerability was the North-East – the highest unemployment region in the UK.

The embeddedness, or lack of it, of foreign semiconductor producers in the UK is further constrained by the weakness of the British semiconductor research base. In Siemens' case, while a 50-person electronics design and development centre was planned for the same site as the Tyneside manufacturing plant, the centre would be dependent on its home (German) base for technological innovations and for its most advanced new products and processes. The role of a potential UK centre would be limited to adoption of basic Germany-originated designs (Lorenz, 1995). With process and design technology changing rapidly in semiconductors, the semiconductor specialist at the NDC, Paul Taylor, argues that if this research is not being carried out in the UK, then the UK will continue to be, or end up being, an offshore industrial park for the US and Japanese (Taylor, 1998).

Government industrial policy is not helping to develop a strong supply and research infrastructure. With regional authorities across the UK and member states within the EU competing to attract semiconductor firms using the carrot of regional aid, semiconductor investment has been scattered throughout the UK and EU. According to Graham (1996b: 21), economic efficiency is reduced as plants have been built at sub-optimal scale and economies associated with clustering may have been lost. Furthermore, as we argued in previous chapters, MNCs locate strategic, high-value added activities in locations benefiting from close links between headquarters, production, development and design and economies of scale, scope and clustering. In reference to the semiconductor industry, Yoffie (1993: 198) notes: 'With few exceptions...core Research and Development activities on semiconductors have remained in the home base throughout the history of the industry.'

With only 5% of the British market UK-owned, the weakness of semiconductor research activities in the UK is not surprising. At the same time, the situation in Britain is compounded by insufficient courses and reduced numbers of graduates entering the industry, which has now created a critical situation in the UK. Germany and Switzerland have nearly 60% more home graduates in engineering and technology than the UK, and the same is true for vocational qualifications (Cooke and Morgan, 1998: 26–7).

The distinguishing advantage of the UK labour market – flexibility – while playing a key role in attracting inward investment, in sectors like automotive and semiconductor manufacturing, also makes it easier for the foreign firms scale down and close operations in the UK relative to other countries in response to market trends or corporate restructuring. Evidence also suggests that a multinational's overseas subsidiaries are closed before those in its home country (Heiduk and Hodges, 1992, cited in Barrell *et al.*, July 1997: 4), with a recent example Renault's controversial closure in 1997 of a major plant in Vilvorde, Belgium as part of the company's rationalisation. Table 7.1 also shows that Japanese MNCs are reducing employment overseas rather than at home. MNCs derive significant economic and political benefits from showing a high commitment to their home country.

In relation to the semiconductor industry, one example, which we referred to above, is Siemens' symbiotic relationship with the German government. Siemens and the government are jointly promoting Dresden and the Saxony region as a centre for semiconductor manufacturing and research. The industrial strategy of the German government is to build on the region's strong electrical engineering and industrial history and develop the region into a cluster of semiconductor activities. With the government channelling both domestic and foreign semiconductor investment into Saxony through regional grants worth up to 50% of investment outlay, turnover from microchip companies increased from DM59 million in 1991 to nearly DM1 billion in 1997. Manufacturers are also attracted by the high unemployment, large pools of skilled labour, and a relatively weak system of collective bargaining.

The federal government, however, favours R&D investment over manufacturing facilities, with R&D investment in East Germany eligible for Research and Technical Development grants up to 60% of expenditure or DM1 million, compared, for example, to grants of only 30% of costs or £150,000 available in Scotland (see Euroconfidential, 1997) – Europe's leading centre for semiconductor manufacturing. Generous grants combined with skilled engineers and the cluster effects of Siemens' research activities are leading to Dresden emerging as a centre for manufacturing *and* R&D. By 1999, 420 technology companies and 2,000 of their suppliers had set up in and around the city. Siemens and California-based Mattson Technology and AMD have their European semiconductor research centres of competence in Dresden (*The Economist*, 1999d). AMD's $1.9 billion investment is particularly impressive. The project is the world's most advanced semiconductor manufacturing facility and will produce 1 gigahertz Athlon microprocessors, which outperform other leading processors including Intel's Pentium III. According to AMD, the investment was driven by access to a large skilled and talented workforce and the presence of the Dresden Design Centre, which is part of the company's European microelectronics centre (*Business Wire*, 1999).

The contrast between the German government's targeted industrial strategy for semiconductors and regional development in Saxony and the apathy of UK industrial policy is clear-cut; while the federal government, the Eastern Länder and its regional partners, and Siemens are working together to promote Saxony as a cluster for semiconductor manufacturing, research and related industries, UK industrial policy is based on the ad hoc attraction of large-scale, job-creating inward investment to create short-term jobs in declining regions. There is no coherent strategy integrating sector targeting and economic development, at least at the central level, and government policy has artificially dispersed foreign companies, missing out on any clustering benefits, which we argued in Chapters 2 and 4 are central to innovation. In the midst of regional rivalries and lack of central co-ordination, it unlikely that the UK government could have adopted the regionally specific, sector-based targeted policy favoured by the Germans in the case of semiconductors, even if it had had the foresight to do so. A similar contrast can be made between the UK government and the approach of Taiwan, where the major policy initiative was the establishment of a science-based semiconductor park (see Hong, 1995), which has now developed into one the world's major centres of semiconductor manufacturing and research activity.

The leader of North Tyneside Council, Brian Flood, believed that, 'Siemens brings us the opportunity to develop 21st century industries' (cited in North Tyneside Council, 1995), and certainly in terms of creating 1,000's of highly trained jobs Siemens was the flag-ship of the region. However, in terms of building on the region's existing industrial base, Siemens was closer to the foreign plants operating in the Mezzogiorno, Italy, described by Rhodes (1995) as 'cathedrals in the desert,' than the JIT-led (Mair, 1993) plant of Nissan.

Although certainly not of branch-plant status, as the fab involved a complete manufacturing process and skilled workers not sweat-shop assembly, the long-term spin-offs of Siemens to the local economy, other than the creation of well-paid jobs, would depend on attracting new inward investors rather than building links with indigenous enterprises. The North-East therefore became more dependent on the commitment of inward investors not on the comparative advantage of indigenous industry, increasing the region's vulnerability to changes in the corporate strategy of MNCs. The ability of regional bodies to build links and work with business to respond to changes in market trends were also reduced, as such links are more difficult to forge with foreign than indigenous firms.

Siemens typified the failure of the UK's exogenous strategy to economic development, illustrating that there is no quick-fix to the long-term process of economic renewal. The government had no regional or sectoral strategy for long-term economic development for either indigenous enterprises or inward foreign investment.

In the following Chapters the inward investment strategy of the UK government and NDC is examined in greater detail. We outline how at the time of Siemens' investment regional policy makers were gradually changing their attitudes away from the unequivocal belief in the benefits of inward investment towards re-orientating efforts to focus on the needs of local industry. The collapse of Siemens' investment is likely to hasten this shift in emphasis.

Part III

Inward Investment Policy and the Impact on Economic Development

9 Inward Investment in the UK

The objective of this chapter is to examine the relationship between inward investment in the UK and the industrial policy of the British government. The chapter is divided into two parts. The first part analyses the role of FDI in the UK economy, and the second part looks at the evolution of UK industrial policy and the role of inward investment in that policy. The analysis of FDI gives a broad picture of the highly significant role of foreign MNCs in the UK economy, which not only reflects the historical openness of British FDI policy, but also influences the context within which present industrial policy is formulated.

We argue that while British industrial policy has been constrained by the importance of inward and outward FDI to the UK economy, the non-regulatory stance of UK policy also represents factors unique to the British political economy. In particular, our analysis of UK industrial policy highlights the impact that the City and the military have had on weakening the UK manufacturing base, leaving policy-makers with fewer alternatives to choosing an exogenous path to economic development. The non-interventionist ideology of successive Conservative governments has also been integral to the emphasis placed on inward investment as the key component of industrial policy.

9.1 EMPIRICAL OVERVIEW OF FDI IN THE UK

In the introduction to this study we noted that the UK is the most penetrated of the major economies by FDI. In this section we first compare the scale of inward FDI in the UK economy relative to other major host countries before analysing in greater detail the role of FDI in the UK. We also consider outward FDI flows because the degree of FDI symmetry is an important determinant of the target of domestic concern in government industrial policy, and therefore influences FDI policy.

Statistical sources of FDI data used include the British Office of National Statistics (ONS), the OECD, and UNCTAD. Recalling the discussion in chapter three, these statistical sources are not precise and suffer from important drawbacks, not least that they do capture new forms of FDI and are heavily influenced by M&As. We therefore also make use of project specific data collected by the Invest in Britain Bureau and Ernst & Young.

9.1.1   The relative FDI position of the UK

In Chapter 4 we analysed the growth of FDI over the last century and saw that the key hosts for FDI have shifted from developing to developed countries and that developed countries have continued to increase their significance as a source of FDI. In particular, Western Europe recorded the biggest percentage increase in its share of the world inward FDI stock. In 1914, Western Europe accounted for 8% of global FDI inflows, by 1967 30% and in 1998 38%. We argued that a key factor in the transformation in FDI location was the shift away from resource to efficiency and especially market seeking corporate FDI strategies. In Europe, regional integration, tariff and NTBs, and the Single European Market increased inward FDI from countries outside of the EU and also facilitated intra-FDI flows between member countries markets as national regulations were replaced by Community-wide policy.[1]

EU member countries were therefore major beneficiaries of changes in the international political economy in terms of attracting inward FDI. The UK, as the biggest economy in Europe until the 1970s, and the third biggest today, attracted a substantial proportion of the FDI flowing into Western Europe. In fact, the UK has been *the* major recipient of inward FDI, accounting for about one-third of FDI in Western Europe during the post-war period up until the 1990s, and one-fifth in the 1990s. Figure 9.1 shows FDI flows into the UK from 1981 to 1998 relative to the G-5 industrialised countries.

In 1981, the UK was the second biggest recipient of FDI in the world with nearly US$6 billion of inward FDI flows. This was over twice the level of France, but only about one-quarter the US level. In per capita terms, however, the UK attracted more FDI than the US. From the mid-1980s, the growth of FDI accelerated, increasing four-fold between 1986 and 1990 and, after falling in the early 1990s, 1997 and 1998 were each record year's for FDI in the UK. In 1997 and 1998, the UK attracted more FDI than Germany, France and Japan combined, reversing the trend in the first half of the 1990s when France attracted more inward FDI that the UK.

Figure 9.1   FDI in G-5 countries, 1981–98 (US$ million)

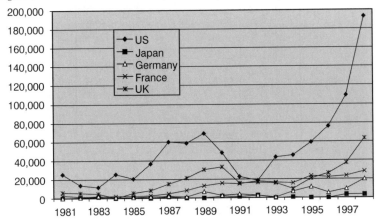

Sources: OECD (1993, 1997b); UNCTAD (1999).

Although official sources do not provide a detailed breakdown of FDI by modality, FDI projects recorded by the IBB, show that since the early 1980s about 50% of FDI inflows have been brown field – expansions by existing investors (Hood and Taggart, 1997; Groom, 1998b; IBB, 1998). Overall, the UK ranks second in the world in terms of FDI inflows, but sixteenth in terms of flows per capita (UNCTAD, 1998) with small, highly open developed countries like Belgium, Netherlands, Ireland, and Switzerland and city-states like Luxembourg and Singapore exceeding UK levels.

Table 9.1 compares official FDI data with Ernst & Young's *European Investment Monitor*, which monitors new and expansion FDI projects in Europe. The table shows a strong correlation between the official and project FDI data, with the UK accounting for around one-quarter of FDI flows and projects in Europe from 1997 to 1999. However, for the developing economies of Hungary and Poland, their share of FDI projects is not reflected in their share of FDI flows. The key reason is that M&As play a minimal role in their economies when compared to the developed countries. The role of M&As is the main reason why the Netherlands accounted for 12.4% of total FDI flows in Europe in 1998, but only 3.8% of FDI projects, with several very large acquisitions of Dutch companies in that year.

If we look at outward FDI in Figure 9.2, we find similar overall trends. The US is the world's major source of FDI, followed by the

Table 9.1 Top 10 locations for FDI projects and FDI flows, 1997–99

	1997			1998			1999		
	Projects	% of total projects	% of total FDI flows	Projects	% of total projects	% of total FDI flows	Projects	% of total projects	% of total FDI flows
UK	**302**	**22.1**	**23.8**	**646**	**28**	**24.6**	**508**	**23.8**	**24.4**
France	110	8.1	14.9	271	11.7	10.9	391	18.3	11.6
Germany	123	9	6.2	196	8.5	7.7	195	9.1	8.0
Spain	58	4.2	4.1	90	3.9	4.4	139	6.5	2.8
R. of Ireland	115	8.4	1.8	116	5.0	2.7	117	5.5	5.4
Belgium	70	5.1	8	132	5.7	8.1	108	5.1	4.7
Hungary	71	5.2	1.3	114	4.9	0.8	89	4.2	0.6
Netherlands	53	3.9	6.1	87	3.8	12.4	86	4	10.0
Austria	17	1.2	1.5	84	3.6	2.3	68	3.2	0.8
Poland	105	7.7	3.2	117	5.1	2	67	3.1	2.2
Other	341	25	29.1	458	19.8	24.1	368	17.2	29.4
Total Europe	**1365**	**100**	**$155.2bn**	**2311**	**100**	**$257.0bn**	**2136**	**100**	**$336.5bn**

Sources: Derived from Ernst & Young cited in Site Selection (2000); UNCTAD (1999); UNCTAD (2000).

Figure 9.2 FDI outflows of G-5 countries, 1981–98 (US$ million)

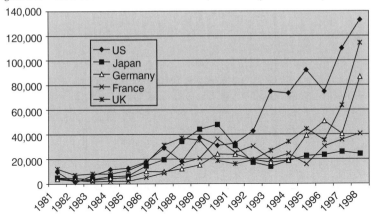

Sources: OECD (1993, 1997b); UNCTAD (1999).

UK. Outward FDI from the UK in almost all periods exceeds inward FDI, and from the mid-1980s the growth of outward FDI accelerated. As with inward FDI in the UK, there was a fall in FDI flows in the early 1990s with the UK recession, and then rapid growth at the end of the 1990s. From 1996 to 1998 UK outward FDI more than tripled. Unlike with inward FDI, UK outward FDI is approaching US levels, due to UK firms leading the world in M&As at the end of the 1990s.

Another major difference between Figures 9.1 and 9.2 is the greater importance of Japan and Germany in outward FDI. During the second half of the 1980s, Japanese outward FDI was the highest in the world, while in the first half of the 1990s German outward FDI was on par with UK and French levels, and has accelerated rapidly in the second half of the 1990s. However, in 1998 UK outward FDI was still more than German and Japanese FDI combined.

The inward and outward FDI stock position of the G-5 can be seen Table 9.2. For all the countries (other than France in 1985), outward FDI exceeds inward FDI in each of the selected years, most marked in the case of Japan.

In Japan, from 1980 to 1998 outward FDI increased by 15 times and in 1998 the outward stock exceeded the inward stock by 10 times. The US is the major home and host country, with nearly US$0.9 trillion inward FDI and close to US$1 trillion outward FDI stock in 1998. UK inward and outward stocks have remained the second highest in the world from 1980 to 1998, with total cumulative inward FDI of

Table 9.2   Inward and outward FDI stocks of G-5 Countries, 1980–98 (US$ million)

Country	FDI stock	1980	1985	1990	1995	1997	1998
US	Inward	83,046	184,615	394,911	535,553	681,651	875,026
	Outward	220,178	251,034	435,219	696,092	860,723	993,552
Japan	Inward	3,270	4,740	9,850	33,531	27,080	30,272
	Outward	19,610	43,970	201,440	238,452	271,905	296,056
Germany	Inward	36,630	36,926	111,232	165,914	208,917	228,794
	Outward	43,127	59,909	151,581	268,419	303,499	390,090
France	Inward	22,862	33,636	86,508	143,670	141,135	179,186
	Outward	17,985	31,458	110,126	184,380	189,681	242,347
UK	Inward	63,014	64,028	218,713	213,850	276,258	326,809
	Outward	80,434	100,313	232,593	311,372	374,431	498,624
World	Inward	506,602	782,298	1,768,456	2,789,585	3,436,651	4,088,068
	Outward	513,105	685,753	1,714,147	2,840,216	3,423,433	4,117,144

Sources: UNCTAD (1998, 1999).

nearly US$1/3 trillion in 1998 and outward FDI of US$0.5 trillion. In terms of FDI inflows, FDI projects and FDI stocks the UK is the leading location for FDI in Europe. In the late 1990s the UK has maintained its position as the most favoured location in Europe, despite rapidly increasing FDI flows and projects in competitor countries.

9.1.2   UK inward and outward FDI by modality and sector

Trends in the location of UK FDI reflect those of developed countries more generally; UK FDI flows are strongly skewed towards other developed countries and, in the 1990s, FDI has been increasingly concentrated in Western Europe. Table 9.3 shows UK FDI by region.

In 1987, just one year after the signing of the Single European Act and its commitment to complete unification of the internal market, half of UK inward investment was of North American origin and over 40% of UK outward FDI was located in the NAFTA. The EU accounted for only one-quarter of UK inward and outward FDI, and only 5% of UK inward FDI was from non-OECD countries. However, by the end of 1996, the EU was the UK's most important FDI partner, and intra-OECD flows represented an even greater proportion of UK FDI stocks. The move to create a Single European Market by the end of 1992, with 95% of the programmes' 300 measures implemented by this date, led to a re-orientation of UK FDI towards other EU members.

The shift towards OECD countries dominating UK inward and outward FDI represents changing motivations for investment from resource to market and efficiency seeking, as argued in chapter 4. If we look at UK FDI by industrial sector, Table 9.4, there a clear trend, with FDI shifting from the primary to the manufacturing and especially the service sector during the 10 years from 1987 to 1998.

Table 9.3   UK inward and outward FDI stock by region, 1985–96

Sector	1987		1995		1996	
	Inward	*Outward*	*Inward*	*Outward*	*Inward*	*Outward*
EU-15	28	25	35	37	33	44
NAFTA	50	43	45	34	41	29
Other OECD	17	13	16	10	22	9
Non-OECD	5	19	4	19	4	18

Sources: derived from OECD (1997b, 1998a).

Inward Investment Policy

Table 9.4   UK FDI stocks (%) by industrial sector, 1987–98

Sector	1987		1995		1998	
	Inward	Outward	Inward	Outward	Inward	Outward
Manufacturing	36	36	31	44	29	39
Services	32	40	47	40	55	45
Primary	27	24	22	16	16	16

Source: derived from OECD (2000). Totals may not add up to 100% due to unallocated parts.

In 1987, one-quarter of UK inward and outward FDI was in the primary sector. By the end of the 1998 this proportion fell to one-sixth. Manufacturing and services each accounted for a over one-third of FDI in 1987 but in 1998 outward manufacturing FDI had increased while inward manufacturing FDI had fallen, indicating a reduced attractiveness of the UK as a location for manufacturing FDI. Services became the major component of FDI. Up until 1995 all of the rapid increase in service sector FDI was accounted for by inward FDI, while from 1995 to 1998 services became the dominant component of both inward and outward FDI.

The growth of service FDI represents the shift to market and efficiency seeking investment and a changing sectoral composition of FDI. In particular, the rapid growth of IT & Software sectors and the increasing importance of call centres and shared service centres led to a rapid growth in service sector FDI in the UK. The UK is also particularly active in service FDI due to the pre-eminence of finance and banking in Britain and the importance of large M&As in this sector. The role of service FDI in the UK mirrors that of trade, where the UK is the second largest trading country in services in the world.

If we look at project data provided by the IBB, Table 9.5, we can see that in the fiscal year 1999/2000 the split between service and manufacturing projects was approximately 50–50. However, the leading sector was information technology and Internet services. The 162 projects in this sector equalled the total number projects in the top three manufacturing sectors (automotive, electronics, engineering).

Data provided by Ernst & Young, Table 9.6, also demonstrates the importance of service sector FDI in the UK. New manufacturing projects accounted for only 11% of total projects recorded in the UK,

Table 9.5   FDI projects in UK in fiscal year 1999/2000 by activity and sector

Activity	% of projects	Sector	Projects
Manufacturing	40	IT/Internet services	162
Services	38	Automotive	70
R&D	9	Electronics	51
E-commerce	4	Engineering	44
Distribution	3	Telecommunications	43
Contact & shared		Finance, management	
service centres	2	and business	41
Assembly	1	Metal products	39
Other	3	Contact and shared	
		service centres	31
Total	100	Food and drink	27
		Chemicals	21
		Other	228
		Total	757

Source: Invest.uk (2000).

Table 9.6   FDI projects in the UK by sector, 1999 (total projects 508)

Sector	Projects	% of total projects
New manufacturing projects	57	11.2
Distribution	25	4.9
Headquarters	80	15.7
Research & Development	55	10.8
New call centres	27	5.3
Customer services/marketing	158	31.1

Source: derived from Ernst & Young cited in Site Selection (2000).

while customer services and marketing projects accounted for nearly one-third of total projects. Indicating the globalisation of technology and innovation and the transfer of strategic decision-making to regional headquarters, R&D projects accounted for 11% of total projects, while headquarters projects accounted for 16%.

In terms of the modality of FDI, IBB data from 1998 to 2000 shows that the new projects, expansions, and M&As each account for around one-third of total projects. The proportion of new jobs in the total of new and safeguarded jobs is less than 40%.

Table 9.7   FDI projects in the UK, fiscal years 1998–2000

	1998–99		1999–2000	
	Total	% of total	Total	% of total
Projects	652	100	757	100
New	204	31.3	269	35.5
Expansions	250	38.3	255	33.7
M&As	198	30.4	214	28.3
Joint ventures	0	0	19	2.5
Jobs	118,753	100	134,194	100
New	44,413	37.4	52,783	39.3
Safeguarded	74,340	62.6	81,414	60.7

Sources: derived from IBB (1999) and Invest.uk (2000).

9.1.3   Inward FDI in the UK by source and location

Table 9.8 shows FDI flows into the UK from 1971 to 1998 by the 10 largest source countries, with the period 1980–97 segmented into three six-year intervals, which indicates four trends:

● From 1971 to 1985 inward FDI was dominated by culturally/ linguistically similar former UK colonies; the US, Canada and Australia accounted for over three-fifths of FDI into the UK.

● From 1986 to 1991 the source of inward FDI shifted dramatically toward European countries and Japan at the same time as the implementation of the SEM progressed. The EU and Japan accounted for half of FDI in the UK.

● From 1992 to 1997 the US again became the major source of FDI, as European and Japanese FDI fell in relative and absolute terms, reflecting in part the massive restructuring in the previous period and also economic recession in Japan and the rapidly growing US economy. In 1998, the US accounted for 55% of FDI in the UK.

● Throughout the period, the Netherlands (and Switzerland to a lesser extent) has served as a major financial entrepôt, channelling FDI flows to the UK. This has distorted country and region-specific data, with, for example, an unspecified volume of US and Japanese FDI emanating from the Netherlands. These two countries are also very active in M&As.

Table 9.8 FDI in the UK by 10 largest sources: average annual flows, 1971–98

	1971–79		1980–85		1986–91		1992–97		1998	
	£m	% total	£m	% total	£m	% total	£m	% total	Flows £m	Stock £m
Australia	21	2.4	–30	–	887	7.7	546	4.4	940	7,861
Bel-Lux	19	2.2	31	1.7	384	3.3	215	1.7	1,003	3,019
Canada	26	3.0	36	2.0	309	2.7	37	0.3	–123	4,878
France	53	6.0	106	5.8	1,162	10.1	1,016	8.1	–470	17,554
Germany	30	3.4	29	1.6	521	4.5	1,014	8.1	205	12,943
Japan	11	1.3	76	4.2	908	7.9	73	0.6	56	7,917
Neths.	18	2.1	–206	–11.3	2,080	18.0	1,211	9.7	343	18,488
Sweden	23	2.6	60	3.3	435	3.8	–3	0	–233	3,170
Switzerland	52	5.9	186	10.2	912	7.9	759	6.1	12,366	13,657
USA	495	56.5	1,158	63.8	2,970	25.8	6,295	50.5	21,533	88,641
EU-14	172	19.6	86	4.7	4,923	42.7	3,991	32.0	2,061	60,689
OECD*	813	92.9	1,530	84.3	11,119	96.4	11,868	95.2	36,547	186,320
World	875	100.0	1,815	100.0	11,529	100.0	12,467	100.0	38,633	196,412

*1971–91 OECD refers to Western Europe, North America, Australia, Japan, and New Zealand.
Sources: derived from HMSO (1985, 1977); ONS (1995, 1998a, 1999a) and OECD (2000).

In absolute terms, annual FDI flows in the UK roughly doubled between 1971 and 1979 and 1980–85 but increased six-fold between the periods 1980–85 and 1986–91. During the mid-1990s inward FDI increased slightly relative to the previous period, but increased rapidly in 1998. On average, since the mid-1980s over £13 billion FDI has flowed each year into the UK.

However, as we discussed in Chapter 3, official FDI statistics should be treated with some caution. While official balance of payments data, from which FDI data is drawn, shows non-portfolio capital flows between countries, it is not necessarily an accurate indicator of the capital investment or the number of inward investment projects each country is 'winning'. Furthermore, official data includes M&As, which have increased exponentially since the 1990s.

M&As have a minimal direct expansionary impact on jobs or investment. The possible contribution of M&As to an economy is more qualitative, involving the transfer of knowledge (technological, marketing, managerial, etc.) and opportunities for economies of scale and greater specialisation between the merged or acquired firms. This may in fact lead to cost-cutting and reduced jobs and output in the local economy as synergies are driven out. Table 9.9 indicates the job losses in several M&A involving UK firms. The merger or acquisition may, though, safe-guard the long term future of the company, leading to the argument that reduced jobs are better than no jobs. However, it should be noted that there is minimal case-study evidence examining the impact of M&As on regional economies.

Governments and investment agencies have therefore been primarily concerned with attracting new investment, which will expand output and employment. In the UK case, the overriding objective in

Table 9.9 Employment cuts in selected cross-border M&As

M&A deal	Industry	Year of deals	No. of job losses
Astra–Zeneca	Pharmaceuticals	1998	6,000
BMW–Rover	Automobile	1994	3,000
British Petroleum–Amoco	Oil	1998	6,000
Goodyear–Sumitomo Rubber Industries	Tyre maker	1999	2,800
Hoechst–Rhone–Poulenc	Pharmaceuticals	1998	10,000

Source: UNCTAD (1999).

attracting and facilitating inward investment has been job creation in peripheral regions. However, the objective of investment agencies across the world has increasingly been to secure re-investment of existing investors as well as attract new investment projects. Using data from the IBB, Table 9.10 provides an analysis of project data recorded over a five-year period by regional investment agencies and the IBB. Its shows the contribution of FDI from the UK's main source countries to new jobs and capital expenditure. Table 9.10 also indicates the significance of M&As.

The top 10 sources of FDI in terms of capital expenditure are different from those given by the official FDI data (Table 9.8), with Australia, Belgium–Luxembourg and Sweden replaced by Ireland, South Korea, and Taiwan. The shares of total capital expenditure as derived from project data are, though, very similar to the shares shown in the official data, with the US the major source of investment, and Germany and France the major sources from Europe. The correlation between capital expenditure and number of investment projects is also strong, but there is a much weaker relationship between the number of projects and capital expenditure and new jobs created.

In particular, South Korea and Taiwan account for the smallest number of projects but created among the highest number of new jobs. This reflects the large size and labour intensity of primarily manufacturing investments. In fact, less than 4% of South Korean and Taiwanese new jobs were in the service sector, compared to over one-quarter for FDI as a whole. For Switzerland, the relationship between capital expenditure and projects and job creation is the reverse, with relatively few jobs created. This reflects the concentration of Swiss investment in capital intensive sectors, in particular industrial equipment and machinery, precision instruments and chemicals.

A major difference between the project and official FDI data is in the significance of Japan. The project data shows that Japanese firms invested or planned to invest over £4.5 billion in the UK from 1994 to first quarter 1999, the second largest source of inward investment in the UK. This compares with less than £0.5 billion Japanese FDI in the UK from 1992 to 1998 according to the official data. One reason for the discrepancy is likely to be disinvestment by Japanese firms, which is recorded in the official not project data. According to ONS (1998a), Japanese FDI in the UK was −£379 million in 1995, while the project data shows that Japanese FDI in the UK was £1.6 billion in that year. It may also be because Japanese firms are raising finance for new investment projects in the UK, rather than transferring capital from Japan.

Table 9.10 FDI in the UK by 10 largest sources of new jobs, 1994–Q1 1999

Country	Projects		New jobs created		Total capital expenditure		Top 5 acquisitions, % of total capital expenditure
	No.	% total	No.	% total	£m	% total	
Canada	101	3.8	6,204	2.8	651	1.4	21.8
France	121	4.5	10,767	4.8	3,555	7.8	70.4
Germany	238	8.9	18,545	8.4	3,992	8.8	42.3
R. of Ireland	84	3.1	3,908	1.8	967	2.1	48.9
Japan	232	8.7	23,912	10.8	4,565	10.0	1.0
Korea	36	1.3	17,316	7.8	2,092	4.6	0
Netherlands	93	3.3	4,451	2.0	2,337	5.1	84.4
Switzerland	74	2.8	2,946	1.3	1,817,	4.0	79.4
Taiwan	39	1.5	11,345	5.1	634	1.4	0
USA	1,326	49.8	104,998	47.3	20,942	45.9	22.3
Others							
Total	2670	100	222,027	100	45,601	100	14.0

Source: derived from IBB project data.

A major advantage of the project data is that it allows us to analyse FDI by modality. In particular, we can examine the role of acquisitions in inward investment. Table 9.10 highlights the role of the top five acquisitions of each country in total capital expenditure. For France, Netherlands and Switzerland the top five acquisitions accounted for between 70% and 84% of total investment, while the figure for Germany and Ireland is over 40%. For total FDI in the UK, the top five acquisitions accounted for 14% of total capital investment, while acquisitions as a whole accounted for over 50% of investment. However, South Korea and Taiwan made no acquisitions and for Japan acquisitions were very marginal. The almost exclusive mode of entry to the UK for Far Eastern firms is greenfield investment. The role of acquisitions makes understanding the motives for investment and comparing the performance of different countries in attracting inward investment potentially ambiguous when using official data.

9.1.4 Weight of FDI in the UK economy

With the rapid growth of FDI flows, the weight of FDI in the UK economy has increased significantly. However, as Table 9.11 shows, the weight of FDI has actually grown faster in Japan and Germany, although from a much lower level.

From 1980 to 1995, cumulative inward FDI in the UK increased by almost 2.5 times as a proportion of UK GDP, accounting for over one-quarter of GDP in 1995. Over the same period, outward FDI almost doubled. While the contribution of inward FDI to GDP fell from 1995 to 1997, the total of inward and outward FDI accounted for over half of UK GDP in 1997. In comparison to Germany, and Japan,

Table 9.11   UK, German and Japanese FDI stock as % GDP, 1980–97

Country		1980	1985	1990	1995	1997
UK:	Inward flows	11.7	14.0	20.8	28.5	21.5
	Outward flows	14.9	21.9	23.4	27.4	29.1
Germany:	Inward flows	4.5	6.0	7.4	6.9	9.9
	Outward flows	5.3	9.5	10.1	10.8	14.4
Japan:	Inward flows	0.3	0.4	0.3	0.3	0.6
	Outward flows	1.9	3.3	6.8	6.0	6.5

Sources: UNCTAD (1998, 1999).

Inward Investment Policy

FDI is far more important to the UK economy. Table 4.6 also shows that in developed and developing countries inward and outward FDI accounted for roughly one-fifth of GDP in 1996 – less than half the UK proportion. In the UK, FDI therefore makes a more significant contribution to GDP than most countries in the world.

If we look at the contribution of FDI to domestic gross fixed capital formation, the same picture is presented, as seen in Table 9.12.

In the UK, by the mid-1990s inward and outward FDI accounted for one-third of gross fixed capital formation, a moderate increase over the 1986–91 period, but in 1997 accounted for over half of gross fixed capital formation. In 1997, inward FDI accounted for 18.6% of fixed capital, 5% higher than 1986–91, but four times higher than the period 1960–86 (Ietto-Gillies, 1992: 193). The transformation in the significance of FDI to investment in the UK economy took place in the second half of the 1980s. In contrast, inward and outward FDI as a proportion of gross fixed capital in Germany exceeded 10% for the first time only in 1997 and in Japan has never exceeded the level of the second half of the 1980s – remaining at less than 2% for most of the 1990s.

Focusing specifically on manufacturing FDI, the role of inward FDI increases in weight. Table 9.13 shows the contribution of foreign owned enterprises to output, investment and employment in the UK manufacturing industry.

In 1963, foreign companies played a relatively small, role in British manufacturing. Over the next 25 years, though, the proportion of output, investment and employment accounted for by foreign companies roughly doubled, and by the mid-1990s foreign companies accounted for one-quarter of manufacturing output, one-third of

Table 9.12   UK, German and Japanese FDI flows as a % gross fixed capital, 1986–97

Country		1986–91 average	1992	1993	1994	1995	1997
UK:	Inward flows	13.6	9.8	10.9	6.1	11.9	18.6
	Outward flows	17.1	11.6	19.0	22.2	25.9	32.0
Germany:	Inward flows	1.1	0.6	–	1.6	2.3	2.3
	Outward flows	6.1	4.3	4.1	4.2	7.5	9.5
Japan:	Inward flows	–	0.2	–	–	–	0.3
	Outward flows	4.0	1.5	1.1	1.4	1.5	2.2

Sources: UNCTAD (1998, 1999).

Table 9.13   Role of foreign-owned firms in the UK
manufacturing economy, 1963–97

Year	Output	Investment	Employment
1963	10	13	7
1987	20	21	15
1994	24	32	18
1995	26	33	17
1997	26	33	17

Sources: Jones (1990: 194); HMSO (1995b); IBB (1995a, 1998);
ONS (1999b).

investment and one-sixth of manufacturing jobs in the UK economy. However, most illustrative of the significance of FDI is its contribution to exports; in 1994, 40% of UK manufacturing exports were attributed to foreign companies (HMSO, 1997: 30).

The increasing significance of foreign companies in the 1980s was due not only to the expansion of inward FDI, but also to the collapse of the local manufacturing sector. In the 1980s, UK manufacturing employment halved, with the loss of over one million jobs, while foreign companies experienced employment growth of 3%. By the end of 1995, 750,000 jobs were provided for in the UK economy as a whole by foreign companies, with over 600,000 created in the last decade (Cooke *et al.*, 1995: 112; HMSO, 1997: 30).

However, the employment in foreign companies varies considerably according to the manufacturing sector. Table 9.14 shows the top eight manufacturing sectors for FDI in terms of employment in foreign companies. The leading sector is motor vehicles, where 130,000 people, or 52% of the UK total, and 73% of output is accounted for by foreign firms. The most penetrated sector is office machinery and computers, where over 50% of UK employment and three quarters of output was controlled by foreign firms in 1997. In fact, by the mid-1990s almost three quarters of all computers manufactured in UK were made by foreign companies (Jones, 1997: 116). Other leading sectors in terms of employment in foreign companies are chemicals and machinery equipment.

The role of FDI in the UK economy also varies according to nationality of the foreign company. As we would expect from our analysis of the main sources of FDI in the UK, Table 9.15 shows that the US accounts for over half of the gross output and value added

Table 9.14   Top 8 FDI sectors in terms of employment
in foreign companies, 1997

Sector	No. of firms	Employment (000s)		Gross output (£m)	
		Total	% of UK	Total	% of UK
Manufacture of motor vehicles, trailers and semi-trailers	113	130.3	52.0	28,236.8	73.1
Manufacture of chemicals and products	270	90.0	33.4	18,468.6	39.8
Manufacture of machinery equipment not elsewhere classified	373	86.5	21.4	10,354.3	28.3
Manufacture of radio, TV, and communication equipment and apparatus	112	58.4	41.0	10,873.7	15.3
Manufacture of food products and beverages	127	57.5	11.8	12,126.2	18.1
Manufacture of rubber and plastic products	164	38.9	14.6	4,035.4	20.2
Manufacture of electrical machinery and apparatus not elsewhere classified	154	37.3	18.9	3,240.0	23.0
Manufacture of office machinery, machinery and computers	42	31.7	50.5	12,046.4	77.4

Source: derived from ONS (1999b).

of foreign companies in the UK and for nearly half of employment and capital expenditure. US companies play a greater role in the UK economy than EU companies by most measures. Japanese and German companies have the greatest weight in the UK economy after the US. By 1998 there were 4,200 US firms, 1,000 Japanese firms, 1,600 German firms and 1,300 French firms in the UK (Valery, 1992; Marsh, 1995; IBB, 1998).

The overall picture is clear: FDI plays a pervasive role in the UK economy. With inward and outward FDI accounting for over half of GDP, the UK is more dependent on FDI than all the other major developed economies in the world. The dependence on foreign companies is amplified in manufacturing and in certain key sectors, in particular in automotive and office equipment and computing, two of

Table 9.15   Role of foreign enterprises in the UK economy
by nationality, 1997 (£m)

Private sector enterprise groups	Employment (000s)	Gross output	Gross value added at basic prices	Net capital expenditure
USA	331.8	78,051.3	19,075.9	3,126.0
Germany	83.9	11,177.7	2,574.2	817.9
Japan	61.6	10,460.7	2,375.7	913.1
France	49.9	9,154.0	2,323.2	261.4
Switzerland	37.3	5,655.4	2,201.7	271.7
Netherlands	36.7	4,248.0	1,497.9	145.4
Canada	34.6	5,378.4	1,681.2	244.2
Sweden	22.9	3,412.4	864.2	110.3
Total EU (14)	250.3	37,654.9	9,269.4	1,685.6
Total all foreign enterprises in UK	745.8	141,732.8	36,171.6	6,501.6
Total all enterprises in UK	4,274.7	449,819.1	143,564.8	19,652.0

Source: ONS (1999b).

the UK biggest export sectors. We also saw in chapter four that one-third of UK manufacturing R&D is accounted for by foreign companies and that over 80% of UK patents are by foreign residents. In manufacturing, the UK depends on foreign companies for technology generation and innovation even more than for employment, output, and investment.

9.2   THE FDI POLICY OF THE UK: THE LAST 70 YEARS

According to the Invest in Britain Bureau, in the mid-1990s the UK accounted for over 40% of Japanese FDI, almost 40% of US FDI, around 50% of South Korean FDI, and 18% of German FDI in the EU (IBB, 1998). However, the British economy is smaller than France's and only 60% the size of Germany's. Key questions, as noted in the introduction to this study, are why the UK attracts a disproportionate share of FDI and, furthermore, what are the implications for economic development? In this section we examine the UK political economy and industrial policy, which sets the context within which foreign companies invest. As Lord (1996: 226) notes,

'It would be naive to claim that the flow of FDI to Britain has not in part been policy-directed.'

In our discussion of government–MNC relations in Chapters 5 and 6, we also saw how government industrial policy and the institutional organisation of the FDI policy making and implementation apparatus are major factors determining the outcome of bargaining between governments and MNCs. The following discussion reviews UK FDI policy and its institutional organisation, highlighting key aspects of UK industrial policy which influence bargaining with multinationals.

We argue that UK policy has been one of continuity, with openness to inward investment. The policy debate over inward investment has changed, though, from one of questioning the benefits of FDI, and hence calling for some regulation of MNCs, to an aggressive policy stance designed explicitly to attract foreign firms, with the government assuming unequivocal benefits deriving from inward FDI. This change is in part an outcome of structural changes in the international political economy and is common to most states, as argued in Chapter 5, but the lack of regulation over foreign MNCs is an outcome specific to the evolution of the UK political economy.

When discussing the relationship between the UK government and foreign MNCs, four features of the UK political economy stand out as having had a major impact on the role of FDI in industrial policy:

- symmetry of FDI flows;
- ideology of the Conservative government;
- influence of the City;
- role of the military.

The first factor, symmetry, has underpinned Britain's open policy to foreign MNC for most of the 20th century, but was more important in the pre-1979 period when overall industrial policy was more interventionist and when there was a greater consensus that inward FDI should be regulated. The second factor, ideology, heightened the significance attached to attracting FDI as a market-friendly policy. The third and fourth factors, the City and the military, have had a broadly similar long term impact on the UK economy – reducing the alternatives to attracting FDI and influencing the quality of inward investment. British FDI policy has therefore emerged as an outcome of the interaction between the evolving *domestic* political economy and structural changes in the *international* political economy.

9.2.1 Policy indifference: the pre-1979 period

Jones (1990, 1996b) argues that historically UK MNC policy has been a non-policy, with subsequent governments sustaining a tradition of open policies. However, the issue of FDI was a subject of serious deliberation in 1929. Bailey *et al.* (1994: 151) argue that Britain's MNC policy has been one of continuity since this date.

Three explicit points emerged from 1929, a debate which took place because of US complaints about discrimination in share-holdings:

- *Fear that some industries may locate all of their R&D in the US*: this relates to the FDI activities of UK MNCs, and the fear was not without justification. We have seen (Table 4.8) that UK MNCs conduct the highest proportion of their patenting activities outside of their home base when compared to 13 of the world's leading innovating economies. In fact, well over half of the patenting activities of UK MNCs are conducted outside of the UK.
- *The growth of inward investment was presumed beneficial*: before 1939 Britain was the world's largest multinational investor, accounting for 45% of the accumulated stock of outward FDI in 1914 (Jones, 1997: 107). At the onset of the Second World War there were already 233 American enterprises operating in Britain (Dicken, 1990a: 163). In terms of the Rugman and Verbeke (1998) model, discussed in Chapter 6, the UK economy was characterised by a high degree of *symmetry* (Clegg, 1996a), favouring an open policy to inward and outward FDI. Jones (1990: 197) cites the 1929 debate concluding that restrictions on inward investment were highly risky because of the 'possibility of retribution by foreign countries and of its serious effect for the UK as a large investor in foreign activities'. Inward and outward FDI was largely presumed to be beneficial.
- *Key or strategic industries (finance, defence and related industries) should not fall under foreign control*: this was particularly emphasised by the British Military service (Jones, 1990: 198). It was not until the late 1970s that government ownership of key strategic industries was discredited in the UK both ideologically and in practice. A government environment permitting foreign ownership of 'British' national champions has been a pre-condition for the large proportion of FDI in the UK that flows in the form of M&As.

Before the Second World War, FDI policy was therefore broadly liberal, with any regulation associated with concerns over the activities of MNCs watered down by a high degree of symmetry. After the Second World War the debate over FDI continued, starting with the Treasury in 1945, who suggested that any manufacturing company in Britain should have a majority British shareholding. The reason was that Britain's balance of payments situation was of major concern and while inward manufacturing FDI was seen as positive in terms of employment, the Treasury questioned whether there would be unambiguous gain for the British balance of payments. This proposal, however, was dropped primarily due to Britain's high degree of FDI symmetry, and additionally because of the possibility of technology transfer and competitive stimulus to local firms, which was identified in late 1940s as potentially positive impacts of inward FDI (Jones, 1990: 198–9).

The payments situation finally led Britain to introduce extensive exchange controls, with the key legislation the Exchange Control Act of 1947, which remained in operation until 1979. The importance of the balance of payments was accentuated by the Bretton Woods exchange rate system, with Sterling set at a fixed rate. Foreign exchange reserves were of overriding concern, at least until Sterling was forced out of the system in 1967. The 1947 Act required Treasury permission for almost any financial transaction involving non-residents or for the import of capital for greenfield investments or acquisitions. However, acquisitions on the stock market were exempt from restrictions, which indicates the influence of the City of London.

Through this Act, the Treasury gained control over FDI policy with the main regulation that the foreign currency inflow had to be equal to the degree of control by the foreign MNC (e.g. 100% control implies 100% external finance). Exceptions were made if particular advantages were apparent, such as a plant in a high unemployment area, and with the balance of payments constraint, export-oriented FDI with 100% local content was particularly welcomed.

However, the Act provided no systematic review mechanism to ensure that the inward investor satisfied government requirements and there was no sanction if these were not met, in contrast to the case in other countries like France (Behrman and Grosse, 1990: 166–79; Sugden, 1990a: 217; Michalet, 1997: 319–20). In practice, obstacles to inward investment were very few and policy was liberal, with no concern for ownership (Bailey *et al.*, 1994: 151–4). The government would only restrict the activities of MNCs if there was no risk of jeopardising the investment (Jones, 1990).

Once established in Britain, foreign companies were treated by the government almost exactly as if they were indigenous firms. Existing restrictions were removed during the 1950s, with, for example, repatriation of funds allowed in 1950 and from 1954 rather than having to demonstrate the investment was advantageous, investors had only to show that their proposed investment was not 'positively disadvantageous'. In 1955, local borrowing was also allowed (Jones, 1990: 201). According to Jones (1990: 201): 'Control remained vague and official attitudes were softened.'

The policy of the UK government up until the late 1970s can be described as 'benign neglect' (Barberis and May, 1993: 58–59), with restrictions placed on inward investors progressively reduced, no enforced investment screening and monitoring, and no pro-active government effort to attract inward investment either. Indifference to foreign MNCs seems to capture UK government attitude and policy.

Even with a new incumbent labour government in 1964, which favoured national industry, policies towards investment did not change significantly with an underlying assumption of a net benefit derived from inward investment (Bailey *et al.*, 1994: 155). In part, this was due to the high productivity, better export performance and perceived technological and managerial expertise of foreign MNCs (Dunning, 1958), and there was no scrutinising machinery anyway, with diffused responsibility throughout government (Bailey *et al.*, 1994: 156–7). In the early 1970s, despite the Labour government being motivated by trade unions and public concern to re-evaluate its relaxed policy, the weak British economy meant new, especially job-creating, export-oriented FDI was highly valued. Fear of retaliation was again a major factor constraining any restrictions on inward investment.

The most visible change in government policy relating to FDI was not so much in terms of regulatory policy but rather of organisation. The institutional structure for decision-making inherited in the post-war period remained complex and fragmented, with a prospective investor having to secure up to six official consents and approvals from different departments and agencies (Jones, 1990: 200–1). In response to pressure from the US government and MNCs, the Board of Trade took responsibility for co-ordinating official negotiations with foreign companies. A further institutional shuffle was initiated by the incumbent Labour government of 1974, in an attempt to counter the diffusion of responsibility for FDI by centralising policy in the new Department of Industry (Bailey *et al.*, 1994: 161–6; Sugden, 1990a: 216). As we argued in Chapter 6, a centralised government agency is most likely to reduce inter-governmental conflicts and be better placed to attract inward investment and negotiate with investors. In 1977 the Invest in Britain Bureau was set up as a single agency to attract foreign direct investment and facilitate the investment process for foreign companies.

According to Dicken and Tickell (1992: 100), the IBB was established 'largely as a response to criticisms that the UK's mechanism for promoting and processing inward investment projects was excessively fragmented'. The centralisation of decision-making can be seen as an attempt to increase the ability of the government to bargain for inward investment. However, centralising FDI policy under one departmental umbrella was not so much about giving the government greater ability to bargain for concessions from multinationals, but rather centralisation was intended to facilitate a faster approval of inward investment cases and reduce red-tape. Centralisation was a move to attract FDI not regulate MNCs more effectively. However, the Labour government did introduce the 1975 Industry Act which gave the relevant Ministry power to prevent any important manufacturing firm from falling under foreign control if this served the national interest. The potential significance for inward FDI of this Act has, however, remained unexploited (Sugden, 1990a: 216–17). With a new government in 1979, and the (associated) collapse in manufacturing, the emphasis on attracting FDI was heightened.

9.2.2 Policy inducement: 1979–2000

The ideology of the Conservative government, in power from 1979 to 1997, was based on the neo-liberal paradigm, which generated hostility towards state intervention. Given this hostility, 'inward investment offered the Thatcher governments a primarily market-led solution to the problem of how to re-enter lost export markets and improve the UK's trade performance' (Lee, 1996: 55).

With the incoming Conservative government of 1979, all remaining exchange control legislation was swept away (Bailey *et al.*, 1994: 170). Patrick Jenkin, the Secretary of State for Industry speaking in 1982, stated the official policy as:

This government, like its predecessors, welcomes inward investment into the UK. Since the lifting of exchange controls in 1979, non-residents have needed no official permission to invest in this country other than those, such as planning consent, which are required of all investors. Foreign investors are assured of receiving equal treatment with their UK counterparts and are eligible for the full range of incentives and benefits provided to investors generally (cited in Cowling and Sugden, 1987: 216).

It was hoped that deregulation would improve the position of the UK relative to other locations for inward investment, and this policy was therefore consistent with the largely non-interventionist policy stance towards foreign investors taken by previous administrations. MNC policy was based on the presumption that inward FDI is unequivocally beneficial to the UK (Safarian, 1993: 340).

The removal of exchange controls was the beginning of the Conservative government's boosted emphasis in attracting inward FDI. In 1982, the importance attached to the role of FDI was explained by the Secretary of State for Industry:

> The government is committed to maintaining and strengthening the operation of market forces in order to improve the country's economic performance. A free flow of inward investment contributes to this central policy by introducing additional productive capacity to compete with established sources in the UK and with imports, as well as to raise exports. Such investment, often bringing new technological skills and managerial expertise, thus tends to increase both the quality and quantity of output and employment in this country (cited in Brech and Sharp, 1984: 19–20).

In the same incumbent party's 1994 Competitiveness White Paper, government industrial policy was to have no strategic intervention in the activities of firms: 'The central thrust of the government's policy for industry should be to maintain and enhance the attractiveness of the UK as a location for manufacturing and other industrial activities' (HMSO, 1994b: 32).

The UK's industrial policy was therefore, in theory, in accordance with the policy prescription of Porter, Reich and Nicolaides, as discussed in Chapter 5, with policy based on upgrading location advantages rather than providing discriminatory support to firms. However, in practice:

- The government's policy tool to 'maintain and enhance the attractiveness of the UK' was not improving the quality of the supply side. The major policy tool was in fact a heightened emphasis on investment promotion activities. The IBB was given increased resources for marketing, and for establishing overseas offices to generate leads, as well as to handle cases. The increased support for inward investment was replicated in RDOs at the sub-national level. Generous financial inducements were also used to attract investment to particular regions and compete with other countries.

- The UK government, through the central role given to attracting FDI in the activities of the IBB and RDOs and the criteria for awarding financial incentives, discriminated against indigenous firms.

The UK government therefore favoured inward investment over domestic investment and relied on incentives explicitly targeted to persuade inward investors to establish operations in poorer regions. Through an industrial policy formulated to favour particular (foreign) companies and influence the location of inward investment in the UK, the government implicitly influenced the strategic orientation of the economy towards an exogenous-led developmental path.

The UK government thought that attracting inward investment would lead to spin-offs for the wider economy through the market mechanism, and that there was no need for a systematic strategy to link inward investment to the competitiveness of local industry. In the 1990s, the perceived contribution attributed to inward FDI by the government was broadened to include not only new technology, management, and output and employment but also the positive impact on local suppliers:

> Inward investment brings world class production techniques, technological innovation and managerial skills, which can be transferred to local companies. It has revived the international competitiveness of some sectors of UK industry, such as vehicles.... Inward investment can also bring spin-off benefits to suppliers. It can provide new markets and help them to improve quality and expand their product range so that they can compete more efficiently in world markets. It raises skill levels in the work force and brings new jobs (HMSO, 1994b: 94).

The UK government therefore thought that market forces would lead to the integration of inward investment with local industry, and in the following year's 1995 Competitiveness White Paper, the spin-offs to local suppliers were spelt out more precisely, with inward investment having:

> a positive impact on the performance and competitiveness of UK suppliers, particularly on their production processes, including quality assurance systems, plant and machinery, delivery times and cost control methods. Product development is also strengthened. Inward investors stimulate UK exports (HMSO, 1995a: 161).

The UK government's industrial policy has therefore centred on the maintenance of a favourable environment characterised by privatisation, deregulation, and investment incentives to attract inward investment to poorer regions in the milieu of competitive bidding between states.

This investor friendly policy was endorsed in the Conservative government's last Competitiveness White Paper, which focused solely on FDI. The DTI outlined that:

> The government's policy is to encourage both inward and outward investment. It is committed to creating an attractive climate for investment in the UK. The most successful companies in all countries have high productivity, high levels of investment and strong growth, and often invest overseas (HMSO, 1996: 1).

The benign approach that had been characteristic of previous UK governments became overt in terms of the commitment in policy and practice to attracting new investment. As well as having a long-standing 'national treatment' policy with virtually non-existent restrictions on FDI, no government agency monitoring FDI activity, and no reporting requirements for foreign investors different from those required of domestic investors (Hamill *et al.*, 1988: 208), government agencies at the central and regional levels have aggressively promoted inward investment. UK industrial policy has favoured foreign over domestic firms and, as our bargaining model analysis in Chapter 6 indicates, the high commitment of the UK government to foreign companies is likely to be a key factor behind the dis-proportionate share of European FDI in the UK.

We also argued in Chapter 6 that governments wishing to attract inward investment should establish a centralised agency, and in this respect the role of the IBB has been important. The IBB is charged with attracting FDI, acting as a centralised agency to promote the

UK globally as an investment location, operating primarily through the Foreign Office's network of embassies, high commissions and consulates (Dicken and Tickell, 1992: 100). The IBB is jointly owned by the DTI and foreign office, following a tie-up with the foreign offices in 1997. According to Chris Fraser, former head of the IBB's Asia-Pacific operation, 'its major role is to sell the UK in competition with other European neighbours as a leading base for European investment....It is organised on a geographical desk basis and is in charge of marketing and case handling' (Fraser, 1998).[2]

The IBB's case handling remit was widened under the Conservative government, with the centralised investment agency given powers and responsibility for co-ordinating the promotional activities of the network of territorial regional development agencies and English regional promotional agencies (IBB, 1995a: 5). Regional agencies, as we discuss in Chapter 10, have adopted central government's emphasis on attracting FDI, which has further increased the significance of the IBB. The IBB therefore stands at the apex of a hierarchical institutional structure of inward investment promotion (Cox and Wood, 1994: 640).

However, the IBB has faced difficulty in containing regional rivalries for inward investment (Cassell, 1995) and, according to Hamill *et al.* (1988: 204), the 'pattern of institutions involved remains complex'. In 1995, nearly 20 years after its establishment, the IBB was still only '*aiming* to introduce a nationally co-ordinated programme' (HMSO, 1995b: 13, emphasis added), and Dicken (1990a: 172–5) argues that for the promotion of UK as base for FDI there is:

> a *confusion* of institutions and agencies which variously compete and collaborate with each other in both a vertical and horizontal dimension....The notion that such competitive bidding is, to any large extent, co-ordinated is wishful thinking.

We can conclude that a policy of aggressively attracting of FDI has underpinned UK industrial policy since 1979, and the new incumbent Labour government appears to share the previous governments commitment to attracting inward FDI and unequivocal belief in the benefits of FDI. As the Labour government's first Competitiveness White Paper states, 'Over the last decade, FDI has not only created over 600,000 jobs but has helped to develop and modernise the industrial base' (HMSO, 1997: 30). British industrial policy has been based on forging a market-led, *exogenous* path to economic development, with no central policy to link inward investment to the performance of local industry.

9.3 INDUSTRIAL POLICY, THE NATIONAL INNOVATION SYSTEM AND INWARD INVESTMENT

In defining industrial policy, most commentators have opted for a general, all-encompassing definition, viewing industrial policy as 'all those microeconomic policies which impact on industrial performance' (Arestis and Sawyer, 1997: 1). A more useful interpretation, however, is provided by Pitelis (1997: 21), who defines industrial policy as 'the government policies intended to affect industry directly and specifically towards achieving a particular objective'.

In most countries, industrial policy is strongly directed toward regional development (Blais, 1986) with main objectives often job creation in high unemployment regions and preferential policies to assist the catch-up of peripheral regions. At the same time, the treatment of foreign capital one of the major issues in industrial policy (Blais, 1986). The UK government has attempted to combine these two dimensions of industrial policy, attracting FDI to peripheral regions through a discriminatory aid regime, with subsidies for inward investment in Assisted Areas. The principal component of industrial policy in the UK has been attracting inward investment, with the key objective job creation in peripheral regions.

Industrial policy can be contrasted with industrial strategy as the former is specific to a particular objective, such as job creation in depressed areas, while the latter is concerned with the government anticipating and making strategic choices for *future* industrial development (Krauss, 1992: 312). One is reactive while the other is pro-active. Pitelis (1997: 21–2) thus defines industrial strategy:

> as the existence, or otherwise, of a well-thought out and reasonably consistent and coherent set of industrial policies (along with the required resources and mechanisms for implementation) which aim at the realisation of a long-term objective concerning industry in particular and, through it, the nation more generally.

Industrial strategy can therefore be seen 'as a broad economy wide program intended to reorient the entire economy' (Adams, 1985: 5), and while almost all countries have some kind of industrial policy, not all have an industrial strategy.

The industrial activities of the UK government have historically been oriented to short-term industrial policies rather than long-term strategies for re-organisation of the economy. Hall (1986: 252) argues that, 'The British state simply lacked the means with which to enforce an active policy of sectoral reorganisation, even if it could have formulated one.' Under the Conservative government, industrial policy shifted from supporting declining industries to market-led policies, including privatisation, deregulation, leveraging private investment, and attracting FDI. In fact, the Conservative government publicly rejected an industrial strategy with Michael Heseltine, former deputy Prime Minister, describing strategy as a 'non-word'.

The lack of an explicit industrial strategy in the UK and the emphasis of industrial policy on inward investment are closely related to the role of the City of London and the Military. They have had a major influence on the UK political economy, affecting the investment climate and the quantity and quality of domestic and foreign investment. We argue that the role of the City and the military in the UK has weakened the British manufacturing industry through their negative influence on the UK's financial and R&D system – key elements in national and regional innovation systems. This has left UK policy makers with less alternatives to the attraction of FDI as the major component of industrial policy.

9.3.1 Productivity deficits and the City

The financial community in the City of London and the stock market more generally have had an enormous impact on the UK economy, favouring market liberalisation, non-discrimination and non-intervention.[3] The UK was one of the first countries to create freely operating money and capital markets with no exchange controls, no limits on profit remittances, royalties, interest payments, or other international financial flows (Behrman and Grosse, 1990: 130). This was not only part of the government's commitment to ensure London as the world's premier financial capital but was also a policy to entice inward manufacturing investment.

With the failure of previous national champions' policy and the together with the Conservative government's neo-liberal ideology, emphasis in Britain shifted towards privatisation and deregulation since no government-led industrial strategy seemed feasible. The deregulation of finance and privatisation has also facilitated cross-border mergers and take-overs, increasing FDI. The growth of M&As intensified the argument made in the Chapter 5 that: 'For internationally dispersed companies, the nationality of ownership does not coincide with the nationality of output.... As foreign companies become global, so do domestic firms making discrimination difficult' (Nicolaides and Thomsen, 1991: 110–11).

However, the influence of finance capital on the UK economy is much more far-reaching. It is widely argued that the financial system has engendered short-termism throughout British industry (Walker, 1993; RSA, 1995; Hutton, 1996). The corporate governance system is dominated by shareholders, with public companies in the UK representing over 80% of GDP, compared to 59% in USA, and 23% in Germany. The threat of hostile take-overs force management to satisfy current shareholders rather than secure the long-term health of the enterprise. A government study found that 90% of finance directors of major British companies believed, 'City institutions are excessively preoccupied with short-term earnings' (House of Commons, 1994, cited in Cooke and Morgan, 1998: 136).

Emphasis on short-term earnings is a major factor behind the weakness of the UK manufacturing economy, with the UK financial sector often criticised for a lack of loyalty on the part of institutional investors to incumbent management in take-overs. Hostile take-overs, aimed at short-term profit, have inhibited investment in fixed capital, skills and R&D (Smith, 1993: 477), and UK multinationals have favoured a finance-driven decentralised organisational form, unlikely to promote sustained innovative capacity (Jones, 1997: 125). The UK has suffered from a productivity and innovation deficit. In the words of the British government:

> We have invested too little in modern plant and machinery, as well as research and development and other intangible assets. Skill levels, including marketing and design skills, are too low across too much of the workforce (HMSO, 1998a).

Looking at Table 9.16 we can see the UK has lagged behind the other G-5 economies in the rate of growth of fixed capital stock, and the gap has widened since the mid-1980s.

Therefore, although the UK recorded a fast rate of productivity growth in manufacturing in the second half of the 1980s (Table 9.17), slower growth in capital investment has limited long term

Table 9.16 Rate of growth of fixed capital stock, 1950–96

	Germany	UK	France	US	Japan
1950–73	5.35	3.28	3.62	3.38	7.98
1973–84	3.39	2.51	4.0	2.79	3.41
1984–96	3.1	2.2	1.5	4.0	4.7

Source: Loewendahl and Hölscher (2001).

Table 9.17 Manufacturing output and output per hour, 1979–98

	1979–98		1979–85		1985–90		1990–98	
	Output	Output per hour	Output	Output per hour	Output	Output per hour	Output	Output per hour
US	2.7	3.1	2.0	3.3	2.2	2.2	3.5	3.4
Japan	3.1	3.5	4.7	3.5	4.8	4.3	0.9	2.9
France	1.3	3.5	−0.4	3.0	2.6	3.4	1.8	3.3
Germany	0.8	2.6	0.2	2.1	2.3	2.2	0.2	3.2
Italy	2.2	3.3	1.7	4.9	3.9	2.5	1.5	2.6
UK	0.8	3.3	−1.2	4.1	3.4	4.1	0.6	2.2
South Korea	8.7	–	8.8	–	13.2	–	5.9	–

Source: BLS (2000).

manufacturing productivity growth in the UK. In fact, as the rate of growth in the UK capital stock fell in the 1990s so has output per hour in manufacturing, which was the lowest in the G-6 from 1990 to 1998. The overall growth in manufacturing output was the joint lowest in the G-6 (together with Germany) from 1979 to 1998.

With lower levels of capital available per worker, absolute levels of labour productivity in the UK are far below its major competitors, and wages are rising much faster than productivity in manufacturing. In fact, Table 9.18 shows UK manufacturing labour productivity is only around half of the US level, while wages are almost 90% of US levels. Only Germany out of the major economies has a wider differential between labour productivity and compensation relative to the US. The contrast with South Korea is particularly stark. Labour productivity in South Korea is only 12% lower than the UK, while compensation per employee is 62% lower.

Table 9.18 Compensation and value added per employee in manufacturing, 1973–98

	1970s		1980s		1998	
	Compensation 1975	*Value added 1973*	*Compensation 1987*	*Value added 1985*	*Compensation*	*Value added*
US	100	100	100	100	100	100
Japan	47	55	49	76	97	79
France	71	68	58	71	98	76
Germany	99	76	73	70	151	68
Netherlands	67	79	140	83	111	80
UK	53	51	48	54	89	53*
South Korea	5	15	9	27	27	41*

*1996.
Sources: BLS (2000); GGDC (2000).

Crucially, UK productivity growth in the 1980s was not investment or output led, but was associated with the shedding of labour – 2.1 million manufacturing jobs were lost from 1979 to 1989 (Jones, 1997: 115) – the scrapping of inefficient plants, and improved management of remaining productive assets (Walker, 1993: 170). As the OECD argues:

> Stronger labour productivity growth has not been linked to capital investment.... Rather it seems linked to changes in work organisation with inflexible and outdated job demarcation giving way to more rational job allocation (1988, cited in Tomaney, 1990: 45–6).

9.3.2   Innovation deficits, the City and the military

As productivity levels improved in the 1980s, firm dividends increased as a proportion of post-tax profits, but at the same time companies reduced their layouts on R&D (Office of Science and Technology, 1995, cited in Cooke and Morgan, 1998: 136). The key reason is outlined by Walker (1993: 171):

> the increased surplus profits generated by higher productivity has tended to be absorbed by higher dividend and interest payments, and by higher taxes, or has been put aside to raise money earnings, or to engage in company purchases.

The role of finance capital is therefore one of the major factors behind the innovation as well as productivity gap between the UK and other economies. Figure 9.3 shows R&D expenditure for the G-5 and South Korea from 1960 to 1996. The UK spends relatively less on R&D than all the other major economies, and the weight of R&D in the UK economy has fallen over the period 1960–98. In 1960, the UK had the second highest R&D as a proportion of GDP, but by the mid-1980s the UK had the lowest R&D in the G-5 countries. In the early 1990s, South Korean R&D surpassed UK levels. Since the mid-1980s the gap between the UK and its major competitors has continued to widen.

As discussed in Chapter 2, R&D underpins both MNC and country competitiveness. However, per capita expenditure on R&D in the UK is also less than any other of the major economies. In 1996 the US spent two times more than the US$362 per capita spent on R&D in the UK, and in 1996 South Korea exceeded UK expenditure (derived from OECD, 1998b).

Britain is the only country where the long term growth in R&D expenditure has been lower than GDP growth (Walker, 1993: 172), which is also true in terms of business expenditure on R&D (Temple, 1999). For example, a recent DTI-sponsored survey of the world's top 300 international companies found that aggregate R&D averaged 4.6% sales, but for UK companies 2.5% – the second lowest after Italian

Figure 9.3   R&D expenditure as a percentage of GDP, 1960–98

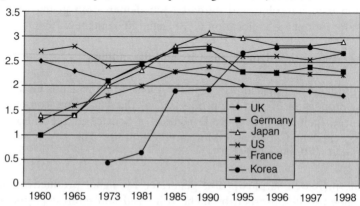

Sources: OECD (1987, 1989, 1998b); Odagiri and Goto (1993); Mowery and Oxley (1995); Chandler and Hikino (1997); IMD (1999, 2000).

MNCs (*The Economist*, 1999d). However, while Italian R&D as a proportion of GDP is lower than the UK, from 1973 to 1992 the Italian manufacturing industry experienced a growth of R&D intensity above every G-5 economy, with Japan having the second highest growth (Temple, 1999). In fact, according to Cooke and Morgan (1998: 137):

> the combined R&D expenditure of just five Japanese companies – Hitachi, Toyota, Matsushita, NEC, and Fujitsu – equals the entire R&D spending of the UK private sector.

The low R&D intensity of UK industry is not only a function of the role that finance capital plays in the UK economy, but is also one of the costs of heavy government spending on defence technology. Edgerton (1991) convincingly argues that the efforts of the Military Ministries and agencies dwarf that of the civil one in science and industrial policy. Britain's defence R&D out of all the major developed countries accounts for the highest proportion of government R&D – over 50% from 1976 to 1981. By the 1990s, the UK government was devoting over 60% of its R&D expenditure to defence and the related aerospace industry (Lee, 1997: 5). More recent data from the OECD (1998b) shows that in 1996, 38% of UK government R&D expenditure was on defence, compared to 30% in France, 10% in Germany, and only 6% in Japan.

As well as channelling government resources away from supporting civilian R&D, Walker (1993) notes three further costs of high defence expenditure:

- High opportunity costs, especially as the UK has a weak skills base.
- Little spin-offs into the civil sector – unlike in France or the US there is no requirement that military technologies should be exploited for commercial advantage.
- A protected defence market lures large firms away from more risky and competitive civilian activities.

According to the UK government, the poor performance in manufacturing of the UK relative and other countries like Germany is due to low R&D and poor productivity (HMSO, 1998a). Smith (1993: 477) argues that 'there are some signs that the UK industry is entering a spiral of decline, arising out of a lack of innovation'. British manufacturing has not been able to compete on the international market.

A key statistic is that from the early 1970s to the early 1990s, UK manufacturing output remained virtually static, compared to increases of 27% in France, 25% in Germany, 85% in Italy and 119% in Japan (Cooke and Morgan, 1998: 135). Furthermore, Edgerton (1991: 164) notes that while the manufacturing industry lost market shares, in armaments Britain's world market share was maintained, increasing the relative importance of military production to the economy.

9.3.3 Implications for inward investment and industrial policy

With the stagnation of manufacturing industry, Walker (1993: 186) argues that, 'Thatcherism was an opportunistic response to failure of the past innovation system.' The policy rhetoric of Thatcher governments was to improve the attractiveness of the UK as a base for investment, with inward FDI seen as the main source of new investment. The emphasis on FDI of the UK government since 1979 can therefore in part be seen as an outcome of the failure of past industrial policies, which favoured the City and the military over the domestic manufacturing industry.

For example, in colour television manufacturing, Cawson *et al.* (1990) describe how in 1967 there were 10 manufacturers in the UK, 8 British and none Japanese, but by the end of the 1980s there were 11, none British but 8 Japanese. In the earlier part of this period, pressure from local industry caused the government to encourage joint ventures rather than greenfield inward investment in the consumer electronics industry. However, the joint ventures collapsed, indigenous industry was not spurred into competitiveness by the Japanese entrants, and combined with intra-EC competition for investment UK policy shifted. As Cawson *et al.* argue (1990: 244–6), 'once there was no indigenous industry to protect logically inward investment seemed good'. Therefore, while 'inward investment, the characteristic policy instrument of the Thatcher era, is frequently cited as a success story in relation to the attraction of electronics firms' (Pratt and Totterdill, 1992: 379), the weakness of indigenous manufacturing belies the success of inward FDI.

The UK government has more recently attempted to compensate for the negative impacts of finance capital and the military, and in doing so is adopting a more targeted industrial policy. In the 1990s, the DTI pinpointed four major sectors in which it hoped to generate business competitiveness in, due to a perceived UK comparative advantage in these sectors and because of their perceived importance for wider competitiveness: communication, computing, new materials and genetics. To advance their competitiveness the Conservative government distributed £6 billion annually to these sectors (IBB, 1995a: 15).

Technology Foresight was also launched in 1994 to promote better technology-transfer networks between government, industry and academia, prioritising 15 key sectors (Cooke and Morgan, 1998: 141). The main aim was to achieve a better allocation of resources through greater co-ordination across scientific and technological programmes, not necessarily enhance the size of technology the base itself (Temple, 1999). Technology Foresight was more pro-active than previous policy initiatives, attempting to identify the future of different industrial sectors in 5, 10 and 15 years' time. Foresight therefore potentially provides the beginnings of a sector-based strategy for the future reorientation of the economy and in North-East England, for example, there is a Regional Foresight Panel, which looks at the message of the national programme and is hoping to reorient local industry accordingly.

The incumbent Labour government, has placed a new emphasis on civilian innovation and SMEs, although attracting inward FDI still remains the key component of industrial policy. Innovation and knowledge were highlighted as central for the future of the UK economy in the government's 1998 Competitiveness White Paper, and SMEs were identified as the sector in need of most government support. Cooke and Morgan (1998: 150) argue that the weak R&D base and small population of SMEs with low capacity for innovation are the two key interrelated weaknesses facing the UK economy.[4] Box 9.1 compares the support for SMEs in the UK with Germany.

The UK government has identified finance capital as a key restraint for SMEs, with the risk-averse financial system making it extraordinarily difficult for SMEs to raise small loans for R&D in the £50,000–£150,000 range (Cooke, 1998a). For example, although venture capital per capita in UK is almost the same as in the US, just 16% is invested in high-tech firms (computer, biotech, electronics and communications sectors), compared to 71% in US (HMSO, 1998a). In 1999 and 2000 the government announced the introduction of several *ad hoc* programmes to support innovation, specifically in SMEs. New initiatives include:

- an extra £1.4 billion for science and engineering;
- an increase of 20% over the next three years in the DTI's innovation budget;

- financial incentives for universities to enhance interaction with business;
- help to a million SMEs to become proficient in information and communications technology;
- establishing a Small Business Service to improve the quality for business support for small businesses, possibly replacing Business Links;
- a new tax credit announced in the March 1999 budget for R&D in SMEs;
- £150 million Enterprise Fund to support SMEs with growth potential, including a joint scheme with six major financial institutions to provide new venture capital.

Box 9.1 Support for SMEs: a comparison of the UK and Germany

German support for SMEs has centred on three key pillars of the German economy:

- **A federal system**: The federal system in German, which is one of the most devolved in the world, has facilitated the development of a regional innovation system which provides comprehensive support to SMEs (Esser, 1988; Herrigel, 1993; Cooke and Morgan, 1998). As Danson (1995a), Hirst and Thomson (1995) and ERT (1998), among many others, argue, it is regional and Local Authorities which are best placed to develop the institutions to deal with the problems of SMEs. In contrast, in the UK central government has been unwilling to devolve strategic powers to the sub-national level, and it was only in 1999 that regional development agencies were established. There is still no elected tier of regional government in England.
- **A banking system attuned to the long-term needs of business**: Long term capital investment and R&D have been encouraged by the financial system in Germany for both large firms and SMEs. Through an alternative banking system and state support to compensate SMEs for the disadvantages of small scale in the credit market (see Bräuling, 1995, for the Eastern Länder), the banking system has been attuned to the needs of SMEs (Lane, 1995: 47–8). This contrasts with the UK, where

commercial banks are prohibited from taking shares in companies (Hall, 1986: 236) and SMEs suffer severe disadvantage in access to finance (Lane, 1995: 47–8). The corporate governance system in the UK has led managers to avoid long-term investment in capital, training and R&D and to the inadequate provision of finance for small firms (Woolcock *et al.*, 1991; Mayes and Hart, 1994; Woolcock, 1996). This is reinforced through the recruitment of accountants as managers. In the 1980s, Britain had 30 times more qualified accountants as Germany, and accountancy training was single most common qualification for British managers (Jones, 1997b: 127). By contrast, in the German chemical industry 95% of top and higher managers typically have German doctoral and professional titles (Lane, 1998: 476).

- **Coherent networking relations**: The close relationship between government, MNCs, SMEs, trade unions, employees, and banks, in the context of a federal system, has fostered the growth of collaborative, cohesive and participatory industrial policy networks at the local and national levels involving both private and public actors. By contrast, in the UK 'local networks, both with other firms, and with state agencies and intermediary organisations, are relatively underdeveloped' (Lane, 1998: 466).

The industrial policies of the UK government are crucial not only in attracting FDI but through initiatives supporting technology, SMEs, and education, they influence the diamond of competitive advantages in the national economy. As noted in Chapter 5, government policy influences the *quality* of inward FDI and contribution to the host economy.

For example, the emphasis of successive administrations on elite science, in part an outcome of the demands of the defence industry, has established the UK as a world centre of excellence in chemicals, pharmaceuticals and military electronics. In the pharmaceutical and related industry, R&D expenditure accounted for over one-quarter of sales in 1996, and the R&D intensity of the industry is higher than all the other major economies (Tarabusi and Vickery, 1996; ONS, 1998b). On the other hand, Britain's has a major weakness in engineering and vocational skills (Walker, 1993). For example, Table 9.19 shows that Germany has almost 40% more science and engineering students as

Table 9.19   Science and technology human infrastructure, 1987–97

	Scientists and engineers in R&D per million people	Technicians in R&D per million people	Science and engineering students as a per cent of total tertiary students
Australia	3,357	797	24
Belgium	2,272	2,201	41
Canada	2,719	1,070	16
France	2,659	2,873	37
Germany	2,831	1,472	47
Ireland	2,319	506	31
Japan	4,909	827	21
Netherlands	2,219	1,358	39
Sweden	3,826	3,166	38
UK	**2,448**	**1,017**	**34**
US	3,676	–	19

Source: World Bank (2000b).

a proportion of total tertiary students than the UK. Japan has double the UK's number of scientists and engineers in R&D per million people, and the US, Sweden and Australia have over 50% more. In terms of technicians in R&D per million people, Belgium and France have over double the number of the UK and Sweden has over three times as many.

The UK's technological human infrastructure is much weaker than other developed countries, in particular its main European competitors like Germany, France and Sweden, which is reflected in much lower levels of overall R&D expenditure. There is growing evidence to suggest that the lack of government support for the UK's technological infrastructure has reduced the quality of FDI in the UK. For example, a 1991 survey found that over 70% of inward investors said that the UK had a shortage of graduate engineers (IBB, 1991), a major constraint to the growth of high value added manufacturing. The OECD (1996: 42) found that R&D as a share of production in foreign companies operating in the UK was only about 1%, only half the intensity of UK business as a whole. Data on US and German FDI in the UK also indicates that the UK has been less successful than competing locations in attracting R&D activities, and data on Japanese FDI shows that the R&D intensity of FDI has decreased over time.

For German foreign direct investment, Barrell *et al.* (1997) observe that there is little evidence of technology sourcing by German MNCs in the UK and a study by Papanastassiou and Pearce (1996) also found very little collaboration between MNCs and research laboratories in the UK. For the UK operations of US foreign affiliates, Table 9.20 shows that the UK is the most important location for US multinationals in terms of sales and employment. However, in terms of sales per employee and R&D intensity (R&D per employee), the UK performs below that of its key competitors for FDI.

Sales per employee in the UK were US$338,000 in 1996 – lower than the average of US$370,000 for Western Europe and less than half of the level of Singapore, Japan and Netherlands. In terms of R&D per employee, the UK performs even worse. R&D per employee in the UK is over one quarter below the European average, less than half the level of Germany and Japan, and less than one-third the R&D intensity in Israel. It is clear that the UK, while the most successful country in the world in terms of attracting US FDI, is not attractive for high value and R&D intensive activities. The UK's key competitors for FDI in Europe – Germany, France, Netherlands and Ireland – are all far more research intensive and, with the exception of France, appear to be attracting high value activities that generate higher sales per employee.

Table 9.20   Sales and R&D in US majority owned non-bank foreign affiliates, 1996

	Sales ($m)	*R&D ($m)*	*Employees (000s)*	*Sales/employee ($000s)*	*R&D/employee ($000s)*
Canada	231,044	1,582	826.6	279.5	1.91
Europe	1,044,697	9,651	2,825.9	369.7	3.42
France	125,164	1,326	410.2	305.1	3.23
Germany	195,221	3,061	556.4	350.9	5.50
Ireland	27,023	193	57.1	473.3	3.38
Netherlands	98,588	545	149.3	660.3	3.65
Spain	41,892	317	135.3	309.6	2.34
UK	**286,954**	**2,133**	**848.7**	**338.1**	**2.51**
Brazil	49,814	489	284.4	175.2	1.72
Israel	3,152	166	29.1	108.3	5.70
Australia	54,198	409	217.3	294.4	1.88
Japan	109,518	1,337	165.0	663.7	8.10
Singapore	72,593	88	99.2	731.8	0.89

Source: derived from BEA (1998).

If we look at number of Japanese design and R&D centres in the EU from 1990–95 (Table 9.21) it appears that the UK has been the most successful country in attracting Japanese R&D. By 1996, the UK had attracted over one-third of Japanese centres in the EU – the same proportion that the UK had attracted in 1990. This is despite the total number of Japanese design and R&D centres in the EU more than quadrupling over this period.

However, if we compare the UK's share of design and R&D centres with its share of the total stock of Japanese FDI in the EU a different picture emerges. By 1990 the UK had attracted 34.3% of Japanese centres in the EU and 31.9% of FDI. But by 1996 the UK's share of design and R&D centres was the same while its share of Japanese FDI had increased by 40% to almost half of the Japanese FDI stock in the EU. By comparison, Germany's share of design and R&D centres was double its share of Japanese FDI and France's share of design and R&D centres was 3.7 times higher than its share of FDI. Hence, while the UK has continued to attract R&D activities, Japanese FDI in the UK is becoming less R&D intensive over time and is far less R&D intensive when compared to Germany and France.

In accordance with Porter (1999), there is strong evidence suggesting that 'too many companies are using the UK as a low cost production site rather than a high value production site'.

The quality of inward FDI in the UK has been reduced by three main factors.

- Weakness in technological infrastructure and skills has negatively affected the supply side location advantages of the UK for high value and R&D intensive inward investment. A weak innovation system is, in turn, a major factor behind the high proportion of innovation undertaken by UK MNCs overseas.
- UK industrial policy has been biased *against* technology-intensive inward investment, with the key financial incentive for FDI based on jobs created not the quality of the investment, as we discuss in more detail in Chapter 10.
- R&D has remained for the most part concentrated in the home bases of MNCs. While globalisation and the emergence of the N-form MNC is leading to the dispersal of R&D activities, MNCs specialise in existing centres of excellence. Hence, the OECD (1996) found that out of the major economies only in the US do foreign companies have a R&D intensity higher than indigenous firms, reflecting the supply and demand side advantages

Table 9.21 Japanese design/R&D centres and FDI stock in Europe: 1990–95

Country	January 1990		January 1992		January 1994		End 1995	
	R&D	*FDI*	*R&D*	*FDI*	*R&D*	*FDI*	*R&D*	*FDI**
UK	34.3%	31.9%	38.1%	37.2%	33.2%	40.5%	34.3%	48.2%
Germany	20.0%	8.6%	20.1%	9.3%	20.1%	9.4%	21.4%	10.0%
France	14.3%	7.2%	15.3%	8.0%	13.6%	7.6%	13.2%	3.6%
Total centres/FDI in EU	70	$40bn	189	$62bn	201	$78bn	307	Y5tn

*1996 data (1995 not available).
Sources: Derived from EC (1998); Harukiyo (1998); OECD (2000).

of the US economy. Inward FDI in the UK has not been sufficient for technological advance.

While Technology Foresight and new initiatives to support innovation in SMEs should therefore be welcomed as positive measures to improve the technological supply-side infrastructure of the UK economy, what is needed is the integration of industrial, technology, education, and regional policy into a coherent strategy for the long term development of the UK economy. An *ad hoc* industrial policy based on attracting inward investment using the key carrots of government aid and labour flexibility does not fit well with the stated strategy of developing a knowledge-driven economy.

Even if the government developed a pro-active, integrated strategy for the future orientation of economy, in order to implement such as strategy 'a government must have capabilities to integrate and motivate the complex organisational structure of its country's political and economic institutions to take concerted action' (Lenway and Murtha, 1994a: 113).

Central government has been lacking in the these capabilities, which require co-ordinated, consensual and coherent industrial policy-making networks, between government, large and small firms, trade unions, and universities at both the central and regional levels within the context of an overall industrial strategy framework. Concerted action depends on trust, which has been eroded both within firms and government. In firms, share-holder capitalism and the anti-unionist policies of the Thatcher government have had the dual impact of reducing the commitment of firms to invest in fixed capital, in R&D and in their workforce and eroding the ability of workers to act as equal partners in adjusting to change. In government, the control exerted by central government and the transfer of power to non-elected bodies has led to a democratic deficit at the sub-national level, weakening the trust between public and private sector bodies at the regional level and between central and local government. In the next chapter we argue that without greater political autonomy passed down to the regional level, the trust and capability necessary for long term economic development policy is unlikely to emerge.

10 Inward Investment in the UK regions

In this chapter we follow a similar line of analysis to Chapter 9. First, we conduct an empirical overview of FDI in the UK regions, before examining the role of inward investment in industrial policy at the regional level. We find that while peripheral regions have been most successful in attracting manufacturing FDI projects, the richer regions have a large share of the manufacturing employment provided by foreign companies in the UK. In terms of service sector FDI projects, the South East dominates as an investment location. This has serious implications for peripheral regions because service sector FDI projects are growing much faster than manufacturing projects, and are likely to provide most of the opportunities for attracting FDI and diversifying regional economies away from low cost manufacturing. Furthermore, the most recent data indicates that manufacturing FDI projects are shifting away from low cost to high cost regions, in particular to the Eastern region.

In policy terms, we argue that regional policy has been a major component of government industrial policy, and that central government has transplanted its emphasis on attracting inward investment down to the sub-national level. This has been achieved through central government controlling the resources and targets of sub-national agencies and the lack of a democratically accountable regional tier of governance has weakened the ability of UK regions to develop an alternative to the exogenous strategy of economic development.

Regional grants directed towards attracting labour-intensive, inwardly investing MNCs have formed the major element of the UK government's regional policy, and our interest is in the peripheral regions eligible to receive these grants. In particular, we focus on Scotland, Wales, and North-East England, and argue that the territorial regions are more autonomous and have received proportionately far more funds than the English regions. The relative improvement in the economic performance of Wales and Scotland has not been replicated in the North-East. We argue that the new regional development agencies, created under EU pressure, do not go far enough in giving the English regions the institutional capacity to break away from an exogenous strategy based on the attraction of inward investment.

10.1 REGIONAL DISAGGREGATION OF FDI IN THE UK

The weight of FDI in the UK economy is amplified at the sub-national level, with the traditional industrial and manufacturing regions of Scotland, Wales, the West Midlands and the North-East among the most successful in attracting manufacturing FDI. As Table 10.1 shows, these four regions accounted for 58% of UK manufacturing FDI projects from 1993 to 1998 – over twice the proportion of their 27% share of the UK population. Peripheral regions have been particularly attractive for manufacturing FDI over the last two decades. Wales and the North-East attracted the highest number of projects per capita, and these are the two poorest regions in the UK, after Northern Ireland. In comparison, the richest and most populous region in the UK, the South East, accounted for only 5.7% of manufacturing FDI projects from 1993 to 1998. This is a reversal from the situation in the first half of the 1980s. In 1984 the South East accounted for 11.6% of total manufacturing projects – a higher proportion than every other region in England. However, by the mid-1990s the North-East was attracting nearly double the number of projects as the South East.

Inward investors have therefore favoured the more peripheral regions for manufacturing investment in the 1990s, and have kept away from the richer regions of the East and South – where most of the UK's R&D activities take place. This is in contrast to the pattern for other countries, with de Vet (1993) finding that in the US, Germany, Netherlands and France FDI is directed to the prosperous regions more so than lagging regions. In de Vet's cross-country comparison, the UK was the only country analysed where Assisted Areas attracted above-average shares of FDI. This supports our conclusion in Chapter 9 that US and Japanese FDI in the UK is less R&D intensive and lower value added than in other European countries. Foreign investors are attracted by the low costs, high unemployment, and flexible labour in peripheral locations and the incentives offered to investors further encourage FDI that is based on cost rather than quality factors, questioning the contribution of inward investment to supporting long term competitiveness in these regions.

If we look at the regional share of manufacturing employment provided by foreign companies, Table 10.2, we see that the South East accounted for over one-quarter of UK employment in foreign manufacturing companies throughout the first half of the 1990s and still over one-fifth in 1997. This was only 2% less than the North-East, Wales and Scotland *combined*, despite these three regions attracting

Table 10.1   Direct manufacturing FDI in UK regions, project successes, 1984–98

Region	1984	1986	1991–92	1993–94	1994–95	1995–96	1996–97	1997–98	% of total 1993–98
North East	24	26	28	35	31	49	36	35	11.1
North West	29	27	61	23	42	24	26	43	9.4
Yorks & Humb.	7	13	15	28	15	33	31	45	9.1
East Midlands	9	9	3	12	28	10	15	12	4.6
West Midlands	11	37	35	63	46	61	50	49	16.1
East*	–	–	5	5	6	7	3	13	2.0
South East*	30	22	17	10	17	26	16	22	5.4
South West	13	8	6	11	18	24	20	22	5.7
Wales	47	45	63	51	41	44	43	50	13.7
Scotland	59	33	31	65	63	57	53	48	17.1
N. Ireland	29	16	10	18	17	22	21	19	5.8
UK	**258**	**236**	**274**	**321**	**324**	**357**	**314**	**358**	**1674**

*Prior to 1990, the East was included in the South East.
Sources: derived from ONS (1996; 1998c; 1999c).

Table 10.2 Regional shares (%) of UK manufacturing employment in foreign enterprises, 1979–97

Region	1979	1990	1991	1992	1993	1994	1997	1997 (all UK based firms)
North East	5.0	6.4	6.4	6.3	6.7	6.6	5.3	4.5
North West	13.8	11.8	12.6	12.5	12.5	11.5	10.2	11.0
Yorks & Humberside	6.5	7.2	7.3	6.8	7.6	7.3	8.2	11.7
East Midlands	4.4	5.8	5.7	6.3	7.0	6.5	6.9	10.0
West Midlands	8.0	11.6	11.3	12.1	11.4	14.4	15.3	13.3
East Anglia	4.3	4.4	3.9	4.0	3.6	3.6	9.7	8.6
South East	35.3	28.4	27.9	26.9	26.2	26.0	19.1	17.9
South West	4.3	5.1	5.5	5.4	5.2	5.9	6.5	7.4
England	81.7	80.8	80.6	80.3	80.2	81.8	81.3	84.4
Wales	5.5	6.4	6.2	6.5	7.5	6.6	7.1	5.1
Scotland	9.8	10.0	9.9	10.1	9.5	9.0	8.9	7.9
Northern Ireland	3.1	2.9	3.2	3.1	2.8	2.6	2.7	2.6
UK	100.0	100.0	100.0	100.0	100.0	100.0	100.0	100.0
							(745,800)	(4,299,300)

Source: derived from ONS (1999b). Data before 1997 provided by Professor Sugden, University of Birmingham.

three times more manufacturing FDI projects than the South East in 1997. In fact, the South East accounts for a higher proportion of UK manufacturing employment in foreign companies than it does UK manufacturing employment in all domestic and foreign companies.

The huge discrepancy between the number of projects won in the 1990s and employment provided can be explained by two factors:

- First, the South East attracted more investment before the 1990s – in 1984, only Wales and Scotland attracted more projects. It is only in the 1980s and 1990s that the peripheral regions have attracted the bulk of new projects. The high share of employment in foreign companies accounted for by the South East therefore represents the *stock* of FDI which the region has attracted. In the 1990s, as the share of projects won by the South East has fallen so has its share of UK manufacturing employment provided by foreign companies, especially from 1994 to 1997.

- Secondly, the data on project successes says nothing about the longevity of projects; much FDI in the peripheral regions has proved highly vulnerable to subsequent closure (Greer *et al.*, 1995; Tomaney, 1995). Morris (1987) found that successive inward FDI in Wales was insufficient to compensate for job loss in traditional industries and in previous rounds of inward investment. Using more recent data provided by Peck and Stone (1996), we can derive that from 1979 to 1993 in the North-East, Wales and Scotland the number of project closures was nearly three-quarters of the total number of new projects. Job losses as a result of closures exceeded job creation from new projects – the employment provided by foreign companies actually *fell* over this period.

One reason for the vulnerability of projects in the peripheral regions to closure is that they were lured to a large extent by the availability of government incentives. While helping the project to reach short-term profitability, incentives are no guarantor of the long-term future of the plant. As Morgan (1997: 78) argues, regional development grants 'offers no guarantee that the plant will continue to find its existing site sufficiently attractive to commit new rounds of investment at that site.' In the UK case, the incentives have been offered on an ad hoc basis, with no industrial strategy for developing sectors or regionally based clusters. Furthermore, we argue that incentives have been based on cost-per-job, not on the quality of the investment or the fit with the industrial structure of regional economies. Multinational

Inward Investment Policy

companies have therefore been artificially dispersed across the UK, reducing any clustering opportunities, and inward investment has been oriented towards labour intensive and low value added activities which are more unstable in the face of exchange rate changes, corporate restructuring and increased competition from other locations.

Hence, Locate in Scotland found that of 62 assisted projects set up during 1981–83, one-third had either failed or did not start at all and a further two-fifths had yet to achieve their own projected job target by 1988 (Peck and Stone, 1996: 56). The Scottish Office also found that only about two-thirds of promised jobs materialise from FDI and, in Ireland, the Industrial Development Authority discovered that only 26% of the jobs promised by foreign investors are actually realised (Wells and Wint, 1991: 33; Buxton, 1997). Similarly, UNCTAD (1998) documents that in Spain in 1995 over one-tenth of FDI was in tax havens – in 1996 over 70% of it was divested and UNCTAD (1998: 145) concludes that 'FDI in tax havens or FDI made in response to incentives is particularly vulnerable'.

However, foreign companies have continuously increased their share of overall manufacturing employment in almost every region over the period 1979–94. This indicates that although the net employment provided by inward investment in some cases may have actually fallen, this decline has been outpaced by jobs losses in indigenous industry. Table 10.3 shows that the North-East, the West Midlands and Wales have seen the fastest rise in the share of foreign companies in manufacturing employment since 1979. In the West Midlands, the share increased by nearly 2.5 times from 1979 to 1994 and in the North the share almost doubled.

The region in the UK with the highest share of R&D expenditure by business, East Anglia, has experienced the greatest fall in the manufacturing employment provided for by foreign companies. This suggests that regions aiming to support technology intensive investment should not necessarily rely on inward manufacturing FDI as the central policy instrument.

From 1994 to 1997, though, the trend of the past 15 years seems to have reversed with almost every region experiencing a declining significance of employment by foreign companies in total manufacturing employment. The major exception was East Anglia, which experienced an almost 10% increase in the role of foreign companies in manufacturing employment. This may indicate that the attractiveness of the traditional manufacturing regions is under threat as cost sensitive greenfield and brownfield FDI shifts to Eastern Europe.

Table 10.3 Regional shares (%) of foreign enterprises in UK manufacturing employment, 1979–97

Region	1979	1990	1991	1992	1993	1994	1997
North	11.8	18.3	19.6	20.2	21.2	22.7	20.4
North West	13.9	15.4	17.4	18.3	18.2	18.0	16.0
Yorks & Humberside	9.3	11.8	12.7	12.4	14.1	13.6	12.3
East Midlands	7.6	9.8	10.2	11.6	12.6	12.1	12.0
West Midlands	8.4	13.7	14.4	16.4	15.6	20.1	20.0
East Anglia	21.2	19.6	18.9	20.1	18.0	17.9	19.6
South East	19.7	19.3	20.4	20.9	21.1	21.3	20.1
South West	10.3	11.3	12.8	13.2	13.2	15.2	15.4
England	13.5	15.2	16.2	17.0	17.2	18.1	16.7
Wales	17.5	21.4	22.0	24.3	28.3	25.2	24.1
Scotland	16.6	20.8	21.7	22.7	21.4	21.2	19.5
Northern Ireland	22.7	19.9	21.8	22.1	19.7	18.6	18.1
Great Britain	13.9	15.9	17.0	17.8	18.1	18.7	17.3

Source: derived from ONS (1999b). Data before provided by Professor Sugden, University of Birmingham.

High value added and R&D intensive manufacturing FDI will congregate to regions which offer a quality supply side technology and innovation infrastructure and sophisticated demand and will be less sensitive to the low cost advantages and incentives of poorer regions in the UK. Hence, from 1997 to 1998 East Anglia gained the largest increase in manufacturing projects in the UK.

Furthermore, the growing importance of service sector FDI also questions the sustainability of peripheral regions to attract high levels of FDI. Table 10.4 shows that nearly 30% of non-manufacturing FDI projects from 1993 to 1998 went to the South East, a far higher concentration than for manufacturing projects in the leading peripheral regions. The three poorest regions in the UK, Northern Ireland, Wales and the North-East, accounted for less than 12% of non-manufacturing projects from 1993 to 1998, while attracting over 30% of manufacturing projects.

While the cumulative number of manufacturing projects in the UK was almost double the number of non-manufacturing projects from 1993–98, the number of non-manufacturing projects increased by 2.4 times over this period while the number of manufacturing projects increased by only 11.5%. In 1999 IT & Software was the leading sector for FDI projects in Europe, accounting for 15% of total

Table 10.4   Direct non-manufacturing FDI in UK regions,
project successes, 1993–98

Region	1993–94	1994–95	1995–96	1996–97	1997–98	% of total 1993–98
North East	5	10	13	10	12	5.9
North West	10	12	13	19	28	9.7
Yorks. & Humb.	12	11	13	5	20	7.2
East Midlands	10	16	11	7	11	6.5
West Midlands	21	16	15	27	32	13.1
East	9	5	9	6	19	5.7
South East	10	23	47	69	95	28.8
South west	1	3	4	9	18	4.1
Wales	13	10	9	2	5	4.6
Scotland	22	18	15	23	28	12.5
N. Ireland	0	6	1	3	5	1.8
UK	**113**	**130**	**151**	**180**	**273**	**846**

Source: derived from ONS (1999c).

projects according to Ernst & Young's European Investment Monitor and in Chapter 9 we saw that IT and Internet services was the leading sector for FDI projects in the UK in 1999/2000. The continued success of peripheral regions in attracting FDI therefore appears to be increasingly questionable as the composition of FDI in the UK shifts towards the service sector and as peripheral regions become less competitive for cost sensitive manufacturing investment.

10.2   REGIONAL POLICY IN THE UK

Meyer-Stamer (1996: 479) states that, 'It is virtually impossible, at least under democratic conditions, to refrain completely from industrial policy', which is perhaps most visible in the area of regional policy, with industrial policy in almost all countries strongly directed toward regional development (Blais, 1986). This is because central government is concerned with aims associated with employment, exports and local development, all of which are central elements in political processes (Brech and Sharp, 1984: 98–101; Hamill *et al.*, 1988: 196).

Regional economic disparities exist in all countries, with divides of particularly high political sensitivity in countries like UK (North–

South), Italy (South–North), and Germany (East–West). At the same time, strong cultural differences are often manifested at the regional level, extreme in the case of the UK, which contains several nations without a state, and also in other countries like the Basques in Spain.

Governments therefore face dual pressures for a regionalisation of institutions and policy. First from the need to compensate for regional disparities and attune development strategies at the local level and second with regions striving for greater cultural autonomy (Cooke and Morgan, 1998: 29). We will see that a third pressure for regionalisation is being exerted on central governments in Europe – from the EU.

Governments across Europe have responded to pressures for region-alisation in different ways. While decentralised institutions and policy appear to have characterised overall developments in Europe (Stoker, 1990; Cole and John, 1995), in the UK central government has been less willing to pass control to regions, especially when compared to Germany, Spain and Switzerland (Sampson, 1992). In Spain, there are 17 autonomous communities with growing autonomy given to regions like the Basque Country and Castile, while in Germany a federal structure was put in place after the Second World War, with each *Länder* given its own parliament and elections.

In part as a consequence of different institutional structures (Rhodes, 1995), regional governments have adopted different devel-opment policies, which can be conceptualised along a scale from endogenous to endogenous-exogenous to exogenous. We can gener-alise that the endogenous strategy has characterised sub-national regions in North Italy with policy focusing on home-grown SMEs, the mixed endogenous-exogenous strategy reflects regions in Germany and France with a mixture of successful indigenous and foreign firms, while in the UK, Southern Italy and Ireland (a regional state) the exogenous path to development has been followed with a height-ened role for inward FDI.

In the following discussion we will give an overview of UK regional policy to understand why the exogenous path to regional development was taken. The subsidies available to businesses investing in periph-eral regions are argued to have represented the corner-stone of UK regional policy, and are examined in detail. The role of the EU and recent moves to pass more power to the regional level in the UK are also discussed, but the key argument is that regional policy has been a major element of UK industrial policy and that the attraction of inward investment through regional grants has been its principal instrument.

10.2.1 Regions in the UK: centripetal forces

Since the early 1980s, sub-national regions have faced four main pressures:

- a central government industrial policy which stresses regional self-reliance;
- reduced central government intervention in the spatial economy;
- increasingly competitive strategies to attract business in other localities;
- deepening industrial recession in the old manufacturing centres.

In response, a growing number of sub-national authorities and agencies devised policies based on the intensified attraction of inward investment and private sector co-operation to re-generate their local economies (Amin and Pywell, 1989; Danson *et al.*, 1992; Shaw, 1993). Central government established new institutions such as Urban Development Corporations (from 1981) to activate urban regeneration in inner-city areas (see Stoker, 1990; Peck and Stone, 1996), and RDOs in the English regions to attract inward investment. In Scotland the Scottish Development Agency (SDA) was established and in Wales the Welsh Development Agency (WDA). Their main aim, like the RDOs, was to attract FDI, although they were given much greater funding and a wider functional remit than the English RDOs.

The government has also more recently set-up a locally sensitive system of enterprise support, involving Training and Enterprise Councils (see Evans, 1991; Jones and Peck, 1995), Business Links, and most recently Regional Supply Offices in 1995 (DTI, 1998). According to central government, the role of Training and Enterprise Councils (TECs), Business Links and RSOs is to work with regional development agencies as part of network to meet the needs of client purchasers (especially inward investors) and develop supply chains (HMSO, 1998a). They represent the government's market-facilitating approach to regional development.

Gibbs (1989) argues that the increasing involvement of local agencies in economic policy making challenges the power of central government. However, in the UK central government policies and budgetary considerations have been constraining (Morris, 1992a: 419; Harding *et al.*, 1996: 20). As more and more responsibilities were given to sub-national government, they were not accompanied by a demonstrable increase in resources (Fenney, 1998: 85), and the emergence of new modes of local governance was the product of accommodation to new central government legislation. Powers and duties have been increasingly transferred to quangos, often appointed by government ministers. The Urban Development Corporations, for example, are not accountable to the local community but directly to the Secretary of State, and the RDOs are also accountable to central government as well as being dependent on centrally allocated funds.

Formally accountable, democratically elected local authority responsibility for policy implementation has been replaced by non-elected, centrally controlled quangos. By the mid-1990s, members of unaccountable quangos outnumbered elected council members by nearly three to one (Fenney, 1998: 86) and in 1999 they employed 70,000 people and controlled £60 billion or one-third of central government spending. Sampson (1992: 147) argues that, 'The British are now almost unique among western nations in the weakness of their local representation', and while RDOs were set up to attract inward FDI there is no parallel network of elected regional governance. As Danson (1995b: 76) points out, 'The UK is exceptional among the larger EC states in not having a network of elected regional authorities.'

Reliance on central resources meant that the rhetoric characterising new sub-national governance mirrored that of central government (Stoker, 1990; Hay, 1995). National government continued to set the policy objectives, targets and expenditure while implementation was devolved to the sub-national level (Harding *et al.*, 1996: 11). The strategic and executive sides of policy were split, allowing the ideology of central government, based on enhancing competitiveness by removing barriers to the efficient operation of markets and attracting FDI, to direct regional policy towards focusing on the primacy of flexible regional responses to market forces (e.g. see Danson *et al.*, 1992).

A key aspect of regional policy has been the promotion of inward investment. With intra-regional competition for inward investment and an increasing role of MNCs in regional economies (Tomaney, 1994a: 545), an emphasis has been placed upon RDOs and Local Authorities to produce cohesive packages of 'before and after' benefits to entice foreign MNCs. Such a 'package' involves private-public co-operation due to the demands of central government and the shift towards flexible production (Stoker, 1990: 252), with agencies co-operating with the business sector to provide the site, infrastructure, supply chain and training requirements to inward investors.

Attracting inward FDI has formed a major part of industrial policy at the regional level, in part because central government control has left English regions without a strong tier of regional government. Together with the emphasis on market-facilitating policies and concomitant reduction in government aid, sub-national agencies have lacked the institutional capacity to design a developmental agenda (Cooke and Morgan, 1998: 135). The regional development grants available to subsidise investment in Assisted Areas symbolise the bias of regional industrial policy towards attracting foreign direct investment rather than supporting indigenous development.

10.2.2   Competing for investment: England versus the territorial regions

The IBB is charged with co-ordinating FDI at the regional level, with the funding of the English regional promotion agencies dependent upon the negotiation of a programme of overseas promotion with the IBB (Dicken, 1990a: 174). According to the government, regional agencies located in every region are partners in a network co-ordinated by the IBB. Their role is to service current and prospective client enquiries, build regional partnerships involving Local Authorities and the private sector, and support links between local academic institutions and businesses (HMSO, 1994b: 95; IBB, 1995: 5). The attraction of inward FDI has, though, dominated the activities of regional agencies.

In theory, with the IBB co-ordinating the regional agencies they in turn are expected to co-ordinate the activities of sub-regional development agencies such as the promotional activities of Local Authorities. However, their mandate is voluntary, and within the UK as a whole there are well over 500 such 'lower tier' authorities, almost all of which are potentially interested in attracting inward investment (Dicken and Tickell, 1992: 100; Cox and Wood, 1994: 640). The overall system is far from co-ordinated, with fragmentation (Tickell *et al.*, 1995) and incoherence (Harding *et al.*, 1996) characterising the plethora of agencies operating at the sub-national level.

There are differences, though, in the role of regional agencies, with the territorial agencies in Wales, Northern Ireland and Scotland acting as more cohesive bodies with a strong and broad co-ordinating role in economic development. As Dicken (1990a: 172) notes, these agencies have a broad *developmental* remit, while in contrast, English agencies have been given a *promotional* remit. With several English regions falling behind Scotland economically, the English Unit at the DTI was established in 1989. The aim of the English Unit was to promote England as a location for inward investment projects working in close partnership with the English regions and the associated development agencies (Collis and Noon, 1994: 846). The Unit was set up in direct competition with the SDA and WDA who are the English region's main competitors for FDI projects. However, Dicken and Tickell (1992: 100) note that the unit was poorly resourced and lacked the developmental powers or political influence of the territorial agencies. It failed to improve the relative position of the poorer English regions.

An earlier agency called English Estates was therefore revamped and in 1993 became known as English Partnerships, with a £250 million investment programme (EP, 1997a). The economic regeneration agency was operational in 1994, with its major emphasis on inward investment, mirroring central government industrial policy:

> English Partnerships' objectives are to promote job creation, inward investment and environmental improvement, through the reclamation and development of vacant, derelict and underused or contaminated land and buildings (EP, 1998).

The unequivocal belief in the benefits of inward investment is made clear by English Partnerships' Chief Executive, Anthony Dunnett, in the opening paragraph of agency's 1997 edition of *England plc*: 'During the last 12 months England has continued to build on its success in attracting investment from major international companies... these decisions benefit the local economy in which their investment is based' (EP, 1997b).

Like the English Unit, English Partnerships was established to allow the English regions to compete better against Scotland and Wales for inward investment (EP, 1997b), and is part of the IBB network. The agency has a greater degree of self-financing and decision-making autonomy than its predecessor and, as with other quangos, it is required to secure private sector co-operation and joint financing of projects (Peck, 1996: 330–1). However, the new Regional Development Agencies, operational from April 1999, are likely to take over many of the functions of English Partnerships.

In terms of financial resources, central government grants to the English regions are dwarfed by those given to the territorial agencies (Table 10.5). For example, in 1997 Scotland received almost 20%

Table 10.5 Economic performance and UK and EU aid in UK regions

Region	GDP/head EU15 = 100 1996	ILO unemployment summary 1998	Population 1996 (m)	DTI Aid* £m 1997–98	EU structural funds (£m at 1994 prices)		
					1999	1998	1997
North East	85	8.7	2.6	38.1	83	86	81
N.West/Mers.	91	7.4	6.9	19.4	204	216	193
Yorks/Humb.	89	8.0	5.0	12.7	88	90	85
E.Midlands	94	5.5	4.1	10.5	30	31	29
W. Midlands	93	6.4	5.3	29.8	104	108	101
Eastern	97	4.6	5.3	2.2	8	8	7
London	140	8.1	7.1	2.7	22	23	22
South East	107	4.6	7.9	5.4	4	4	4
South West	95	4.9	4.8	4.5	36	36	35
Wales	83	7.6	2.9	172.6	71	72	69
Scotland	98	7.7	5.1	132.5	155	162	150
N. Ireland	81	8.3	1.7	156.1	157	170	145

*Regional preferential assistance to industry.
Source: derived from *The Economist* (1999b); ONS (1998c; 1999c).

more UK government and EU aid per capita than the North-East, despite Scotland's per capita income being 13% higher than the North East and its unemployment rate 1% lower. In fact, in 1996 Scotland had the third highest per capita income in the UK after London and the South East. In 1997, Wales received 45% more UK government and EU aid per capita than the North-East, although Welsh unemployment is over 1% lower than in the North-East and per capita incomes only 2% lower.

In terms of GDP per capita, out the assisted areas in the UK eligible for UK aid and EU structural funds only Scotland has closed the gap significantly with the UK, with per capita incomes increasing from 94.6% of UK levels in 1987 to 99.1% in 1996. In every English region north of the Midlands GDP per capita as a proportion of the UK average has fallen in the last 10 years, in the North-East from 85.7% in 1987 to 84.7% in 1996 (data from DTI, 1999a). At the same time, as Table 10.5 shows, these regions also have the highest unemployment, with the North-East having the highest unemployment in the UK.

Central government's expenditure on regional preferential assistance to industry is heavily weighted against the English regions. However, according to the NDC, the key reason for the catch-up of Scotland and Wales and convergence towards UK income and employment levels was not only their higher funding but also the role of the more powerful and autonomous SDA and WDA:

> In fact in 1973 Scotland and Wales had the highest levels of unemployment in Britain. Today, both these regions operate at or near the national average on a number of economic indicators, and it can be argued that this economic improvement can be attributed to the presence of development agencies, which have had wide responsibilities for economic development strategies and programmes in these territories. These agencies have been able both to combine resources and target them in areas where there was the greatest economic gain (NDC, 1998f).

With regions like the North-East continuing to lag behind the rest of the UK and with the far greater resources handed out to the territorial regions, central government has been placed under considerable pressure to establish a new regional tier of governance in England to fill the gap in the existing central-local dichotomy. The Chief Executive of the NDC argues that 'A Northern Development Agency is the vehicle to secure continued economic success' (cited in EP, 1997a), which is justified in the NDC's proposals for new regional development agencies (RDAs) in England:

> Indigenous companies will benefit from a strategy that meets the particular needs of regional companies rather than having to fit into a national system. It will enable the Region to become more competitive and ensure that local companies are able to develop into world class ones (NDC, 1998b).

10.2.3   Europe of the regions: centrifugal forces

The EU also advocates more autonomy for regions in Europe, with the Maastricht Treaty introducing the principle of subsidiarity. At the same time the influence of EU industrial policy over the regions is also increasing. From Table 10.5 we can see that the contribution of EU structural funds to UK regions greatly exceeds that of central government. For the UK as whole, from 1994 to 1996 the UK share of EU funds targeted specifically at regional development was roughly £980 million per year – 3.5 times more than regional policy expenditure by DTI and Welsh and Scottish Offices (Lloyd and Meegan, 1996). In England, the significance of EU funds is more pronounced. In the mid-1990s the EU allocated structural funds of over £1/2 billion each year to England, four times more than central government's regional assistance. The UK government has tried to substitute EU funds for government funds (Fenney, 1998), with central government regional assistance to industry falling from over £600 million in the late 1980s to under £400 million by the early 1990s (data from ONS, 1998c).

The EU is committed to a 'Europe of the Regions' with regionally based policies for economic and social cohesion (Lloyd and Meegan, 1996), and through the operation of the structural funds has raised the status of peripheral regions. Even though the 170 billion ECU in funds allocated for 1994 to 1999 accounts for only 0.45% of EU GDP (Cooke and Morgan, 1998: 215), we have seen that the EU is a more important source of finance for UK regions than the British government. Furthermore, to gain assistance from the structural funds regions have to submit Single Programming Documents detailing regional plans and strategies for economic development and regeneration (see Lloyd and Meegan, 1996), and according to Amin and Tomaney:

in many European regions where regional institutions are weak (such as the UK) the existence of EU regional policy has been the catalyst to the development of local planning structures which are essential if regional structural problems are to be effectively tackled (1995b: 308).

However, with the UK central government controlling regional policy and at the same time imposing central control on Local Authorities and regional quangos, the English regions have lacked the autonomy to design and implement the developmental strategy, which the EU advocates. As Lloyd and Meegan (1996: 88–9) argue, Regional Government Offices:

> in every case in the English regions have reserved to themselves the role of Secretariat to manage the on-going operations of the [structural funds] programme. This has the effect of reinforcing a strong bias toward central government control at every stage . . . it would be our view that opportunities for a strong degree of regional ownership and institutional capacity building are foregone. In particular, the failure to engage representatives of local SMEs, the voluntary sector and trade unions more directly seems to deny the entire process not only an important element of skill and local knowledge but also the potential for wider political legitimacy.

The institutional system of regional governance in the UK is out of line with the rest of Europe. Even in France, generally perceived as highly centralised and *dirigiste*, a far greater significance for the regions is given, first through the 1982 laws on decentralisation (Dunford, 1995) and second with France's 22 regions having their own governments chosen by direct elections since 1986 (Sampson, 1992: 148). Not only have English peripheral regions been unable to develop an endogenous approach to regional economic development, but the lack of a strong, accountable regional tier of government has placed the regions in a weak position relative to other member countries in the competition for European funds (Elcock, 1997) and in their influence over the formulation of national positions on Community policies (Hart and Roberts, 1995: 105). The new RDAs created in 1999, while representing moves to devolve greater power to the regions, do not put in place a regionally elected tier of governance.

10.2.4 The regional development agencies and inward investment

The new incumbent Labour government responded to pressures for regionalisation by setting out in their first Competitiveness White Paper (HMSO, 1997) proposals for establishing a network of new RDAs across England. The aim of the nine English RDAs, operational from April 1999, is to co-ordinate regional economic development, attract inward investment and support the small business sector (Pike, 1997), with the key objective to even out the persistent economic disparities between regions. To this end, RDAs are to have a broad developmental remit, similar to their Welsh, Scottish and Irish counterparts, rather than the promotional remit encouraged under the Conservative government. As the Labour government states, RDAs will have 'leadership in developing and implementing *regional economic strategies...*in an expanded form of the function now carried out by the Government Offices' (HMSO, 1997: 44).

The rationale underlying the establishment of RDAs is the principal that a region knows best its own strengths, weaknesses and priorities, which are most efficiently implemented through partnership at the regional level. As the Labour Party outlined in 1995 before coming into power:

> Organisational capacity, in terms of political and economic institutions, will be a key determiner of economic success. It is crucial to have the right institutions at regional level, so that they can bring together all the key participants in each region's economy (cited in Harding *et al.*, 1996: 67).

While the rhetoric surrounding the establishment of the RDAs suggests a fundamental break with previous centrally determined, locally implemented policy, central government sees the RDAs as a more effective mechanism for attracting inward investment – an integrated one-stop shop – rather than as strategic agencies who can potentially break-away from the government's exogenous approach for regional development.

The key function of the RDAs, according to central government, is to strengthen the organisational capacity of English regions to attract inward investment, with the 1997 Competitiveness White Paper on the regions explaining:

> The Regional Development Agencies will take the lead on the handling of significant internationally-mobile investment projects within

their regions (subject to UK-wide controls to achieve cohesive promotion of the UK abroad and avoiding wasteful competition at home). This work will include assembling the 'package' of support offered to firms qualifying for assistance, to include training, recruitment, site availability and assembly, infrastructure, services, locating suppliers, private finance, and liaison with regulatory bodies... RDAs will have the task of co-ordinating such projects and capturing the maximum benefit from them for the region as a whole (HMSO, 1997: 30–1).

To develop an integrated, single-thread approach to inward investment, the RDAs will absorb the RDOs, English Partnerships, Regional Supply Offices, TECs and Rural Development Corporations and will also have responsibility for technology policy. The RDAs will therefore have the remit to integrate marketing, infrastructure, training, supply chain and technology activities to attract and add value to inward FDI. In fact, an NDC publication states that the formation of RDAs was precisely to improve the ability to the regions to bid for inward investment:

> The Government's policy of welcoming inward investment has led to a proposal for new Regional Development Agencies in England and the strengthening of development agencies in Scotland and Wales (NDC, 1998d: 4).

To retain central control over the RDAs, the agencies will not be democratically nor regionally accountable. Unlike their territorial counter-parts, the English RDAs will not receive a block grant and there will be no regional equivalent in the English regions to the Scottish and Welsh Assemblies. The RDAs will remain dependent on central government departments for their total budget of £800 million (*The Economist*, 1999e) and this dependence is reinforced with the RDAs accountable to the Department of Environment, Transport and the Regions, not to the local community. The RDAs will therefore have less autonomy than the territorial RDAs and they may lack the political legitimacy to develop and implement an economic development strategy for the whole region.

The institutional fragmentation of the English regions will remain, with elected Local Authorities continuing to lobby for the establishment of a regional assembly to control the RDAs. The only lines of regional accountability will be through the voluntary Regional

Chamber – made up of Local Authorities and regional partners. However, the Chamber will only give a 'view' of the RDAs' regional plan, and will have no formal legitimacy to intervene in its activities.

The establishment of the new RDAs should facilitate a more integrated economic policy at the regional level, fostering the development of self-contained policy communities sharing a common focus, but without comparable political institutions it is unlikely that any body will have the political legitimacy to bring together *all* the major participants at the regional level and co-ordinate policy effectively with central government. Unless the RDAs are publicly accountable they will lack the political legitimacy which is necessary for real autonomy.

This suggests that the motivation for creating RDAs is primarily to enable England to fit into the EU's concept of a 'Europe of Regions' and to counter criticism that territorial agencies are better placed in the competition for inward investment. The importance of the institutional machinery in attracting FDI has been particularly heightened with increased competition for FDI and inward investors demanding a more sophisticated package. As the analysis of regional incentives in the next section suggests, attracting FDI is still the key component of industrial policy for the regions.

10.3 REGIONAL GRANTS AND INWARD INVESTMENT

The principal policy for economic development in the peripheral regions of the UK has been the attraction of inward investment, through the key instrument of regional investment incentives. In the next parts, we will look at how the system of regional grants has changed over time and examine both the institutional structure and the allocation criteria through which regional incentives are awarded. Our key argument is that regional incentives continue to be biased towards job creating multinationals rather than aimed at developing and sustaining the competitiveness of peripheral regions.

10.3.1 Regional selective assistance: a value for money approach

From 1947 material incentives, such as government-financed trading estate factories in Scotland, and from the 1960s a wide variety of financial incentives were available to lure foreign investors to poorer regions (Jones, 1990: 202–3). Until 1988, Regional Development Grants (RDGs) were the major form of assistance available in Assisted Areas, and were mandatory grants intended to be straightforward, predictable and quickly administered so that businesses could easily integrate them into business appraisals. Grants peaked at £2 billion per year or £35,000 per job created, in 1998 prices (Groom, 1998d).

However, there was criticism that RDGs were not based on jobs, but were being used by large firms in Assisted Areas to finance capital intensive investment leading to job-shedding (Hamilton, 1987: 189), and that RDGs were being given to firms when they would have invested anyway. The Conservative government also wanted to reduce the incentives offered, and maintain them within EU limits (HMSO, 1995b: 6). In the 1988 White Paper (cm278), RDGs were phased out and replaced by RSA. RSA is the last substantive instrument for regional policy in UK (Lloyd and Meegan, 1996: 79) and is granted to businesses according to a centrally determined criteria.

The allocation of RSA is discretionary, with no pre-committed grants, and the central government criteria for a project to be awarded RSA requires eligible projects to meet five requirements:

- It must make economic and commercial sense. The project must be viable, requiring assistance only once.
- It must take place in an Assisted Area, which in 1998 covered 34% of the working population in the UK.
- It must involve capital expenditure and create or safeguard jobs in the area.
- It should lead to a substantial improvement in performance and should strengthen the regional and national economies.
- It must demonstrate the need for assistance – how the grant will enhance the project, for example, by allowing it to go ahead in the UK as opposed to an alternative location, or by compensating for additional risk.

RSA is administered by central government, through a tripartite structure involving the DTI, IBB and the regional Government Offices. However, the system that operates in England is different to that in the territorial agencies. In England, the allocation of RSA is the stated responsibility of the Secretary for Trade and Industry. Government Offices in England have responsibility for grants up to £2 million, with grants above £2 million referred to the IBB. This £2 million cut-off point for local control has remained at the same level for over 10 years. The IBB then handles these larger cases, with advice from the DTI. The Industrial Development Unit at the DTI has final responsibility for awarding grants, and in big cases makes an 'economic efficiency test' – estimating how much taxation the project will generate for the government in 5–10 years and calculating the balance of payments impact. Ultimately, though, the Secretary of State has the final say.

In the territorial agencies, the responsibility for allocating RSA shifts to the respective Secretaries of States for Wales, Scotland and Northern Ireland (Lee, 1997: 28), giving them more autonomy to bid for investment. With inter-regional competition for inward investment, at the end of 1998 the government was proposing a concordat between the territorial regions, with a new national committee, outside of DTI auspices, established to examine projects involving over 500 jobs (Groom, 1998c). This represents the government's concern over internal, zero-sum competition for investment and is basically intended to ensure value for money. However, the proposal will not cover the new RDAs in England, the establishment of which, according to the Chairman of the new North-East Development Agency (One North-East), will potentially increase bidding between regions (Bridge, 1998b).

10.3.2 Regional selective assistance: an employment subsidy for MNCs

Although the institutional structure for allocating RSA differs between England and the territorial regions, the criteria for RSA has remained the same, with grant limit for RSA set at 22% of investment costs. However, projects perceived to promote national competitiveness can receive above average grants, as discussed in debates between the Trade and Industry Select Committee and the government, recorded in *Regional Industrial Policy* (HMSO, 1995b: 6). This gives the DTI and Government Offices considerable flexibility in determining the level of grants. However, the grant should be limited to the minimum necessary to allow the project to proceed. Therefore RSA should only be provided when it is essential to secure projects, and then be specially tailored for site provision and training programs (through English Partnerships and the TECs in England).

In theory, the discretionary nature of RSA should allow projects that contribute to the long term development of local economies to be prioritised and attract more grants. However, according to the government RSA does not officially differentiate between companies and Sheehan (1994: 513) argues that while:

> government policy officially changed to that of assistance only to offset market failure and the key objective of industrial development policy should be increasing the competitiveness of existing companies.... Job creation still remained the ultimate goal.

In practice, according to Rick O'Farrel, Head of Inward Investment, RSA and Technology at the Government Office for the North-East, 'cost-per-job is the base agent' (O'Farrel, 1998), and job creation is the key objective. As the DTI (1995) states, RSA 'is the government's main regional support measure. Grants may be offered for projects which create or safeguard jobs in the Assisted Areas,' and the government's 1997 Competitiveness White Paper outlines in more detail that:

> Regional Selective Assistance (RSA) is available to companies in Assisted Areas on a discretionary basis to help them carry out investment projects that create or safeguard jobs. It takes the form of Government grant, generally ranging between 5% and 15% of the project's fixed costs (HMSO, 1997: 31).

The level of RSA offered is subject to negotiations between the government and the potentially investing firm (Hill and Munday, 1994: 69), and the emphasis on job creation, cost-per-job, and the minimum grant needed to secure the project – 'most for least' – introduces the possibility that certain types of firms are able to bargain for higher levels of incentives, for two major reasons. First, while the government argues that RSA is non-discriminatory, regional grants through their emphasis on jobs are geared to labour-intensive rather than high value added activities. Second, because MNCs have more alternatives than domestically-based firms. It is precisely the alternatives available which can be crucial in the awarding of RSA as the level of aid offered is an outcome of bargaining between the government and the inward investor. As we argued in Chapter 6, alternatives are a fundamental dimension determining relative bargaining power.

State aid in the UK has therefore become polarised, with job-creating MNCs gaining at the expense of indigenous SMEs. As Rick O'Farrel (1998) explains, 'it is inevitably easier for inward investors to make a case for assistance. They are more flexibly mobile'. The chief executive of the IBB, Andrew Fraser, also concedes that:

> First, the fact that the capacity of Governments to constrain – or even monitor – activities of the global corporation is diminishing; and Secondly, the 'balance of power' has shifted substantially (Fraser, 1995: 3).

Labour-intensive, mobile MNCs have been able to bargain for higher levels of RSA, which discriminates against indigenous firms. As Oman (2000: 115) argues, incentives discriminate against smaller firms, local firms, and firms in non-targeted sectors. Since 1987, nearly £1.5 billion in regional aid has been used to subsidise foreign companies and in the first half of the 1990s over £700 million in RSA was used to attract inward investment, with over half of the allocation concentrated in Wales and Scotland (Barnett, 1996; Lee, 1997). Roughly half the value of regional development aids in Great Britain went to FDI from 1984 to 1995 (Batchler *et al.*, 1998, cited in Oman, 2000: 68) and nearly half of all inward investment recorded by the IBB has received RSA (HMSO, 1995c).

Regional incentives have favoured not only FDI in general, but also large, job creating investment projects in particular. Table 5.2 in Chapter 5 shows that in the 1990s major projects in the UK received from US$30,000 to US$200,000 per new job. This compares with an average amount of RSA given in England of US$6,000 per job in 1996. Projects such as Samsung's electronic plant, Siemens' semi-conductor plant and LG's electronics complex were all large scale, job creating projects. Critically, at the same time these projects were mobile. In the cases of Samsung and Siemens, the NDC and the Government Office for the North-East told the DTI that the MNCs would invest elsewhere if high grants were not forthcoming. For example, Samsung claimed to be considering a site in Spain (Tighe, 1994), and Siemens was appraising locations globally.

The case of the Taiwanese firm Acer – the world's third largest producer of computers – was particularly contentious. In 1998, Acer planned a £25 million investment creating 1,000 jobs in monitor assembly, and was seemingly investing in the North-East. According to senior executives at English Partnerships, Acer had even started to look for houses for its managers (Bowman, 1998). However, despite the IDU and IBB informing Acer that it would get the same money from every region, Wales virtually doubled the grant offered and won

Figure 10.1 Regional assistance to industry, 1988–98 (£m)

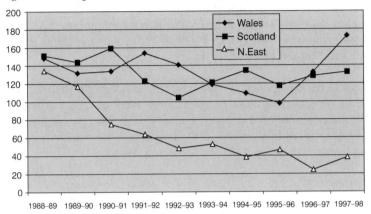

Sources: ONS (1998c, 1999c).

the investment (Lee, 1997: 26), although the exact amount paid was never disclosed. According to several government officials, the WDA collaborated with the IBB, shifting the project to Wales.

Scotland, Wales and Northern Ireland are able to out-bid regions in England first because the block grant given to the territorial regions allows the respective Government Offices to vire between their budgets, and second because they are allocated a far greater share of RSA. As figure 10.1 shows, in 1988, the North-East received only 10% less RSA than Wales, and roughly double the amount allocated to Scotland in per capita terms. However, since 1988 the assistance given to the North-East has decreased by 3.5 times from £134 million to only £38 million in 1998. By comparison, assistance in Wales increased by 16% to £173 million in 1998 and assistance in Scotland fell by only 12% to £133 million in 1998.

Over the period 1988–98, Wales and Scotland each received over £1.3 billion, over double the £638 million received in the North-East. Regional economic policy in the UK, as illustrated by RSA, has been highly politically motivated to appease territorial nationalism, and has not reflected economic fundamentals in different regions.

10.3.3 Regional policy in the UK: a lever for competitiveness?

The subsidy element of regional policy has been pivotal to the industrial policy of central government in the post-war period. In fact,

Tomaney (1995: 110) argues that the contemporary regional policy of central government was little different in the 1980s and 1990s when compared to the 1960s and 1970s, with regional grants based on dispersing industrial activities evenly to reduce unemployment. As Cooke and Morgan (1998: 151) describe in more detail:

> Classical regional policy in Britain was essentially a glorified subsidy regime for attracting mobile capital... it was not designed to engage with the organisational structures, managerial cultures, and absorptive capacities of firms in the assisted regions, issues which lie at the very heart of the economic development process.

The incentives offered by 'Locate in Scotland,' for example, were based on the assumption that the national economy was growing and basic problem was the spatial distribution of economic growth. According to Moore (1995: 232), this led to zero-sum competition and dependency on externally controlled industry. Similarly, in Northern Ireland, the key economic policy for regional development has been attracting inward investment: As the Industrial Development Board (1990) states, its objective has been:

> to encourage the introduction and development of internationally competitive companies in the manufacturing and tradable service sectors in Northern Ireland so as to create the conditions for growth in durable employment (cited in NIEC, 1992: 47–8).

The Northern Ireland Economic Council, an independent think-tank set up to advise the Secretary of State, more recently argued that the grants on offer to inward investors in Northern Ireland are still being used as a straight government subsidy with the result that the government approach has, 'failed to produce an economy which can sustain high wages in the tradable sector' (cited in Brown, 1997). The Confederation of British Industry has also criticised the lack of emphasis within regional programmes on promoting competitiveness (Wighton, 1997).

The large regional selective subsidies offered to inwardly investing MNCs are not only discriminating against indigenous firms, but they have also been targeted at job creating projects rather than investments which will build upon and develop the long term competitiveness of regions. One reason is that the efficiency test is based on the government's historical concern with the balance of payments and more recent emphasis on value for money rather than the contribution of the project to long term economic development. Hence, RSA is biased towards high revenue earning projects i.e., large scale manufacturing operations. Projects that do not yield high tax revenues fail the efficiency test.

Another major reason for the absence of a RSA system linked to supporting regional competitiveness is that the UK government and sub-national agencies have generally believed inward investment to be unequivocally beneficial for the economy. All that needs to be done is to make the MNC aware of the investment opportunities in the UK, offer incentives to compete with other locations giving incentives and attract FDI to peripheral regions, and then leave the rest to market forces. The IBB (1998), for example, notes that foreign companies pay higher wages and have higher productivity, among other advantages, indicating the benefits of inward investment. However, as we concluded in chapter nine, a non-interventionist industrial policy based on attracting labour-intensive inward investment does not synergise well with an increasingly interventionist technology policy aimed at creating a knowledge-driven economy.

Underpinning the government's assumption of the benefits of inward investment is its definition of competitiveness. The UK appears to have defined competitiveness as the ability of the local economy to attract and retain firms that are successful global competitors and which have high productivity. The UK government highlights the impact of Japanese FDI, with the influx of high productivity Japanese investment in the automotive industry. While Michael Porter also sees competitiveness as basically a proxy for productivity, productivity is increasingly driven by innovation (Porter, 1999). As we discussed in Chapter 2, innovation takes place within an innovative milieu based on spatial proximity and the exchange of tacit knowledge through co-operative, trust based networks operating within clusters linking suppliers, customers, and institutions at the local, national and international levels. The emphasis placed by the UK government on attracting inward investment and dispersing it artificially is therefore unlikely to contribute to innovation, long term productivity growth and to overall competitiveness unless it is integrated into an innovative milieu. Hence, we saw in Chapter 9 that the UK's overall manufacturing productivity, and R&D performance is below that of other developed economies and that the UK has also under-performed in attracting R&D intensive FDI.

Furthermore, Maskell *et al.* (1998: 12–13) also suggest that:

> productivity is a measure of the rate at which output flows from
> the use of a given amount of factors of production. It is thus a
> gauge of the efficiency by which the contemporary best technology
> is employed...high levels of productivity might infer very low
> income to some factors of production.

They define competitiveness as, 'a sustained above-average income
for all employed factors of production' (Maskell *et al.*, 1998: 13). For
example, the higher wages paid by foreign companies may reflect low
costs gained through forging new subcontracting relations and by
using a divide and rule strategy to pass costs of production to supplier
companies (e.g. see Cowling and Sugden, 1987; Turok, 1993b). The
high wages of foreign companies may therefore be subsidised by low
wages in their supplier firms. Higher wages may reflect other factors
such as greater work intensity, less job security, an increase in the
duration of work or fewer benefits as a result of a non-union plant
being established. The incentives given to MNCs may also subsidise
high wages and the poaching of employees from smaller, indigenous
firms. Similarly, higher productivity may represent more flexible
practices due to lack of union representation and Pike (1996) argues
that over time the initial productivity advantages of a new plant is
eroded, questioning the long-term benefits of greenfield inward FDI.

Pitelis (1997) also argues that 'competitiveness is the improvement
of a subjectively defined welfare indicator for a country, over time
and/or in relation to other countries'. At a sub-national level, in terms
of closing the gap in the income per head between the Assisted and
non-assisted regions in England and Wales, regional policy based on
the attraction and subsidisation of inward investment has failed to
increase competitiveness.[1]

11 Inward Investment and Regional Development in North-East England

In this chapter we analyse the role of inward investment in regional economic policy in the North-East (and Cumbria) region. We have seen that the North-East has attracted the largest number of manufacturing FDI projects per capita in England and is more dependent on the employment provided by foreign companies than any other UK region, except Wales. We have also seen than the region has attracted two of the UK's biggest ever 'flagship' manufacturing projects, Nissan and Siemens, each with contrasting impacts on the economy. Nissan spurred the development of a regional supplier industry and is the one of the biggest employers and the biggest exporter in the region, while Siemens' major impact would have been on upgrading the quality of work and increasing disposable income in the region, through its demand for a highly trained work-force.

Nissan has expanded its investment continuously over the last 15 years and has become embedded into the region. On the other hand, the closure of Siemens' Tyneside plant and the collapse of semiconductor manufacturing in the region questions the benefits of a RED policy based solely on the attraction of inward investment. In Chapter 10 we saw that the North-East remains the poorest region in England and has the highest unemployment in the UK. The North-East, having experienced the costs as well as benefits of inward investment to a greater extent than most regions, is therefore an ideal case study to examine the role of inward FDI in policy at a sub-national level.

Using project data, our empirical overview of inward FDI in the North-East provides more detailed evidence that Japanese firms prefer greenfield ventures and that the bulk of Japanese FDI took place in the second half of the 1980s. German FDI in the region also followed the national trends, and was highest in the second half of the 1990s. Japanese and German MNCs in the North-East are concentrated in industries in which they have a comparative advantage, and we find that Japanese MNCs have made a larger contribution to new job creation and new investment than either German or US MNCs. However, we reveal that new investment and jobs in the region are dominated by only a few investors, indicating the vulnerability of the region to dis-investment by foreign multinationals.

After analysing the empirical data, we examine the changing inward investment policy of the NDC, the RDO in the North-East. While public bodies in the region, including the Government Office–North-East (GO–NE) and local authorities, also play a significant role in attracting inward investment, we focus on the NDC for two main reasons. First, the NDC was given the remit from the DTI to explicitly attract FDI and Local Authorities are discouraged by central government from acting independently to attract inward investment (Dicken and Tickell, 1992: 104). Secondly, the NDC makes up half the workforce of the new RDA, set-up in April 1999. The Chief Executive of the NDC has also become the Chairman of the new RDA, and the RDA itself is based in the NDC's headquarters in Newcastle-upon-Tyne. The NDC will have *the* major impact on the Regional Economic Strategy being developed for the whole region.

From over 50 hours of open-ended interviews with senior officials at the NDC, the GO–NE and English Partnerships in the region, and full access to NDC documents, we analyse inward investment policy in the region. Until the 1990s, we find the NDC to be a purely marketing-based organisation, aimed at attracting inward FDI, but that in the first of half of the 1990s the NDC's remit broadened to secure the commitment of multinationals to re-invest in the region. A key policy initiative has been to integrate inward investors with the local supply base in order to embed MNCs. In the second half of the 1990s we observe that the NDC shifted towards a more pro-active, targeted strategy aimed at using inward investment to build up the local supplier base.

As the NDC is merged into the new RDA, the policy attitude in the region is shifting away from the belief that inward FDI is sufficient for economic development towards the view that the key strategy should be to facilitate the growth and competitiveness of SMEs and increase R&D. While central governments views the establishment of RDA's as a more effective vehicle to attract and add value to FDI and compete for EU structural funds, the NDC hopes that the RDA will facilitate a shift towards a more endogenous approach to economic development. However, despite the NDC's recent emphasis on endogenous development, we find that technology policy in the region is fragmented with no coherent strategy to support R&D in SMEs and MNCs. We argue that RDAs must develop a targeted regional development strategy linking inward investment, technology policy, and RSA. This can only be achieved through strong partnership between the public and private sectors in the region and a change in policy in central government.

11.1   AN EMPIRICAL OVERVIEW OF FDI IN THE NORTH-EAST

The role of the inward investment in the Northern economy increased rapidly in the 1980s. Foreign enterprises accounted for 11.8% of manufacturing employment in the North-East and Cumbria in 1979, 18.3% in 1990, and by 1994 nearly 23% of manufacturing employment was in foreign companies, almost double the level of 1979. At the same time, between 1979 and 1994 the North-East increased its proportion of total UK manufacturing employment in foreign companies by 1.6%, a bigger increase than any other UK region outside the Midlands. However, by 1998 the region's share had fallen to pre-1990 levels. In terms of the region's share of inward foreign manufacturing projects, in 1984 the North-East accounted for 9.3% of the UK total, while at its peak in 1995–96, the North-East accounted for 13.7% of projects – the third highest in the UK. From 1993 to 1998 the North-East's share of manufacturing projects was 11.1%, the fourth highest in the UK, while the North-East accounted for only 4.4% of UK employment and an even lower share of UK GDP. By most measures, the region has been among the most successful in the UK in attracting manufacturing FDI. While the region has been far less successful in attracting service sector FDI – accounting for 5.9% of non-manufacturing projects in the UK from 1993 to 1998 – this proportion is still higher than the North-East's share of UK population and GDP.

11.1.1   The growth of FDI and contribution to job creation and investment

Table 11.1 shows the growth of inward investment in the North-East and Cumbria from 1985 to 1997 using case-by-case project data provided by the NDC. Since 1989, the number of projects and new jobs created per annum has on average been roughly double the number of 1985 and new investment has been nine times higher. By the end of 1997, there was a total of 568 inward investment projects creating over 45,000 new jobs and investing £8.7 billion. By mid-1998, there were 486 overseas owned companies in the North of England,

Table 11.1　Inward foreign investment projects in the
North, 1985–97

Year	No. of projects	New jobs	Investment (£m)
1985	25	1,867	96.53
1986	28	3,698	338.46
1987	28	2,857	303.39
1988	30	3,351	96.61
1989	45	4,433	526.04
1990	51	2,853	416.28
1991	49	2,302	677.41
1992	39	2,981	548.85
1993	43	2,128	147.06
1994	56	6,113	1,006.17
1995	58	5,597	3,130.08
1996	60	3,652	667.22
1997*	46 (56)	3,199	744.20
Total	558 (568)	45,031	8,698.30

*1997 statistics are under-estimated as out of the
56 projects in that year, data is available for only 46.
Source:　derived from NDC project data.

of which 185 were US, 56 Japanese and 49 German, with these three
countries accounting for 60% of the total.

Table 11.2 shows in more detail the projects, jobs and investment
associated with new investments, expansions, acquisitions and joint
ventures. Expansions by existing investors is the major type of FDI,
accounting for 47% of total projects, 42% of new and safeguarded
jobs, and 40% of investment. This is in line with figures for the UK
economy as whole, with about 50% of FDI re-investment.

New investment is the biggest source of new jobs, indicating the
initial job creation of greenfield investments, and acquisitions the
are main source of safeguarded jobs, accounting for 17% of projects
and 60% of safeguarded jobs. However, acquisitions only account for
4% of new jobs, and therefore the 22% of total FDI in the North in
the form of acquisitions has had a minimal impact on job creation.

Joint ventures have had a more positive impact per project on new
jobs and investment than acquisitions. Each joint venture project on
average created 56 new jobs compared to only 21 for acquisitions.
Joint ventures are also more capital intensive than acquisitions,
expansions or new investment. For regional development organisations hoping to generate jobs and investment in their region, targeting

Table 11.2 FDI in the North by type, projects, jobs and capital, 1985–97

FDI by type	Projects		New jobs		Safe jobs		Investment (£m)	
	No.	% total	No.	% total	No.	% total	Amount	% total
New	177	32	21,467	48	0	0	2,799	32
Expansion	263	47	20,406	45	15,343	39	3,467	40
Acquisition	97	17	1,992	4	23,549	60	1,906	22
Joint Venture	21	4	1,166	3	323	1	527	6
Total	558 (570)	100	45,031	100	39,215	100	8,698	100

Source: derived from NDC project data; there were 570 projects from 1985 to end 1997, but adequate data for only 558.

or at least supporting joint ventures would appear to have positive impacts, if successful. Joint ventures are also important for the transfer of technology between firms, as we saw in chapter four.

If we focus on new FDI projects, expansions, and joint ventures, then new jobs and new investment are dominated by only 14 projects from just three companies – Nissan, Fujitsu and Siemens. Over the period 1985–97, their cumulative investment reached £3.6 billion – over half of the total – and they created well over 10,000 jobs – nearly one-quarter of the total. Nissan alone accounts for over £1.2 billion investment and nearly 6,400 jobs. As we saw in Chapter 10, Fujitsu and Siemens have now closed their plants, leaving the North-East highly dependent on Nissan for investment and jobs.

11.1.2   The sectoral composition of FDI

In terms of the sectors favoured by inward investors, the vast majority of projects in the North are in manufacturing – 89% of total projects compared to only 6.5% in services. This is in total contrast to the picture for the UK and world economy as whole where we have seen that only 40% of FDI flows and projects are in manufacturing. It is therefore not surprising that the North has the highest proportion of employment in industry in the UK, after the Midlands (ONS, 1998c). Within industry, foreign investment in the North is concentrated in several major manufacturing sectors as Table 11.3 shows.

The chemical sector (NACE 24) accounts for the largest number of projects, nearly 12% of the total, but only 3.6% of total jobs created. The high number of projects reflects the concentration of around 60 companies working in this sector on Teeside, which employ 11,000 people directly with an extended support industry employing over 25,000 in the North (Chexal, 1997b; TECs, 1998). World leading companies including ICI, DuPont, BASF and Merck have a major presence in the region. The relatively small number of new jobs represents the high capital and research intensity of the industry and also the fact that over one-quarter of foreign projects in this sector have been acquisitions, compared to 17% for all sectors.

The sector in which foreign companies have had the major impact is the manufacture of motor vehicles and trailers (NACE 34). This industry sector accounts for almost 11% of total projects and one-quarter of all new jobs created. As noted, Nissan dominates this sector, but major supplier firms from Germany, the US, Japan and France, including Lucas, Calsonic, Valeo, Tallent and TRW have

Table 11.3 FDI in the North by sector, projects and jobs created, 1985–97

Classification		Projects		Jobs created	
NACE	Industry	No.	% of total	No.	% of total
24	Manufacture of chemicals	66	11.8	1,617	3.6
25	Manufacture of rubber and plastics	41	7.3	611	3.6
28	Manufacture of fabricated metal products (not machinery)	39	7.0	2,030	4.5
29	Manufacture of machinery and equipment	52	9.3	6,527	14.5
31	Manufacture of electrical/electronic equipment	25	4.5	2,252	5.0
32	Manufacture of radio, television and communication equipment and electronic components	50	9.0	9,234	20.5
34	Manufacture of motor vehicles and trailers	61	10.9	11,343	25.2 (76.9%)

Source: derived from NDC project data.

consolidated the foreign presence in the sector. TRW, for example, has 5 auto plants in the region, the first established in 1988 and the most recent in 1996, and its success in the region has led to production shifting from Germany, France and Italy to the North-East.

The next most favoured sector for foreign investment is NACE 32, which includes electronics components and consumer electronics and accounts for 9% of total projects and one-fifth of total jobs created. Major investors include Siemens and Fujitsu in semiconductors and Samsung, Onwa Electronics and Philips in consumer electronics. The manufacture of machinery and equipment (NACE 29) is the fourth main sector, accounting for over 9% of total projects and 14.5% of jobs created. Major companies in this sector include Komatsu, Parsons and Electrolux.

These four manufacturing sectors – covering chemicals, vehicles, consumer electronics, electronic components, machinery and equipment – together account for 41% of total projects and nearly 64% of jobs created. German and US MNCs dominate chemicals, Japanese

MNCs motor vehicles, Far Eastern producers consumer electronics, while investment in machinery and equipment is distributed more evenly across all the major investors.

11.1.3 Japanese, German and US FDI

Table 11.4 shows FDI in the region by the three main source countries – the US, Japan and Germany. Table 11.4 divides the period 1985–97 into two, allowing us to identify changing FDI trends since the mid-1980s. If we look first at the number of projects by MNCs from each country over the whole period 1985–97, 186 were of US origin, 87 were from Japan and 60 from Germany. Overall, these three countries accounted for 60% of all foreign FDI projects in the North-East and Cumbria – an identical proportion to the number of US, Japanese and German MNCs in the region. In accordance with our analysis of Japanese and German investment in the UK in Chapter 9, Japanese projects in the North peaked in the period 1985–91 and German projects were highest between 1992 and 1997.

Over half of Japanese projects in the first period were new investments, illustrating the Japanese preference for greenfield investments and the relative newness of Japanese FDI. Also of interest are Japanese joint ventures, which out-numbered German and US joint ventures combined. This probably reflects Japanese investors' lack of information on the host market, encouraging joint ventures to gain immediate access to local know-how. In contrast, less than one-quarter of German projects were greenfield and there were only 2 joint ventures from 1985–97. However, in the second period, 1992–97, only one-quarter of Japanese projects were new investments, with over two-thirds expansions, indicating that in this latter period Japanese firms were consolidating their previous investment rather than making new investment.

German projects from 1992 to 1997 exceeded the number of Japanese projects in this period, and the most interesting observation is the high number of acquisitions. Acquisitions accounted for nearly one-third of German projects in the second period, a higher proportion than for US MNCs, which are traditionally more active in M&As. Lane (1998: 478) and Schröter (1993: 45) both argue that German MNCs prefer greenfield investments to acquisitions in order to retain close links with subsidiaries and internalise activities in order to maintain quality. However, from 1992 to 1997 German acquisitions in the North were over twice the number of new investments.

Table 11.4 German, Japanese and US FDI in the North, 1985–97

	Japan			Germany			United States		
	1985–91	1992–97	Total	1985–91	1992–97	Total	1985–91	1992–97	Total
Projects	55	32	87	25	35	60	73	113	186
New	28	8	36	9	5	14	18	30	48
Expansion	20	22	42	11	18	29	41	47	88
Acquisition	1	1	2	4	11	15	10	32	42
Joint venture	6	1	7	1	1	2	4	4	8
Jobs	10,442	3,996	14,438	1,864	5,975	7,839	8,745	16,854	25,599
New	10,310	3,729	14,039	938	3,062	4,000	4,656	5,464	10,120
Safeguarded	132	267	399	926	2,913	3,839	4,089	11,390	15,479
Investment £m	1,242	1,534	2,776	141	1,242	1,383	1,058	1,592	2,649
NACE projects									
24	0	0	0	3	7	10	15	17	32
25	1	2	3	1	4	5	3	6	9
28	5	0	5	3	4	7	6	4	10
29	5	2	7	4	3	7	12	4	16
31	3	1	4	0	0	0	7	7	14
32	6	4	10	2	1	3	3	8	11
34	15	12	27	4	4	8	8	9	17

Source: derived from NDC project data.

The importance of acquisitions indicates that German MNCs do not view internalisation as crucial for quality maintenance, perhaps representing the high quality levels achieved in the North-East by investors like Nissan, and that German MNCs are willing to form new network relations through the acquisition of foreign firms. In most cases, though, German firms are the dominant partner. The growth of acquisitions also shows that German MNCs are rapidly increasing their market presence in the UK, as we saw with Siemens in Chapter 8. Acquisitions are a strategy to gain better market access and expertise and control of firms operating in a lower cost environment.

If we look now at job creation, the most significant observation is the high proportion of new jobs created by Japanese investors. In just 7 years from 1985 to 1991, Japanese firms created over 10,000 new jobs – more than the total number of new jobs created by US investors *over the whole period* 1985–97. In contrast, from 1985 to 1997 safeguarded jobs by Japanese firms numbered less than 400 – almost 10 times less than the number of jobs safeguarded by German firms and nearly 39 times less than the figure for US firms. The major reason is the relative preference of US and German firms for acquisitions and the high number of greenfield plants established by Japanese MNCs from 1985 to 1991. Notably, the number of new investments by Japanese firms fell by three-and-a-half times from 1992 to 1997 compared to the first period and at the same time job creation also fell, by over two-and-a-half times. Key reasons include the Japanese economic crisis and the end of the 'first wave' of Japanese investment in Europe.

In the second period, new job creation by German firms, at over 3,000, was approaching the Japanese level and US job creation exceeded the Japanese level by 46.5%. In terms of new jobs per project, though, Japanese firms created far more than either Germany or the US. From 1985 to 1997, Japanese firms on average created 161 new jobs per project, exactly double the average for all FDI projects in the North. Job creation by German and US firms was well below the average, and Japanese firms created almost three times more jobs per project than US firms. A key reason is that Japanese companies are the most export intensive and are generally investing to supply the whole EU market. An empirical study by Papanastassiou and Pearce (1995, 1996) found that out of 145 MNCs in the EU, Japanese subsidiaries were the most export intensive – relying on the host country market for only 12.5% of sales, compared to 24.3% for US firms and 50% for EU firms. The average size of projects is therefore larger for Japanese FDI than for US and German MNCs. If job creation and exports are key goals of regional authorities, targeting new investment, expansions and joint ventures by Japanese MNCs appears to be most productive, judging by the experience of the 1990s. Table 11.4 also shows that Japanese firms are far more capital intensive than either German or US firms. In fact, from 1985 to 1997 the £2.8 billion invested by Japan's 87 projects exceeded the total investment of the 186 US-sourced projects. A large proportion of German and US capital investment is also in the form of acquisitions. For example, in the second period from 1992 to 1997 if we discount Siemens investment due to its subsequent closure, then nearly half of total FDI by German firms was accounted for by a single acquisition. Similarly, nearly two-fifths of US FDI in the second period was accounted for by just four acquisitions. Japanese FDI has therefore been more productive in terms of capital investment and job creation, than either German or US FDI both in project and absolute terms.

However, nearly three-fifths of total new jobs and 44% of FDI by Japanese firms can be attributed to Nissan and Fujitsu's original investment and subsequent expansion. Similarly, 71% of German FDI in the first period was accounted for by just two firms, BASF and TRW, and in the second period Siemens alone accounted for almost three-fifths of new jobs and 89% of capital investment by German firms. Perhaps more important than attracting a certain type of investment or FDI from a particular country is ensuring the long term commitment of major investors to re-investment in the region, a point we discuss in more detail later in this chapter.

11.2   CHANGING FDI POLICY AT THE NDC

The role of inward FDI in development policy in the North-East since the 1980s, as epitomised by the activities of the Northern Development Company, can be divided into three periods:

- From the early 1980s to the start of the 1990s policy was characterised by a high dependency on inward FDI as the major source of new investment and attracting foreign MNCs was the principal tool of economic development.
- In the first half of the 1990s policy shifted in emphasis from attracting FDI to embedding existing investors to secure future re-investment.

● From the mid-1990s a competitiveness strategy is being developed, concentrating on supporting indigenous firms, R&D and targeting inward investment to meet the needs of local economy.

The shift in policy has been largely reactive – responding to a changing economic environment – rather than part of a deliberate, coherent strategy for long-term economic development. However, the lack of institutional autonomy and dependence on a central government industrial policy which stressed the leverage of private investment and failed to develop a strategy for long term regional development, left peripheral region's like the North-East with few alternatives to pursuing an exogenous strategy based on attracting inward investment.

11.2.1 Development policy in the North: attracting inward investment (early 1980s–early 1990s)

An underlying problem of the Northern regional economy has been lack of sectoral diversification, with employment in its staple industries – mining, metal manufacture, shipbuilding and marine engineering – declining from one-quarter to one-sixth of total employment between 1961 and 1981. Between 1977 and 1985 one in three manufacturing jobs disappeared, three quarters from the region's staple industries. In 1975, the coal, steel and shipbuilding industries employed 35% of all people in the manufacturing and extractive industries. Today this figure is 1%, with 180,000 jobs lost between 1978 and 1983 largely due to industries like shipbuilding declining, alternative fuel sources (gas and nuclear) replacing coal, major productivity gains in the steel industry, and a rationalisation of industry following reduced government support and privatisation. There was no small firm sector capable of generating new employment. Proportionately, the North lost more of its manufacturing base in the 1970s and early 1980s than any other region in the UK, with one-third of the region's capacity in manufacturing, construction and primary sectors lost in the early 1980s.[1]

By 1978, the majority of manufacturing employment in the North-East was in foreign companies (Goddard, 1990: 189), however many were truncated, factory-based production outlets with no higher order functions such as R&D or company headquarters, and structural problems remained (Amin and Pywell, 1989: 464–7). The legacy of the collapse of traditional manufacturing industry and dependence on branch plants was a rapid rise in unemployment (average regional unemployment was close to 20% by 1984 with unemployment almost twice this level in inner-city areas), large amounts of derelict and often polluted land, a poor physical infrastructure, a narrow skills base, low rates of business survival and new firm formation (the lowest in the UK in 1981), and little evidence of innovation or technology transfer (Harding *et al.*, 1996: 25; NDC, 1998a).

According to the NDC, the principle solution had to lie in the creation of new jobs, and jobs can only come from three sources: inward investment, indigenous business growth and new firm formation (NDC,1998a). With the collapse of traditional industry and the lowest rate of new firm formation and R&D in the UK in the early 1980s, according to the Chief Executive of the NDC, Dr Bridge, 'the policy view in the region was that we had to try and secure inward investment to act as a stimulus to regional development' (Bridge, 1998b).

This policy view also reflected the broader non-interventionist industrial policy rhetoric of the Conservative government, which was eager to attract inward investment to the many regions in the UK that suffered the consequences of a hollowing-out, or total collapse, of traditional manufacturing industry – a decline induced by the new policies of privatisation, closure of nationalised industries and reduced subsidisation (Sadler, 1992a: ch. 5). As we saw in Chapter 10, central government more or less imposed its market-facilitating ideology onto the UK regions, leaving sub-national agencies in peripheral regions with few alternatives to attracting inward FDI.

The North-East, designated as an Assisted Area, therefore followed the same path as other peripheral regions, using the availability of government regional development assistance, low wages, and infrastructure improvements to forge a low-cost advantage and successfully attract FDI through partnership between various regional bodies. High unemployment and labour flexibility were also key carrots on offer to inward investors, and were crucial factors behind the investment of Japanese and German companies like Nissan and Siemens.

The Northern economy received £100 million per annum in EU funding, the biggest proportion under Objective 2, which is aimed at areas suffering from unemployment as a result of industrial decline. While EU rules prohibit the use of structural funds as a subsidy for individual firms, the £1 billion in EU structural funds given since 1989 played an important role in upgrading the infrastructure and cultural facilities, increasing the attractiveness of the region to inward investors.[2]

A major infrastructure initiative to attract FDI is the Hadrian Business Park, which was created to attract manufacturing firms. The Enterprise Zone status of the park means that for 10 years the capital costs of buildings can be charged to tax at 100%, offering significant cost benefits for large investments. Exemption from business rates and a simplified planning regime are further incentives for investment. More recent examples include the Teesside Chemical Initiative, whose objective is to solve infrastructure weaknesses and attract more chemical companies (Tighe, 1995b), and the £7.7 million North-East Microelectronics Institute Centre for Advanced Industries in North Tyneside, paid for by EU structural funds, which opened in 1998 to support a cluster of projects in electronics, microelectronics and in advanced engineering design (NDC, 1997a; Linford, 1998). The key aim was to attract inward investment, with officials hoping the Centre would demonstrate to inward investors that the region possessed a good technological infrastructure.

From the early 1980s several factors combined to make conditions conducive to attracting FDI. On the demand side, the globalisation of production was leading to a rapid growth in mobile investment projects and demand for host locations. On the supply side, the North-East had access to the UK and European market and was attractive to new, job-creating manufacturing investment due to the region's low cost and flexible labour market and the availability of financial incentives and susbidised factories, sites and infrastructure. According to the chairman of the NDC, 'All you needed in-between was a marketing function to encourage people to look at the North and the NDC's role was to do precisely that' (Bridge, 1998b).

The NDC was formed in 1986 as a tripartite owned intermediary institution uniting the public and private sectors and unions in order to secure major inward investments for the North-East and Cumbria. According to Dr Bridge:

> The reason for its development was really brought about by the very successful development of Nissan. . . . In order to secure the Nissan investment, a fairly large multidisciplinary team was put together representing a very large range of interests from central and local government . . . to people involved in skills, training, supplies and so on and it worked (Bridge, 1998b).

To unite the public and private sectors, the NDC's Board is tripartite and consists of representatives from local political parties, trade unions and the business community (Tighe, 1996a; Corcoran and Liddle, 1997: 16). The NDC is a relatively powerful and cohesive development corporation, which has 100% membership (non-compulsory) from its Local Authorities. The NDC has an extensive network of overseas offices generating awareness of investment possibilities and when combined with site and labour availability, RSA, and collaboration with other organisations in the region to provide the infrastructure for multinationals the North-East is able to successfully bid for manufacturing FDI.

While the NDC is supported by Local Authorities and trade unions in the region, it has less finance than the WDA and Scottish Enterprise, and is partly funded from central government through the DTI via the IBB (Grant, 1989: 110; Peck, 1996: 331). The NDC receives £6 million per annum in total support from all sources, compared to grant aid of £380 million per year for Scottish Enterprise (Harding *et al.*, 1996: 57). Roughly one-third of the NDC budget comes from Central Government, through the IBB and Regional Supply Office (RSO), another one-third from local authority and private sector contributions, sponsorship and sales of business services, and the remainder comes from the EU and other activities (NDC, 1997c). The dependence of the NDC and other development bodies in the North-East on negotiating government finance limits their autonomy and coherence. As Harding *et al.* (1996: 44) argue, 'In the North-East, as in most English regions, institutional arrangements for economic development are complex and responsibilities fragmented.'

However, the NDC is an important link in a regional policy network evolving in the region, which includes local Councils, Urban Development Corporations, trade unions, leading businesses, the North of England Assembly of Local Authorities, and the Northern Business Forum (Dicken and Tickell, 1992; Cole and John, 1995; Corcoran and Liddle, 1997). This network alleviates to some extent the fragmented responsibilities and lack of autonomy in the region. One reason for the ability to form a relatively cohesive and unified network is the keen sense of regional identity in the North-East (Harding *et al.*, 1996: 39; Dicken and Tickell, 1992), with an informal policy network engendered as cultural and leisure facilities, such as Newcastle Football Club, act as focus points for informal meetings between leading public and business figures.

The regional network is also strengthened by consensus over the main economic problems in the region and how they should be tackled. A local growth coalition emerged with a shared aim to reduce unemployment through attracting inward investment. Attracting FDI to create jobs reflected not only the nature of the economic problems in the region, as highlighted above by the NDC, but also central government policy, with Hudson (1991) pointing out:

> As the political economy of Thatcherism switched the emphasis to regional self-reliance and to competition between places as the only route to economic growth, revived sorts of corporatist bodies... emerged to sell the region, or particularly locations within it, to potential private investors (cited in Shaw, 1993: 258).

The new growth coalition has become crucial; in order to attract inward investment regional and local bodies must offer an overall 'package' quickly and flexibly and one which is perceived more favourable than packages available in other competing locations. An *a priori* for such a package, as argued by Regulation and Flexible Specialisation theorists, is the ability to engender co-operation and trust between and within local business, labour interests, education and research, and government (see King, 1990; Hirst and Zeitlin, 1992; Mair, 1993; Jessop, 1994).

The policies pursued by this coalition are *reacting* to market forces and are not so different from the past, with the key aim to use investment incentives, marketing tools and the provision of supporting infrastructures to attract investment and then leave it to market forces to deliver positive outcomes.

There was no criticism of, or alternatives considered to, the market-led, exogenous regional development policy. Hence, a detailed study by Dicken and Tickell (1992, 1993) of Local Authorities in Northern England and the IBB found overwhelming support for attracting inward investment. They found that 75% of local authorities regarded the attraction of FDI as desirable, 58% of local economic development officers gave the promotion of inward investment at least equal top priority in economic development strategies, and 59% thought new jobs was the main perceived benefit of inward investment. Unemployment was a key factor influencing perceptions. High unemployment Local Authorities desired FDI while those with low jobless rates did not desire foreign investment. Dicken and Tickell (1993) note a key reason is that only high unemployment areas are eligible for RSA, which continues to be perceived by officials in the region as very important for attracting inward investment. Central government regional policy, through the RSA system, was therefore a powerful determinant of the emphasis given to attracting FDI in the North-East and other peripheral regions in the UK.

With attracting inward investment the key policy for economic development in the North-East region, the importance of the NDC was reinforced as the organisation, with its 65 staff, was charged with the task of securing FDI. In fact, as we saw in the last section, the NDC and its regional partners were very successful in attracting inward investment; from 1985 to 1990 there were 235 FDI projects in the North-East and Cumbria, creating over 19,000 new jobs with capital investment of £1.8 billion. The NDC was filling a marketing and co-ordinating role, aiming to secure an initial foreign investment enquiry and then make sure that the various bodies in the region provided a good service to the prospective investor. The success in attracting FDI gave the NDC and the region as a whole confidence in their policy.

11.2.2 Embedding inward investors: new NDC initiatives (early 1990s–mid-1990s)

By the early 1990s, the NDC began to shift its focus away from a purely exogenous strategy aimed at attracting inward investment towards a strategy to support integration between foreign MNCs and local industry. Five key trends were combining to encourage a redirection in NDC inward investment policy:

- Unemployment had fallen steeply in the North-East, and the gap with the UK level closed slightly during the 1990–92 recession. The urgency to create jobs fell and at the same time gross value-added per worker in manufacturing had risen above UK levels (EP, 1997a; TECs, 1998), vindicating for policy makers in the region that attracting inward investment had increased regional competitiveness.
- It was becoming apparent that the expansion of existing investors was a key source of jobs and investment; by 1991, over 40% of new projects, jobs and investment had come from re-investment at existing plants.
- The NDC was becoming aware that plants were vulnerable to closure (NDC, 1997e) and, while the NDC does not record data on closures, Smith and Stone (1989) document that in the North-East from 1978 to 1989 the number of Japanese firms increased

from one to fifteen, creating 5,000 jobs, but over this period 35 US plants closed in the region with the loss of 15,000 jobs.

- The NDC's own research showed that total expenditure of the top 250 companies in North-East on suppliers is £4 billion, but that 80% is sourced outside of the region (Sherburn, 1998). This reinforced the results of an earlier academic study by Phelps (1993), which found that of 200 greenfield manufacturing plants in the Northern Region from 1979 to 1989 the sourcing of material inputs from the region *decreased* from 21% to 20% and from the UK fell from 70% to 69%.

- Restructuring, rationalisation and vertical disintegration in MNCs involves reducing the number of suppliers and moving to long term relationships with those remaining. Final producers are concentrating on their core competencies and sharing the risks of new product and process development with first tier suppliers. The local supplier industry therefore became more important to inward investors.

While the NDC was traditionally concerned with attracting inward investors, the emphasis shifted to embedding them as well. Without the urgency to secure short-term jobs, in this second phase of policy the NDC diverted resources from attracting inward investment to developing the first Investor Development Programme in the UK, which enables the NDC to remain in contact with around 400 strategically important companies (NDC, 1997f). The NDC collaborates with MNC subsidiaries to help them meet their competitive needs, such as developing supply chains, cutting costs or preparing business cases to their parent companies. The key aims are to guard against the risk of dis-investment and job loss through committing major investors to re-investment in the region and supporting investors in the face of demands for rationalisation or closure from the parent company. As we saw in Chapter 10, FDI in peripheral regions has proved highly vulnerable to closure. The emphasis of the NDC was therefore shifting to 'after-care' policies, which, according to UNCTAD (1995b) and Hood and Young (1993, 1995), are crucial for upgrading or retaining inwardly investing multinationals.

To support investor development, supply chain programmes were created in 1992, with a team of business development managers interfacing between the major investors and the SME sector (Bridge, 1998a). The aim is to facilitate upgrading the quality of local suppliers to enable local industry to meet the needs of major investors.

The NDC hoped that supply chain programmes would support local sourcing, increasing the embeddedness of MNCs by raising their exit costs. As the NDC, in its research on supply chain dynamics, argues:

> Investment can come from a number of sources and viewed from a large company point of view, the local SME supplier capability is a critical factor in the decision.... The unique characteristic that supply chain analysis can bring to bear is the embedding of investment into the local supply base (NDC, 1998a).

Furthermore, through helping local suppliers to upgrade and become first tier suppliers, the NDC hoped that this would improve the attractiveness of the region to inward investment, with a senior business development manager at the NDC explaining that:

> Discerning investors increasingly want to map out their supply chains ahead of the decision to invest in a region and the UK as a whole.... The supplier base is now almost as important as labour issues (Sherburn, 1998).

The NDC therefore developed a strategy focused on competencies in two key areas: investor development and supply-chain development, and the core function of the NDC was now not only to secure inward investment but to add value to it in order to embed MNCs into the local economy. This was a major change from existing policy in the North-East, with Dicken and Tickell (1992) finding that only one-third of Local Authorities in the region made any attempt to maintain contact with foreign firms in their area once located there. By the mid-1990s, the NDC had operations across three main areas:

- Regional Investment Team and Investor Development;
- Supply Chain and Cluster Development Team;
- International Business Opportunities Team.

This Regional Investment Team works in partnership with other regional organisations in both the public and private sector to secure new foreign direct investment. The NDC has branches in 6 foreign markets – North America, Taiwan, Japan, Korea, Continental Europe and India – to generate investment leads. Once a potential project is located, either through the overseas branches or via the IBB, a business case is made for potential MNCs to invest in the North of

England. If the firm invests, the Investor Development team tries to keep in regular contact with local managers and assists in future development and expansion needs. In the first six years since investor development started, the NDC cites that it has been involved in projects that have created more than 9,000 jobs and safeguarded more than 8,137 jobs.

Within the NDC, a team of business development managers has been created to work on Strategic Supply Chain Development to help OEMs reduce costs and assist local suppliers in entering the supply-chain. In 1997 and 1998 each manager was tasked with developing a thorough understanding of the supply chains of ten Ordered-Export Manufacturers (OEMs) or primary suppliers of sub-assemblies in their sector. They will identify twenty potential regional suppliers and profile their capability. Each of the eight managers, who have procurement and production engineering backgrounds, will work on 30 supply chains as a result of this activity (NDC, 1997c). According to the NDC, this:

> is a critically important element of the process that creates the infrastructure to support and sustain inward and indigenous investment. It is also a very important element of the business case presented to potential investors whose projects are dependent on sourcing competent and capable suppliers (NDC, 1998d).

The qualification process for suppliers uses the *Supply-Chain Assessment Tool* (SCAT), developed in conjunction with Glasgow University, and the Promotion of Business Excellence (PROBE), a wider-based management tool developed by the National Manufacturing Council in the UK (NDC, 1998a). SCAT, for example, examines four main areas of the potential supplier's business:

- company strategy: vision, business planning, market position;
- management: financial outputs, organisation, structure, planning and human resources;
- process: R&D, new product introduction, manufacturing quality, sales and marketing;
- metrics: measurement of performance, quality, delivery and cost.

Each area is becoming more important as OEMs channel higher value added activities to first tier suppliers and at the same time expect suppliers to continuously reduce costs.[3] The business development managers provide the critical interface only with OEMs and first-tier suppliers, as the NDC's remit is to work with large businesses. The results of SCAT are, however, fed into the local DTI-controlled Business Links partnership, which assists supplier capability upgrading of small firms with less than 250 people (Taylor, 1998a). Training weaknesses identified by the NDC's business development managers are passed on to local TECs. While the various business support bodies co-operate, there is no single body to co-ordinate and make policy – until the formation of the RDA in 1999.

The third dimension of the NDC's operations is international business opportunities, with the key objective to secure exports and local orders for the region's companies. Often, the contacts made lead to future inward investment (Jones, 1998). International business opportunities include:

- *Export missions*: over 200 from 1986 to 1999, taking 4,000 companies overseas to obtain business valued at approaching £1 billion – the NDC is the largest organiser of export missions in the UK and the North-East is proportionately the UK's biggest exporter (Wilson, 1998; NDC, 1999).
- *Exhibitions*: 423 exhibitors have been taken to 23 exhibitions around the world from 1993 to 1998, leading to initial orders of over £15 million and estimated future business worth £93 million.
- *RSO North-East and RSO North West Cumbria*: Established in 1995 by the DTI to match purchasers and suppliers, and run by the NDC. They now also help the business development managers, using SCAT to find deficiencies in local suppliers if the order is over £100,000. Every enquiry is passed to Business Links, which has more local knowledge (Jones, 1998). The Northern RSO's have secured business worth over £25 million, which compares favourably to the £33 million secured by the West Midlands RSO (WMRDA, 1998), which operates in a region with over double the GDP of the Northern region.

By the mid-1990s, about half of the NDC's inward investment work was focused on existing investors, and less than one-third of resources went to the attraction of FDI (NDC, 1997a). From 1996 to 1997 the Investor Development and Supply Chain Programmes helped to contribute nearly £1 billion to the regional economy – more than inward FDI, as shown in Table 11.5.

Table 11.5 Embedding MNCs: jobs and investment in the North by source: 1996–97

	Overseas inward investment	Invester development	Supply-chain programmes	Total
Projects	54	26	117	197
New jobs	3,487	2,036	–	5,523
Safe jobs	4,474	1,360	–	5,834
Investment	£653 m	£558 m	£380 m	£1,591

Source: data from NDC (1997a).

The NDC's embedding initiatives – investor development and supply chain development – became more important than attracting inward FDI not only to the NDC's activities but also in terms of their contribution to the regional economy. Investor development created more new jobs and more investment per project than inward investment, while the £380 million in expenditure resulting from supply chain programmes represents new business generated for the region's SMEs.

Although it is too early to say whether or not the NDC's new initiatives have 'embedded' MNCs into the local economy to any lasting effect, as the interface between the NDC and OEMs intensifies and as local suppliers are integrated into MNC supply chains there are definitely increased opportunities for securing the commitment of foreign companies to the region. Anecdotal evidence also suggests that investor development and supply chain programmes have prevented the dis-investment and closure of plants in several cases. Box 11.1 shows the example of Black & Decker.

However, while the investor development and supply chain programmes were arguably successful in facilitating the integration of MNC subsidiaries with local industry, in particular in the automotive industry, any positive benefits on the indigenous SME sector were really side-impacts of the main aim which was to encourage the re-investment of MNCs and improve the attractiveness of the region to new inward FDI. The benefits of inward investment were not questioned and in cases like Siemens and Fujitsu where there was no local industry capable of meeting the major supply needs of the MNCs, the NDC could only have minimal influence. Additionally, many MNCs are reluctant to disclose potentially strategic information, limiting the potential for Investor Development activities. Hence, when Siemens

Box 11.1   Embedding multinationals: the case of Black & Decker

In 1998 the corporate headquarters at the US MNC Black & Decker announced that it was going to close the North East plant as part of world-wide rationalisation. The NDC, which had built up a good relationship with local management at Black & Decker through the investor development programme, offered to help. The Operations Director at the North East plant had no personal influence in the headquarters, so the NDC helped Black & Decker prepare a business plan to submit to the HQ, outlining how Black & Decker would cut costs through the supply chain and would establish a supplier village at the plant to attract international quality firms. Instead of closing the plant, the head office closed its Italian branch, shifted production to the North East and established a design, research and development centre to develop products specifically for the European market. The 1998 expansion involved new investment of £17 million, which created 350 new jobs and safeguarded 775 jobs. The possibility of substantial job loss was very real. In the region, Black & Decker now produces 11 million professional power tools per annum with 75% of output being exported to all parts of the world and its product development and manufacturing operations based in Spennymoor, County Durham are the largest within Black & Decker world-wide. The North East plant is emerging as a leading implementer plant for the MNC.

Source: NDC (1998a, f); Sherburn (1998)

decided to close its plant there was no consultation with the NDC beforehand; it was a decision made in the German corporate headquarters to decide the fate of an overseas subsidiary which had very little 'embeddedness' in the local economy.

In the first half of the 1990s, inward investment remained pivotal to the NDCs and the region's economic development strategy. As the NDC said in a 1994 House of Commons Select Committee: 'The task for the region is to use inward investment as means of developing a strong internal dynamic which can lead to long-term self-sustaining growth' (cited in Tomaney, 1995: 109). No alternatives to an exogenous strategy of regional development were considered, with the strategy to continue the previous success in attracting FDI, but only now to ensure that inward investment remains in the region rather than being dis-invested at a later date.

11.2.3   Re-evaluating the role of FDI: the NDC's pro-active strategy (mid-1990s–)

By the second half of the 1990s the NDC had begun to question the sustainability of a development policy centred on inward investment. This was in large part a response to a changing economic environment, but also an outcome of the NDC's more pro-active efforts to evaluate the competitiveness of the region and develop a long term strategy for sustainable economic development.

Since the mid-1990s the exogenous development strategy of the NDC has been put under pressure from four angles:

- *At the national level*: a period of sustained growth helped to lower unemployment in the North-East, reducing the urgency to secure short-term jobs through inward FDI.
- *At the international level*: the inward investment market for manufacturing FDI is becoming more competitive.
- *At the regional level*: the North-East is not closing the economic gap with the UK as a whole.
- *At the NDC level*: moves to formulate a long term competitiveness strategy are re-focusing efforts on indigenous rather than foreign enterprises, a shift in emphasis reinforced as the NDC becomes subsumed into the new RDA.

After a prolonged period of growth in the UK economy, unemployment in the North-East fell from 12.5% in Spring 1994 to 8.2% in Spring 1998 (ILO cited in DTI, 1999). According to a senior investment manager who has been at the NDC since its foundation, 'in the past we did not look at the quality of jobs provided by inward investors, but as unemployment has fallen we began to be more selective'. The benefits of inward investment are now being questioned, not only by investment managers responsible for attracting FDI, but also by business development managers who work with MNCs in the post-investment period. For example, one senior business development manager at the NDC commented:

> Present industries in the North-East are not better than in the past. In the past, heavy engineering involved highly skilled workers, much more skilled than those employed by companies like Samsung. Heavy engineering was also more capital intensive....Low skilled jobs are not the way to raise economic development of a region.

There is, therefore, a growing emphasis on the 'quality' of inward investment in the region and its ability to upgrade the skills of the work force. The changing attitudes of the regional supply office in the region also suggests that increasing emphasis is being placed not only on the skill implications of FDI but also the impact on the quality of indigenous suppliers. At the RSO the help given to foreign OEMs to find suppliers is becoming more selective, with the RSO now refusing to support 'warehouse' production. An indication of this more selective, quality-driven approach is that in the past there were over 100 inquiries handled a month, whereas now there are about 30 and at the same time the pound boundaries on component expenditure in order to qualify for help has been raised (Jones, 1998).

In the second half of the 1990s, manufacturing FDI, especially quality projects, has become more difficult to attract. In the first place, the Asian crisis has led to a slow-down in FDI from the Far East and the increase in the value of Sterling has also made the North-East less attractive. But most significant, for the long term, is increasing competition to attract inward FDI from other countries. As we argued in chapter five, governments across the world are shifting to a more open policy towards inward FDI, with France, for example, making a U-turn in policy and establishing a centralised investment agency to actively attract inward investment. In fact, France attracted more inward FDI flows than the UK in the first half of the 1990s and its share of European FDI projects is increasing every year. With over 1,000 development agencies across Europe bidding for inward investment, the NDC is facing greater competition for FDI projects from other locations.

Competition for projects is not only intensifying from developed countries, like France and Ireland, but also from developing countries, especially with the break-up of the Soviet Union. As a secondee from Barclay's Bank to the NDC notes:

> Competition for internationally mobile investment is intense, particularly from Central Europe, China and North America, which are increasingly important locations for companies with global business strategies (Docherty, 1997).

Similarly, in the NDC's quarterly reports to the IBB, it is argued, 'Major competition has been experienced from Eastern Europe, specifically Hungary and the Czech Republic' (NDC, 1997d) and 'we perceive a threat emerging from low cost locations in Central Europe who are providing an attractive option to existing OEM's in regard to the manufacture of key components' (NDC, 1997f).

By the mid-1990s Eastern Europe became major competitors for labour intensive investment in Europe in sectors such as automobiles, electronics and textiles. Hungary, Poland, the Czech Republic, Turkey, Estonia, Slovakia, and Slovenia offer generous incentives, Enterprise Zones for inward investors, and have wages a fraction of the North-East level. German firms are shifting production to Eastern Europe in order to lower costs (especially for SMEs) and penetrate the market (Estrin *et al.*, 1997; Larcon, 1998), leaving fewer opportunities for the North-East. According to PricewaterhouseCoopers (1999), Eastern Europe's share of European FDI projects has increased from 5% to 15% in second half of 1990s, driven by their lower costs, strategic location, much improved regulatory situation, and accession prospects with EU. In Table 4.10 we also saw that in 1999 Poland, Hungary and the Czech Republic were all in the top 5 locations for European FDI projects in manufacturing and Hungary was in the top 10 locations for R&D projects. According to executives at the NDC, increasing competition for inward FDI is leading to a greater concentration on indigenous enterprises.

The optimism of the late 1980s and early 1990s regarding the ability of inward FDI to sustain regional development was also being eroded by the mid-1990s as the North-East failed to catch-up with the UK by most economic and social measures. In chapter ten, we saw that the North-East is the poorest region in England and it was becoming clearer that using inward investment as the sole agent for achieving economic development in the North had not been effective in catching-up with the rest of the UK. Unemployment continued to be several percentage points above the UK average and The North-East Labour Market Report found that in terms of incomes 'the region is not making progress in narrowing the gap ... Earnings in the region are on average 10.3% below the national average' (TEC, 1998). Grant (1997) also shows that economic performance of North-East continues to below other UK regions. Figure 11.1 shows GDP per head in the North-East from 1986 to 1996 compared to its main rivals for inward FDI – Scotland and Wales – and the UK average.

The trend over the period 1986–96 is clear; the gap between the North-East and the UK is widening and Scotland has caught up with the UK average. While GDP per head in Wales has remained roughly at the level of the North-East, Wales has lower unemployment than either the North-East or Scotland. In 1986, GDP per head in the

Figure 11.1 GDP/head in the North East, Scotland, Wales and the UK, 1986–96 (£)

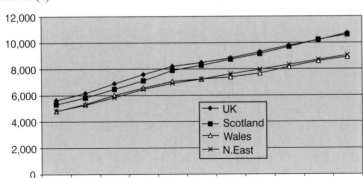

Source: ONS (1998c).

North-East was 86% of the UK average, but in 1996 it had fallen to 84%, indicating that while inward investment had arguably spearheaded new job creation in the North-East, it had failed to converge the region towards UK levels of income.

According to the Financial Times, commenting in 1998 on the collapse of many inward investment projects in the North-East, the region 'has the UK's highest regional unemployment rate, its worst educational attainment record, the lowest household weekly income and the lowest business survival rate. It also has England's lowest regional GDP.' If we define competitiveness as the ability to increase both labour productivity and factor incomes (Hitchens *et al.*, 1993), the policy based on inward investment failed to increase the competitiveness of the region relative to the rest of the UK. The Welsh Development Agency appears to have come to the same conclusion in the case of Wales. In its 2000–2003 Corporate Plan, the agency concludes that: 'Restructuring around infrastructure development, financial incentives and the attraction of foreign capital has not, however, narrowed the GDP gap' (WDA, 2000: 8).

In response to the poor performance of the North-East economy, intensifying competition for new inward FDI projects and increasing dissatisfaction over the quality of jobs created, the NDC's strategy of using inward investment as the pivot for developing the regional economy is slowly being re-appraised, although certainly not rejected. As Dr Bridge notes, 'the NDC was largely focused on attracting new,

mobile, international investment. . . . In 1998, the focus is much wider'
(Bridge, 1998a: 12) and in a subsequent interview he emphasised, 'I
don't think anyone would argue that you would want a regional policy
which was entirely based upon inward investment' (Bridge, 1998b).
The collapse of Siemens and Fujitsu has hastened the change in
attitudes over the role of inward investment in regional development.

The NDC is now entering a third stage of policy, focusing more on
indigenous enterprises (NDC, 1997b, 1998e). Investor development
and supply chain programmes, while increasing the spin-offs from
inward investment for local suppliers, were primarily aimed at attracting and embedding inward FDI in order to secure new and re-investment by foreign subsidiaries. Inward investment was at the centre of
development policy. Now the emphasis is reversing; local suppliers are
not seen so much as a means to secure MNC investment but rather
MNCs are seen as a way to improve the competitiveness of indigenous
industry. Perceptions over the drivers of long term, sustainable economic development are changing from MNCs to SMEs, where the NDC
believes the bulk of future jobs will come from (NDC, 1997e). As an
internal study of research in the NDC found in 1998:

> The third and largest group of projects [50%] consists of research
> activities that are . . . less linked to NDC's traditional role in attract-
> ing inward investment, but draw on NDC's increasing role in devel-
> oping indigenous industry and point toward the future role of a
> RDA (Hamilton, 1998).

The Raising Regional Competitiveness Project, which began in 1996,
is playing an important role in re-directing support to local industry.
The Competitiveness Project is managed by NDC on behalf of partners in region – Business Links, Local Authorities, Northern Business
Forum, Chamber of Commerce, Regional Technology Centre, GO–NE
and higher education institutions – and is the largest project of its
kind in the UK (NDC, 1998d). The stated goal is, 'To Create continuously improving sustainable competitiveness through common
understanding and synergy' and the project looks at the underlying
causes of non-competitiveness and identifies mechanisms for improving competitiveness. The activities of the project include company
bench-marking, regional bench-marking and business support process
improvement and the emphasis is strongly on indigenous business. In
fact, John Armstrong, the leading personality in the project, argues
that indigenous business must be at the centre of any long term strategy

for raising competitiveness in the region, and in a recent interview he stated that, 'if you can't do it with indigenous business fast enough then attract FDI as a tactical move for the short term (Armstrong, 1998). FDI is not seen as a long term substitute for regional development based on endogenous growth.

To upgrade the quality and performance of the local supplier base the NDC is in the process of developing a targeted strategy for attracting FDI and the issue of how to increase the R&D capability of both local industry and MNCs is at the centre of present debate. The first moves towards a targeted FDI strategy came when the NDC shifted from a geographic-desk basis to a sector-approach to understand and help sectors individually. As the NDC's expertise concerning the strengths and weaknesses of each major sector built-up, there was greater pressure to identify areas within each sector in need of improvement and target inward investment accordingly. For example, the NDC's 1998/99 strategic market plan for the automotive industry states:

> It is no longer acceptable for inward investment to be seen as the only fix for unemployment. Attracting any investment that comes along without ensuring that it fits the regional profile is at best a short term fix. Waiting to be given opportunities through IBB or our own overseas offices is not enough....Finding companies capable of filling national gaps is an imperative....All inward investment **must** add additional value to the current infrastructure....It is absolutely necessary to ensure that any OEM targeted by NDC meets the needs of the region and the supplier base (Hall, 1997).

The Director of Investment Services at the NDC, Chris Fraser, argues that the aim should be not only to identify and compensate for weaknesses in each sector, but to ensure that the areas in which the region has strengths in are fully developed:

> We have to be pro-active...to sell the region in competition with other regions, build on our strengths (e.g. pharmaceuticals) and also to fill in gaps in infrastructure...supply gaps and new sectors (Fraser, 1998).

Project management teams will not wait for incoming inquiries but will be given a certain number of countries to target and they will have to contact a selection of companies and ask them whether or not they would be interested in locating in the North of England. According to the NDC (1998g), 'What is going to happen is that each member of the PMT will try to be more pro-active than reactive.'

As part of the emerging pro-active, sector-based strategy, the NDC is also working on an initiative to prioritise the response to potential investment projects, either from a company or the IBB. Prioritisation assesses how much resources and effort to commit and will check whether the project is of high or low priority for NDC teams. According to Aisbitt (1998) and Gartland (1998), who are working on prioritisation at the NDC, at present as much effort goes into bad as good inquiries and with 500 inquiries a year and only 8 investment managers, the aim is to match the money to the priorities. Prioritisation will be based on three key criteria:

● the probability of winning the investment;
● the value of the investment;
● the fit with overall strategy.

Prioritisation will be computerised to facilitate speedy decisions about how much resources to commit. Additionally the NDC's overseas posts will have to understand which projects are most suitable, which doesn't happen now. The foundations are being laid to attract inward investment as part of a sector-based regional development strategy. At the heart of the emerging regional strategy for the North-East appears to be the aim to target foreign companies according to their potential contribution to the long term sustainable development of indigenous industry.

This would represent another major break with the policy of the 1980s and 1990s, as identified by Dicken and Tickell (1992). Dicken and Tickell's first major criticism of Local Authorities in the North-East was that they did not maintain contact with foreign companies in the region once they invested and their second major criticism was that they found only 25% of Local Authorities claimed to adopt a targeted strategy to attract particular types of investment, which they described as 'a short-sighted policy without knowledge of integration into local economy'. The NDC is combating both of these criticisms through its embedding policies and emerging targeting strategy.

With the NDC, and its present staff of 105, accounting for over half the personnel of the new North-East RDA and with the Chief Executive of the NDC becoming Chairman of the new RDA, it is very likely the NDC's embedding and more pro-active targeting strategy will be central to the Regional Economic Strategy of the RDA and therefore to the region as a whole. This strategy will be based as much on indigenous SMEs as inward investment, with the Chairman of the NDC, George Russel, stating:

> we still need to attract mobile investment into the Region, but, just as important, we need to retain and improve our existing investor base and secure the critical value-added from this investment by growing our small and medium-sized enterprises. This is a challenge to the existing economic development partnership, but must also be at the core of the New Agency (Russel, 1997: 1).

11.3 TECHNOLOGY POLICY, INWARD INVESTMENT AND THE RDAS

With greater focus on the quality of inward FDI and the link between MNCs and the competitiveness of indigenous enterprises, the key inter-related problem with both inward investment and SMEs is increasingly viewed in the NDC to be weakness in R&D activities and capability. For example, in life sciences, the NDC argues in its Regional Sector Strategy for Improved SME Performance that:

> potential exists for further SME development by promoting the regional R&D base, pro-actively pursuing new investment initiatives, bridging links between university centres of excellence ... and the wider network aimed at research for start up, joint venture and strategic alliance opportunities (NDC, 1997b).

The need for similar action has been recently identified in other region's of the UK that have followed an exogenous path to economic development. For example, the Welsh Development Agency argues 'Small and Medium Sized Enterprises (SMEs) are under-performing in several crucial respects, including new firm formation, innovation and R&D, investment in physical and human capital and international trade' (WDA, 2000). The implications have been highlighted in the NDC's 1998/99 strategic sector plans for electronics (Grosvenor and Malloy, 1997), life science (Chexal, 1997a), and the automotive sector (Hall, 1997) – without the development of R&D capabilities and the introduction of new technologies and products in SMEs, local linkages in the region will remain weak and there will be continued dependence on large, mobile multinational investors.

As we can see from Table 11.6, at present the North-East fares badly compared to other UK regions in terms of the R&D expenditure and employment provided by manufacturing enterprises. In 1996, only 3,000 people were employed in R&D in the North-East compared to over three times more in the North West, Midlands and South-West, four times more in London, six times more in the Eastern region and seven times more in the South East. Each of these regions also had far higher per capita employment in R&D. Only the territorial regions had lower R&D employment per person than the North-East.

If we look at R&D expenditure, the gap between the North-East and other English regions is even wider, and R&D expenditure in the North-East as a proportion of GDP is lower than every English region, with the exception of Yorkshire and Humberside. Only 0.7% of GDP was accounted for by the R&D of manufacturing enterprises in the North-East in 1996, almost half the UK average. Manufacturing businesses in the region spent only 2.9% of valued added on R&D

Table 11.6 R&D expenditure and employment of manufacturing businesses in UK regions, 1996

	R&D employment	Expenditure on R&D by manufacturing enterprises (£m)		
		Total	% GDP	% gross value added
North East	3,000	187	0.7	2.9
North West	10,000	1,064	1.4	5.8
York & Hum	5,000	275	0.5	2.2
E. Midlands	10,000	710	1.4	5.7
W. Midland	11,000	628	1.0	3.8
Eastern	18,000	2,057	2.8	17.0
London	12,000*	889	0.8	8.1
South East	21,000	2,207	1.9	13.4
South West	9,000	726	1.3	7.1
Wales	2,000	117	0.4	1.5
Scotland	4,000	357	0.6	3.0
N. Ireland	2,000	83	0.5	2.7
UK	105,000	9,301	1.3	6.7

*all sectors.
Source: ONS (1998b,c) and DTI (1999a).

compared to 6.7% for the UK as a whole and 17% in the Eastern region.

The NDC argues that the R&D capability in SMEs is crucial for their long term competitiveness, and low levels of R&D reduce the opportunities for innovative new firm start-ups and is a key reason for the poor quality of jobs and low incomes in the region. For example, in 1997 an R&D worker in the North-East would earn £574 per week – well over three times higher than an unskilled production worker and over twice as high as a skilled worker (derived from NDC, 1998e). Furthermore, minimal R&D in the region by MNCs lowers the costs of exit for existing foreign investors and is a major constraint to sustainable investment (Hall, 1997; NDC, 1997b).

Table 11.7 shows R&D projects in the Northern region by foreign MNCs from 1985 to 1997. Over this period there were just 14 overseas R&D projects – only 2.5% of the 568 FDI projects in the region. Inward R&D projects created 624 new jobs, 1.4% of total, with investment of £47 million. This represents only 0.5% of total FDI in the region since 1985.

The major foreign investors in R&D were Japanese firms, which reflects the growth of Japanese R&D in Europe as a whole in the 1990s. Japanese R&D projects are concentrated in the automotive sector, following the lead of Nissan, who established a European Technology Centre in the region in 1988. In fact, as with FDI as a whole, Nissan dominates foreign R&D projects in the region, accounting for 40% of total R&D investment and almost one-quarter of the associated jobs. This is despite the fact that Nissan's main R&D activities take place in Cranfied, UK. R&D projects by foreign companies of non-Japanese origin are primarily focused on the pharmaceuticals sector, where the region has a cluster of manufacturing and research activities revolving around the presence of ICI. The chemical sector dominates overall R&D in the North-East, accounting for £100 million of £175 million expenditure on R&D in 1996 (ONS, 1998b).

Although the NDC has been emphasising the importance of technology for several years, there has been very little support for R&D in the region. One significant factor is that central government policy appears to have amplified the low levels of R&D in the North-East. While total business expenditure on R&D in 1996 was the lowest in England and 10 times lower than the South East, government expenditure on R&D in the region, at only £16 million, was over 40 times lower than in the South East, and nearly one-third of expenditure in Yorkshire and Humberside (derived from EP, 1997a). In fact,

Table 11.7 Overseas R&D projects in the North East and Cumbria, 1985–97

Country	Company	Year	Type FDI	New jobs	Capital (£m)	Activity
Japan	Nissan European Technology Centre	1988	New	200	1.5	Car design (Washington, Tyne & Wear)
Japan	Calsonic Technical Centre	1989	New	15	0	Autocomponents R&D (Washington, Tyne & Wear)
Japan	Ikeda Technology	1989	New	50	10	Car Seats R&D (Washington, Tyne & Wear)
Japan	Nissan European Technology Centre	1990	New	0	8	Car design (Washington, Tyne & Wear)
Japan	Hashimoto	1991	Exp.	120	10	Vehicle R&D (Boldon, Tyne & Wear)
USA	Sterling Research	1991	Exp.	160	0	Drug R&D Centre (Alnwick, Northumberland)
Japan	Ikeda Technology Europe	1991	Exp.	30	3	Automotive R&D (Newcastle, Tyne & Wear)
Japan	Komatsu	1991	New	15	3	Earth-moving equipment R&D (Birtley, Tyne and Wear)
Hong-Kong	GPT/HP Electronics	1991	Acq.	0	0	Telecommunications R&D (Aycliffe, Durham)
Austria	PAA Biologics	1992	New	20	0	Genetic Engineering (Consett, Durham)
Taiwan	Synpac	1994	Exp.	14	2.5	Pharmaceuticals R&D (Cambois, Northumberland)
France	Sterling Organics	1994	Exp.	0	9	Pharmaceuticals R&D (Dudley, Northumberland)
France	Sterling Research/ Sanofi	1994	Acq.	0	0	Pharmaceuticals R&D (Alnwick, Northumberland)

Source: derived from NDC project data.

government R&D expenditure in each of the Eastern, South East, and South-West regions exceeds *business* R&D expenditure in the North-East. Higher education R&D expenditure in the North-East is also by far the lowest in England.

Another important factor is that central government separated FDI and technology policy at both the national and regional levels. At the regional level, the RDOs had responsibility for inward investment, while the Government Offices were in charge of technology, making it difficult to develop and implement a strategy for regional development based on integrating FDI and technology. In the North-East, as in other regions, there was no strategy to link inward investment to technological upgrading and what evolved was a series of ad hoc initiatives, largely driven by the European Union, rather than national government.

The European structural funds made large amounts of cash available for R&D type activities, and the NDC won an EU contract to develop a Regional Innovation and Technology Transfer Strategy. However, unlike in Wales where a similar contract led to additional European funding and to the launch in 1996 of a Regional Technology Plan, at the NDC no strategies or action plans were produced. It was left to the Government Office to develop some sought of strategy for technology in the region.

A Regional Innovation and Technology Strategy was developed by the GO–NE in 1992 to reduce the fragmentation in university–business–government links. A partnership of universities, further education colleges and several independent private sector providers identified the key issues facing the region in terms of R&D and what sort of infrastructure they wanted to put into place. This framework was then used to bid for European funds and decide which projects to support. Through accessing European structural funds the technology team at the Government Office hoped to encourage businesses to tap into R&D support services and to develop the infrastructure to make R&D available to businesses. Three main initiatives have come out of the Regional Innovation and Technology Strategy:

● Knowledge House;
● Regional Technology Centre;
● Three Rivers Strategy.

Knowledge House is the most recent strategy and is hailed as best practice by central government. It was developed in the mid-1990s, and involves an individual placed in each university in the region whose prime role is to help businesses gain the support they might need from that university. A central clearing house for the whole region was set-up to allow businesses to use the universities to find solutions for research problems. The role of the Regional Technology Centre – a small operation established in 1980s – was also significantly increased. One of the projects it undertakes is to identify ideas and help develop them into small businesses.

The third main technology project is the Three Rivers Strategy, which aimed to build-up university expertise according to business clusters in the region, as previously much university research was perceived as irrelevant to the needs of business. Three clusters were identified coinciding with the three major rivers in the region. On Teeside, the chemical industry dominates, on the Wear there is a cluster of automotive activities revolving around Nissan, and on the Tyne there is what is left of rig constructors and shipbuilding. Specialist centres of expertise were established – at Newcastle University a Regional Centre for Innovation and Design, at Sunderland University a Centre for Automotive (Advanced) Manufacturing Management and a Centre for European Process Industries was also set-up. The idea was to direct structural funds to develop existing clusters.

According to Rick O'Farrel, Head of Technology at the Government Office-North-East, these initiatives have not been as successful as they would have liked. The centres of education and research in the North-East have little R&D capability and there is no long term government aid to support the expansion of the research base. As with central government technology policy, the emphasis has been on an efficient allocation of resources within the existing R&D base.

Apart from the above three *ad hoc* initiatives, there has also been no integrated strategy for technology transfer with the region lacking an innovative support system of intermediate organisations (Rhodes, 1995: 341). If we compare the technology initiatives in the North-East with those in Wales, as documented by Huggins (1996), and Cooke (1998a) then it is clear that the North-East failed to develop a technology strategy based on the partnership that was achieved in Wales. As the NDC states in relation to technology policy, 'Key public and private sector organisations within the region are operating in isolation' (Chexal, 1997a).

In Wales, the WDA, the Welsh Office and about 600 public and private organisations in an EU sponsored Regional Technology Plan identified 66 projects ranging from technology transfer, supply chains, finance for innovation, skills and so on. Sectors were targeted and networking relations were developed in the 1990s, with initiatives including the Technology Forum to promote the horizontal interaction of firms and institutions (similar to Knowledge House), the Welsh Medical Technology Forum, the Welsh Opto-Electronics Forum, the Automotive Training Centre to help training in SMEs, and various Innovation Centres (see Cooke, 1997; Cooke and Morgan, 1998). At the same time, the WDA also has similar supply chain initiatives to the NDC, forming 20 supplier associations in 1996 in the automotive and electronics sectors to improve local supplier capabilities and integrate MNCs into the local economy (Morgan, 1996; Pyke, 1997a).

A key advantage for Wales was the greater autonomy of the WDA and the Welsh Office relative to the respective bodies in the North-East. Finance of £7 billion through a block grant gives the Welsh Office greater leeway to tailor central government initiatives to local needs and to vire between its budgets – for example, in order to attract a major inward investment project. The Welsh Office and WDA also have a greater functional remit than the NDC or Government Office-North-East and Wales has been better placed to bid for European funds, being seen as a clearly recognised 'region' of Europe. In bidding for European structural funds, a greater degree of partnership has been engendered.

The establishment of RDAs in English Regions in 1999 should put the North-East in a better position to develop a more coherent economic strategy for the region and bid for European funds (Elcock, 1997), although the approximate £500 million under the control of the RDA will not take the form of a block grant, which may weaken the ability of the Agency to co-ordinate programmes in the region. The RDA in the North-East will include the NDC, the RSO, English Partnerships, and the Rural Development Commission, and it will have a significant role in overseeing the strategic plans of the TECs (or their future replacement).[4] Responsibility for taking forward technology policy in the region is passing from the Government Office to the North-East RDA and, following the launch of Regional Innovation Strategies in the EU in 1997, a Regional Innovation Strategy is being developed, which will form an integral part of the Regional Economic Strategy of the new RDA.

At present, while the NDC is targeting sectors so that inward investment will meet the needs of indigenous industry, this targeted strategy is not fed into the RSA offered by the Government Office while, at the same time, the technology strategy of the Government

Office is not necessarily reflected in the NDC's targeted strategy for inward investment. Both the NDC and Government Office are emphasising the 'quality' of inward investment, especially in the wake of the DTI's vision of a knowledge-driven economy, but there is no co-ordination between the two organisations to define what 'quality' actually means. The assumption is that an investment providing technology, high skills and good training is a 'quality' project, and that SMEs should be favoured over multinationals. But, unless a criteria is developed to determine the allocation of RSA, cost-per-job and the bargaining power of MNCs are likely to continue to be the main factors behind who gets the money.

The RDAs offer a major opportunity to integrate inward investment with technology policy as part of an overall development strategy and to ensure that RSA is allocated according to this strategy. While formal communication between the RDA and Government Offices is envisaged, with each RDA having representatives on the DTI's industrial advisory board in the Government Office, we suggest that a coherent strategy needs to be put in place to prioritise the allocation of RSA according to a targeted sector based strategy for regional development. Strong partnership is therefore a requirement for economic development, which perhaps is best achieved through an elected regional assembly which would make the RDA accountable to a legitimate regional government rather than to Ministers in central government.

12 Conclusions and Policy Recommendations

In this book we have covered a wide range of research topics relating to the activities of MNCs. We analysed structural changes and their impact on the strategy and organisation of MNCs, the globalisation of technology, and bargaining between MNCs and governments. We discussed in detail inward investment in the UK and UK industrial policy at the national and regional levels, with case studies of Nissan, Siemens, and regional development in North East England.

We conclude in this chapter by summarising the main findings of our study, addressing the five research questions outlined in our introduction in chapter one. In the first section of our conclusion we examine the implications of our research for the role of inward investment in regional development, and in the second section we outline policy recommendations for improving the contribution of MNCs to regional economic development.

The main argument is that if left to market forces attracting inward investment is unlikely address the disadvantaged position of peripheral regions and that a new strategic framework is needed to position the policy of attracting FDI into a wider strategy for endogenous economic development. We argue that a new framework should integrate policy across five dimensions:

- technology, SMEs and training;
- after-care policy;
- investor targeting;
- incentives;
- bargaining with MNCs.

We suggest that such a framework would be most effective if an elected regional assembly was created in the English regions, but also that a greater role for the EU is desirable.

333

12.1 INWARD INVESTMENT AND ECONOMIC DEVELOPMENT: RESEARCH FINDINGS

Attracting inward investment has been the British government's key industrial policy instrument for regional development in peripheral regions. Reducing unemployment has been the dominant objective in attracting inward investment, reflected in the allocation criteria for regional selective assistance. In terms of reducing unemployment and weathering the decline of traditional industry, the policy has met with some success. In Wales, inward investment reversed manufacturing decline (Cooke and Morgan, 1998) and in Scotland, the performance of foreign companies has been better than indigenous plants (Turok, 1993b).

Similarly, our study of the North East showed that inward investment has created new jobs, new investment and facilitated the growth of new industrial sectors, in particular the automotive industry. In fact, the North East's share of UK manufacturing output increased by over 25% in the 1990s (NDC, 1998c), and the region is the UK's most successful exporter – in large part due to the high export intensity of multinationals in the region. For example, Nissan's North East plant exports over three times more than Siemens 12 manufacturing plants in the UK combined.

In relation to our first research question – *what is the role of government inward investment policy in attracting FDI* – UK regional policy has effectively channeled inward investment to peripheral regions. Furthermore, our case studies of Intel and Siemens demonstrate that a professional facilitative service offered by government to inward investors can influence the location of investment, especially towards the final stages of the MNC decision-making process. The case of Siemens in particular illustrates the importance of a coherent, coordinated and rapid response to meeting the needs of inward investors at the central, regional and local levels. Our example of French policy in chapter five and Nissan's investment in chapter seven also highlights the importance of central government policy and attitudes. Government inward investment policy can therefore have a major influence on attracting FDI. Table 6.1 lists some of the key factors influencing the institutional capability of an inward investment agency to successfully attract FDI.

Our study of inward investment in the North East, however, showed that despite central government's emphasis on attracting new FDI, in the 1990s the focus of the NDC shifted from luring inward investment to supporting existing investors. The change in policy reflected the vulnerability of existing investment to closure. For example, net job creation by foreign companies (excluding acquisitions) in the North was only 958 from 1979 to 1992, while Scotland and Wales registered net job *losses* of nearly 32,000 and over 2,000 respectively (derived from Peck and Stone, 1996). The performance of foreign only appears positive in the light of the collapse of the domestic manufacturing industry.

In the North East, we saw that an important initiative to support inward investors was the NDC's supply chain programme. The main motivation was to counter the low levels of local sourcing by MNCs. Local content for foreign companies in the North East is only about 20%, and in Scotland it is even less (Turok, 1993a,b; Buxton, 1995b). Market forces did not lead inward investors to develop close linkages with domestic suppliers – an important factor behind the vulnerability of foreign companies to closure.

In relation to our second research question – *how, if at all, has inward investment policy and incentives been linked to an overall industrial strategy to maximise the benefits of foreign direct investment?* – the UK government's market-led philosophy and belief in the unequivocal benefits of inward investment resulted in an industrial policy which made no attempt to link FDI to the competitiveness of indigenous industry. At the sub-national level, regions like the North East, which have bared the cost of central government's policy apathy, realised in the 1990s that the benefits of inward investment were dependent upon redirecting money and effort away from attracting FDI and towards integrating foreign companies into the regional economy. Two major initiatives to link FDI to local industry have been investor development and supply chain development programmes.

However, there has been minimal support both in central government and in the North East to develop and link technology in MNCs and SMEs. We found the R&D activities of foreign companies to be minimal in the North East, which appears to be the pattern for other regions. Studies of Scotland (Turok, 1993b), Ireland (O'Malley, 1990), and a major study looking at FDI in five European regions (Amin *et al.*, 1994) all concluded that the R&D of MNCs and innovation capacity of regions was limited. In the UK as a whole, our research showed that R&D by foreign companies is low relative to both indigenous firms and especially to other countries.

The weak R&D activities of MNCs in the UK, especially in peripheral regions, are inter-linked to the low levels of local sourcing. The importance of product design being done locally is that the supplier of high value components for a product is usually chosen by its designers. Buxton (1995b) notes that if products are designed in the US then the designers will usually specify suppliers based there and Taylor (1998) points-out that in the automotive and engineering industries designers and suppliers are linked, with the project engineer or designer choosing local suppliers, often within a 50 mile radius. The link between R&D and high value added production is discussed by DuBois *et al.*, who observe that:

> technology-intensive products tend to be manufactured close to the R&D function as a result of the need to troubleshoot production processes during the product's early life.... In addition, there is a critical need for proximity to the state-of-the-art development in product design and product technology (1993, cited in Tan and Vertinsky, 1996)

With low levels of local sourcing, the impact of FDI on the trade balance is likely to be negative (Loewendahl, 1996). Moran (1996: 428) and Estrin *et al.* (1997: 25) note that the literature shows the propensity to import from established foreign suppliers is high and Tarabusi and Vickery (1996: 96–8) give evidence linking countries with high shares of foreign companies to high shares of foreign sourcing. Embeddedness of multinationals is therefore linked more to innovation and production than to market variables (Hood and Taggart, 1997: 148).

Both innovation and production are dependent on R&D. The global–local strategies of MNCs are leading to the establishment of more overseas R&D centres, as we saw chapter four, and emergence of the N-form will create more opportunities for overseas subsidiaries to play a strategic role in innovation. But the R&D activities of MNCs are kept primarily at home, and the globalisation of technology is associated more with M&As of research-intensive firms, cross-border co-operative alliances, and other strategic relations than direct, greenfield FDI. Only subsidiaries operating in highly networked localities with clusters of supporting institutions and SMEs and a strong technological infrastructure will have the possibility to become 'contributor' or 'strategic leader' plants. Centres of research excellence, often revolving around universities, appear to be vital to developing host base clusters of MNC research activities.

The R&D capability of SMEs has become additionally important with changes in the production structure. As we saw in chapter four,

MNCs are passing more responsibility for higher-value added manufacturing and R&D to first tier suppliers and in other industries, like pharmaceuticals, rationalisation means that only the most capable suppliers will survive. For the UK as a whole, and for sub-national regions like the North East, we have argued that R&D and SMEs have been largely neglected, with policy favouring the attraction of labour-intensive inward FDI. The result has been minimal pressures for the technological integration of MNCs with the supplier base and increased vulnerability of projects to closure or dis-investment.

Weakness in engineering and technical skills and availability reduces the long-term commitment of inward investors. While we argued that Nissan is a successful example of embeddedness, the future of Nissan in the UK will depend on the manufacturing and research capabilities of suppliers and the availability of trained workers, as well as the British government's commitment to being at the centre of European integration. Even then, Nissan is a manufacturing plant – a super-systems integrator – with limited possibilities for increasing its strategic remit. The case of Siemens starkly illustrates the impact of limited technological integration with the supplier base on the vulnerability of a subsidiary that is not a key weapon in the multinational's armoury. Other FDI projects, like Samsung in the North East, are of branch-plant status making minimal contribution to the regional economy, even though attracting generous government incentives.

The key historic location advantage of the UK has not been its technological or skill infrastructure, but rather institutional openness to FDI and new work practices and a cost advantage connected with low relative labour costs and the availability of government incentives. While FDI in the UK is likely to be associated with organisational innovation, as MNCs like Nissan introduce new work practices and supplier relations, flexibility and cost-oriented investment motivations are unlikely, in-themselves, to lead to technological innovation and integration with local industry. As Lall (1995b: 8) argues, 'In responding to free market forces, foreign investors would focus on activities that exploit a host country's given competitive advantages rather than those that could be developed with some additional effort.' The positive contribution of Nissan to the local supplier base is the exception rather than the rule. Furthermore, labour market flexibility makes it easier for foreign companies to dis-invest and close their operations, as the examples of Siemens and Fujitsu in 1998 and BMW (Rover) and Ford (Dagenham) in 2000 illustrate.

The UK's economic development policy, based on inward FDI, has failed to increase the competitiveness of peripheral regions. Only in Scotland has income per capita converged with the UK average; in the North East it has actually declined over time, indicating the failure of British regional policy.[1] While central government continued to believe that market forces would lead to beneficial outcomes from inward investment, in the North East the NDC has reacted with after-care, supplier development and a more targeted FDI strategy, with similar initiatives being implemented in Wales.

However, these initiatives do not go far enough. A coherent strategy is needed for integrating industrial, technology and regional policy and determining the role that inward investment should play. The recent emphasis of both central and regional government on technology and SMEs is disingenuous to an industrial policy that stresses the attraction of job-creating inward FDI in peripheral regions based on the carrot of labour flexibility and cost-related location advantages.

The integration of foreign companies with local industry depends not only on the corporate strategies of MNCs but also on the quality of the existing SME, skill, and research infrastructure. In relation to our third research question – *how do foreign MNCs contribute to the development of the national technology base?* – our main conclusion is that on the one hand the contribution of inward investment depends on the strategy and organisation of MNCs, while on the other hand it depends on the location advantages of the host country. Multinational companies, as they move towards the network-form, are making greater efforts to leverage innovation world-wide and specialise R&D activities and world product mandates in centres of excellence globally, as we saw for both ABB and Siemens. This creates more opportunities for government's to attract inward R&D investment and for subsidiaries to play a strategic role and upgrade to higher value added activities.

To benefit from inward investment and the transition to the N-form, it is essential that the investor development and supply chain initiatives, as being developed at the NDC, are strengthened to encourage subsidiary evolution. After-care policies must also be integrated to incentives, and to a strategy for increasing skills, technology and support for SMEs. Inward FDI is not a substitute to endogenous-based development policy; the success of inward investment depends on it.

In the case of the North East, we found no link between a fragmented technology policy and the attraction of inward investment and, furthermore, minimal effective co-ordination between the incentives offered to multinationals by the Government Office and the increasingly targeted sector-based inward investment strategy of the NDC. In our interviews, officials at the NDC stated that they did not even know the Government Office North East's allocation criteria for RSA. While both the NDC and the Government Office hope to attract quality FDI, there has been no attempt to define a 'quality' investment and link this to the incentives offered to investors.

We propose a new strategic framework for making and implementing policy towards inward investment and regional development. This can only be achieved by a change in inward investment policy and a greater degree of autonomy, partnership and trust at the regional level. In the next section we give policy recommendations to our fourth research question – *what are the policy options for linking inward investment to economic development?*

12.2 INWARD INVESTMENT AND ECONOMIC DEVELOPMENT: POLICY RECOMMENDATIONS

Our research has suggested that a key question for central government and peripheral regions is what alternatives are there to attracting inward investment as the principal policy for regional development? Giunta and Martinelli (1995: 255) conclude that 'there is no viable alternative for peripheral regions, at least in the medium term, to offering traditional cost advantages', which points to the lack of options for less-advantaged regions. Neither in the North East, nor in other peripheral regions like Wales, is there a 'Cambridge' or a 'MIT' which can be leveraged to develop a research-intensive SME sector and high-tech start-ups. The lack of world-class centres of research expertise and clusters of innovative SMEs in turn reduces the possibilities for attracting the higher value added activities of MNCs.

The perception that there were no alternatives to attracting inward investment was seen in our study of the NDC's development policy. Although we found an emerging consensus in the NDC and Government Office in the region that R&D and SMEs must be prioritised over FDI, the reality was that few officials thought there were any alternatives to FDI and many acknowledged the difficulty in attracting 'quality' investments. In our interviews, a senior investment manager argued that, 'The North East is the most disadvantaged region in the

UK and therefore cannot afford to be so selective and must be realistic', and a business development manager stated, 'the North East cannot attract a headquarters'. The key strategist at the NDC, John Armstrong, uses an analogy to highlight the problems in attracting high quality investments:

> the star player in a football team will not go to a lower division, whatever money is offered, unless he can be convinced that there are other good players, fans, and a history at that club (Armstrong, 1998).

There were minimal opportunities for attracting high quality investment, not only because of the weakness of the innovation, supplier and skill base in the region, but also because competition is extremely intense for the few 'flagship' investments that have the potential to develop new technologies, skilled jobs and act as catalysts for supply chain development. Rather than targeting specific types of investment project, the NDC traditionally welcomed all inward FDI, particularly large, job creating manufacturing investment. In common with developments in Wales and Scotland, the NDC introduced investor development and supply chain after-care initiatives to embed MNCs and hoped that its institutional support for suppliers would also increase the attractiveness of the region to new FDI. The NDC was therefore following the policy prescription of Amin *et al.* (1994), who argue that upgrading existing plants is perhaps more crucial than attracting particular investments in the first place. The first major alternative to attracting new FDI is therefore supporting the competitiveness of existing foreign companies through creating supply chain linkages with local industry.

However, after-care policy is aimed at adding value from inward investment rather than providing alternatives to a regional economic development policy based on FDI. The evidence in this study suggests that the exogenous path to RED has not, and will not, be sufficient for increasing the competitiveness of peripheral regions, i.e. for reducing unemployment and driving both productivity *and* income up to the national average. MNCs are poor catalysts for increasing R&D, and will transfer strategic and high value added activities overseas only to locations that have a *pre-existing* R&D base.

Even though low costs and work-force flexibility remain the key location advantage of peripheral regions in the UK, we argue that it is critical for regions like the North East to put in place a strategic framework for building new sources of comparative advantage both to upgrade existing investors and develop alternatives to attracting FDI. This requires a new inward investment strategy as part of an exogenous-endogenous approach to regional economic development. To develop a regional development strategy which breaks away from the exogenous policy of the past decades, central and regional tiers of governance in the UK face five pressing challenges:

● *Increasing the size of the technology base and intensity of links between research institutions, SMEs, and MNCs* in order to support the upgrading of plants and the sustained growth of SMEs. Enlarging the size and quality of the UK education and vocational skills base to meet the needs of industry now and in the future is critical, as is ensuring that peripheral region's have a world class telecommunications and internet infrastructure, which is increasingly vital for both manufacturing and service companies.

● *Expanding investor development and supply chain after-care policies* through building much closer links between the RDAs and MNCs and committing more resources to developing networks and supporting indigenous suppliers.

● *Developing a pro-active, sector-based FDI strategy*, which targets inward investors to meet the needs of local industry, and in particular addresses the historic lack of policy emphasis on service sector FDI in peripheral regions.

● *Changing the system of regional incentives* through prioritising the allocation of regional assistance according to an overall strategy for endogenous (SMEs, technology, training) and exogenous (inward investment) development in each region.

● *Strengthening the institutional system of FDI decision-making* to control competitive bidding and secure long term benefits from MNCs and the incentives offered.

To meet these challenges, we propose a framework that integrates technology, SMEs, training, FDI policy and incentives into a mutually reinforcing and coherent vision for the future direction of the regional and national economy. We would stress that each region should formulate its own vision based on their own strengths and weaknesses and the democratic wishes of the region. This requires a degree of regional autonomy, which does not exist in the English regions.

While the establishment of RDAs will increase the intensity of interactions at the regional level, which is crucial for trust (see Cooke and Morgan, 1998: 31), constant dialogue is required between all parties. Evidence suggests that the establishment in the English regions of elected regional assemblies would give the RDAs greater regional accountability and the political legitimacy to bring together the public and private sectors and build the consensus to make and implement a regional economic development strategy for each region.

12.2.1 Technology, SMEs and training

In Chapter 2, we argued that innovation, knowledge and learning are key sources of competitiveness and we saw that technological change is a major driver of globalisation. Technology is at the heart of core industries like semiconductors and R&D is essential for innovation and economic growth. In chapter nine we found that the UK performs worse than every other major economy in terms of business R&D expenditure and the UK is also behind countries like Germany, Japan, and Sweden in terms of human technological infrastructure. We also saw in Chapter 10 that government R&D in peripheral regions in the UK is dwarfed by that in the richer East and South. This has compounded the weak technology base in poorer regions and the reluctance of multinationals to engage in R&D, which in turn limits the spin-offs of inward investment to SMEs leading to a cycle of low innovation and vulnerability of foreign companies to closure.

With developed countries, like France, shifting to an aggressive FDI promotion policy and with the emergence of low-cost locations in Eastern Europe competition for FDI is intense. Europe-wide competition for inward investment is hastening the shift of peripheral regions in the UK towards a more endogenous approach to regional development. Central to a new exogenous-endogenous approach must be a technology policy based on upgrading existing plants, supporting indigenous SMEs, and developing a world class telecommunications and internet infrastructure.

Trends in international business are also pushing MNCs like Siemens, Daimler Benz and Chrysler towards restructuring, rationalisation and subcontracting. Subsidiaries are at risk if they do not upgrade and suppliers must have advanced manufacturing, research and networking capabilities if they are to become higher tier suppliers. Regional policy needs to support technology linkages between research institutes, SMEs and MNCs, and provide incentives for SMEs and MNCs to expand R&D activities. The supply chain initiatives of the RDAs and RSOs in the UK need to be expanded and combined with technology support policies.

In the North East, a technology policy has put in place ad hoc initiatives designed to help companies exploit better the research potential of universities. However, to integrate MNCs with indigenous companies it crucial that extra-firm institutions are established for supporting technology transfer between universities and SMEs and encouraging co-operation between SMEs so that they have the capability to supply both inputs and technological know-how to MNCs (Esser, 1988; Herrigel, 1993). As argued by cluster, innovation and evolutionary theories, innovation involves interdependence, requires collaboration, and is favoured by geographically proximate networks of SMEs, intermediary institutions and MNCs.

Studies have shown that 72% of firms acquire technology transfer from other firms, firm associations or universities (Cooke, 1998a: 259), about 50% of SMEs state proximate customers and competitors as an important source of technological knowledge (Hassink *et al.*, 1995: 74), and the OECD finds that over 80% of transfers of scientific and technological information from higher education institutes to SMEs involves government assistance (cited in Hassink, 1996: 169). A major change in policy of the UK government is therefore needed; while government's and many academics may argue that companies not countries compete, which favours a non-interventionist policy because of the 'who is us?' conundrum, SMEs are nationally rooted and dependent on government support for competitiveness.

Supporting technology and innovation in SMEs is crucial if SMEs, the engines of growth, are to act as high quality suppliers for disintegrated larger firms and if clusters of competing and co-operating firms are to emerge. Only then can alternatives to the cost and labour flexibility based comparative advantage of peripheral regions develop. Crucially, as the appropriation and generation of technology involves interdependence between firms and collaboration, intermediary institutions are needed to broker horizontal and vertical networks and provide financial, marketing and organisational support for innovation in SMEs (see Hassink, 1996).

Models to follow could be the regionally based 'innovation centres' in the Netherlands to support the technological capabilities of SMEs (Pyke, 1997a), the US$30 million SME network project in Denmark (Henriksen, 1995), the Steinbeis Foundation 'Transfer Centres' for technology transfer to SMEs in Germany (Cooke and Morgan, 1994; Cooke *et al.*, 1995), or the Local Industry Upgrade Programme in Singapore, which stimulates technology transfer between suppliers and MNCs (Peters, 1995).

A successful technology support policy for SMEs must combine networking and R&D programmes with finance, training and risk taking and co-ordinate needs at the local, regional and national level (Eisenschitz and Gough, 1993). A strong regional policy is crucial to reduce the risk and costs for SMEs and hence nurture new firm start-ups (Danson, 1995a; Rhodes, 1995).[2] Developing an entrepreneurial culture is increasingly being identified as essential for new firm formation and innovation (Maskell et al, 1998; Rhodes, 1995).

Government support is also crucial for the provision of qualified scientists and engineers to SMEs and MNCs (Morgan, 1997; Hassink, 1996; Saxenian, 1992). Successful examples include Ireland and Singapore (notably regional states), who evolved their education and vocational training systems as part of an overall strategy to guide MNCs to higher value added activities (Lall, 1997; Görg and Ruane, 1997). For peripheral regions, whose location advantage will depend on lower costs for a considerable time, a large supply of engineers and technicians with good vocational skills is especially important. The key reason is that low labour costs and subsidiary evolution in 'implementer' manufacturing plants like Nissan, TRW and Black & Decker in the North East depends on the availability of skilled workers.

Our argument for increased government support for SMEs, technology and training points to the importance of developing a regional innovation system (Cooke and Morgan, 1998) and a networked region (Tomaney, 1994a) for increasing R&D and the integration of MNCs in peripheral regions. In chapter two we argued that innovation depends on knowledge flows, trust, and co-operation which is most effectively engendered at the sub-national level, and in chapter nine we saw how the federal system in Germany facilitated effective support for SMEs.

The region is the most appropriate governance level for delivering to MNCs and SMEs locally responsive support services and technology transfer, tailoring training to meet the present and future needs of regional industry, brokering vertical and horizontal network relations between firms and institutions, and developing partnership between public and private bodies to create a regionally sensitive strategy for economic development.

As well as integrated support for SMEs, R&D and training, we also emphasise that region's need to develop a world class telecommunications and internet infrastructure. As Gatrell (1999) argues, 'the key to facilitating the exchange of ideas and multifaceted linkages between firms...is the development of a stable, efficient, and cost effective IT infrastructure'. A quality IT&T infrastructure is critical for attracting service sector activities, and is increasingly important for manufacturing operations as final producers and their network of suppliers become linked through e-business. New business growth, in particular the formation of 'new economy' firms, depends on availability of a low cost, reliable, and high speed telecommunications and internet infrastructure.

12.2.2 After-care

A recurring theme in this study has been the political nature of the MNC. In Chapter 1 we defined the MNC as a heterogeneous actor, in chapter four our discussion of the N-form noted the importance of creating a common culture throughout the multinational to counter political pulls for autonomy from overseas subsidiaries. Most explicitly, in Chapter 6, we defined the MNC as a global political actor involved in power relations internally and externally.

For regions like the North East, increasing the commitment of existing foreign investors to re-invest, upgrade value-added activities, and integrate with suppliers has become a major component of regional development policy and is vital for deriving sustained benefits from inward investment.

There are two sides to the commitment of inward investors:

● The linkages between regional authorities and management in foreign-owned companies.
● The linkages between local subsidiary managers and their corporate headquarters.

The commitment of inward investors is therefore dependent on the channels of political influence between the region, the foreign subsidiary and their parent firm.

It is vital for regional development agencies to forge close relations with inward investors, allowing a joint response to changes in headquarters' corporate decision-making and market conditions. Investor development is a major part of the embedding process, as Ferner (1997b) explains:

National subsidiaries and their managers are enmeshed in local networks of influence and exchange – with local and national political structures, customers, suppliers, employees and unions. In cases of relocation, the interests and loyalties of local MNC managers may lie with other local actors rather more than with corporate headquarters in the home country. Such 'embeddedness' provides the conditions for the construction of interest coalitions to respond to the decisions of MNCs.

One mechanism promoted in several countries to forge interest coalitions has been to encourage indigenous managers to take management positions in foreign OEMs. Indigenous managers should be more committed to the region and, as the ERT (1998: 93–4) argues, 'it is the enthusiasm and commitment of local management that determine whether local relationships will succeed or fail... It is local managers and local communities that play the vital role in forging links'.[3]

In Ireland, Amin *et al.* (1994) argue that indigenous managers and the after-care support of the Irish Development Agency supported the political bargaining of these managers and ensured a long-term and positive commitment of MNCs to the Irish economy. In Singapore, Lall (1995a; 1995b) argues that indigenous managers committed to the local economy facilitated closely-knit and long term relationships between government FDI representatives and inwardly investing MNCs, ensuring that the technological upgrading of the local economy was consistent with the competitiveness of MNCs. And Peters (1995) finds that the aspirations of senior site management in the host country, as well as relatively cheap but capable engineering skills, led to the time taken for technological upgrading in foreign companies in Singapore and Taiwan to be half as long as in the UK.

Notably, both Ireland and Singapore have centralised and well co-ordinated FDI promotion agencies and extensive post-investment servicing. The Irish Development Agency and Singapore Economic Development Board integrate inward investment and industrial development strategy into a coherent framework for fast-track economic development. As we emphasised in Chapter 6, a single body with a well-defined role and a functional mandate has the greatest capacity to make and implement policy, and attract and co-ordinate enquiries with MNCs. In the UK, the RDAs are envisaged to play this role, in collaboration with the IBB, and we suggest that they should follow the example of Ireland and Singapore by intensifying their hands-on interaction with MNCs which, as Wells and Wint (1991), Wint (1993) and Lall (1995b) argue, also facilitates a subtle form of monitoring.

Monitoring of the purchasing, R&D and training performance of investors, as well as supply chain programmes, are key facets of good institutional practice towards mobile investment (see Amin *et al.*, 1994; Amin and Tomaney, 1995a). It helps secure the upgrading of MNCs into higher value-added activities while at the same time acting in the interests of the multinationals.

However, our research in the North East found that both the NDC and the North East RSO complained that foreign investors do not provide enough feedback on suppliers to allow strategic supply chain development to be totally effective and that gaining access to information for investor development is a major obstacle. Furthermore, according to the Investor Development and Monitoring Manager at the NDC, compared to indigenous firms foreign companies are less embedded into the decision-making process of their corporate headquarters as there is greater separation of ownership and control and more management tiers to go through (Boughton, 1998). Moore (1995: 235–6) also found that 'the high degree of external control limited the scope of the SDA to effectively influence decisions about sourcing.'

We therefore recommend that the tools available for investor development and supply chain programmes are strengthened. In particular, a comprehensive system of technology support should be available to help upgrade the activities of MNCs, perhaps through establishing regional innovation centres, in order to increase the commitment of the subsidiary and its role within the parent company as a whole. Regular contact with MNCs should be mandatory for the RDAs and perhaps also for inward investors, with the mutual interest stressed. It would appear from the examples of Ireland and Singapore that emphasising the appointment of indigenous managers could be a productive mechanism to increase links between the RDAs and MNCs.

However, we noted there are two sides to the commitment of MNCs, and indigenous local managers may not necessarily be an advantage as a foreign manager may have direct feedback to the headquarters. As MNCs converge towards the N-form, it is likely, though, that an international management structure will be placed in more and more multinationals to engender the growth of personal networks throughout the company. While perhaps reducing the commitment of local management to the host region, this eventuality should increase the voice of local management in the corporate headquarters.

The globalisation strategies of MNCs are also likely to be associated with a greater regionalisation of strategic functions. More opportunities exist for regions to co-operate with each-other. For example, the North East could co-operate with London to attract and influence strategic decision-making functions and with the Eastern region to attract R&D intensive activities to the UK. In the case of Nissan, its European Technology Centre in Cranfield represents a competitive advantage for NMUK while, in turn, the success of NMUK increases the importance of the Technology Centre. Developing networks between the different RDAs across the UK would facilitate investor development at both the regional and national scales. Furthermore, we argue below that co-operation between RDAs should be part of a targeted strategy for attracting FDI.

12.2.3   A targeted FDI strategy

In our analysis of FDI in the North East, we found a marked difference in FDI projects depending on the nationality of MNCs. Japanese MNCs are concentrated in the automotive and electronics industries while German multinationals focus far more on the chemicals industry. American and German MNCs are more prone to invest via acquisitions, while Japanese MNCs favour greenfield investments and joint ventures. Japanese projects are larger both in terms of jobs created and capital invested, and also the majority of overseas R&D projects since the mid-1980s have been by Japanese multinationals. Our examination of Nissan and Siemens revealed the contrasting impacts on regional development in the North-East. Nissan led to the development of a new supplier industry while the lessons from the collapse of Siemens Tyneside investment can be summarised in the words Porter (1998: 89): 'Businesses involving advanced technology succeed not in a vacuum but where there is already a base of related activities in the field.'

Inward investment projects vary according to the modality of FDI and the activity and sector involved. The nationality of the enterprise is likely to be a significant determinant of modality, activity and sector. At the same time, we have argued that the location advantages of the region are a major determinant of the quality of inward investment and that investor development and supply chain initiatives influence the strategic evolution of an FDI project and its contribution to the region over time. There is therefore much scope to target inward investment according to the location advantages of the region or those advantages that may be developed with support from regional development agencies.

In the UK, we found that although attracting FDI was at the centre of the government's industrial and regional policy, there was no strategy to target FDI according to its contribution to the competitiveness of the UK economy at a national or regional level. The emphasis has been on attracting large-scale, job creating manufacturing projects to peripheral regions through the use of financial incentives biased towards labour intensive mobile multinationals. We argue for two major changes in inward investment policy:

● Central government, through the IBB, should target and allocate FDI projects according to the synergy between projects and regions.
● RDAs should target FDI as part of a pro-active, sectoral strategy for regional development.

The present system under which the IBB attracts and often influences the location of a project has meant that the IBB can to some extent pick and choose where it puts major facilities, without necessarily understanding the benefits of the investment for the region or benefits of the region for the investment. With the IBB involved in 1769 active projects from 1991 to 1997 – more than Locate in Scotland and the WDA combined – a major opportunity has been lost to build on the strengths or fill in the weaknesses of individual regions and develop clusters of related activities. We therefore concur with Porter (1998) when he argues that subsidies to Assisted Areas disperse companies artificially and that government 'should reinforce and build on existing and emerging clusters rather than attempt to create entirely new ones'. For example, we saw in Chapter 8 that the federal German government adopted a targeted strategy to attract semiconductor activities to Dresden, building on the comparative advantage of the Saxony region, and the case of Ireland is discussed on Box 12.1.

For the UK to emulate the targeted policy of Germany or the IDA requires a degree of co-operation between the regions and central government which has not been forthcoming. In the UK, there is no functional equivalent of the centralised IDA and we would not recommend the establishment of a similar body as the essence of the RDAs is that they are best placed to develop regional strategies. For a medium sized country like the UK, what is needed is inter-RDA co-operation which, in co-ordination with the IBB, could more effectively attract and influence the location of facilities.

Box 12.1   Ireland's integrated, sector-based FDI targeting strategy

In Ireland, the IDA implemented a targeted, cluster-based FDI strategy in the late 1980s and has re-evaluated its target sectors as the economy moved up the value chain and as new opportunities for attracting FDI arose. Initially, the IDA targeted US FDI in electronics and pharmaceuticals, but in the 1990s focused on software and internationally traded services. In 2000 the IDA is targeting IT, multi-media and e-business. The IDA's targeted policy has been integrated with skills, technology and after-care policies and has met with huge success (see Tomaney, 1995; Barry and Bradley, 1997; Görg and Ruane, 1997). Ireland has become the leading location in Europe for high value added international service sectors, IT & Software and for R&D projects. For example, in 1999 Ireland attracted 117 FDI projects according to Ernst & Young, of which 15% were in R&D – a higher proportion than for any other country in Europe (derived from Site Selection, 2000). In 1975 Ireland's per capita GDP was only 63% of the EU average, but in 1996 was 90% (Pitelis, 1997: 10). In 1999, Ireland's per capita income was the twelfth highest in the world, after 20 years of average annual GDP growth exceeding 7%, and unemployment was less than 6% (IMD, 1999).

Source: Loewendahl (2001).

The trust needed to develop a high degree of co-operation is clearing lacking, especially given the animosity between regions like the North East and Wales. With each region aiming to serve their own interests and with central government unable or unwilling to foster greater co-operation between its regional components, the problem mirrors that of a large MNC aiming to create synergistic networks throughout its dispersed operations. The response of the N-form MNC has been to create a federal structure, specialised activities across its network, and introduce international management structures with a strong emphasis on shared commonalities or normative integration.

Central to international management structures in MNCs is the transfer of personnel between units and across functions, particularly notable in Japanese companies. The headquarters takes on the role of a strategic co-ordinating centre, ensuring co-operation and competition between its constituent parts and the transfer of best practices. To engender co-operative networks across RDAs one recommendation could therefore be to dispatch staff between RDAs and also to central government so that personal networks are formed and a greater degree of trust and understanding can develop. Such a proposal could also be used to limit RDA competition for projects and the bidding-up of incentives. The RDOs in the English regions already co-operate through overseas offices to attract FDI and we recommend that this co-operation is expanded to facilitate a regionally-sensitive, sector-based targeted strategy for attracting FDI on a national scale.

The N-form MNC specialises activities across its federal structure, with the headquarters preventing duplication of resources and providing support for world leading centres of excellence centres to develop. Another recommendation for developing coherent and co-ordinated objectives for a targeted investment promotion strategy could therefore be to develop a similar structure at the central and regional levels in the UK. The IBB would be responsible for achieving agreed national objectives for attracting FDI based on a coherent industrial strategy and focusing on target sectors. Each RDA would then be given the opportunity to participate in national investment promotion activities for those sectors which meet their own FDI and development objectives. For example, lets say that the IBB has 20 target sectors,[4] agreed with stakeholders, then each RDA must decide how many and which of these sectors it wants to 'buy into.' The RDAs could be required to contribute resources, sector expertise, regional information, and transfer staff with the IBB in their chosen sectors, encouraging the RDAs to focus on those sectors in which they have a actual or potential international competitive advantage. The IBB and RDAs could develop regionally specific investment offer packages and forge closer co-ordination on project handling. The IBB would therefore market the UK in target sectors and when it generates investment leads across its 20 sectors regions will automatically be suggested to the investor as investment locations depending on their sectoral focus. In this way, regional differentiation and specialisation would be encouraged and wasteful competition between regions would be reduced and perhaps also the amount of incentives needed to attract FDI to particular regions could also be scaled down. This recommendation would encourage a co-ordinated sector based investment promotion strategy based on the comparative advantage of each region and the UK as a whole.

To determine priority sectors at the regional level, a targeted strategy should involve the matching of local strengths to the profile of

Figure 12.1   Sector evaluation matrix

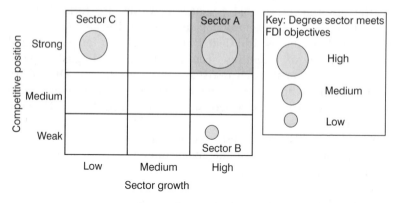

inward investors. Similar to Porter's cluster theory, the idea would be to build on what you have and target inward FDI with synergy to this, which is exactly what the NDC plans to do. Inward FDI should be targeted on a sector-basis, with an analysis of the strengths, weaknesses, opportunities and threats (SWOT) of each sector to identify areas in which inward investment can contribute. As Morgan (1996: 709) argues, a targeted FDI strategy is therefore 'concerned with type of FDI, which with appropriate policies can be used to help give the indigenous production system critical mass'.

There should also be scope to target inward investment to fill in gaps in the supply infrastructure or to leverage an existing strong supply infrastructure by attracting a major investor. At the same time, target sectors need to be matched to opportunities in the market-place for attracting projects and the probability of being able to attract those projects, which depends on the competitive position of the region relative to competing locations. Figure 12.1 indicates diagrammatically how target sectors can be identified.

The aim is to identify sectors in the right-hand corner that meet investment objectives. The evaluation matrix positions sectors according to:

- *Sector growth* – analysis of target sectors with the best potential for mobile projects. The key aim is to identify sectors that are growing and mobile. Effective targeting therefore requires an understanding of the size and growth characteristics of sectors and their structural characteristics (Young *et al.*, 1994) and identifying sectors that will be internationally mobile.

● *Competitive position* – the strength of the location *vis-à-vis* competing locations for the sector. It is important to identify sectors where the host region has an existing competitive strength or one that can be built-upon through attracting FDI and through product development activities.

● *Degree meets FDI objectives* – the extent to which the sector meets the overall objectives in attracting FDI. These objectives should be an integral part of an overall development strategy.

We have argued that FDI objectives should focus not on job creation, but prioritise sectors and activities which take into account and capitalise on the strength of indigenous industry, form dynamic relationships with regional SMEs, exploit skilled labour and domestic R&D capability, and help build networks among innovative firms. One recommendation could be to target joint ventures between MNCs and SMEs. Our discussion of technology in chapter's two and four emphasised the importance of joint ventures and other forms of collaboration in the access and generation of technology for businesses. In fact, Belderbos (1997) found that joint ventures have a higher R&D intensity than other forms of FDI, but Harukiyo (1998) found that of Japanese R&D centres in Europe in 1994, only 12.6% in the UK were joint ventures compared to 29.7% in France and 36.7% in Germany. There is therefore a strong justification for encouraging and supporting joint ventures which facilitate access to technology and know-how and contribute to the transfer of technology between MNCs and SMEs. A targeted FDI strategy should therefore be an integral part of a wider regional strategy for economic development encompassing SMEs and technology.[5]

In the North East and other peripheral regions there also needs to be a recognition that a targeted FDI strategy does imply focusing solely on manufacturing firms. We have seen in previous chapters that service sector FDI projects are the fastest growing in Europe and in the UK. There is also growing evidence to suggest that a competitive service sector is increasingly important for attracting and embedding manufacturing investment (Lyons, 1995; MacPherson, 1997) and that peripheral regions have increased opportunities to attract high value added services, with the Republic of Ireland perhaps the most successful example. Gatrell (1999) also argues that the decentralisation of economic activities, in areas such as call centres, shared service centres and information technology and software, may benefit high value added activities setting up in peripheral regions and that attracting business services can support the competitiveness of the whole economy.

We also recommend that a targeted FDI strategy is linked to the allocation of regional incentives.

12.2.4   Prioritising the allocation of investment incentives

In Chapter 10 we argued that RSA has been used as an employment subsidy for MNCs, embellishing the labour flexibility and cost advantages of peripheral regions, rather than as a lever for developing regional competitiveness. There has been no systematic link between the incentives offered to inward investors and the contribution they would make to regional economic development. The UK government has been more concerned with minimising cost-per-job and maximising the tax revenue accruing to central government (the 'efficiency criteria') than using incentives to develop a sustainable location product in peripheral regions. The rationale for making available incentives for investment in Assisted Areas was to compensate for the disadvantaged position of many regions and while incentives played an important role in attracting FDI to peripheral regions, they addressed 'the symptoms rather than the underlying causes of peripherality' (Cooke and Morgan, 1998: 135).

With the collapse in 1998 of many high profile investments that had received RSA, central government is questioning the merits of the whole regional incentive system, and is considering cutting or even phasing out RSA. However, we found that incentives can and do make a difference to company decision-making. What needs to change is the not regional aid per se but rather the institutional structure and criteria for allocating financial incentives. The closure and dis-investment of major FDI projects in 1998, including Siemens, Fujitsu, Grove Europe, Lite-On, National Semiconductor, Visasystems, and Mitsubishi in the North East and Scotland, indicates the vulnerability of projects attracted by low costs, labour flexibility and the availability of cost-based regional incentives. The large incentives 'offered' to multinational investors is also a reflection of the bargaining power of MNCs, an issue we address in the next section.

Amin and Tomaney (1995a: 217–18) put forward the case that policy should calibrate regional incentives to the quality of mobile investment and tie the offer of discretionary awards to agreed quality targets. In our case study of the North East, although we found increasing concern at the NDC and Government Office that incentives should reflect the quality of investments, there was no commonly agreed definition of what a 'quality' project looks like. Amin *et al.* (1994) define a quality project according to five measures: management functions and decision-making autonomy, innovation capacity, training intensity, quality of labour, and local content and supplier linkages. Similarly, Rhodes (1995) argues that incentives should encourage projects that have opportunities for greater task sophistication and operational autonomy, skill formation, technology transfer and the creation of market opportunities. One straightforward method adopted by several US states to help ensure the quality of FDI is to link incentives to the average wages levels of new jobs created, with FDI often having to create jobs paying at least 10% above the average wage to qualify for incentives. The IDA also monitors the pay levels provided by inward investors. However, there is no guarantee that inward investors will not poach employees from indigenous firms and pay higher wages subsidised by the incentives offered by government, unless greater monitoring of MNCs takes place.

We would also stress that the criteria for allocating incentives should depend on the 'fit' of the project with the sector-based strategies of the region. It would be very unlikely for a region like the North East to realistically attract projects embodying each of Amin *et al.*'s five measures. Therefore the region must prioritise which dimensions of quality are most important for each sector. In the North East, we could envisage that attracting R&D activities would be of the greatest priority in the pharmaceuticals sector, while attracting components suppliers would have had the highest priority in the semiconductor sector – until the closure of Siemens and Fujitsu. Clearly, an element of realism is involved – regions must balance the type of project they would like with the probability that are able to attract that project.

To allow the system of RSA to be linked to the regionally-sensitive economic strategies being developed by the RDAs, we recommend that greater autonomy for allocating RSA is passed to the regional level. For example, the threshold for projects handled by the Government Office's could be increased from its present £2 million ceiling to £10 million, with only very large, mobile FDI projects handled centrally by the DTI. Increasing the ceiling would pass more responsibility down to the regional level and at the same time would allow a single thread approach to be given to investors, reducing the time-scale of negotiations and increasing policy certainty. While the Government Offices would continue to retain the power to support projects financially, which gives the RDAs impartiality, encourages strategies based on regional strengths not the money available, and controls the amount of grant awarded, there should be formalised and robust communication channels between the Government Offices and the RDAs to prioritise the allocation of RSA.

If incentives were allocated according to the fit of projects with sector-based strategies, then it is much more likely that incentives will favour SMEs and high-value added activities over the large-scale, manufacturing plants that the present job oriented RSA is biased towards. With increasing emphasis on technology in both central and regional government, the financial incentives awarded could be changed from one-off grants to discretionary, long-term incentives. One example to follow could be Singapore, where financial incentive systems, involving both grants and tax breaks, encourage progressive upgrading and technology transfer to local firms (Peters, 1995: 272). However, this shift in emphasis will require the bargaining power of MNCs to be balanced.

12.2.5 Bargaining with multinationals: levelling the playing field

Our theoretical and empirical discussion of bargaining and case studies of Nissan and Siemens addressed our fifth research question – *what factors influence the bargaining relationship between governments and MNCs*. We found international capital mobility and control over core technologies as two key changes increasing the *structural power* of MNCs. Changes in the international political economy have also led national governments to view more favourably inwardly investing multinationals, in part because both developed and developing countries increasingly became major sources of outward FDI. The increased commitment of governments strengthened the bargaining power of MNCs. We argued that the bargaining power of multinationals is additionally heightened through their greater degree of institutional and decision-making autonomy relative to more institutionally fragmented governments. Our political economy bargaining model of MNC–government relations therefore emphasised two fundamental dimensions that determine the path and outcome of negotiations between governments and MNCs:

- *Potential power* – the alternatives and commitment of each actor.
- *Actual power* – the ability and willingness to exercise potential power, which depends on overall perceptions and the interest and institutional structure of each actor.

In relation to our fifth research question – *what are the implications for of bargaining for inward investment and economic development policy?* – MNCs have exercised their bargaining power, in particular relating to their greater number of alternative investment locations in regional integration areas, to play-off regions, bidding-up the level of incentives offered. The cross-border mobility of MNCs has led to a fear by governments that, unless they offer 'just enough,' their position will be harmed in future investment bargaining (Mueller, 1996: 346). At the same time, to avoid precedents being set for future investors, incentives have become discretionary and increasingly outside the public domain. This has reduced the accountability of government, and heightened the importance of bargaining power in determining the level of incentives.

We saw that the Taiwanese computer giant, Acer, played-off the North East and Wales, exploiting the weakness in the UK's institutional structure for FDI decision-making. It is thought that Acer doubled the amount of incentives forthcoming, although the actual figure was never released. Siemens also put pressure on the UK government to increase its incentives 'offer', referring to the higher incentives available from alternative investment locations in Holland and Ireland.

More recently, in June 1999, BMW was able to increase the UK government's initial aid offer by nearly £40 million, to £152 million in regional incentives for re-investment at Rover's Longbridge plant in Birmingham. BMW's key source of bargaining power was its threat to shift output to a new plant in Eastern Europe.

Although the UK government is proposing a concordat between regions to prevent competitive bidding in the case of large FDI projects, a more appropriate level for controlling the incentives offered to multinationals is the European Commission. In developing our bargaining model in chapter six, we found that in order to increase bargaining power and at the same time gain agreement (i.e. encourage more FDI) and actor should increase the commitment and reduce the alternatives of the other party. A UK concordat would reduce the opportunities for MNCs to play-off alternative locations on a national scale, whereas an EU concordat would effectively reduce the bargaining power of MNCs on a pan-EU scale through reducing their alternatives. MNCs are also highly commitment to the EU market, giving an EU body greater bargaining power.

To convert potential into actual bargaining power our analysis of the political economy of bargaining showed that a single, centralised agency with a clear functional remit and independent access to expertise and information is crucial if the agency is to have the ability and autonomy to negotiate effectively. We therefore recommend that an FDI monitoring agency be established at the EU level to negotiate with MNCs and co-ordinate similar agencies at the national level. In turn, national level agencies would co-ordinate the RDAs. If a RDA feels that a MNC is playing-off regions it could approach the national agency and then, if the MNC is seemingly using its cross-border capital mobility to bid up incentives, the case would be referred to the EU FDI monitoring agency. The monitoring agencies would also ensure that RDAs and national governments are also not inflating the incentives offered above the economic benefit of the investment.

At present, the EU does not have an official FDI policy and there are no mechanisms for policy co-ordination or for monitoring the benefits of FDI (Grimes, 1993; Hood et al., 1996). The EU does, though, place limits on regional incentives and controls the use of regional structural funds (see Woolcock and Wallace, 1985; Groenewegen and Beije, 1992; Blanchard, 1995), and in recent years has attempted to exercise greater monitoring of incentives (Nicolaides and Thomsen, 1991: 108). For example, following an independent investigation and ruling by Brussels, Toyota had to pay the Derbyshire County Council an additional £4.2 million when land was sold below the market price (McCooey, 1991: 71), and the UK government's aid package to BMW was rejected by the EU. The EU has also reduced the proportion of a project's eligible costs that can be given as incentives from 75% to 50% in least favoured regions and from 30% to 20% in development areas (Oman, 2000: 68).

However, the EU does not control local and regional packages which are less transparent and in the public eye and may encourage governments to shift to other state aids, in particular tax incentives as in Ireland and Hungary (see Oman, 2000: 71–4). In our case studies, we saw that Nissan received a purpose built site at below market value and Siemens received a whole package of non-grant incentives. The EU largely responds to complaints from other companies, such as Porsche in the case of BMW–Rover, and lacks the information, which is crucial to monitor effectively the incentives offered (Van Herwaarden, 1995; Ietto-Gillies, 1997b; Oman, 2000). The EU has failed to control the use of structural funds and has been largely unsuccessful in curtailing bidding for inward investment (Hood and Young, 1993; Hood et al., 1996). There is therefore a strong rationale for establishing an EU FDI monitoring agency to strengthen existing policy.

We would also recommend that the remit of the proposed FDI agencies should go beyond the monitoring of incentives, and also include the monitoring of other dimensions of MNC activity, gathering of information, and ensuring that performance requirements are adhered to. For example, we found that the NDC did not record closures of foreign companies, as it would have 'hurt morale,' making a critical analysis of the contribution of FDI and recent after-care policies very difficult.

An EU monitoring unit could therefore collate and discuss information on MNCs (Sugden, 1990b: 84–5) and national and EU FDI agencies could give weight to the policies recommended in this Chapter for technology, SMEs, training, after care, and regional incentives. For example, it could be made mandatory for MNCs to meet with regional representatives to discuss ways of upgrading plant quality and utilising local suppliers. If RDAs decide to initiate a system of long-term incentives linked, for example, to MNCs increasing R&D, training, and technology transfer to local suppliers, the FDI monitoring agencies could act as enforcement bodies. If the RDAs actually prove reluctant to ensure that incentives offered to multinationals are tied to a performance criteria other than job creation, the national or EU FDI agency could apply penalties on the RDAs.

If restrictions are placed on MNCs to encourage progressive plant upgrading or integration with local industry then the EU FDI agency would become crucial to ensure that the MNCs do not shift activities to another location. As Bellak (1997: 21) argues, 'Unilateral actions by national governments to restrict TNCs must fail, because it will lead to an outflow of indigenous and foreign investment and with it employment.' However, we recommend that the approach of Singapore – aggressive co-operation with multinationals for the mutual interest of the host country/region and the MNC – might be preferred to imposing outright restrictions.

The success of Singapore's approach is premised on its integrated framework towards inward investment, which combines highly focused sector and company based targeting and investment promotion with investor development, supply chain development, R&D support services, and a long-term technology and training strategy. If RDAs, supported by central government and the EU, develop a similar integrated framework for inward investment, such as that outlined in this chapter, then arguably restrictions on MNCs would not be needed, especially as they move towards the N-form structure.

In fact, if the institutional system of FDI policy in the EU is strengthened considerably to level the playing-field with multinationals, RDAs should not be given the freedom to impose restrictions on MNCs, under the umbrella of the EU. Rather, the EU FDI agency should encourage regions to develop their endogenous location advantages (SMEs, IT&T infrastructure, technology and innovation base, and skills and training) and implement a comprehensive aftercare policy to make it in the interests of MNCs to upgrade their plant and forge greater production and technological links with local suppliers. Only in extreme cases of MNC competitive bidding and non-co-operation should the EU FDI agency intervene and impose restrictions.

As we pointed out in our bargaining analysis in chapter six, the translation of potential to actual bargaining power depends not only on institutional *ability* but also *willingness* to exercise bargaining power. At each of the three levels of regional, central and supranational government there appears to be an increasing willingness to strengthen the institutional structure of FDI and to formulate a new framework for inward investment and regional development to improve the trade-off between the incentives offered to MNCs and their contribution to regional economies.

In the UK, we found growing emphasis on R&D and supporting SMEs at the central and regional levels. The NDC has initiated programmes to embed MNCs and is presently developing a sector-based, targeted strategy for FDI to support indigenous industry. In the North East there are concerns that the allocation of RSA should reflect the 'quality' of FDI, and there are high tensions surrounding competitive bidding for investment. In the EU, the regional commissioner has stated that, 'We want to promote regional development... but pure profiting from aid needs to be ruled out' (cited in Ferner, 1997b).

Across all levels of governance there is widespread agreement that incentives need to be controlled and channelled to projects which provide the best opportunities to develop regional competitiveness. The establishment of FDI monitoring bodies at the national and EU level is necessary to reduce the bargaining power of MNCs by changing the structural context and to monitor both MNCs and RDAs.[6] We recommend that initiatives to attract and secure benefits from inward investment should be an integral part of an overall strategy based on combining endogenous and exogenous approaches to regional economic development.

12.3 THEORETICAL REFLECTIONS AND FURTHER RESEARCH

The international political economy framework discussed in Chapter 1 directed our research towards examining what is happening, how and why. IPE states that economics and politics and the domestic and international levels cannot be separated and that research should focus on structural changes and the role of the state. Through utilising an IPE framework, the aim was to critically analyse the role of inward investment in regional development, and reveal the power relations surrounding the relationship between MNCs and governments. IPE promotes research that questions the existing order and provides alternative policy options.

We underlined that globalisation offers benefits to some regions but not to others and that MNCs are increasing their structural power over governments, leading to regional aid being diverted away from indigenous firms to multinationals. We also saw that central government in the UK is engaged in power relations with sub-national government, and is unwilling to pass substantial political autonomy down to the regional level. In our conclusion, we have outlined five policy initiatives to address the asymmetrical power relations and provide alternatives to existing policy.

The inter-disciplinary nature of this study has facilitated a broad, holistic understanding of the relationship between MNCs, economic development and government policy. While we are aware that the large volume of information brought together might have in parts lacked a coherent structure with a single underlying research question, we hope the benefits derived from adopting a critical, inter-disciplinary approach outweigh the costs. An alternative approach would have been tightly focused on, for example, the factors determining bargaining or the role of regional incentives in inward investment decisions or inward investment policy in the North East. Such an approach would have facilitated a precise research methodology and more detailed concrete analysis. The aim of this study, though, was to draw together theoretical and empirical research from various disciplines and, combined with our original case study research, to examine different levels of analysis in order to understand how the whole system works and its consequences, which is the essence of IPE.

We believe that this study makes four main original contributions to empirical and theoretical research, which underpin our policy recommendations:

- First, it is one of the most comprehensive studies to date examining FDI. We focused on the growth FDI, the globalisaton of technology and innovation, and the investment strategies of Nissan and Siemens, as well as giving a detailed analysis of FDI in the UK and its regions. We developed a new model of FDI location, based on the conditions that allow firms to become multinational, the corporate and FDI strategy of the firm, and project specific requirements and decision making stage. The model was used in our analysis of bargaining to understand the commitment of MNCs to invest in a particular location. Our primary research on FDI gave new insights into the motivations for investment in the UK and the changing face of German business in particular. We linked lean production to labour flexibility as a key explanation for why the UK is a favoured location within the EU for Japanese automotive investment. Our analysis of Siemens provides new research pointing-to the 'Anglo-Saxonisation' of German corporate governance and we provided evidence that MNCs are moving toward the network-form of organisation.

- Secondly, we hope that our analysis of bargaining in Chapter 6 makes an important original contribution to the theoretical understanding of the why and how of MNC-government bargaining. Through incorporating the insights of economic and dependency theories of bargaining with political economy we developed a new model, which we hope will be used as a conceptual tool to analyse bargaining relations and investment decisions. The model is based on the underlying factors (commitment and alternatives and interest and institutional structure) that determine the investment decision making process and hence can be used to examine inward investment over time.

- Thirdly, we provide the most recent analysis of inward investment policy in North East England and challenge previous critical academic research. We give new evidence that policy in the North East, as represented by the activities of the NDC, is shifting away from an exogenous developmental approach based on attracting FDI towards embedding multinationals through supply chain programmes and investor development and supporting indigenous industry through a targeted FDI strategy.

- Fourthly, we develop a framework for exogenous-endogenous development in peripheral regions.

This study has covered many areas of academic research and has involved theoretical and primary research examining different aspects of the MNC. Hence, many avenues for further research have been identified, which we will limit here to three major areas that particularly lack existing research.

A first important research topic would be to compare and contrast the impact of different types of FDI. Our study of FDI in the UK highlighted the importance of M&As as a source of inward invetsment and our case study of the North East showed that the employment and investment implications of FDI varied according to type. In this chapter we suggested that joint ventures should be investigated further as a mechanism to support the technological activities and links between MNCs and SMEs. An interesting topic of research would therefore be to analyse the motivations behind different types of FDI and examine the impact on sustainable investment, jobs and the upgrading of value-adding activities at the regional, national, or cross-national levels. This would require the use of both official and project-by-project data and detailed comparative case-study research. There is also a need for research providing policy recommendations on how investment agencies can encourage and promote their location for new forms of investment.

A second area of increasing importance but where detailed academic research is lacking concerns the supplier and investor development activities of the RDAs. A major area for future research should be evaluating the impact of these initiatives on local sourcing and the embeddedness of MNCs. Research could look at whether local content is increasing, if local linkages involve high value added activities, and also analyse the balance of payments implications. The investor development activities of the RDAs could be assessed through both case-study research and by examining whether the intensity of interactions between the RDAs and foreign companies are increasing and if plants are becoming less vulnerable to closure. Future research should also focus on how to upgrade existing plants and research relating to technology transfer policies in other countries could be developed into a best practice model, in order to provide solid recommendations for a technology policy linking FDI and SMEs in peripheral regions.

A third area for further research relates to our recommendation to establish FDI monitoring agencies. Detailed research is needed on how to establish such agencies at the national and most importantly EU level. Issues of functional mandate, the powers of the agencies, and their accountability need to be addressed in more detail. Future research on establishing FDI monitoring agencies should focus not only on controlling incentives and supporting the long term development strategies of regions, but also on the potential role for such agencies to collect information and monitor the power-seeking strategies of MNCs relating to labour. Only then can we hope to reduce the negative distributional consequences associated with the bargaining power of multinationals.

Notes

Chapter 1

1. In July 1999 the author completed a PhD at the Institute for German Studies, University of Birmingham, titled 'Bargaining with Multinationals: The Investment of Siemens and Nissan in North East England'. This book as an updated and abridged version of the PhD. Please refer to PhD thesis for additional chapters on the semiconductor and automotive industry and Japanese and German FDI.
2. See Wendt (1987) for a classic text examining the relationship between structure and agency, concluding that 'the basic analytical objective is to join agents and structures in a "dialectical synthesis" that overcomes the subordination of one to the other'. Also see: Scott and Storper, 1986a; Avery and Rapkin, 1989; Giddens, 1990.

Chapter 2

1. Argued by Dicken (1994); Dunning and Sauvant (1996); Jones (1996b); Lawton (1997).
2. Porter (1999) defines a cluster as 'a geographical concentration in a particular country – or region within a country – of a group of related and supporting firms...[which] create information flows, incentives, spin-offs, new companies – an innovative vitality'. The OECD (1999b: 36) defines clusters as 'networks of suppliers, customers, and knowledge-creating institutions which together create value-added'.
3. According to Lung (1992: 72), learning is not available on the market and competitive advantage can be derived from learning in product, process, management, and horizontal and vertical integration.
4. Innovation is the commercialisation of new, probably patented, knowledge (Cooke, 1996: 54). There are many types of innovation (Huggins, 1996: 757). Narrowly defined, innovation refers to the generation of new technologies and radical product innovations. Liberally defined, incremental product innovation, new work practices, supplier relationships, forms of industrial organisation, and synergies between public and private sectors are all innovation (Cooke and Morgan, 1998: 134). However, innovation is more than new ideas – there must be broader normative support for the adoption, adaptation and diffusion of innovations (Powell and Smith-Doerr, 1994: 388; Asheim, 1996: 381).
5. For convergence, see: Jessop (1994); Abdullah and Keenoy (1995: 759); Lucio and Blyton (1995); MacDuffie (1995: 75); Mittelman (1996a: 11); Masayuki (1998: 186).

6. For example, see Piore and Sabel (1984); Scott and Storper (1986b); Moulaert and Swyngedouw (1991); Stopford and Strange (1991); Jessop (1994); Cox (1996); Gill (1996); Dunning (1998).
7. Technology is applied and applicable knowledge, permitting the development of new products and processes (Lawton, 1997: 5). Technological change is a dynamic, multi-faceted process, encompassing invention, innovation, transfer and diffusion of technology (Parayil, 1993 cited in Lawton, 1997: 6).
8. E-business can be defined as the application of information technologies to facilitate the buying and selling of products, services, and information over public networks. E-business is *not* a new business, but a way *to do* business

Chapter 3

1. See UNCTAD, *World Investment Report*, OECD *International Direct Investment Statistics Yearbook*, and EUROSTAT *European Union Direct Investment*.
2. We can identify seven major potential contributions of FDI to economic development: capital, technology transfer, access to market expertise and links in foreign markets, skills transfer and access to new management techniques, employment creation, industrial and export diversification, and enhanced competition in domestic markets. For a detailed discussion see: Balasubramanyum *et al.* (1996); Blomstrom (1996); IFC (1997); OECD (1998c; 1998d); UNCTAD (1999); Thomsen (2000).
3. For example, over 45% of the financing of the overseas subsidiaries of Japanese MNCs was from host country sources in 1995 (UNCTAD, 1999).
4. For example, establishing the source of inward FDI in the UK is difficult because of distortions caused by investments channelled through the Netherlands, which counts as Dutch, but are mostly by Japanese and US companies (Brown, 1999).
5. For example, in central and eastern Europe from 1988 to 1995 over 45% of FDI inflows were received through privatisation sales compared to 15% in Latin America (IFC, 1997: 43–4). Also see Loewendahl and Ertugal-Loewendahl (2000).
6. For the case of German firms see Schröter (1993), Ferner and Quinta-nilla (1998), and Loewendahl (1999). Also see Sally (1994) and Ruigrok and Van Tulder (1995) for detailed theoretical and case study analysis.
7. Thomsen and Woolcock (1993) and Eurostat (1997) give evidence for the role of proximity in market seeking strategies. For example, Eurostat notes that Italian firms have taken a 'special interest' in Greece, Portugal and Spain, and the huge two-way FDI flows between the UK and US is another key example.
8. See Barrell and Pain (1997) for the case of German FDI in the EU.
9. Key location factors derived from KPMG (1991); Ernst & Young (1992; 1993); Chesnais (1993); Papanastassiou and Pearce (1994); Arthur Anderson (1996); Malachuk (1998); OECD (1999b).

Chapter 4

1. For example, increasing competition and rising domestic costs stimulated German FDI in lower cost European countries (Fisher and Lindeman (1995); Lindeman (1995); Betz (1996); *The Economist* (1996a); Commerzbank, 1997 cited in OECD (1997a: 32–3); Landsbury and Pain (1997); and Hong Kong and Taiwanese FDI in mainland China (Baldwin, 1992; Chiu, 1994; Chang, 1995; So and Chiu, 1995).

2. Between one-half and three-fifths of capital and knowledge flows are internalised within MNCs (Dunning, 1998).

3. Cantwell (1996: 153–7), however, argues that the issue of appropriability and information leakage is not normally the overriding concern. Knowledge created by an in-house R&D facility is generally of greatest relevance to the same firm's learning process and the most efficient and effective way to exploit this knowledge is through its contribution to innovation within the same company.

4. For example, 60% of world computer industry R&D is undertaken in the US (Vickery, 1996: 111).

5. We need to be aware of the measurement problems discussed in Chapter 3 when making these calculations.

6. These division have strategic responsibility for the production, research and marketing of groups of products in different countries and has become the dominant form of international organisation (Ferner and Quintanilla, 1998).

7. Hungary is also in the process of positioning the supply and demand side of its economy to compete for technology and innovation based activities. It is therefore too early to assess the impact on GDP.

8. Direct grants, tax reductions, and training grants tailored to R&D in target sectors.

Chapter 5

1. For example, number of states offering incentives in the US doubled between 1977 and 1996 and the average number of incentive programmes in each state has also doubled (Oman, 2000: 60).

Chapter 6

1. Jones (1990), Hill and Munday (1994) and Yeung (1996) find that bureaucratic competence is an important factor determining the location of inward investment.

2. The information for Intel's negotiations with Costa Rica is drawn from *Caribbean Update*, 1998; *Latin Trade*, 1998; Spar, 1998; *Sun-Sentinel*, 1998; *Wall Street Journal*, 1998; UNCTAD, 1999.

3. To analyse the full bargaining context behind inward investment in the UK and France we would also have to consider the alternatives and commitment of MNCs investing in each country and the political economy

of bargaining. We would need to look at the institutional structure of FDI decision-making and the influence of political constraints in France and the UK.

Chapter 7

1. Renault, Peugeot, Fiat and VW lobbied for protection from Nissan. Italy limited the number of Japanese cars to 1% of its market and France to 3%. In Britain and Germany, the Japanese agreed to limit market share to 11% and 15% (Camerra-Rowe, 1994: 9–11). In 1991 the EU also agreed a temporary ceiling on Japanese imports into the EU of 1.23 million vehicles per year until the end of 1999 (Islam, 1996). Japanese market share in restricted markets is therefore a fraction of what it would other wise have been. Japanese market share in unrestrained European markets is up to 30%, in the US is 24%, and in many Asian markets is overwhelming (Nakamoto *et al.*, 1998). In fact, the success of Europe's biggest producer, VW, has largely been achieved in restricted markets.
2. In 1987, the EU decision to regulate Japanese so-called 'screw-driver' plants led to the Japanese taking the EU to the General Agreement on Tariffs and Trade (GATT) in 1988 and winning the case in 1990 (Hook, 1998: 24).
3. In terms of quality, a recent study of 88,000 company cars found that Rover had the second worse reliability – over 30 breakdowns per 100 vehicles, compared with Mitsubishi's 5.8 breakdowns per 100 vehicles (Griffiths, 1998).
4. However, Peck and Stone (1993), from a study of 84 new greenfield ventures in the North East, argue that the influence of the overall Japanese presence in the region on the adoption of new practices in other firms is very unclear.

Chapter 8

1. The following discussion draws on Loewendahl (1999).
2. See Wendt (1987) for a classic text examining the relationship between structure and agency, concluding that the basic analytical objective is to join agents and structures in a 'dialectical synthesis' that overcomes the subordination of one to the other? Also see Giddens (1990); Avery and Rapkin (1989); Scott and Storper (1986a).
3. As with Siemens, Hyundai played off different countries in Europe to gain higher incentives. There were reports of US$190,000 per job. Germany and Austria made higher offers but did not make short list due to higher production costs and the large UK 'offer' was decisive in Scotland winning over Ireland (Batchler *et al.*, 1998, cited in Oman, 2000: 69).

Chapter 9

1. See EC (1998) and Bende-Nabende (1999) for empirical studies. See Nicolaides and Thomsen (1991) and Clegg (1996b) for the impact of

regional integration on Japanese and US FDI in the EU and Landsbury and Pain (1997) and Allen *et al*. (1998) for the impact on German FDI.

2. In Summer 2000 the IBB changed its name to Invest.uk and merged with British Trade International.

3. However, while the government has permitted the foreign acquisition of dominant UK firms (Bailey *et al*., 1994: 173–4), 1987 legislation gave the Bank of England the power to block the purchase of over 15% of the shares of a UK bank from any source (Hood and Young, 1997: 257), indicating the role of the financial community in industrial policy formation.

4. In 1994, firms employing between 100 and 499 employees in continental Europe accounted for almost 30% of employment, whereas the British share was only 16% (*The Economist*, 1994a). As well as weakness in employment, R&D in the UK is concentrated in large firms more than most other OECD countries. Cooke and Morgan (1998: 137) note that 95% of manufacturing R&D is carried out by just 100 firms in the UK.

Chapter 10

1. The counter-proposition is that we need to know what would have happened to peripheral economies in the absence of an exogenous led development policy – which is extremely difficult to evaluate.

Chapter 11

1. See Amin and Pywell (1989) and Sadler (1992b) for a discussion of industrial crisis in the North East.

2. See Martin and Townroe (1992) for the importance of 'hard' and 'soft' infrastructure in RED policy and inward investment and see Peck (1996) for the increasing role of customised infrastructure in attracting MNCs.

3. See Battat *et al*. (1996); Bridge (1997); and Handfiled *et al*. (2000) for the latest research on supplier development.

4. As well as the more strategic RDA, private and public sectors on the Tees are lobbying to create a single executive body which would merge the activities of the TECs, Business Links, the inward investment and tourism activities of the Local Authorities and the Tees Valley Development Company.

Chapter 12

1. Scotland's better performance may be attributed to the high levels of government money injected into the economy, a higher quality skills base (Peters, 1995; Hood and Young, 1997), and the greater autonomy of the SDA, which permitted a more targeted strategy aimed at strengthening existing clusters (Scottish Enterprise, 1993; Peters, 1995; Pyke, 1997a).

2. For example, the ERT (1998) reports that large businesses face 600 ECU's per employee per year in administrative costs compared to

3,500 ECU's in smaller businesses. A study of SMEs in the UK found that higher education institutes are reluctant to collaborate in technology with smaller firms due to their lower levels of capital and technology (Rothwell and Dodgson, 1991, cited in Hassink, 1996).

3. Lawton (1997: 162) notes that, 'Since its inception in 1983, European Round Table (ERT) has been one of the most influential forces in industrial lobbying at an EC level.'

4. In practice, the term 'sector' is often referring to a particular 'activity.' For example, the Netherlands and Scotland target call centres, Sweden and Denmark promote themselves as a location for e-business, shared service centres and distribution and logistics projects, while French, Canadian and German regions have a specific focus on attracting R&D projects. These targets are generally not sector or industry specific.

5. In addition, we found joint ventures in the North East to yield better returns in terms of capital invested per project than other types of FDI and also to make a positive contribution to new jobs – creating twice as many new jobs per project as acquisitions. Our analysis of the closure of Siemens Tyneside plant also revealed that Siemens joint venture in France with IBM reduced the vulnerability of the plant to closure in the face of rationalisation.

6. Ultimately, the rationale for establishing an EU FDI monitoring agency should be extended to the international level through the wider multi-lateral investment agreement. The MAI would therefore look not only at issues like public procurement, state ownership and privatisation, but also incentives, other locational policies, performance requirements and the conduct of MNCs in host countries (Moran, 1993: 18; Hood *et al.*, 1996: 245).

References

AAMA (1998) *World Motor Vehicle Data*. Detroit: American Automobile Manufacturers Association.

Abrahams, P., Hess, J. & Simonian, H. (1998) 'Inside the Fuyo Keiretsu: Nissan Could be the Trigger for Crisis', *Financial Times*, 28 October.

Abdullah, S.R.S. & Keenoy, T. (1995) 'Japanese Managerial Practices in the Malaysian Electronics Industry: Two Case Studies', *Journal of Management Studies*, Special Issue 32 (6): 747–66, November.

Ackroyd, S., Burrell, G., Hughes, M. & Whitaker, A. (1988) 'The Japanisation of British Industry?', *Industrial Relations Journal*, 19 (1): 11–23.

Adams, F.G. (1985) 'Empirical Analysis of Industrial Policies: The Challenges', in Adams, F.G. (ed.), *Industrial Policies for Growth and Competitiveness: Volume 2*. Lexington, Mass.: Lexington.

Agarwal, J.P. (1997) 'European Integration and German FDI: Implications for Domestic Investment and Central European Economies', *National Institute Economic Review*, 2 (160): 100–10, April.

Aglietta, M. (1976; published 1979) *A Theory of Capitalist Regulation: The US Experience*. London: New Left Books.

Aisbitt, K. (1998) Senior Project Manager. Northern Development Company. Private Interview, July.

Allen, C., Gasiorek, M. & Smith, A. (1998) 'European Single Market: How the Programme has Fostered Competition', *Economic Policy*: 440–86.

Altvater, E. (1992) 'Fordist and Post-Fordist International Division of Labour and Monetary Regimes', in Scott, A.J. & Storper, M.J. (eds), *Pathways to Regionalisation and Industrial Development*. London: Routledge.

Alvstan, C. (1993) 'The Impact of FDI on the Geographical Pattern of Foreign Trade Flows in Asia with Special Reference to Taiwan', in Dixon, C. *et al.* (eds), *Economic and Social Development in Pacific Asia*. London: Routledge.

Amin, A. & Malmberg, A. (1992) 'Competing Structural and Institutional Influences on the Geography of Production in Europe', *Environment and Planning*, March, *A* 24: 401–16.

Amin, A. & Pywell, C. (1989) 'Is Technology Policy Enough for Local Economic Revitalisation?: The Case of Tyne and Wear in the North East of England', *Regional Studies*, 23: 463–77.

Amin, A. & Tomaney, J. (1995a) 'The Regional Development Potential of Inward Investment in the Less Favoured Regions of the European Community', in Amin, A. & Tomaney, J. (eds), *Behind the Myth of the European Union: Prospects for Cohesion*. London: Routledge.

Amin, A. & Tomaney, J. (1995b) 'A Framework for Cohesion', in Amin, A. & Tomaney, J. (eds), *Behind the Myth of the European Union: Prospects for Cohesion*. London: Routledge.

Amin, A., Bradley, D., Howells, J., Tomaney, J. & Gentle, C. (1994) 'Regional Incentives and the Quality of Mobile Investment in the Less Favoured Regions of the EC', *Progress in Planning*, 41 (1): 1–112.

Amoore, L. (1997) 'Deconstructing Global "Best Practice:" Institutions, "Embedded Practice" and the Reorganisation of Work', paper presented at the First Annual Postgraduate Conference, 'Globalisation Versus Regionalism: New Trends in World Politics', Centre of Globalisation, University of Warwick, 10–11 December.

Anderson, J.A. (1996) 'German Industry and the European Union in the 1990s', in Berghahn, V.R. (ed.), *Quest for Economic Empire: European Strategies of German Big Business in the Twentieth Century*. Oxford: Berghahn.

Archibugi, D. & Michie, J. (1995) 'The Globalisation of Technology: A New Taxonomy', *Cambridge Journal of Economics*, Special Issue on Technology and Innovation, 19: 121–40, February.

Arestis, P. & Sawyer, M. (1997) 'The Macroeconomics of Industrial Strategy'. paper presented at EUNIP 'Practical Proposals for Industrial Policy in Europe'. Warwick University, 11–15 December.

Armstrong, J. (1998) Regional Industrial Adviser (key strategy adviser at NDC and former senior executive in a US automobile MNC). Northern Development Company. Private Interview, July.

Armstrong, P., Edwards, P.K., Marginson, P. & Purcell, J. (1995) 'Extending Beyond Borders: Multinational Companies and the International Management of Labour', *The International Journal of Human Resource Management*, 6 (3): 702–19, September.

Arthur Andersen (1996) *Global Opportunities in Business Location – Being in the Right Place at the Right Time*.

Ascarrelli, S. (1996) 'Siemens Shareholders Set To Give Executives A Tough Ride Today', *WSJE*, 12 December.

Asheim, B.T. (1996) 'Industrial Districts as "Learning Regions": A Condition for Prosperity', *European Planning Studies*, 4 (4): 379–400.

Atkins, R. (1998) 'Munich Head Office Sees Closure as Logical Sacrifice', *Financial Times*, 1–2 August.

Atkinson, M.M. & Coleman, W.D. (1985) 'Corporatism and Industrial Policy', in Cawson, A. (ed.), *Organised Interests and the State: Studies in Meso-Corporatism*. London: Sage.

Atkinson, M.M. & Coleman, W.D. (1989) *The State, Business, and Industrial Change in Canada*. London: University of Toronto Press.

Avery, W.P. & Rapkin, D.P. (1989) 'Markets, Politics, and Change in the Global Political Economy', in Avery, W.P. & Rapkin, D.P. (eds), *Markets, Politics, and Change in the Global Political Economy*. London: Lynne Rienner.

Bacharach, S.B. & Lawler, E.J. (1981) *Bargaining: Power, Tactics and Outcomes*. London: Jossey-Bass.

Bailey, D. (1997) 'A European Transnationals Monitoring Unit', paper presented at EUNIP 'Practical Proposals for Industrial Policy in Europe'. Warwick University, 11–15 December.

Bailey, D., Harte, G. & Sugden, R. (1994) *Transnationals and Governments: Recent Policies in Japan, France, Germany, the United States and Britain*. London and New York: Routledge.

Balasubramanyam, V.N., Salisu, M. & Sapsford, D. (1996) 'Foreign Direct Investment and Growth in EP and IS Countries', *The Economic Journal*, 106: 92–105, January.

Baldwin, R.E. (1992) 'Regional Economic Blocs and the Asian Dynamic Economies', in 'Seminar on Regional Economic Blocs and the Asian Dynamic Economies: Conference' Series No.8. Taipei: Chung-Hua Institute for Economic Research, April.

Bannister N. (1996) 'Siemens Pledges to Expand its £1bn Tyne', 13 December.

Barber, K. & Enderwick, P. (1992) 'International Human Resource Management in the 1990s', in Hamill, J. & Hood, S. (eds), *Europe and the Multinationals: Issues and Responses*. Aldershot: Edward Elgar.

Barberis, P. & May, T. (1993) *Government, Industry and Political Economy*. Buckingham: Oxford University Press.

Barnett, A. (1996) 'Cut-Price Britain Luring Investors', *Observer*, 14 July.

Barone, C.A. (1985) *Marxist Thought on Imperialism: Survey and Critique*. Basingstoke: Macmillan.

Barrell, R. & Pain, N. (1997a) 'The Growth of Foreign Direct Investment in Europe', *National Institute Economic Review*, 2 (160): 63–75, April.

Barrell, R. & Pain, N. (1997b) 'Foreign Direct Investment, Technological Change, and Economic Growth within Europe', *Economic Journal*, 107 (445): 1770–86, November.

Barrell, R., Hubert, F. & Pain, N. (1997) 'Innovation and the Regional and Industrial Patterns of German Foreign Direct Investment', mimeo, July.

Barrie, C. & Milner, M. (1996) 'British Jobs at Risk from Chip Glut', *The Guardian*, 16 July.

Barry, F. & Bradley, J. (1997) 'FDI and Trade: The Irish Host-Country Experience', *Economic Journal*, 107 (445): 1798–811, November.

Bartlett, C.A. & Ghoshal, S. (1989) *Managing Across Borders: The Transnational Solution*. Boston: Harvard Business School Press.

Bartlett, C.A. & Ghoshal, S. (1990) 'Managing Innovation in the Transnational Corporation', in Bartlett, C.A., Doz, Y. & Hedlund, G. (eds), *Managing the Global Firm*. London: Routledge.

Bartlett, C.A. & Ghoshal, S. (1993a) 'Beyond the M-Form: Towards a Managerial Theory of the Firm', *Strategic Management Journal*, 14: 23–46

Bartlett, C.A. & Ghoshal, S. (1993b) 'The Multinational Corporation as an Interorganisational Network', in Ghoshal, S. & Westney, D.E. (eds), *Organisation Theory and the Multinational Corporation*. Basingstoke: Macmillan.

Bass, S.J. (1998) 'Japanese Research Parks and Local Development', *Regional Studies*, 32 (5): 391–403, July.

Bates, T. (1996) 'Locate in North East: Feeding the Insatiable Hunger of the Giants – Overseas Investors Are Not Only Creating Jobs, But Huge Opportunities for Local Suppliers Too', *Daily Telegraph*, 29 May.

Battat, J., Frank, I. & Shen, X. (1996) 'Suppliers to Multinationals: Linkage Programmes to Strengthen Local Companies in Developing Countries', *FIAS Occasional Paper 6*. Foreign Investment Advisory Service, International Finance Corporation and World Bank, September.

BEA (1998) 'US Multinational Companies: Operations in 1996', *Survey of Current Business*, September.

Begg, H. & McDowall, S. (1987) 'The Effect of Regional Investment Incentives on Company Decisions', *Regional Studies*, 21 (5): 459–70.

Behrman, J.N. & Grosse, R. (1992) 'Theory in International Business', *Transnational Corporations*, 1(1): 93–126, February.

Behrman, J.N. & Grosse, R. (1990) *International Business and Governments: Issues and Institutions*. Columbia: South Carolina.

Belderbos, R.A. (1997) *Japanese Electronics Multinationals and Strategic Trade Policies*. Oxford: Clarendon Press

Bellak, C. (1997) 'Reeling in the Transnationals', *New Economy*, 4 (1): 17–21, Spring.

Belussi, F. (1996) 'Local Systems, Industrial Districts and Institutional Networks: Towards a New Evolutionary Paradigm of Industrial Economics', *European Planning Studies*, 4 (1): 5–26.

Bende-Nabende, A. (1999) *FDI, Regionalism, Government Policy and Endogenous Growth*. Ashgate: Aldershot.

Bennett, R.J. & Krebs, G. (1994) 'Local Economic Development Partnerships: An Analysis of Policy Networks in EC–LEDA Local Employment Development strategies', *Regional Studies*, 28 (2): 119–40.

Best, M.H. (1990) *The New Competition: Institutions of Industrial Restructuring*. Cambridge: Polity Press.

Betz, H-G. (1996) 'German Model Reconsidered', *German Studies Review*, xix (2): 302–20, May.

Birkinshaw, J. & Hood, N. (eds) (1998) *Multinational Corporate Evolution and Subsidiary Development*. Basingstoke: Macmillan.

Blais, A. (1986) 'Industrial Policy in Advanced Capitalist Democracies', in Blais, A. (Research Co-ordinator) *Industrial Policy*. Toronto: Toronto University Press.

Blanchard, G. (1995) 'The Single Market Revisited', *EIU European Trends*, 3rd quarter.

Blomstrom, M. (1996) 'The Impact of Foreign Investment on Host Countries: A Review of the Empirical Evidence', Stockholm School of Economics, December.

Blomstrom, M. & Lipsey, R. (1993) 'The Competitiveness of Countries and Their Multinational Firms', in Eden, L. & Potter, E.H. (eds), *Multinationals in the Global Political Economy*. New York: St. Martin's Press.

BLS (2000) US Bureau of Labour Statistics, *http://stats.bls.gov*.

Boddewyn, J.J. & Brewer, T.L. (1994) 'International-Business Political Behaviour: New Theoretical Directions', *Academy of Management Review*, 19 (1): 119–43, January.

Boughton, L. (1998) Investor Development Monitoring Management. Northern Development Company. Private Interview, July.

Bowles, D. (1998) Director of Operations. Northern Development Company. Private Interview, July.

Bowley, G. & Wagstyl, S. (1998) 'A Strategist Who Has Everything to Play For: Profile Heinrich Von Pierer, Chief Executive, Siemens', *Financial Times*, 20 April.

Bowman, D. (1998) Senior Project Executive (handled Siemens enquiries). North East English Partnership. Private Interview, July.

Boyer, R. (1990) *The Regulation School: A Critical Introduction*. New York: Columbia University Press.

Braczyk, H-J. & Heidenreich, M. (1998) 'Regional Governance in a Globalized World', in Braczyk, H-J., Cooke, P. & Heidenreich, M. (eds), *Regional*

Innovation Systems: The Role of Governance in a Globalized World. London: UCL Press.

Brainard, S.L. (1993) 'Comment' in Froot, K.A. (ed.), *Foreign Direct Invest-ment*. London: University of Chicago Press.

Bräuling, G. (1995) 'An Innovation-Based Strategy for the New German *Länder*' *European Planning Studies*, 3(4): 511–29.

Braczyk, H.-J., Cooke, P. & Heidenreich, M. (eds) (19??) *Regional Innovation Systems: The Role of Governance in a Globalized World*. London: UCL Press.

Brech, M. & Sharp, M. (1984) *Inward Investment: Policy Options for the UK*. London: Routledge and Kegan Paul.

Breitenfellner, A. (1997) 'Global Unionism: A Potential Player', *International Labour Review*, 136 (4): 531–55, Winter.

Brewer, T.L. (1992) 'An Issue-Area Approach to the Analysis of MNE–Government Relations', *Journal of International Business Studies*, 23(2): 295–310, 2nd quarter.

Brewer, T.L. & Young, S. (1995) 'Towards a Multilateral Framework for Foreign Direct Investment: Issues and Scenarios', *Transnational Corporations*, 4 (1): 69–83, April.

Bridge, J. (1997) 'Supply-Chain Dynamics – A case Study of the Automotive Sector', *World Bank Workshop for Practitioners in Cluster Formation*. Chihuana, Mexico: 17–20 November.

Bridge, J. (1998a) 'Innovative Policy Networks and Local Development Initia-tives: A Case Study of the North of England', *Global Production and Local Jobs: New Perspectives on Enterprise Networks, Employment and Local Government Policy*. Geneva: ILO: 8–10 March 1998.

Bridge, J. (1998b) Chief Executive of Northern Development Company/ Chairman of North East Regional Development Agency. Private Interview, May.

Brown, J.M. (1997) 'Aid may have been Bad for Northern Ireland', *Financial Times*, 9 May.

Brown, K. (1999) 'Britain Focuses on Securing Follow-On Investment to Stay Top of the League', *Financial Times*, 4 March.

Brunskill, I. (1992) 'The Electronics Industry: Inward Investment Versus Indigenous Development – the Policy Debate', *Environment and Planning C: Government and Policy*, 10: 439–50.

Buckley, P.J. & Casson, M.C. (1976) 'A Long Run Theory of the MNE', in Buckley, P.J. & Casson, M.C. (eds), *The Future of the MNE*. London: Macmillan.

Buckley, P.J. & Casson, M.C. (1985) *The Economic Theory of the Multi-national Enterprise*. London: Macmillan.

Buckley, P.J. & Casson, M.C. (1998) 'Models of the Multinational Enterprise', *Journal of International Business Studies*, 29 (1): 21–44, 1st quarter.

Buckley, P.J. & Glaister, K.W. (1996) 'Strategic Motives for Alliance Forma-tion', *Journal of Management Studies*, 33: 301–2, May.

Burt, T. (1996) 'Outsourcing: An Inexorable Trend', *Financial Times*, UK Engineering Survey, 26 June.

Burt, T. & Kampfner, J. (1997) 'Toyota Considers Building Pounds 1bn Car Plant in France: Move Could Hit Tories in Light of EMU Stance', *Financial Times*, 17 March.

Burt, T. & Nakamoto, M. (1997) 'Toyota Focuses on Grand Plan for Lens', *Financial Times*, 17 March.

Business Week (1995) 'Siemens Shapes Up', 1 May.

Business Week (1998) 'Daimler and Chrysler' and 'A Giant Leap for the New Europe', 18 May.

Business Wire (1999) 'AMD Opens World's Most Advanced Fab in Dresden', 20 October.

Buxton, J. (1995a) 'The Importance of Choosing the Right Site', *Financial Times*, Business Locations in Europe Survey, 24 October.

Buxton, J. (1995b) 'New Monarchs of the Glen', *Financial Times*, 15 November.

Buxton, J. (1997) 'Scottish Inward Investment at Record Pounds 3.1bn', *Financial Times*, 17 June.

Camerra-Rowe, P. (1994) 'The Political Response of Firms to the 1992 Single Market Program: The Case of the German Automobile Industry', *Program for the Study of Germany and Europe, Working Paper Series 3.1*. Duke University and Ohio State University.

Cane, A. & Jones, S. (1998) 'Siemens to Close Tyneside Plant', *Financial Times*, 1/2 August.

Cantwell, J. (1995) 'The Globalisation of Technology: What Remains of the Product Cycle Model?', *Cambridge Journal of Economics*, Special Issue on Technology and Innovation, 19: 155–74, February.

Cantwell, J. (1996) 'Transnational Corporations and Innovative Activities', in *Transnational Corporations and World Development*. London: International Thomson Business Press; UN.

Capello, R. (1996) 'Industrial Enterprises and Economic Space: The Network Paradigm', *European Planning Studies*, 4 (4): 485–98.

Caribbean Update (1998) 'Intel Starts Production at its new $500 million, 30,000 sq-m Costa Rica Plant', May.

Cassell, M. (1995) 'Inward-Looking Perspectives: Regional Rivalries Should not Undermine the National Effort to secure Foreign Investment', *Financial Times*, 5 December.

Cave, A. & Potter, B. (1997) 'Nissan Puts £215 Million into UK To Build New Car for Europe', *Daily Telegraph*, 22 January.

Caves, R.E. (1982) 'The Multinational Enterprise as an Economic Organisation', in Frieden, J.A. & Lake, D.A. (eds) (1995) *International Political Economy: Perspectives on Global Power and Wealth*, 3rd Edition. London: Routledge.

Cawson, A., Holmes, P. & Stevens, A. (1987) 'The Interaction Between Firms and the State in France: The Telecommunications and Consumer Electronics Sectors', in Wilks, S. & Wright, M. (eds), *Comparative Government–Industry Relations: Western Europe, the United States, and Japan*. Oxford: Clarendon.

Cawson, A., Holmes, P., Morgan, K., Stevens, A. & Weber, D. (1990) *Hostile Brothers: Competition and Closure in the European Electronics Industry*. Oxford: Clarendon.

Cerny, P.G. (1993) (ed.) *Finance and World Politics*. Cheltenham: Edward Elgar.

Chan, S. (1996) 'Introduction: Foreign Direct Investment in a Changing World', in Chan, S. (ed.), *Foreign Direct Investment in a Changing Global Political Economy*. Basingstoke: Macmillan.

Chandler, A.D. (1962) *Strategy and Structure*. Cambridge, Mass.: Harvard UP.

Chandler Jr, A.D. (1997) 'The United States: Engines of Economic Growth in the Capital-Intensive and Knowledge-Intensive Industries', in Chandler Jr, A.D., Amatori, F. & Hikino, T. (eds), *Big Business and the Wealth of Nations*. Cambridge: CUP.

Chandler Jr, A.D. & Hikino, T. (1997) 'The Large Industrial Enterprise and the Dynamics of Modern Economic Growth', in Chandler Jr, A.D., Amatori, F. & Hikino, T. (eds), *Big Business and the Wealth of Nations*. Cambridge: CUP.

Chandler Jr, A.D., Amatori, F. & Hikino, T. (1997) 'Historical and Comparative Contours of Big Business', in Chandler Jr, A.D., Amatori, F. & Hikino, T. (eds), *Big Business and the Wealth of Nations*. Cambridge: CUP.

Chang, M.H. (1995) 'Greater China and the Chinese "Global Tribe"', *Asian Survey*, XXXV (10): 955–67, October.

Chesnais, F. (1993) 'Globalisation, World Oligopoly and Some of Their Implications', in Humbert, M. (ed.), *The Impact of Globalisation on Europe's Firms and Industries*. London and New York: Pinter.

Chexal, J. (1997a) *NDC Strategic Market Plan 1998/1999: Life Sciences Sector*. Newcastle-upon-Tyne: Northern Development Company, November.

Chexal, J. (1997b) *NDC Strategic Market Plan 1998/1999: Chemical Sector*. Newcastle-upon-Tyne: Northern Development Company, November.

Chexal, J. (1998) Senior Investment Manager (led Siemens regional team). Northern Development Company. Also Chairperson of German-British Chamber in North East England & Cumbria. Private Interview, July.

Chiu, L-i, C. (1994) 'The Economic Reunification of Taiwan and mainland China: The Impact on Industrial Development', in Wang, C-n. (ed.), *Globalisation, Regionalisation and Taiwan's Economic*. Taipei: Chung-Hua Institute for Economic Research, December.

Church, R. (1994) *The Rise and Decline of the British Motor Industry*. Basingstoke: Macmillan.

Clegg, J. (1996a) 'The United Kingdom: A Par Excellence Two-Way Direct Investor', in Dunning, J.H. & Narula, R. (eds), *Foreign Direct Investment and Governments: Catalysts For Economic Restructuring*. London and New York: Routledge.

Clegg, J. (1996b) 'US Foreign Direct Investment in the EU – the Effects of Market Integration in Perspective', in Burton, F., Yamin, M. & Young, S. (eds), *International Business and Europe in Transition*. Basingstoke: Macmillan.

Coase, R.H. (1937) 'The Nature of the Firm', *Economica*, IV: 386–405.

Coase, R.H. (1960) 'The Problem of Social Cost', *The Journal of Law and Economics*, 3: 1–44, October.

Cole, A. & John, P. (1995) 'Local Policy Networks in France and Britain: Policy Co-ordination in Fragmented Political Sub-Systems', *West European Politics*, 18 (4): 89–109, October.

Collis, C. & Noon, D. (1994) 'Foreign Direct Investment in the UK Regions: Recent Trends and Policy Issues', *Regional Studies*, 28 (8): 843–8.

Cooke, P. (1996) 'Building a Twenty-First Century Regional Economy in Emilia-Romagna', *European Planning Studies*, 4 (1): 53–62.

Cooke, P. (1997) 'Regions in a Global Market: The Experiences of Wales and Baden-Württemberg', *Review of International Political Economy*, 4 (2): 349–81, Summer.

Cooke, P. (1998a) 'Global Clustering and Regional Innovation: Systemic Integration in Wales', in Braczyk, H-J., Cooke, P. & Heidenreich, M. (eds), *Regional Innovation Systems: The Role of Governance in a Globalized World*. London: UCL Press.

Cooke, P. (1998b) 'Introduction: Origins of the Concept', in Braczyk, H-J., Cooke, P. & Heidenreich, M. (eds), *Regional Innovation Systems: The Role of Governance in a Globalized World*. London: UCL Press.

Cooke, P. & Morgan, K. (1994) 'Growth Regions Under Duress: Renewal Strategies in Baden-Württemberg and Emilia-Romagna', in Amin, A. & Thrift, N. (eds), *Globalisation, Institutions, and Regional Development in Europe*. Oxford: OUP.

Cooke, P. & Morgan, K. (1998) *The Associational Economy: Firms, Regions, and Innovation*. Oxford: OUP.

Cooke, P., Price, A. & Morgan, K. (1995) 'Regulating Regional Economies: Wales and Baden-Württemberg in Transition', in Rhodes, M. (ed.), *The Regions and the New Europe: Patterns in Core and Periphery Development*. Manchester: Manchester UP.

Corbridge, S. (1993) *Debt and Development*. Oxford: Blackwell.

Corcoran, J. & Liddle, J. (1997) *A Regeneration Regime in the North East of England?: Inter-Agency Partnerships and the Case of Siemens UK*. PSA Conference Paper, University of Ulster, 8–10 April.

Corporate Location (2000a) Quarter I.

Corporate Location (2000b) Quarter II.

Cowling, K. (1990) 'A New Industrial Strategy: Preparing Europe for the Turn of the Century', *International Journal of Industrial Organisation*, 8: 165–83.

Cowling, K., Oughton, C. & Sugden, R. (1997) 'A Reorientation of Industrial Policy? Horizontal Policies and Targeting', paper presented at EUNIP 'Practical Proposals for Industrial Policy in Europe'. Warwick University, 11–15 December.

Cowling, K. & Sugden, R. (1987) *Transnational Monopoly Capitalism*. Brighton: Wheatsheaf.

Cowling, K. & Sugden, R. (1996) 'Beyond Capitalism and State Socialism', in Jacobsen, A., Höelscher, Y., Tomann, H. & Weisfeld, H. (eds), *Conditions of Economic Development in Central and Eastern Europe*. Marbury: Metropolis-Verlag.

Cox, K.R. & Wood, A. (1994) 'Local Government and Local Economic Development in the United States', *Regional Studies*, 28 (6): 640–5.

Cox, R.W. (1981) 'Social Forces, States and World Orders: Beyond International Relations Theory', in Keohane, R. (1986) (ed.), *Neorealism and Its Critics*. New York: Columbia UP.

Cox, R.W. (1987) *Production, Power, and World Order*. New York: Columbia UP.

Cox, R.W. (1994) 'Global Restructuring: Making Sense of the Changing International Political Economy', in Stubbs, R. & Underhill, G.R.D. (eds), *Political Economy and the Changing Global Order*. Basingstoke: Macmillan.

Cox, R.W. (1996) 'A Perspective on Globalisation', in Mittelman, J.H. (ed.), *Globalisation: Critical Reflections*. London: Lynne Rienner.

Crowther, S. & Garrahan, P. (1988) 'Corporate Power and the Local Economy', *Industrial Relations Journal*, 19(1): 51–9, Spring.

Cusumano, M.A. (1985) *The Japanese Automobile Industry: Technology and Management at Nissan and Toyota*. London: Harvard UP.

D'Cruz, J. & Rugman, A. (1997) 'The Theory of the Flagship Firm', *European Management Journal*, 15 (4): 403–12, August.

Daily Telegraph (1996a) 'Siemens Sees Further Room for Growth in UK Market', 12 January.

Daily Telegraph (1996b) 'Siemens Sees Further Room for Growth in UK Market', 12 June.

Daily Telegraph (1997) 'Nissan Can Motor On', 22 January.

Dankbaar, B. (1997) 'Lean Production: Denial, Confirmation or Extension of Sociotechnical Systems Design', *Human Relations*, 50 (5): 567–83, May.

Danson, M. (1995a) 'New Firm Formation and Regional Economic Development: An Introduction and Review of the Scottish Experience', *Small Business Economics*, 7: 81–7.

Danson, M. (1995b) 'Spatial Impact of the Social Chapter', in Hardy, S., Hart, M., Albrechts, L., and Katos, A. (eds), *An Enlarged Europe: Regions in Competition?* London: Jessica Kingsley.

Danson, M.W., Lloyd, M.G. & Newlands (1992) 'Regional Development Agencies on the United Kingdom', in Martin, R. & Townroe, P. (eds), *Regional Development in the 1990s: The British Isles in Transition*. London: Jessica Kingsley.

Deeg, R. (1993) 'The State, Banks, and Economic Governance in Germany', *German Politics*, 2 (2): 149–76, August.

Deeg, R. (1996) 'German Banks and Industrial Finance in the 1980s', *Discussion Paper FS*. Berlin: Wissenschaftszentrum Berlin für Sozialforschung: 96–323, October.

Defraigne, P. (1984) 'Towards Concerted Industrial Policies in the EC', in Jacquemin, A. (ed.), *European Industry: Public Policy and Corporate Strategy*. Oxford: Clarendon.

Dent, C.M. & Randerson, C. (1996) 'Korean Foreign Direct Investment in Europe: The Determining Forces', *The Pacific Review*, 9 (4): 531–52.

Di Mauro, F. (1999) 'The Effects of Economic Integration on FDI Flows: An Empirical Analysis and a Comparison with Trade', Centre for European Studies Working Document 135.

Dicken, P. (1990a) 'Seducing Foreign Investors – the Competitive Bidding Strategies of Local and Regional Agencies in the United Kingdom', in Hansen, J.C. & Hebbert, M. (eds), *Unfamiliar Territory: The Reshaping of European Geography*. Aldershot: Avebury.

Dicken, P. (1990b) 'The Geography of Enterprise: Elements of a Research Agenda', in de Smidt, M. & Wever, E. (eds), *The Corporate Firm in a Changing World Economy: Case Studies in the Geography of Enterprise*. London: Routledge.

Dicken, P (1992a) *Global Shift: The Internationalisation of Economic Activity*, 2nd Edition. London: Paul Chapman.

Dicken, P (1992b) 'Europe 1992 and Strategic Change in the International Automobile Industry', *Environment and Planning, A* 24: 11–31, January.

Dicken, P (1994) 'The Roepke Lecture in Economic Geography Global–Local Tensions: Firms and States in the Global Space-Economy', *Economic Geography*, 70: 101–28.

Dicken, P. (1997) 'Transnational Corporations and Nation-States', *International Social Science Journal*, 151: 77–89, March.

Dicken, P. & Tickell, A. (1992) 'Competitors or Collaborators? The Structure of Inward Investment Promotion in Northern England', *Regional Studies*, 26 (1): 99–106.

Dicken, P. & Tickell, A. (1993) 'The Role of Inward Investment Promotion in Economic Development Strategies: The Case of Northern England', *Local Economy*, 8 (3): 197–208, November.

Dicken, P., Forsfren, M. & Malmberg, A. (1994) 'The Local Embeddedness of Transnational Corporations', in Amin, A. & Thrift, N. (eds), *Globalisation, Institutions, and Regional Development in Europe*. Oxford: OUP.

DiGiovanna, S. (1996) 'Industrial Districts and Regional Economic Development: A Regulation Approach', *Regional Studies*, 30 (4): 373–86, July.

Dixon, C. & Drakakis-Smith, D. (1993) 'The Pacific-Asia Region', in Dixon, C. *et al.* (eds), *Economic and Social Development in Pacific-Asia*. London: Routledge.

Docherty, J. (1997) *NDC Secondee to Develop Proposal for Regional Agency*. Newcastle-upon-Tyne: Northern Development Company, July.

Dohse, K. (1987) 'Innovations in Collective Bargaining Through the Multinationalisation of Japanese Auto Companies: The Cases of NUMMI (USA) and Nissan (UK)', in Trevor, M. (ed.), *The Internationalisation of Japanese Business*. Colorado: Westview Press.

Dosi, G. (1997) 'Organisational Competencies, Firm Size, and the Wealth of Nations: Some Comments from a Comparative Perspective', in Chandler Jr, A.D., Amatori, F. & Hikino, T. (eds), *Big Business and the Wealth of Nations*. Cambridge: CUP.

Doz, Y.L. & Prahalad, C.K. (1980) 'How MNCs Cope with Host Government Intervention: Matching Bargaining Power and Strategic Response Is Not Enough', *Harvard Business Review*: 149–55, March/April.

DTI (Department of Trade and Industry) (1995) 'Siemens Brings £1.1 Billion Plant to the North East – UK Now the Semiconductor Centre in Europe', Press Notice, 4 August.

DTI (Department of Trade and Industry) (1998) *Regional Supply Network: Your Source of Help in Purchasing and Supply*. London: Business Link Directorate, DTI.

DTI (Department of Trade and Industry) (1999) *http://www.dti.government.uk/sd/rci*

Dunford, M. (1995) 'Rhône-Alps: A Dynamic Region in an Age of Crisis', in Rhodes, M. (ed.), *The Regions and the New Europe: Patterns in Core and Periphery Development*. Manchester: Manchester UP.

Dunford, M. & Perrons, D. (1992) 'Strategies of Modernisation: The Market and the State', *Environment and Planning C: Government and Policy*, 10 (4): 387–405.

Dunning, J.H. (1958) *American Investment in British Manufacturing Industry.* London: Allen and Unwin.

Dunning, J.H. (1977) 'Trade, Location of Economic Activity and the MNE: A Search for an Eclectic Approach', in Hesselborn, P.O., Ohlin, B. & Wijkman, P.M. (eds), *The International Allocation of Economic Activity.* London: Macmillan.

Dunning, J.H. (1981) *International Production and the Multinational Enterprise.* London: Allen & Unwin.

Dunning, J.H. (1983) 'Changes in the Level and Structure of International Production: The Last One Hundred Years', in Casson, M. (ed.), *The Growth of International Business.* London: Allen & Unwin.

Dunning, J.H. (1986) *Japanese Participation in British Industry: Trojan Horse or Catalyst for Growth.* London: Croom Helm.

Dunning, J.H. (1988) *Explaining International Production.* London: Unwin Hyman.

Dunning, J.H. (1991) 'Governments–Markets–Firms: Towards a New balance?', *CTC Reporter*, 31: 2–7, Spring.

Dunning, J.H. (1992a) 'The Political Economy of International Production', in Moran, T.H. (1993) (ed.), *Governments and Transnational Corporations, United Nations Library on Transnational Corporations*, Vol. 7. London and New York: Routledge.

Dunning, J.H. (1992b) 'The Competitive Advantage of Countries and the Activity of Transnational Corporations', Review Article *Transnational Corporations*, 1: 135–68, February.

Dunning, J.H. (1992c) 'The Global Economy, Domestic Governance, Strategies and Transnational Corporations: Interactions and Policy Implications', *Transnational Corporations*, 1(3): 7–45, December.

Dunning, J.H. (1993a) *Multinational Enterprises and the Global Economy.* Reading: Addison-Wesley.

Dunning, J.H. (1993b) 'Governments and Multinational Enterprises: From Confrontation to Co-operation?', in Eden, L. & Potter, E.H. (eds), *Multinationals in the Global Political Economy.* New York: St. Martin's Press.

Dunning, J.H. (1998) 'Location and the Multinational Enterprise: A Neglected Factor', *Journal of International Business Studies*, 29 (1): 45–66, 1st quarter.

Dunning, J.H. & Narula, R. (1996) 'The Investment Development Path Revisited: Some Emerging Issues', in Dunning, J.H. & Narula, R. (eds), *Foreign Direct Investment and Governments: Catalysts For Economic Restructuring*, London and New York: Routledge.

Dunning, J.H. & Sauvant, K.P. (1996) 'Introduction: Transnational Corporation in the World Economy', in *Transnational Corporations and World Development.* London: International Thomson Business Press; UN.

Dyer, J.H. (1996a) 'Specialized Supplier Networks as a Source of Competitive Advantage: Evidence from the Auto Industry', *Strategic Management Journal*, 17: 271–91.

Dyer, J.A. (1996b) 'How Chrysler Created an American Keiretsu', *Harvard Business Review*, 42–56, July–August.

Dyer, J.H., Sung Cho, D. & Chu, W. (1998) 'Strategic Supplier Segmentation: The Next "Best Practice", in Supply Chain Management', *California Management Review*, 40 (2): 57–77, Winter.

Eason, K. (1997) 'UK Carmaking Resurgence Driven by the Japanese', *The Times*, 3 March.

EC (European Commission) (1990) *The Effect of Different State Aid Measures on Intra-Community Competition*. Luxembourg: Commission of the European Communities.

EC (European Commission) (1998) 'The Impact on Trade and Investment: Foreign Direct Investment', *The Single Market Review*, 1 (IV).

Economist, The (1981a) 'Japanese Cars at the Cross-Roads', 11 July.

Economist, The (1981b) 'Nissan Promises To Build Cars More British than the British', 5 December.

Economist, The (1982a) 'Nissan in Britain: More Cash, and We'll Come', 6 March.

Economist, The (1982b) 'No Nissan for Britain?', 10 July.

Economist, The (1983a) 'Nissan Reshuffles and Turns Up Trumps for Britain', 2 July.

Economist, The (1983b) 'Nissan Shifts Gear', 29 October.

Economist, The (1983c) 'Detroit's Comeback', 29 October.

Economist, The (1984) 'Nissan: Mini-Deal', 4 February.

Economist, The (1985) 'Nissan: Rising Sun Over Industrial Relations', 27 April.

Economist, The (1986a) 'Nissan: Watching the Yen', 14 June.

Economist, The (1986b) 'Nissan: Bluebirds over the Problems at Rover', 13 September.

Economist, The (1992a) 'Japanese Business Methods: Couldn't We All Do a Little Bit Worse?', 4 April.

Economist, The (1992b) 'Chip Diplomacy: A Spate of Joint-Venture Deals to Develop and Manufacture Microchips Marks a Turning Point for the World's Electronics Industry', 18 July.

Economist, The (1994a) 'Business in Britain', 24 May.

Economist, The (1994b) 'Europe's Would-Be Champions: New Optimism Among European Semiconductor Manufacturers', 27 August.

Economist, The (1996a) 'Is the Model Broken?: Germany's Social-Market System – Which Has Delivered Enviable Stability and Prosperity for Decades – Is in Worse Shape than It Looks', 4 May.

Economist, The (1996b) 'Japanese Semiconductors: Flat as a Pancake', 4 May.

Economist, The (1997) 'Toyota: On the March', 22 March.

Economist, The (1999a) 'Foreign Investment: Ruling the Merger Wave', 23 January.

Economist, The (1999b) 'A Federal Europe', 27 March.

Economist, The (1999c) 30 January.

Economist, The (1999d) 'Who's Clueless Now', 22 May.

Eden, L. (1991) 'Bringing the Firm Back In: Multinationals in International Political Economy', *Millennium: Journal of International Studies*, 20 (2): 197–224.

Edgerton, D. (1991) 'Liberal Militarism and the British State', *New Left Review*, 185: 138–70.

Edwards, P., Ferner, A. & Sisson, K. (1996) 'The Conditions for International Human Resource Management: Two Case Studies', *International Journal of Human Resource Management*, 7 (1): 20–40, February.

Edwards, T. (1998a) 'Multinationals, Labour Management and the Process of Reverse Diffusion: A Case Study', *The International Journal of Human Resource Management*, 9 (4): 696–709, August.

Edwards, T. (1998b) 'Multinational Companies and the Diffusion of Employment Practices: A Survey of the Literature', *Warwick Papers in Industrial Relations*, 61. School of Industrial and Business Studies, University of Warwick, November.

Eisenschitz, A. & Gough, J. (1993) *The Politics of Local Economic Policy: The Problems and Possibilities of Local Initiative*. Basingstoke: Macmillan.

Elcock, H. (1997) 'The North of England and the Europe of the Regions, or, When is a Region not a Region?', in Keating, M. & Loughlin, J. (eds), *The Political Economy of Regionalism*. Frank Cass: London.

Elliot, M. (1995) 'UK Looks Good for Siemens Chip Fab', *Electronic Weekly*, 26 July.

Encarnation, D.J. & Wells, Jr. L.T. (1985) 'Sovereignty En Garde: Negotiating With Foreign Investors', *International Organisation*, 1: 47–78, Winter.

Encarnation, D.J. & Wells, Jr. (1986a) 'Competitive Strategies in Global Industries: A View from Host Governments', in Porter, M.E. (ed.), *Competition in Global Industries*. Boston: Harvard Business School.

Encarnation, D.J. & Wells, Jr. (1986b) 'Evaluating Foreign Investment', in Moran, T.H. (1993) (ed.), *Governments and Transnational Corporations, United Nations Library on Transnational Corporations*, Vol. 7. London and New York: Routledge.

Enderwick, P. (1993) 'Introduction: Transnational Corporations and Human Resources: The Issues', in Enderwick, P. (ed.), *Transnational Corporations and Human Resources, United Nations Library on Transnational Corporations*, (16). London & New York: Routledge.

EP (English Partnerships) (1997a) *North East: A Comprehensive Guide to the Business Region*. Manchester: Newsco.

EP (English Partnerships) (1997b) *England: Economic Regeneration in England and Its Regions*. Manchester: Newsco, March.

EP (English Partnerships) (1998) *English Partnerships: Investment Guide Summary, North East Region*.

Ernst & Young (1992) *Regions of the New Europe*. Corporate Location: London.

Ernst & Young (1993) *New Location Factors for Mobile Investment in Europe*. Netherlands Economics Institute and Ernst & Young for European Commission: Luxembourg.

ERT (European Round Table of Industrialists) (1998) 'A Stimulus to Job Creation: Practical Partnerships Between Large and Small Companies', *European Business Journal*, 10 (3): 92–9.

Esser, J. (1988) 'Does Industrial Policy Matter? Land Governments in Research and Technology Policy in Federal Germany', in Crouch, C. & Marquand, D. (eds), *The New Centralism: Britain Out of Step in Europe?* Oxford: Basil Blackwell.

Estrin, S., Hughes, K. & Todd, S. (1997) *Foreign Direct Investment in Central and Eastern Europe: Multinationals in Transition*. London: The Royal Institute of International Affairs, Pinter.

EUBIR (2000) *The European Union Business Incentives Report 2000*, 6 (2). Inward Investment Europe: London.

Euroconfidential (1997) *Practical Guide to Foreign Direct Investment in the European Union*. Belgium: Euroconfidential.

European Round Table of Industrialists (ERT) (1998) 'A Stimulous to Job Creation: Practical Partnerships Between Large and Small Companies', *European Business Journal*, 10 (3): 92–9.

Eurostat (1997) *Globalisation Through Trade and Foreign Direct Investment*. EC: Luxembourg, October.

Evans, R. (1991) 'Training and Enterprise Councils: An Initial Assessment', *Regional Studies*, 24: 173–84.

Fatouros, A.A. (1995) 'Towards an International Agreement on Foreign Direct Investment?', *ICSID Review: Foreign Investment Law Journal*, 10 (2): 181–207, autumn.

Fenney, R. (1998) *Essential Local Government*. London: Nuffield.

Ferner, A. (1997) 'Multinationals, "Relocations", and Employment in Europe', paper for IESE Third International Conference, 'Job Creation: The Role of Labour Market Institutions'. Barcelona, 19–20 June.

Ferner, A. & Quintanilla, J. (1998) 'Multinationals, National Business Systems, and the Management of HRM: The Enduring Influence of National Identity or a Process of "Anglo-Saxonisation"', *International Journal of Human Resource Management, Special Issue*, 9 (4), August.

Financial Times (1995) 'Silicon on Tyneside', 7 August.

Financial Times (1998a) 'The Essential Guide to Heinrich Von Pierer', 20 April.

Financial Times (1998b) 'Siemens: Lex Column', 24 April.

Financial Times (1998c) 'The Chips are Down: Lex Column', 1–2 August.

Financial Times (1998d) 'Car Component Makers Face Consolidation', 21 May.

Financial Times (1999) Lex Column: Renault/Nissan', 16 March.

Fisher, A. (1998) 'Siemens receives mixed reaction to Acer deal', *Financial Times*, 24 April.

Fisher, A. & Lindeman, M. (1995) 'International Company News: Daimler's Bad Case of a German Affliction – the D-Mark is Driving Industry Abroad', *Financial Times*, 29 June.

Fong, C-O. (1992) 'FDI in Malaysia: Technology Transfer and Linkages by Japan and the Asian NIEs', in Tokunaga, S. (ed.), *Japan's Foreign Investment and Asia Economic Interdependence*. Tokyo: University of Tokyo.

Francks, P. (1992) *Japanese Economic Development: Theory and Practice*. London: Routledge.

Frank, A.G. (1969) *Capitalism and Underdevelopment in Latin America*. London: Modern Review Publishers.

Fraser, A. (1995) 'National Governments and the Global Corporation', *British Foreign Policy Study Group*, November.

Fraser, C. (1998) Director of Investment Services. Northern Development Company. 1995–1998 Head of IBB Asia-Pacific Office. Private Interview, July.

Freeman, C. (1995) 'The "National System of Innovation", in Historical Perspective', *Cambridge Journal of Economics*, 19: 5–24.

Fuchs, M. & Schamp, E. (1990) 'Standard Elektrik Lorenz: Introducing CAD into a Telecommunications Firm: Its Impact on Labour', in de Smidt, M. &

Wever, E. (eds), *The Corporate Firm in a Changing World Economy: Case Studies in the Geography of Enterprise*. London: Routledge.

Fukai, S. (1994) 'Prospects for an Asian Trade Bloc: Japan, the Association of South East Asian Nations and the Asian Newly Industrialising Economies', in Mason, T.D. & Turag, A.M. (eds), *Japan, Nafta and Europe: Trilateral Cooperation or Confrontation?* Basingstoke: St. Martin's Press.

Fukao, M. (1995) *Financial Integration, Corporate Governance, and the Performance of Multinational Companies*. Washington, DC: The Brookings Institution.

Gales, A. (1997) 'Huge Welcome for Nissan Boost', *Evening Chronicle*, 21 January.

Garmise, S.O. (1995) 'Economic Development Strategies in Emilia-Romagna', in Rhodes, M. (ed.), *The Regions and the New Europe: Patterns in Core and Periphery Development*. Manchester: Manchester UP.

Garrahan, P. (1986) 'Nissan in the North-East of England', *Capital and Class*, 27: 5–13, Winter.

Gartland, H. (1998) Project Executive. Northern Development Company. Private Interview, July.

Gatrell, J.D. (1999) 'Re-Thinking Economic Development in Peripheral Regions – Part 1', *Social Sciences Journal*, November.

Geroski, P.A. (1990) 'European Industrial Policy and Industrial Policy in Europe', in Cowling, K. & Tomann, H. (eds), *Industrial Policy After 1992: An Anglo-German Perspective*. London: Anglo-German Foundation.

GGDC (2000) Groningen Growth and Development Centre *www.rug.nl/ggdc*

Ghoshal, S. & Westney, E. (1993) 'Introduction and Overview', in Ghoshal, S. & Westney, D.E. (eds), *Organisation Theory and the Multinational Corporation*. Basingstoke: Macmillan.

Gibbs, D.C. (1989) 'Government Policy and Industrial Change: An Overview', in Gibbs, D. (ed.), *Government Policy and Industrial Change*. London: Routledge.

Giddens, A. (1990) *The Consequences of Modernity*. Cambridge: Polity Press.

Gill, S. (1991) 'Historical Materialism, Gramsci, and International Political Economy', in Murphy, C.N. & Tooze, R. (eds), *The New International Political Economy*. Boulder, Col.: Lynne Rienner.

Gill, S. (1995) 'Globalisation, Market Civilisation, and Disciplinary Neoliberalism', *Millenium: Journal of International Studies*, 24 (3): 399–423, Winter.

Gill, S. (1996) 'Globalisation, Democratisation, and the Politics of Indifference', in Mittelman, J.H. (ed.), *Globalisation: Critical Reflections*. London: Lynne Rienner.

Gittleman, M. & Wolff, E.N. (1995) 'R&D Activity and Cross-Country Growth Comparisons', *Cambridge Journal of Economics*, Special Issue on Technology and Innovation 19: 189–207, February.

Giunta, A. & Martinelli, F. (1995) 'The Impact of Post-Fordist Corporate Restructuring in a Peripheral Region: The Mezzogiorno of Italy', in Amin, A. & Tomaney, J. (eds), *Behind the Myth of the European Union: Prospects for Cohesion*. London: Routledge.

Goddard, J.B. (1990) 'Positioning Older Industrial Regions in Relation to the Emerging Information Economy: The Case of North-East England', in Hansen, J.C. & Hebbert, M. (eds), *Unfamiliar Territory: The Reshaping of European Geography*. Aldershot: Avebury.

Godsmark, C. (1997) 'Nissan in Profit as New UK Car is Confirmed', *Independent*, 22 January.

Gold, D. (1991) 'The Determinants of FDI and their Implications for Host Developing Countries', *CTC Reporter*, 31: 21–24, Spring.

Gomes-Casseres, B. (1990) 'Firm-Ownership Preferences and Host Government Restrictions: An Integrated Approach', in Gomes-Casseres, B. & Yoffie, D.B. (eds), (1993) *The International Political Economy of Direct Foreign Investment, Vol. II*. Aldershot: Edward Elgar.

Goodhart, D. (1994) *The Reshaping of the German Social Market*. London: Institute for Public Policy Research.

Goodwin, M. & Painter, M. (1995) 'Local Governance and Concrete Research: Investigating the uneven Development of Regulation', *Economy and Society*, 24 (3): 334–356, August.

Goold, M. & Campbell, A. (1998) 'Desperately Seeking Synergy', *Harvard Business Review*: 131–43, September–October.

Görg, H. & Ruane, F. (1997) 'The Impact of Foreign Direct Investment on Sectoral Adjustment in the Irish Economy', *National Institute Economic Review*, 160: 76–84, February.

Goto, M. (1987) 'Nissan's International Strategy', in Trevor, M, (ed.), *The Internationalisation of Japanese Business*. Colorado: Westview Press.

Graham, E.M. (1991) 'Strategic Management and Transnational Firm Behaviour: A Formal Approach', in Pitelis, C.N. & Sugden, R. (eds), *The Nature of the Transnational Firm*. London: Routledge.

Graham, E.M. (1996) 'Should There Be Multilateral Rules in Foreign Direct Investment', in Burton, F., Yamin, M. & Young, S. (eds), *International Business and Europe in Transition*. Basingstoke: Macmillan.

Grant, S. (1997) 'Northern Ireland: Regional Policy and Economic Development', *British Economy Survey*, 26 (2): 1–4, Spring.

Grant, W. (1982) *The Political Economy of Industrial Policy*. London: Butterworths.

Grant, W. (1989) *Government and Industry: A Comparative Analysis of the US, Canada and the UK*. Aldershot: Edward Elgar.

Grant, W. (1990) 'Government–Industry Relations in the British Chemical Industry', in Chick, M. (ed.), *Governments, Industries and Markets: Aspects of Government–Industry Relations in the UK, Japan, West Germany and the USA since 1945*. Aldershot: Edward Elgar.

Gray, P.H. (1995) 'The Modern Structure of International Economic Policies', *Transnational Corporations*, 4 (3): 49–66, December.

Greer, J.V., Murray, M.R. & Walsh, J.A. (1995) 'Economic Restructuring Within the European Periphery: The Experience of Ireland', in Hardy, S. *et al.* (eds), *An Enlarged Europe: Regions in Competition?* London: Jessica Kingsley.

Griffiths, J. (1998) 'Imported Japanese Cars More Reliable', *Financial Times*, 6 February.

Grimes, S. (1993) 'Indigenous Entrepreneurship in a Branch Plant Economy: The Case of Ireland', *Regional Studies*, 27: 484–9.

Groenewegen, J. & Beije, P.R. (1992) 'The European Answer to the Dilemmas of Competition, Co-operation, and Mergers', *Journal of Economic Issues*, XXVI (2), June.

Groom, B. (1998a) 'Decision Threatens Inward Investment Record', *Financial Times*, 1 August.

Groom, B. (1998b) 'Job Creation Still Strong as Investments Flow: The UK Continues to Attract Foreign Companies, in Spite of Asia's Economic Woes and the Problems of a Strong Pound. But, although New Statistics may Please the Government they Fail to Convince Everyone', *Financial Times*, 16 July.

Groom, B. (1998c) 'Infighting Poses Its Threats', *Financial Times*, 16 July.

Groom, B. (1998d) 'Ageing Regional Aid Policy Is Feeling the Strain: Economic Slowdown Shines an Unwelcome Spotlight on Policy as Grant-Aided Factories Are Forced to Close', *Financial Times*, 19 October.

Grosvenor, P. & Malloy, J. (1997) *NDC Strategic Market Plan 1998/1999: Electronics Sector*. Newcastle-upon-Tyne: Northern Development Company, November.

Grubaugh, S.G. (1987) 'Determinants of Direct Foreign Investment', *The Review of Economics and Statistics*, LXIX (1): 149–52, February.

Grunberg, L. (1996) 'The IPE of MNCs', in Balaam, D.N. & Veseth, I. (eds), *Introduction to International Political Economy*. New Jersey: Prentice Hall.

Guisinger, S. (1985) *Investment Incentives and Performance Requirements*. New York: Praeger.

Hakanson, L. (1990) 'International Decentralisation of R&D? The Organisational Challenges', in Bartlett, C.A., Doz, Y. & Hedlund, G. (eds), *Managing the Global Firm*. London: Routledge.

Hall, N. (1997) *NDC Strategic Market Plan 1998/1999: Automotive Sector*. Newcastle-upon-Tyne: Northern Development Company, November.

Hall, N. (1998) Senior Investment Manager. Northern Development Company. Private Interview, July.

Hall, P. (1986) *Governing the Economy: The Politics of State Intervention in Britain and France*. Oxford: OUP.

Ham, R.M., Linden, G. & Appleyard, M.M. (1998) 'The Evolving Role of Semiconductor Consortia in the United States and Japan', *California Management Review*, 41 (1): 137–63, autumn.

Hamann, H. (1998) Siemens UK Chief Financial Controller. Private Interview, July.

Hamill, J. (1992) 'Cross-Border Mergers, Acquisitions and Alliances', in Hamill, J. & Hood, S. (eds), *Europe and the Multinationals: Issues and Responses*. Aldershot: Edward Elgar.

Hamill, J., Hood, N. & Young, S. (1988) *Foreign Multinationals and the British Economy: Impact and Policy*. New York: Croom Held.

Hamilton, A. (1998) *Research Strategy – Report on Phase 1: Survey of NDC Research Projects* (internal distribution only). Newcastle-upon-Tyne: Northern Development Company, July.

Hamilton, F.E.I. (1987) 'Multinational Enterprises', in Lever, W.F. (ed.), *Industrial Change in the United Kingdom*. Harlow: Longman.

Handfiled, R., Krause, D., Scannell, T. & Monczka, R. (2000) 'Avoid the Pitfalls in Supplier Development', *Sloan Management Review* (electronic version from Dow Jones).

Hanson, C. (1995) 'Jobs: Rethinking EU Policies', *Director*, 49 (4): 29, November.

Harding, A., Evans, R., Parkinson, M. & Garside, P. (1996) *Regional Government in Britain: An Economic Solution*. Bristol: Policy Press.

Harnischefeger, U. (1999a) 'Siemens Wins Approval for Plan to List in US', *Financial Times*, 19 February.

Harnischefeger, U. (1999b) 'Siemens Chief Sets New Profit Targets', *Financial Times*, 22 February.

Hart, J.A. (1992) 'The Effects of State–Societal Arrangements on International Competitiveness: Steel, Motor Vehicles and Semiconductors in the United States, Japan and Western Europe', in Grant, W. (1995) *Industrial Policy: The International Library of Comparative Public Policy*. Aldershot: Edward Elgar.

Hart, T. & Roberts, P. (1995) 'The Single European Market: Implications for Local and Regional Authorities', in Hardy, S. *et al.* (eds), *An Enlarged Europe: Regions in Competition?* London: Jessica Kingsley.

Harukiyo, H. (1998) 'Japanese Global Strategies in Europe and the Formation of Regional Markets', in Harukiyo, H. & Hook, G.D. (eds), *Japanese Business Management: Restructuring for Low Growth and Globalisation*. London: Routledge.

Haslam, C., Williams, J. & Williams, K. (1987) *The Breakdown of Austin Rover*. Leamington Spa: Berghahn.

Hassink, R., Dankbaar, B. & Corvers, F. (1995) 'Technology Networking in Border Regions: Case Study of the Euroregion Maas-Rhine', *European Planning Studies*, 3 (1): 63–83.

Hassink, R. (1996) 'Technology Transfer Agencies and Regional Economic Development', *European Planning Studies*, 4 (2): 167–84.

Hausmann, R. & Fernandez-Arias, E. (2000) *Foreign Direct Investment: Good Cholesterol?* Inter-American Development Bank: New Orleans, 26 March.

Hay, C. (1995) 'Re-stating the Problem of Regulation and Re-regulating the Local State', *Economy and Society*, 24 (3): 387–407, August.

Hedlund, G. (1986) 'The Hypermodern MNC – A Heterarchy', *Human Resource Management*, 25: 9–35.

Hedlund, G. (1993) 'Assumptions of Hierarchy and Heterarchy, with Applications to the Management of the Multinational Corporation', in Ghoshal, S. & Westney, D.E. (eds), *Organisation Theory and the Multinational Corporation*. Basingstoke: Macmillan.

Heidenreich, M. (1996) 'Beyond Flexible Specialisation: The Rearrangement of Regional Production Orders in Emilia-Romagna and Baden-Württemberg', *European Planning Studies*, 4 (4): 401–19.

Heintz, J.J. (1994) 'Multinational Corporations at the Interstices of Domestic and International Politics – The Case of the HJ-Heinz Company in Zambia and Zimbabwe', *Journal of Commonwealth and Comparative Politics*, 32 (2): 200–29, July.

Hennart, J.F. (1989) 'Can the "New Forms of Investment", Substitute for the "old forms?": A Transaction Costs Perspective', *Journal of International Business Studies*, 20 (2): 211–34, Summer.

Hennart, J.F. (1991) 'The Transaction Cost Theory of the MNE', in Pitelis, C.N. & Sugden, R. (eds), *The Nature of the Transnational Firm*. London: Routledge.

Hennart, J.F. (1993) 'Control in Multinational Firms: The Role of Price Hierarchy', in Ghoshal, S. & Westney, D.E. (eds), *Organisation Theory and the Multinational Corporation*. Basingstoke: Macmillan.

Hennart, J.F. & Park, Y.R. (1994) 'Location, Governance, and Strategic Determinants of Japanese Manufacturing Investment in the United States', *Strategic Management Journal*, 15: 419–36.

Henriksen, L.B. (1995) 'Formal Cooperation Among Firms in Networks: The Case of Danish Joint Ventures and Strategic Alliances', *European Planning Studies*, 3 (4): 254–60.

Herrigel, G. (1993) 'Large Firms, Small Firms, and the Governance of Flexible Specialisation: The Case of Baden Württemberg and Socialised Risk', in Kogut, B. (ed.), *Country Competitiveness: Technology and the Organising of Work*. Oxford: Oxford University Press.

Herrigel, G. (1996) *Industrial Constructions: The Sources of German Industrial Power*. New York: CUP.

Van Herwaarden, E. (1995) 'The Variety of Aid Schemes Grows', *Financial Times*, Business Locations in Europe Survey, 24 October.

Hill, S. & Munday, M. (1992) 'The UK Regional Distribution of Foreign Direct Investment: Analysis and Determinants', *Regional Studies*, 26 (6): 535–44.

Hill, S. & Munday, M. (1994) *The Regional Distribution of Foreign Manufacturing Investment in the UK*. Basingstoke: Macmillan.

Hirst, P. & Thompson, G. (1995) 'Globalisation and the Future of the Nation State', *Economy and Society*, 24 (3): 408–42, August.

Hirst, P. & Zeitlin, J. (1992) 'Flexible Specialisation Versus Post-Fordism: Theory, Evidence, and Policy Implications', in Scott, A.J. & Storper, M. (eds), *Pathways to Industrialisation and Regional Development*. London & New York: Routledge.

Hitchens, D.M.W.N., Birnie, J.E. & Wagner, K. (1993) 'Competitiveness and Regional Development: The Case of Northern Ireland', *Regional Studies*, 26 (1): 106–14.

HMSO (1977) *Business Monitor: Overseas Transactions*, MA4. London: HMSO.

HMSO (1985) *Business Monitor: Overseas Transactions*, MA4. London: DTI.

HMSO (1994a) *Competitiveness of UK Manufacturing Industry: Second Report*. Trade and Industry Committee, House of Commons (2R, ETC). London: HMSO, April.

HMSO (1994b) *1994 Competitiveness White Paper: Helping Business to Win* (Cm 2563). London: HMSO, May.

HMSO (1995a) *1995 Competitiveness White Paper: Forging Ahead* (Cm 2867). London: HMSO, May.

HMSO (1995b) *Regional Industrial Policy: Government's Response to the 4th Report of the House of Commons*. Trade and Industry Select Committee, 1994–1995 Series (Cm 2910). London: HMSO, July.

HMSO (1995c) *Regional Policy: 4th Report (1994–1995) Volume 1*. Trade and Industry Committee (Hc 356-I). London: HMSO, 29 March.

HMSO (1996) *1996 Competitiveness White Paper: Study on Outward Investment*. London: DTI/HMSO.

HMSO (1997) *1997 Competitiveness Paper – Building Partnerships for Prosperity: Sustainable Growth, Competitiveness and Employment in the English Regions*. Cm 3814, December, London: DTI/HMSO.

HMSO (1998a) *1998 Competitiveness White Paper – Our Competitive Future: Building the Knowledge Driven Economy* (with E-Commerce and Analytical Reports). Find at: *http://www.dti.gov.uk/public/search.html*

HMSO (1998b) *Business Monitor: Overseas Trade Statistics of the United Kingdom with the World*, MA20. London: HMSO.

Hofstede, G. (1980) *Cultures Consequences*. Beverly Hills, CA: Sage.

Hollingsworth, J.R., Schmitter, P.C. & Streeck, W. (1994) 'Capitalism, Sectors, Institutions, and Performance', in Hollingsworth, J.R., Scmitter, P.C. & Streeck, W. (eds), *Governing Capitalist Economies: Performance and Control of Economic Sectors*. Oxford: OUP.

Holtbrügge, D. & Welge, M.K. (1997) 'Germany', in Dunning, J.H. (ed.), *Governments, Globalisation, and International Business*. Oxford: OUP.

Hong, S.G. (1995) 'Do Institutions Matter?: A Case of Taiwan's Semiconductor Industry', *Issues and Studies*, 31(11): 16–39, November.

Hood, C., Hood, N. & Young, S. (1996) 'Transatlantic Perspectives on Inward Investment and Prospect for Policy Reconciliation', in Burton, F., Yamin, M. & Young, S. (eds), *International Business and Europe in Transition*. Basingstoke: Macmillan.

Hood, N. & Taggart, J.H. (1997) 'German Foreign Direct Investment in the UK and Ireland: Survey Evidence', *Regional Studies*, 31 (2): 139–50.

Hood, N. & Young, S. (1993) 'Inward Investment Policy in the European Community in the 1990s', *Transnational Corporations*, 2 (2): 35–62, August.

Hood, N. & Young, S. (1995) 'Attracting, Managing and Developing Inward Investment in the Single Market', in Amin, A. & Tomaney, J. (eds), *Behind the Myth of the European Union: Prospects for Cohesion*. London: Routledge.

Hood, N. & Young, S. (1997) 'The United Kingdom', in Dunning, J.H. (ed.), *Governments, Globalisation and International Business*. Oxford: OUP.

Hoogvelt, A. & Yuasa, M. (1994) 'Going Lean or going Native?: The Social Regulation of "Lean", Production Systems', *Review of International Political Economy*, 1 (2): 281–303, Summer.

Hook, G. (1998) 'Japanese Business in Triadic Regionalisation', in Harukiyo, H. & Hook, G.D. (eds), *Japanese Business Management: Restructuring for Low Growth and Globalisation*. London: Routledge.

Hotten, R. (1995) 'Britain Now Favourite to Win Siemens Plant', *Independent*, 3 July.

Hu, Y-S (1992) 'Global or Stateless Corporations are National Firms with International Operations', *California Management Review*, 107–26, Winter.

Huggins, R. (1996) 'Innovation, Technology Support and Networking in South Wales', *European Planning Studies*, 4 (6): 757–68

Humphrey, J. (1995) 'The Adoption of Japanese Management Techniques in Brazilian Industry', *Journal of Management Studies*, Special Issue, 32 (6): 767–87, November.

Hurrell, A. & Woods, N. (1995) 'Globalisation and Inequality', *Millenium: Journal of International Studies*, 24 (3): 447–470, Winter.

Hutton, W. (1996) *The State We're In*. London: Jonathon Cape.

Hymer, S.H. (1959, published 1976) *The International Operations of National Firms: A Study of Direct Foreign Investment*. Cambridge: The MIT Press.

IBB (Invest in Britain Bureau) (1991) *Inward Investment in the UK: A Market Report*. London: IBB, July.

IBB (Invest in Britain Bureau) (1995a) *Europe's Competitive Base, Annual Report*. London: DTI.

IBB (Invest in Britain Bureau) (1995b) 'Siemens Invests $1.7 billion in North-Eastern England', *Briefing on Britain*, 20 October.

IBB (Invest in Britain Bureau) (1996) *Review of Operations*. London: IBB.

IBB (Invest in Britain Bureau) (1997) *Report on Auto Industry*. Home page, 27 August.

IBB (Invest in Britain Bureau) (1998) 'Address by Mr Henderson at the IBB Annual Review Launch', 15 July.

IBB (1999) *Operations Review*. Invest in Britain Bureau.

Ietto-Gillies, G. (1992) *International Production: Trends, Theories, Effects*. Cambridge: Polity Press.

Ietto-Gilles, G. (1996) 'Widening Geographical Trends in UK International Production: Theoretical Analysis and Empirical Evidence', *International Review of Applied Economics*, 10 (2): 195–208.

Ietto-Gilles, G. (1997a) 'Working with the Big Guys', *New Economy*, 4 (1): 12–16, Spring.

Ietto-Gilles, G. (1997b) 'Industrial Strategy in the Era of Transnationals: Issues of Analysis and Policy', paper presented at EUNIP 'Practical Proposals for Industrial Policy in Europe'. Warwick University, 11–15 December 1997.

IFC (1997) 'Foreign Direct Investment', *Lessons of Experience*, 5. International Finance Corporation and Foreign Investment Advisory Service, World Bank: Washington DC.

Industry Week (1999) *World's Top 1000 Industrial Firms*, 7 June.

Invest.uk (2000) *IBB Operations Review*.

Islam, S. (1996) 'Soft Talk, No Stick: Europe's New Approach Towards Japan Pays Off', *Far Eastern Economic Review (FEER)*, 16 May.

Jack, A. (1995) 'Peaceful Brittany Wins Japanese Company', *Financial Times*, Business Locations in Britain Survey, 24 October.

Jack, A. (1996) 'Climate Becomes More Inviting', *Financial Times*, France Survey, 20 June.

Jacobson, C.K., Lenway, S.A. & Ring, P.S. (May 1993) 'The Political Embeddedness of Private Economic Transactions', *Journal of Management Studies*, 30 (3): 453–78.

Jenkins, B. (1986) 'Re-examining the "Obsolescing Bargain:" A Study of Canada's National Energy Program', *International Organisation*, 40 (1): 139–65, Winter.

Jessop, B. (1992) 'Post Fordism and Flexible Specialisation: Incommensurable, Contradictory, or Just Plain Different Perspectives?', in Ernste, H. & Meire, V. (eds), *Regional Development and Contemporary Industrial Response: Extending Flexible Specialisation*. London & New York: Belhaven.

Jessop, B. (1994) 'Post-Fordism and the State', in Amin, A. (ed.), *Post-Fordism: A Reader*. Oxford: Blackwell.

Jessop, B. (1995) 'The Regulation Approach, Governance and Post-Fordism: Alternative Perspectives on Economic and Political Change', *Economy and Society*, 24(3): 307–31, August.

Jones, G. (1990) 'The British Government and Foreign Multinationals before 1970', in Chick, M. (ed.), *Governments, Industries and Markets: Aspects of*

Government–Industry Relations in the UK, Japan, West Germany and the USA since 1945. Aldershot: Edward Elgar.

Jones, G. (1996a) 'Transnational Corporations – A Historical Perspective', in *Transnational Corporations and World Development*. London: International Thomson Business Press; UN.

Jones, G. (1996b) *The Evolution of International Business*. London: Routledge.

Jones, G. (1997) 'Great Britain: Big Business, Management, and Competitiveness in Twentieth-Century Britain', in Chandler Jr, A.D., Amatori, F. & Hikino, T. (eds), *Big Business and the Wealth of Nations*. Cambridge: CUP.

Jones, G. (1998) RSO Manager. Northern Development Company (Regional Supply Office), North East, July.

Jones, G. & Schröter, H.G. (eds) (1993) *The Rise of the Multinational in Continental Europe*. Vermont: Edward Elgar.

Jones, J. & Peck, J. (1995) 'Training and Enterprise Councils: Schumpterian Workfare State or What? *Environment and Planning, A* 27 (9): 1361–96, September.

Julius, D. (1990) *Global Companies and Public Policy: The Growing Challenge of FDI*. London: Pinter Publishers.

Kaminski, B. & Riboud, M. (1999) *Foreign Investment and Restructuring: The Evidence from Hungary*. World Bank.

Karl, J. (1996) 'The Promotion and Protection of German Foreign Investment Abroad', *ICSID Review: Foreign Investment Law Journal*, 11 (1): 1–31, Spring.

Keck, O. (1993) 'The National System for Technical Innovation in Germany', in Nelson, R.R. (ed.), *National Systems of Innovation: A Comparative Analysis*. Oxford: OUP.

Kehoe, L. (1998) 'Siemens Chip Business to be Spun Off', *Financial Times*, 5 November.

Kehoe, L., Munchau, W., Taylor, P. & Tighe, C. (1995) 'Siemens to Build Pounds 1bn Microchip Plant in Britain: North-East Site Will Create 1,800 Jobs', *Financial Times*, 5 August.

Keohane, R.O. & Nye, J. (1975) *Power and Independence: World Politics in Transition*. Boston: Little Brown.

Kindleberger, C.P. (1969) *American Business Abroad*. New Haven, CT: JAI Press.

King, D.S. (1990) 'Economic Activity and the Challenge to Local Government', in King, D.S. & Pierre, J. (eds), *Challenges to Local Government*. London: Sage.

Kline, J.M. (1991) 'The Inverse Relationship Between Nation-States and Global Corporations', in Belous, R.S. & McClenahan, K.L. (eds), *Global Corporations and Nation-States: Do Companies or Countries Compete*. Washington, DC: National Planning Association.

Knickerblocker, F.T. (1973) *Oligopolistic Reaction and the MNE*. Cambridge, MA: Harvard University.

Kobrin, S.J. (1987) 'Testing the bargaining Hypothesis in the Manufacturing Sector in Developing Countries', *International Organisation*, 41(4): 609–38, Autumn.

Kocka, J. (1978) 'Entrepreneurs and Managers in German Industrialisation', in Matias, P. & Postan, M.M. (eds), *The Cambridge Economic History of*

Europe Volume VII, The Industrial Economies: Capital, Labour and Enterprise Part 1: Britain, France, Germany, and Scandinavia. Cambridge, Cambridge University Press.

Kogut, B. (1993) 'Learning, or the Importance of Being Inert: Country Imprinting and International Competition', in Ghoshal, S. & Westney, D.E. (eds), *Organisation Theory and the Multinational Corporation.* Basingstoke: Macmillan.

Kogut, B. & Chang, S.J. (1991) 'Technological Capabilities and Japanese Foreign Direct Investment in the United States', *The Review of Economics and Statistics*, LXXIII (3): 401–13, August.

Köppen, M. (1996) 'Strategies of German Big Business in their International Setting during the 1980s', in Berghahn, V.R. (ed.), *Quest for Economic Empire: European Strategies of German Big Business in the Twentieth Century.* Oxford: Berghahn.

Kozul-Wright, R. (1995) 'Transnational Corporations and the Nation State', in Michie, J. & Smith, J.G. (eds), *Managing the Global Economy.* Oxford: OUP.

KPMG (1991) *Perceptions of England as an Investment Location: A Survey.* DTI: London.

Krauss, E.S. (1992) 'Political Economy: Policymaking and Industrial Policy in Japan', in Grant, W. (ed.), (1995) *Industrial Policy: The International Library of Comparative Public Policy.* Aldershot: Edward Elgar.

Krugman, P. (1991) 'Increasing Returns and Economic Geography', *Journal of Political Economy*, 99 (3): 83–99.

Kume, G. & Totsuka, K. (1993) 'Japanese Manufacturing Investment in the EC: Motives and Locations', in Sumitomo-Life Research Institute with Yoshitomi, M. *et al.*, *Japanese Direct Investment in Europe: Motives, Impact and Policy Implications.* Aldershot: Avebury.

Lahiri, S. & Onu, Y. (1998) 'Foreign Direct Investment, Local Content Requirement, and Profit Taxation', *The Economic Journal*, 108: 444–57.

Lall, S. (1995a) 'Employment and Foreign Investment: Policy Options for Developing Countries', *International Labour Review*, 134 (4–5): 521–40.

Lall, S. (1995b) 'Industrial Strategy and Policies on Foreign Direct Investment in East Asia', *Transnational Corporations*, 4 (3): 1–26, December.

Lall, S. (1997) 'East Asia', in Dunning, J.H. (ed.), *Governments, Globalisation and International Business.* Oxford: OUP.

Lall, S. & Streeten, P. (1977) *Foreign Investment, Transnationals and Developing Countries.* London: Macmillan.

Landsbury, M. & Pain, N. (1997) 'Regional Economic Integration and Foreign Direct Investment: The Case of German Investment in Europe', *National Institute Economic Review*, 2: 87–99, April.

Lane, C. (1995) *Industry and Society in Europe: Stability and Change in Britain, Germany and France.* Aldershot: Edward Elgar.

Lane, C. (1998) 'European Companies between Globalization and Localization: A Comparison of Internationalization Strategies of British and German MNCs', *Economy and Society*, 27 (4): 462–85, November.

Larcon, J. (1998) 'After the Iron Curtain: Golden Opportunities', *Financial Times*, 3 April.

Larrain, J. (1989) *Theories of Development: Capitalism, Colonialism and Dependency.* Cambridge: Polity Press.

Latin Trade (1998) 'Costa Rica should Double its Current Export Value of $3 bn by 2000 due to Intel's Investment', August.

Lawton, T.C. (1997) *Technology and the New Diplomacy: The Creation and Control of EC Industrial Policy for Semiconductors*. Aldershot: Avebury.

Lee, S. (1996) 'Manufacturing' in Coates, D. (ed.), *Industrial Policy in Britain*. Basingstoke: Macmillan.

Lee, S. (1997) 'The Competitive Disadvantage of England', paper presented at EUNIP 'Practical Proposals for Industrial Policy in Europe'. Warwick University, 11–15 December.

Lenway, A. & Murtha, T.P. (1994a) 'Country Capabilities and the Strategic State: How National Political Institutions Affect Multinational Corporations Strategies', *Strategic Management Journal*, 15, Special Issue: 113–29, Summer.

Lenway, A. & Murtha, T.P. (1994b) 'The State as Strategist in International Business Research', *Journal of International Business Studies*, 25 (3): 513–35, 3rd quarter.

Leong, S.M. & Tan, C.T. (1993) 'Managing Across Borders: An Empirical Test of the Bartlett and Ghoshal Organisational Typology', *Journal of International Business Studies*: 449–64, 3rd quarter.

Lerner, A.M. (1991) 'The Benefits and Costs of Global Corporations', in Belous, R.S. & McClenahan, K.L. (eds), *Global Corporations and Nation-States: Do Companies or Countries Compete*. Washington, DC: National Planning Association.

Lewin, T. (1996) 'Nissan Puts Quality First', *The European*, 25–31 July.

Lim, L.Y.C. & Fong, P.E. (1991) *FDI and Industrialisation in Malaysia, Singapore, Taiwan and Thailand*. Paris: OECD.

Lindeman, M. (1995) 'World Trade News: German "Job Exporting" Debate Is Renewed – Record Outward Investment Figures Focus Attention on Employment Costs', *Financial Times*, 2 November.

Linford, P. (1998) 'Report Tells of Bleak Future without EU Aid', *The Journal*, 24 July.

Lipietz, A. (1986a) 'Behind the Crisis: The Exhaustion of a Regime of Accumulation: A 'Regulation School' Perspective on some French Empirical Works', *Review of Radical Political Economics*, 18 (1–2): 13–33.

Lipietz, A. (1986b) 'New Tendencies in the International Division of Labour: Regimes of Accumulation and Modes of Regulation', in Scott, A.J. & Storper, M. (eds), *Production, Work, Territory: The Geographical Anatomy of Industrial Capitalism*. London: Allen & Unwin.

Lipsey, R. (1997) 'Globalisation and National Government Policies: An Economist's View', in Dunning, J.H. (ed.), *Governments, Globalisation, and International Business*. Oxford: OUP.

Lloyd, P. & Meegan, R. (1996) 'Contested Governance: European Exposure in the English Regions', *European Planning Studies*, 4 (1): 75–97.

Loewendahl, H.B. (1996) 'Foreign Direct Investment in Pacific-Asia Since Plaza: The Impact on Trade Flows', Paper for Department of Politics and International Studies, University of Warwick (unpublished).

Loewendahl, H.B. (1998) 'Lean Production and Labour: Lessons from Japanese Investment in the UK', *IGS Discussion Paper in German Studies*, No.IGS98/18. Institute for German Studies, University of Birmingham, December.

Loewendahl, H.B. (1999) 'Siemens "Anglo-Saxon" Strategy: Is Globalising Business Enough?', *German Politics*, 8 (1): 89–105, April.

Loewendahl, H.B. (2001) *A Framework for Investment Promotion* Transnational Corporations, United Nations, April.

Loewendahl, H.B. & Ertugal-Loewendahl, E. (2000) *Turkey's Performance in Attracting Foreign Direct Investment: Implications of EU Enlargement*, CEPS Working Document 157, Centre for European Policy Studies, November.

Loewendahl, H.B. & Hölscher, Y. (2001) 'Anglo-German Economic Relations and Comparative Performance', in Wend, P., Nokes, J. & Wright, D. (eds), *Germany and Britain in Europe* (forthcoming). Oxford: Oxford University Press.

Lord, C. (1996) 'Industrial Policy and the European Union', in Coates, D. (ed.), *Industrial Policy in Britain*. Basingstoke: Macmillan.

Lorenz, C. (1995) 'Global Webs Still Spun from Home – the Significance of Siemen's new UK Design Centre Should not be Exaggerated', *Financial Times*, 18 August.

Lorraine, D. (1996) 'Embedding Inward Investors: Greenfield Barriers and Bridges', *Nissan*, 12 June.

Lovegrove, N.C., Fidler, S., Harris, V.J., Mullings, H.M., Lewis, W.W., & Scott, D.A. (1998) 'Why Is Productivity in the United Kingdom so Low?', *The McKinsey Quarterly*, 4: 44–57, *http://www.mckinseyquarterly.competitiveness/economic/whla98.htm*.

Lucio, M.M. & Blyton, P. (1995) 'Constructing the Post-Fordist State?: The Politics of Labour Market Flexibility in Spain', *West European Politics*, 18 (2): 340–60, April.

Lundvall, B-A. (1992) 'Introduction' in Lundvall, B-A. (ed.), *National Systems of Innovation: Towards a Theory of Innovation and Integrative Learning*. London: Pinter.

Lung, Y. (1992) 'Global Competition and Transregional Strategy: Spatial Reorganisation of the European Car Industry', in Dunford, M. & Kafkalas, U. (eds), *Cities and Regions in the New Europe*. London: Betharen Press.

Lyons, D. (1995) 'Agglomeration Economies Among High Technology Firms in Advanced Production Areas: The Case of Denver/Boulder', *Regional Studies*, 29: 265–78.

Maanen van, J. & Laurent, A. (1993) 'The Flow of Culture: Some Notes on Globalisation and the Multinational Corporation', in Ghoshal, S. & Westney, D.E. (eds), *Organisation Theory and the Multinational Corporation*. Basingstoke: Macmillan.

MacPherson, A. (1997) 'The Role of Producer Services Outsourcing in the Innovation Performance of New York State Manufacturing Firms', *Annals of the Association of American Geographers*, 87: 52–71.

Malachuk, D. (1998) 'Sense of Place', Arthur Andersen HR Director, Autumn/Winter, *www.arthurandersen.com*

Marshall, A. (1890) *Principles of Economics*, 8th edn, 1920; repr. 1990. London: Macmillan.

McCooey, C. (1991) 'Japan: Business, Golf and Gardens', *Accountancy*: 70–1, November.

MacDuffie, J. (1995) 'International Trends in Work Organisation in the Auto Industry: National-Level vs. Company-Level Perspectives', in Wever, K. &

Turner, L. (eds), *The Comparative Political Economy of Industrial Relations*. Madison: IRRA.

McGrew, A.G. (1992) 'Conceptualising Global Politics', in McGrew, A.G. & Lewis, P.G. *et al.* (eds), *Global Politics: Globalisation and the Nation State*. Cambridge: Polity Press.

Macher, Jeffrey T., Mowery, David C. & Hodges, David A. (1998) 'Reversal of Fortune?: The Recovery of the U.S. Semiconductor Industry', *California Management Review*, 41 (1): 107–36, Autumn.

McRae, H. (1997) 'The Other Problem with the Jobs Bought from the Japanese', *The Independent*, 31 January.

Mair, A. (1993) 'New Growth Poles?: Just-in-Time Manufacturing and Local Development Strategy', *Regional Studies*, 27: 207–21.

Management Accounting (1992) 'Competition and Industrial Policy in the European Community', October.

Mardon, R. (1990) 'The State and the Effective Control of Foreign Capital: The Case of South Korea', *World Politics*, 43(1): 111–38, October.

Marginson, P. & Sisson, K. (1996) 'Multinational Companies and the Future of Collective Bargaining: A Review of the Research Issues', *European Journal of Industrial Relations*, 2 (2): 173–97, July.

Markusen, A. (1996) 'Interaction between Regional and Industrial Policies: Evidence from Four Countries', *International Regional Science Review*, 19 (1 & 2): 49–77.

Marsh, P. (1995) 'Contact Between Cultures: A Look at How Many UK Companies Have Benefited From a German Management Perspective', *Financial Times*, 29 May.

Marsh, P. (1997a) 'A Shift to Flexibility: Peter Marsh on the Factors Behind a Ground-Breaking German Deal to establish New Working Patterns', *Financial Times*, 21 February.

Marsh, P. (1997b) 'Inward Investment Boosts Work Practices: Wide Impact of Management Ideas from Foreign Companies is a "Big Factor" in Fast Productivity Growth since Mid-1980s', *Financial Times*, 13 May.

Marshall, A. (1890) *Principles of Economics*, 8th edn 1920, reprinted 1990. London: Macmillan.

Martin, G. & Beaumont, P. (1998) 'Diffusing "Best Practice" in Multinational Firms: Prospects, Practice and Contestation', *The International Journal of Human Resource Management*, 9 (4): 671–95, August.

Martin, R. & Townroe, P. (1992) 'Agenda for the Nineties', in Martin, R. & Townroe, P. (eds), *Regional Development in the 1990s: The British Isles in Transition*. London: Jessica Kingsley.

Masayoshi, I. (1998) 'Globalisation's Impact upon the Subcontracting System', in Harukiyo, H. & Hook, G.D. (eds), *Japanese Business Management: Restructuring for Low Growth and Globalisation*. London: Routledge.

Masayuki, M. (1998) 'The End of the "Mass Production System" and Changes in Work Practices', in Harukiyo, H. & Hook, G.D. (eds), *Japanese Business Management: Restructuring for Low Growth and Globalisation*. London: Routledge.

Mascarenhas, B., Baveja, A. & Jamil, M. (1998) 'Dynamics of Core Competencies in Leading Multinational Companies', *California Management Review*, 40 (4): 117–32, Summer.

Maskell, P., Eskelinen, H., Hannibalsson, I., Malmberg, A. & Vatne, E. (1998) *Competitiveness, Localised Learning and Regional Development: Specialisation and Prosperity in Small Open Economies.* London & New York: Routledge.

Mayes, D. & Hart, P. (1994) 'The UK and German Economies', in Hart, P. & Mayes, P. (eds), *The Single Market Programme as a Stimulous to Change.* Cambridge: CUP.

Meyer-Stamer, J. (1996) 'Industrial Policy in the EU: Old Dilemmas and New Options', *European Planning Studies*, 4 (4): 471–84.

Michalet, C-A. (1997) 'France', in Dunning, J.H. (ed.), *Governments, Globalisation, and International Business.* Oxford: OUP.

Miller, K.L. (1995) 'Siemens Shapes Up', *Business Week*, 1 May.

Miller, W.R. (1991) 'The Role of Global Corporations', in Belous, R.S. & McClenahan, K.L. (eds), *Global Corporations and Nation-States: Do Companies or Countries Compete?* Washington, DC: National Planning Association.

Millward, T. (1995) 'The $17 Billion Search', *Corporate Location*, September/ October.

Milner, H.V. (1988) *Resisting Protectionism: Global Industries and the Politics of International Trade.* Princeton, New Jersey: Princeton UP.

Mittelman, J.H. (1996a) 'The Dynamics of Globalisation', in Mittelman, J.H. (ed.), *Globalisation: Critical Reflections.* London: Lynne Rienner.

Mittelman, J.H. (1996b) 'How Does Globalisation Really Work', in Mittelman, J.H. (ed.), *Globalisation: Critical Reflections.* London: Lynne Rienner.

Mody, A. & Wheeler, D. (1992) 'International Investment Location Decisions: The Case of US Firms', *Journal of International Economics*, 33: 57–76.

Moore, C. (1995) 'Scotland and the SDA': In Rhodes, M. (ed.), *The Regions and the New Europe: Patterns in Core and Periphery Development.* Manchester: Manchester UP.

Moore, L. (1994) 'Developments in Trade and Trade Policy', in Artis, M.J. & Lee, N. (eds), *The Economics of the European Union: Policy and Analysis.* Oxford: OUP.

Moran, T.H. (1974) *Multinational Corporations and the Politics of Dependence: Copper in Chile.* Princeton: Princeton UP.

Moran, T.H. (1993) 'Introduction: Governments and Transnational Corporations', in Moran, T.H. (ed.), *Governments and Transnational Corporations, United Nations Library on Transnational Corporations*, Vol. 7. London & New York: Routledge.

Moran, T.H. (1996) 'Governments and Transnational Corporations', in *Transnational Corporations and World Development.* London: International Thomson Business Press: UN.

Moran, T.H. (1999) *Foreign Direct Investment and Development.* Institute for International Economics: Washington.

Morgan, K. (1996) 'An Endogenous Approach to Regional Economic Development: The Emergence of Wales', *European Planning Studies*, 4 (6): 705–15.

Morgan, K. (1997) 'Regional Animateur: Taking Stock of the Welsh Development Agency', *Regional and Federal Studies*, 7 (2): 70–94, Summer.

Morris, J. (1987) 'Industrial Restructuring, Foreign Direct Investment, and Uneven Development: The Case of Wales', *Environment and Planning*, A 19: 205–24.

Morris, J. (1988) 'The Who, Why and Where of Japanese Manufacturing Investment in the UK', *Industrial Relations Journal*, 19 (1): 31–40.

Morris, J. (1992a) 'Flexible Internationalisation in the Electronics Industry: Implications for Regional Economies', *Environment and Planning C: Government and Policy*, 10: 407–21.

Morris, J. (1992b) 'Flexible Specialisation or the Japanese Model: Reconceptualising a New Regional Industrial Order', in Ernste, H. & Meire, V. (eds), *Regional Development and Contemporary Industrial Response: Extending Flexible Specialisation*. London & New York: Belhaven.

Morris, J. & Wilkinson, B. (1995) 'The Transfer of Japanese Management to Alien Institutional Environments', *Journal of Management Studies*, Special Issue 32 (6): 719–30, November.

Moulaert, F., Swyngedouw, E. & Wilson, P. (1988) 'Spatial Responses to Fordist and Post-Fordist Accumulation and Regulation', *Papers of the Regional Science Association*, 64: 11–23.

Moulaert, F. & Swyngedouw, E. (1991) 'Regional Development and the Geography of the Flexible Production System: Theoretical Arguments and Empirical Evidence', in Hilpert, U. (ed.), *Regional Innovation and Decentralisation: High Tech Industry and Government Policy*. London: Routledge.

Mowery, D.C. & Oxley, J.E. (1995) 'Inward Technology Transfer and Competitiveness: The Role of National Innovation Systems', *Cambridge Journal of Economics*, Special Issue on Technology and Innovation 19 (1): 67–93, February.

Mucchielli, J.L. (1991) 'Strategic Advantages for European Firms', in Burgenmeir, B. & Mucchielli, J.L. (eds), *Multinationals and Europe 1992: Strategy for the Future*. London Routledge.

Mueller, F. (1996) 'National Stakeholders in the Global Contest for Corporate Investment', *European Journal of Industrial Relations*, 2 (3): 345–68, November.

Mueller, F. & Purcell, J. (1992) 'The Europeanisation of Manufacturing and the Decentralisation of Bargaining: Multinational Management Strategies in the European Automobile Industrial', *The International Journal of Human Resource Management*, 3 (1): 15–34, May.

Munchau, W. (1995) 'World Trade News: Scramble for Ultra High-Tech Microchip Plant', *Financial Times*, 3 August.

Murphy, C.N. & Tooze, R. (1991) 'Introduction', in Murphy, C.N. & Tooze, R. (eds), *The New International Political Economy*. Boulder, Colorado: Lynne Rienner.

Nakamoto, M., Jowit, J. & Wagstyl, S. (1998) 'Toyota Plant in Wales to Create 300 Jobs', *Financial Times*, 10 January.

Nakamoto, M. (1999) 'Time to Pick Up the Pieces and Find Other Sources of Funds', *Financial Times*, 11 March.

NDC (Northern Development Company) (1996) 'Siemens Microelectronics Ltd Fact File'.

NDC (Northern Development Company) (1997a) *Annual Review 1996–1997*. Newcastle-upon-Tyne: Northern Development Company.

NDC (Northern Development Company) (1997b) *A Regional Sector Strategy for Improved SME Performance: Co-operating to Compete*. Newcastle-upon-Tyne: Northern Development Company.

NDC (Northern Development Company) (1997c) *NDC Vision Statement 1997–1998*. Newcastle-upon-Tyne: Northern Development Company, December.

NDC (Northern Development Company) (1997d) *Report to the Invest in Britain Bureau from the Northern Development Company*. Newcastle-upon-Tyne: Northern Development Company, January–March.

NDC (Northern Development Company) (1997e) *An Outline Concept for a Northern Development Agency*. Newcastle-upon-Tyne: Northern Development Company, February.

NDC (Northern Development Company) (1997f) *Report to the Invest in Britain Bureau from the Northern Development Company*. Newcastle-upon-Tyne: Northern Development Company, April–June.

NDC (Northern Development Company) (1998a) *Supply Chain Dynamics*. Newcastle-upon-Tyne: Northern Development Company.

NDC (Northern Development Company) (1998b) *The Case for a Regional Development Agency in the North: A Northern Development Company Response to the RDA Issues Paper*. Newcastle-upon-Tyne: Northern Development Company.

NDC (Northern Development Company) (1998c) *Profitable Business in the North – Strengths*. Newcastle-upon-Tyne: Northern Development Company.

NDC (Northern Development Company) (1998d) *Profitable Business in the North – Programme and Budget*. Newcastle-upon-Tyne: Northern Development Company.

NDC (Northern Development Company) (1998e) *A Presentation on the North of England by the Northern Development Company (Agency for Development in the North of England)*. Newcastle-upon-Tyne: Northern Development Company, June.

NDC (Northern Development Company) (1998f) *Main Issues for the RDA*. Newcastle-upon-Tyne: Northern Development Company, July.

NDC (Northern Development Company) (1998g) *Executive Group Meeting – Regional Investment*. Newcastle-upon-Tyne: Northern Development Company, 24 February.

NDC (Northern Development Company) (1999) *Export Trade Mission Newsletter: 1999–2000 Programme*. Newcastle-upon-Tyne: Northern Development Company.

NEI (1992) (in co-operation with Ernst & Young) *New Location Factors for Mobile Investment in Europe*. Final Report for the European Commission. DG XVI, Brussels: CEC.

Nelson, R.R. (1992) 'National Innovation Systems: A Retrospective Study', *Industrial and Corporate Change*, 1: 347–74.

Nelson, R.R. (1994) 'Evolutionary Theorising About Economic Change', in Smelser, N.J. & Swedberg, R. (eds), *Handbook of Economic Sociology*. Princeton, NJ, Princeton UP.

Nelson, R. & Winter, S. (1982) *An Evolutionary Theory of Economic Change*. Cambridge, Mass: HUP.

Nicolaides, P. (1993a) 'Preface', in Nicolaides, P. (ed.), *Industrial Policy in the European Community: A Necessary Response to Economic Integration?* Netherlands: Martinus Nijhoff.

Nicolaides, P. (1993b) 'Industrial Policy: The Problems of Reconciling Definitions, Intentions and Effects', in Nicolaides, P. (ed.), *Industrial Policy in the*

European Community: A Necessary Response to Economic Integration? Netherlands: Martinus Nijhoff.

Nicolaides, P. (1993c) 'Industrial Policy and Foreign Direct Investment', in Nicolaides, P. (ed.), *Industrial Policy in the European Community: A Necessary Response to Economic Integration?* Netherlands: Martinus Nijhoff.

Nicolaides, P. & Thomsen, S. (1991) *The Evolution of Japanese Direct Investment in Europe: Death of a Transistor Salesman.* London: Harvester Wheatsheaf.

NIEC (Northern Ireland Economic Council) (1992) *Inward Investment in Northern Ireland.* Northern Ireland Economic Development Office, Report 99: Belfast, November.

NIER (1998) 'The Internationalisation of German Companies', R&D', *National Institute Economic Review*, January.

Nissan (1995) Untitled.

Nissan (1998a) 'Background Brief'.

Nissan (1998b) 'Nissan to Build Third Major Model in the UK', *Nissan Press and Public Relations*, 21 January.

Nissan (1998c) 'Minister Unveils First UK-Built Nissan Estate Car', *Nissan Press and Public Relations*, 26 January.

Nixson, F. (1988) 'The Political Economy of Bargaining With TNCs: Some Preliminary Observations', *Manchester Papers on Development*, IV (3): 377–90, July.

Nonaka, I. (1990) 'Managing Globalisation as a Self-Renewal Process: Experiences of Japanese MNCs', in Bartlett, C.A., Doz, Y. & Hedlund, G. (eds), *Managing the Global Firm.* London: Routledge.

Norman, P. (1998) 'Germany to Subsidise Chip Industry', *Financial Times*, 13 January.

North Tyneside Council (1995) 'Siemens – Developing 21st Century Industries on Tyneside', News Release, 4 August.

O'Brien, T.F. (1989) '"Rich Beyond the Dreams of Avarice": the Guggenheims in Chile', in Jones, G. (1993) (ed.), *Transnational Corporation: A Historical Perspective. Volume 2.* London and New York: Routledge.

Odagiri, H. & Goto, A. (1993) 'The Japanese System of Innovation: Past, Present, and Future', in Nelson, R.R. (ed.), *National Systems of Innovation: A Comparative Analysis.* Oxford: OUP.

OECD (1987) *Main Science and Technology Indicators 1981–87.* Paris: OECD.

OECD (1989) *Main Science and Technology Indicators 1989.* Paris: OECD.

OECD (1992) *Globalisation of Industrial Activities: Four Case Studies: Auto Parts, Chemicals, Construction and Semiconductors.* Paris: OECD.

OECD (1993) *International Direct Investment Statistics Yearbook.* Paris: OECD.

OECD (1996) *Globalisation of Industry: Overview and Sector Reports.* Paris: OECD.

OECD (1997a) *Economic Survey Germany.* Paris: OECD.

OECD (1997b) *International Direct Investment Statistics Yearbook 1997.* Paris: OECD.

OECD (1998a) *International Direct Investment Statistics Yearbook 1998.* Paris: OECD.

OECD (1998b) *Main Science and Technology Indicators.* Paris: OECD.

OECD (1998c) *Foreign Direct Investment and Economic Development: Lessons from Six Emerging Economies*. OECD: Paris

OECD (1998d) 'Survey of OECD Work on International Investment', *Working Papers on International Investment*, 1. OECD: Paris.

OECD (1999a) 'Internationalisation of Industrial R&D' and 'Foreign Ideas', *OECD Observer*, 217/218: 98, Summer.

OECD (1999b) *Globalisation of Industrial R&D: Policy Issues*. OECD: Paris.

OECD (2000) *International Direct Investment Statistics Yearbook 1998*. Paris: OECD.

O'Farrel, R. (1998) Head of Inward Investment, Technology and Regional Selective Assistance at the Government Office for the North East. Private Interview, July.

Ohmae, K. (1990) *The Borderless World*. New York: HarperCollins.

Ohmae, K. (1995) *The End of the Nation State: The Rise of Regional Economies*. London: HarperCollins.

O'Malley, E. (1990) 'Multinational Versus Indigenous Industry in the Republic of Ireland', in Hansen, J.C. & Hebbert, M. (eds), *Unfamiliar Territory: The Reshaping of European Geography*. Aldershot: Avebury.

Oliver, N. & Wilkinson, B. (1988) *The Japanisation of British Industry*. Oxford: Basil Blackwell.

Oman, C. (2000) *Policy Competition and Foreign Direct Investment: A Study of Competition Among Governments to Attract FDI*. OECD: Paris.

Onimode, B. (ed.), (1989), *The International Monetary Fund, the World Bank and the African Debt Crisis. Volume 1: the Economic Impact*. London: Zed Books.

ONS (1995) *Business Monitor: Overseas Transactions*, MA4. London: Office of National Statistics.

ONS (1996) *Regional Trends*, *31*. London: Office of National Statistics.

ONS (1998a) *First Release: Overseas Direct Investment 1997*. London: Office of National Statistics. 14 December.

ONS (1998b) *Research and Development in UK Businesses 1997*, MA14. London: Office of National Statistics.

ONS (1998c) *Regional Trends*, *33*. London: Office of National Statistics.

ONS (1999a) *First Release: Overseas Direct Investment 1998*. London: Office of National Statistics. 14 December.

ONS (1999b) *Manufacturing: Production and Construction Inquiries–Summary Volume*. PA1002. London: ONS.

ONS (1999c) *Regional Trends*.

Ostry, S. (1998) 'Technology, Productivity and the Multinational Enterprise', *Journal of International Business Studies*, 29 (1): 85–99, 1st quarter.

Oughton, C. & Whittam, G. (1997) 'Competition and Co-operation in the Small Firm Sector', *Scottish Journal of Political Economy*, 44 (1): 1–30, February.

Owen, G. (1997) 'From Mass-Market Manufacturer to Niche Player: Product and Marketing Strategy at British Leyland/Rover from 1968–1995', in Abe, E. & Gourvish, T. (eds), *Japanese Success? British Failure?: Comparisons in Business Performance Since 1945*. New York: OUP.

Papanastassiou, M. (1995) 'Governments and Multinational Enterprises (MNEs); Partners in Search of Competitiveness? Confusion or Limpidity in the Determination of Technological Strategies? The Case of the UK'. *Discussion Papers in International Investment and Business Studies*, University of Reading, Department of Economics. No.1999: Series B Vol. VIII (1995/1996), June.

Papanastassiou, M. & Pearce, R.D. (1994) 'The Internationalisation of Research and Development by Japanese Enterprises', *R&D Management*, 24 (2): 155–6, April.

Papanastassiou, M. & Pearce, R. (1995) 'European Markets, and the Strategic Roles of Multinational Enterprise Subsidiaries in the UK', *Discussion Paper in International Investment and Business Studies*, 208. University of Reading, November.

Papanastassiou, M. & Pearce, R. (1996) 'The Creation and Application of Technology by MNEs' Subsidiaries in Europe', in Burton, F., Yamin, M. & Young, S. (eds), *International Business and Europe in Transition*. Basingstoke: Macmillan.

Patel, P. (1995) 'Localised Production of Technology for Global Markets', *Cambridge Journal of Economics*, Special Issue on Technology and Innovation 19: 141–53, February.

Pauly, L.W. & Reich, S. (1997) 'National Structures and Multinational Corporate Behaviour: Enduring Differences in the Age of Globalisation', *International Organisation*, 51 (1): 1–30, Winter.

Peck, F. (1996) 'Regional Development and the Production of Space: The Role of Infrastructure in the Attraction of New Inward Investment', *Environment and Planning*, A 28 (2): 327–39, February.

Peck, F. & Stone, I. (1993) 'Japanese Inward Investment in the Northeast of England: Reassessing "Japanisation"', *Environment and Planning C: Government and Policy*, 11 (1): 55–67.

Peck, F. & Stone, I. (1996) 'The Foreign-Owned Manufacturing Sector in UK Peripheral Regions, 1978–1993: Restructuring and Comparative Performance', *Regional Studies*, 30 (1): 55–68, February.

Peck, J.A. & Tickell, A. (1995) 'Social Regulation *After*, Fordism: Regulation Theory, Neo-Liberalism and the Global-Local Nexus', *Economy and Society*, 24 (3): 357–84, August.

Perlmutter, H.V. (1969) 'The Tortuous Evolution of the Multinational Corporation', *Columbia Journal of World Business*, 4: 9–18.

Peters, E.H. (1992) 'The Computer Industry and the European Community: Issues and Responses in the 1990s', in Hamill, J. & Young, S. (eds), *Europe and the Multinationals: Issues and Responses for the 1990s*. Aldershot: Edward Elgar.

Peters, E.H. (1995) 'Restructuring of Scotland's Information Technology Industries: Strategic Issues and Responses', in Amin, A. & Tomaney, J. (eds), *Behind the Myth of the European Union: Prospects for Cohesion*. London: Routledge.

Peterson, J. (1995) 'Policy Networks and European Union Policy Making: A Reply to Kassim', *West European Politics*, 18 (2): 389–407, April.

Phelps, N.A. (1993) 'Branch Plants and the Evolving Spatial Division of Labour: A Study of Material Linkage Change in the Northern Region of England', *Regional Studies*, 27 (2): 87–101.

Phelps, N.A. (1997) *Multinationals and European Integration: Trade, Investment and Regional Development*. London: Jessica Kingsley.

Pianta, M. (1995) 'Technology and Growth in OECD Countries, 1970–1990', *Cambridge Journal of Economics*, Special Issue on Technology and Innovation, 19 (1): 175–87, February.

Pike, A. (1996) 'Greenfields, Brownfields and Industrial Policy in the UK', *Regional Studies*, 30 (1): 69–77, February.

Pike, A. (1997) 'Flexible Line on Regions Promised: Minister Says Developmental Agencies will be Allowed Arrangements that Suit Local Circumstances', *Financial Times*, 12 June.

Pilkington, A. (1996) *Transforming Rover: Renewal Against the Odds 1981–1994*. Bristol: Bristol Academic Press.

Pilkington, A. (1998) 'Manufacturing Strategy Regained: Evidence for the Demise of Best-Practice', *California Management Review*, 41 (1): 31–42, Autumn.

Piore, M. & Sabel, C. (1984) *The Second Industrial Divide: Possibilities for Prosperity*. New York: Basic Books.

Pitelis, C.N. (1993) 'Transnationals, International Organisation and Deindustrialisation', *Organisation Studies*, 14: 527–48.

Pitelis, C.N. (1997) 'Productivity, Competitiveness and Convergence in the Global Economy: The Role of the Supply Side', paper presented at EUNIP 'Practical Proposals for Industrial Policy in Europe'. Warwick University, 11–15 December.

Porter, M.E. (1986) *Competition in Global Industries*. Boston: Harvard Business School.

Porter, M.E. (1990a) *The Competitive Advantage of Nations*. New York: The Free Press.

Porter, M.E. (1990b) 'The Competitive Advantage of Nations', *Harvard Business Review*, March–April.

Porter, M.E. (1996) 'Competitive Advantage, Agglomeration Economies, and Regional Policy', *International Regional Science Review*, 19 (1 & 2): 85–94.

Porter, M.E. (1998) 'Clusters and the New Economics of Competition', *Harvard Business Review*: 77–90, November–December.

Porter, M.E. (1999) 'Creating Innovative Capacity', Presentation to the World Productivity Congress, Institute of Management Services. Edinburgh, October.

Poulantzas, N. (1975) *Classes in Contemporary Capitalism*. London: New Left Books.

Powell, W.W. & Smith-Doerr, L. (1994) 'Networks and Economic Life', in Smelser, N.J. & Swedberg, R. (eds), *Handbook of Economic Sociology*. Princeton, NJ, Princeton UP.

Poynter, T.A. (1985) *Multinational Enterprises and Government Intervention*. London: Croom Felm.

Prahalad, C.K. & Doz, Y.L. (1987) *The Multinational Mission: Balancing Local Demands and Global Vision*. New York: Free Press.

Pratt, A.C. & Totterdill, P. (1992) 'Industrial Policy in a Period of Organisational and Institutional Change: The Case of Inward Investment and the Electronics Sector', *Environment and Planning C: Government and Policy*, 10: 375–85.

PricewaterhouseCoopers (1999) *Solutions for Business Location Decisions*.

Pyke, F. (1997a) 'Networks, Development and Change', paper Prepared for The International Institute for Labour Studies, October.

Pyke, F. (1997b) 'Local Development Initiatives and the Management of Change in Europe', paper Written for The Employment Department of the International Labour Office. Geneva, December.

Ramsay, H. (1995) '*Le Défe Européen*: Multinational Restructuring, Labour and EU Policy', in Amin, A. & Tomaney, J. (eds), *Behind the Myth of the European Union: Prospects for Cohesion*. London: Routledge.

RSA (1995) *Tomorrow's Company: The Role of Business in a Changing World*. London: Royal Society for the Encouragement of Arts, Manufactures and Commerce.

Rehder, R. (1990) 'Japanese Transplants: After the Honeymoon', *Business Horizons*, 33: 87–98.

Rehder, R.R. & Thompson, J.K. (1994) 'Nissan UK: The Japanese Transplant Beachhead in Europe', *Columbia Journal of World Business*, 29(3): 92–106, Autumn.

Reich, R.B. (1990) 'Who is Us?', in Grant, W. (1995) *Industrial Policy: The International Library of Comparative Public Policy*. Aldershot: Edward Elgar.

Reich, R.B. (1991) *The Work of Nations: Preparing Ourselves for 21st Century Capitalism*. New York: Alfred Knopf.

Reich, S. (1996) '"Manufacturing" Investment National Variations in the Contribution of Foreign Direct Investors to the US Manufacturing Base in the 1990s', *Review of International Political Economy*, 3 (1): 27–64, Spring.

Rhodes, M. (1995) 'Conclusion: The Viability of Regional Strategies', in Rhodes, M. (ed.), *The Regions and the New Europe: Patterns in Core and Periphery Development*. Manchester: Manchester UP.

Riley, S.P. (1993) (ed.), *The Politics of Global Debt*. Basingstoke: Macmillan.

Roxborough, I. (1987) 'Cardosa and Faletto: Multiple Paths', in Archetti, E.P., Cammack, P. & Roberts, B. (eds), *Sociology of "Developing Societies:" Latin America*. New York: Monthly Review Press.

Ruigrok, W. & Tulder, R. van (1995) *The Logic of International Restructuring*. London: Routledge.

Ruggie, J.G. (1996) 'At Home Abroad, Abroad at Home: International Liberalism and Domestic Stability in the New World Economy', *Millenium: Journal of International Studies*, 24 (3): 507–26, Winter.

Rugman, A.M. & Verbeke, A. (1998) 'Multinational Enterprise and Public Policy', *Journal of International Business Studies*, 29 (1): 115–36, 1st quarter.

Russel, G. (1997) 'Chairman's Statement', *Northern Development Company Annual Review 1996–1997*.

Sabel, C.F. (1989) 'Flexible Specialisation and the Re-emergence of Regional Economies', in Hirst, P. & Zeitlin, J. (eds), *Reversing Industrial Decline? Industrial Structure and Policy in Britain and Her Competitors*. Oxford: St. Martin's Press.

Sabel, C. (1995) 'Bootstrapping Reform', *Politics and Society*, 23: 5–48.

Sabel, C.F., Herrigel, G., Kazis, R. & Deeg, R. (1991) 'Regional Prosperities Compared: Massachusetts and Baden-Württemberg', in Hilpert, U. (ed.), *Regional Innovation and Decentralisation: High Tech Industry and Government Policy*. London: Routledge.

Sadler, D. (1992a) *The Global Region: Production, State Policies and Uneven Development*. Oxford: Pergamon.

Sadler, D. (1992b) 'Industrial Policy of the European Community: Strategic Deficits and Regional Dilemmas', *Environment and Planning*, 24: 1711–30.

Sadler, D. (1994) 'The Geographies of Just-in-Time: Japanese Investment and the Automotive Components Industry in Western Europe', *Economic Geography*, 70: 41–59.

Safarian, A.E. (1993) *Multinational Enterprise and Public Policy: A Study of the Industrial Countries*. Aldershot: Edward Elgar.

Sally, R. (1994) 'Multinational Enterprises, Political Economy and Institutional Theory: Domestic Embeddedness in the Context of Internationalisation', *Review of International Political Economy (RIPE)*, 1(1): 161–92, Spring.

Sally, R. (1995) *States and Firms: Multinational Enterprises in Institutional Competition*. London & New York: Routledge.

Sampson, A. (1992) *The Essential Anatomy of Britain: Democracy in Crisis*. London: BCA.

Saxenian, A. (1992) 'Divergent Patterns of Business Organisation in Silicon Valley', in Scott, A.J. & Storper, M. (eds), *Pathways to Industrialisation and Regional Development*. London & New York: Routledge.

Sayer, A. (1986) 'Industrial Location on a World Scale: The Case of the Semiconductor Industry', in Scott, A.J. & Storper, M. (eds), *Production, Work, Territory: The Geographical Anatomy of Industrial Capitalism*. London: Allen & Unwin.

Schwab, K. & Smadja, C. (1994) 'Power and Policy: The New Economic World Order', *Harvard Business Review*, 72 (6): 40–50, November–December.

Schienstock, G. (1992) 'The Brave New World of the Multinational Corporation', *International Sociology*, 7 (4): 461–79, December.

Schoenberger, E. (1988) 'From Fordism to Flexible Accumulation: Technology, Competitive Strategies, and International Location', *Environment and Planning D: Society and Space*, 6: 245–62.

Schröter, H.G. (1993) 'Continuity and Change: German Multinationals Since 1850', in Jones, G & Schröter, H.G. (eds), *The Rise of the Multinational in Continental Europe*. Vermont: Edward Elgar.

Scott, A.J. (1996) 'Regional Motors of the Global Economy', *Futures*, 28 (5): 391–411.

Scott, A.J. & Storper, M. (1986a) 'Production, Work, Territory: Contemporary Realities and Theoretical Tasks', in Scott, A.J. & Storper, M. (eds), *Production, Work, Territory: The Geographical Anatomy of Industrial Capitalism*. London: Allen & Unwin.

Scott, A.J. & Storper, M. (1986b) 'Industrial Change and Territorial Organisation: A Summing Up', in Scott, A.J. & Storper, M. (eds), *Production, Work, Territory: The Geographical Anatomy of Industrial Capitalism*. London: Allen & Unwin.

Serapio, M., Dalton, D. & Yoshida, P.G. (2000) 'The Globalisation of R&D Enters a New Stage as Firms Learn how to Integrate Technology Operations on a World Scale', *Research Technology Management*. January/February.

Scottish Enterprise (1993) *The Competitive Advantage of Scotland: Identifying Potential for Competitiveness.* Glasgow: Scottish Enterprise.

Shaw, K. (1993) 'The Development of a New Urban Corporatism: The Politics of Urban Regeneration in the North East of England', *Regional Studies*, 27: 251–9.

Sheehan, M. (1993) 'Government Financial Assistance and Manufacturing Investment in Northern Ireland', *Regional Studies*, 27 (6): 527–40.

Sheehan, M. (1994) 'The Investment Decision-Making Process and Investment Determinants in the Northern Ireland Manufacturing Sector', *Regional Studies*, 28 (5): 511–20.

Sherburn, T. (1998) Senior Business Development Manager, Northern Development Company. Private Interview, July.

Shoichi, Y. (1998) 'Japanese Investment Strategy and Technology Transfer in East Asia', in Harukiyo, H. & Hook, G.D. (eds), *Japanese Business Management: Restructuring for Low Growth and Globalisation*. London: Routledge.

Siemens (1995a) 'Building for the Future: Siemens Microelectronics Centre Dresden – Technology from Saxony for the World Market', *Siemens News Release* (internal).

Siemens (1995b) 'Siemens Expands Semiconductor Production Capacity', *Siemens News Release*, 4 August.

Siemens (1995c) 'Major Investment Programme in Semiconductor Manufacturing Brings New Semiconductor Plant to the United Kingdom', *Siemens News Release*, 4 August.

Siemens (1996) 'Siemens in the United Kingdom', *Siemens Annual Review*.

Siemens (1997) '150 Years: Visions Become Reality', *Siemens CD-Rom*.

Siemens (1998a) 'SiemensWorld: International Edition'. Munich: Siemens, 2nd quarter.

Siemens (1998b) 'Siemens Forced by Global Market Conditions to Reduce Semiconductor Manufacturing Capacity', *Siemens Press Release*, 31 July.

Siemens (1998c) *Siemens UK*, 3 June.

Simonian, H. (1999) 'Under Siege', *Financial Times*, 8 February.

Site Selection (2000) *www.siteselection.com*, July.

Smidt, M. de & Wever, E. (1990) 'Firms: Strategy and Changing Environments', in de Smidt, M. & Wever, E. (eds), *The Corporate Firm in a Changing World Economy: Case Studies in the Geography of Enterprise*. London: Routledge.

Smith, H.L. (1993) 'Externalisation of Research and Development in Europe', *European Planning Studies*, 1 (4): 465–82.

Smith, I. & Stone, I. (1989) 'Foreign Investment in the North: Distinguishing Fact from Hype', *Northern Economic Review*, 18: 50–61, Autumn.

Smith, T. (1994) 'Flexible Production and the Capital/Wage Labour Relation in Manufacturing', *Capital & Class*, 53: 39–63, Summer.

SMMT (2000) *Monthly Statistical Review*, Society of Motor Manufacturers and Traders, Ltd, February.

So, A.Y. & Chiu, S.W.K. (1995) *East Asia and the World Economy*. London: Sage.

Spar, D. (1998) 'Attracting High Technology Investment: Intel's Costa Rican Plant', *FIAS Occasional Paper 11*. Foreign Investment Advisory Service, International Finance Corporation and World Bank, April.

Steinmetz, G. (1995) 'Siemens Plans Big Chip Plant in Cheaper UK', *Wall Street Journal*, 7 August.

Stoker, G. (1990) 'Regulation Theory, Local Government and the Transition from Fordism', in King, D.S. & Pierre, J. (eds), *Challenges to Local Government*. London: Sage.

Stopford, J.M. (1993) 'European Multinationals Competitiveness: Implications for Trade Policy', in Anderson, K. *et al.* (eds), *The External Implications of European Integration*. London: Harvester Wheatsheaf.

Stopford, J.M. (1994) 'The Growing Interdependence Between Transnational Corporations and Governments', *Transnational Corporations*, 3(1): 53–76, February.

Stopford, J.M. (1997) 'Implications for National Governments', in Dunning, J.H. (ed.), *Governments, Globalisation, and International Business*. Oxford: OUP.

Stopford, J.M. & Strange, S. (1991) *Rival Sates, Rival Firms: Competition for World Market Shares*. Cambridge: CUP.

Storper, M. (1995) 'The Resurgence of Regional Economies, Ten Years Later: The Region as a Nexus of Untraded Interdependencies', *European Urban and Regional Studies*, 2 (3): 191–221.

Strange, R. (1993) *Japanese Manufacturing Investment in Europe: Its Impact on the UK Economy*. London and New York: Routledge.

Strange, S. (1988) *States and Markets*. London: Pinter.

Strange, S. (1991a) 'An Eclectic Approach', in Murphy, C.N. & Tooze, R. (eds), *The New International Political Economy*. Boulder, Col.: Lynne Rienner.

Strange, S. (1991b) 'Big Business and the State', *Millennium Journal of International Business*, 20 (2): 257–67.

Strange, S. (1994a) 'Rethinking Structural Change in the International Political Economy: States, Firms, and Diplomacy', in Stubbs, R. & Underhill, G.R.D. (eds), *Political Economy and the Changing Global Order*. Basingstoke: Macmillan.

Strange, S. (1994b) 'Wake Up Krasner! The World Has Changed', *Review of International Political Economy (RIPE)*, 1 (2): 209–19, Summer.

Strange, S. (1995) 'Political Economy and International Relations', in Booth, K. & Smith, S. (eds), *International Relations Theory Today*. Cambridge: Polity Press.

Strange, S. (1997) 'An International Political Economy Perspective', in Dunning, J.H. (ed.), *Governments, Globalisation, and International Business*. Oxford: OUP.

Streeck, W. (1989) 'Successful Adjustment in Turbulent Markets: The Automobile Industry', in Katzenstein, P.J. (ed.), *Industry and Politics in West Germany: Towards the Third Republic*. Ithaca: Cornell UP.

Streeck, W. (1996) 'Lean Production in the German Auto Industry: A Test Case for Convergence Theory', in Berger, S. & Dore, R. (eds), *National Diversity and Global Competition*. Cornell UP.

Strong, J. (1997) 'Siemens Sticks to its Second Phase Plans', *The Journal*, 17 January.

Stubbs, P. & Saviotti, P. (1994) 'Science and Technology Policy', in Artis, M.J. and Lee, N. (eds), *The Economics of the European Union: Policy and Analysis*. Oxford: OUP.

Stubbs, R. & Underhill, G.R.D. (1994) 'Introduction: Global Issues in Historical Perspective', in Stubbs, R. & Underhill, G.R.D. (eds), *Political Economy and the Changing Global Order*. Basingstoke: Macmillan.

Sugden, R. (1990a) 'The Warm Welcome for Foreign-Owned Transnationals from Recent British Governments', in Chick, M. (ed.), *Governments, Industries and Markets: Aspects of Government–Industry Relations in the UK, Japan, West Germany and the USA since 1945*. Aldershot: Edward Elgar.

Sugden, R. (1990b) 'Strategic Industries, Community Control and Transnational Corporations', *International Review of Applied Economics*, 4 (1): 72–94, January.

Sun-Sentinel (1998) 'Major Investments by US Companies Like Intel Are Catapulting Cost Rica's High-Tech Industry', 7 February.

Takeuchi, A. (1990) 'Nissan Motor Company: Stages of International Growth, Locational Profile, and Subcontracting in the Tokyo Region', in de Smidt, M. & Wever, E. (eds), *The Corporate Firm in a Changing World Economy: Case Studies in the Geography of Enterprise*. London: Routledge.

Tan, B. & Vertinsky, I. (1996) 'Foreign Direct Investment by Japanese Electronics Firms in the United States and Canada: Modelling the Timing of Entry', *Journal of International Business Studies*, 27 (4): 655–81, 4th quarter.

Tarabusi, C.C. & Vickery, G. (1996) 'Globalisation in the Pharmaceutical Industry', in OECD, *Globalisation of Industry: Overview and Sector Reports*. Paris: OECD.

Tarzi, S.M. (1991) 'Third World Government and Multinational Corporations: Dynamics of Host's Bargaining Power', in Frieden, J.A. & Lake, D.A. (eds), (1995), *International Political Economy: Perspectives on Global Power and Wealth*, 3rd edn. London: Routledge.

Tatoglu, E. & Glaister, K.W. (2000) *Dimensions of Western Foreign Direct Investment in Turkey*. London: Quorum.

Taylor, P. (1997a) *NDC Strategic Market Plan 1998/99: Semiconductor Sector*. Newcastle-upon-Tyne: Northern Development Company, November.

Taylor, P. (1997b) 'Siemens Launches Logic Chip Sales Drive', *Financial Times*, 21 February.

Taylor, P. (1998) Investment Manager and Procurement Co-ordinator in Siemens Project Team Office, Northern Development Company. Private Interview, July.

TECs (Training and Enterprise Councils) (1998) *North East Labour Market Report 1997/8*.

Temple, P. (1999) 'The Knowledge Driven Economy: Fact or Fantasy', *Economic Outlook*, 23 (3): 7–12.

Thiran, J.M. & Yamawaki, H. (1995) 'Regional and Country Determinants of Locational Decisions: Japanese Multinationals in European Manufacturing'. IRES – Department of Economics – UCL (Belgium), Discussion Paper no.9517, June.

Thomas, K.P. (1996) 'Auto Bargaining in Canada, 1965–87', in Chan, S. (ed.), *Foreign Direct Investment in a Changing Global Political Economy*. Basingstoke: Macmillan.

Thomsen, S. (2000) 'Investment Patterns in a Long Term Perspective', *Working Papers on International Investment*, 2000/2, OECD, April.

Thomsen, S. & Woolcock, S. (1993) *Direct Investment and European Integration: Competition Among Firms and Governments*. London: Pinter.

Thorpe, N. (1997) 'Workers who Rise and Shine', *The Scotsman*, 7 February.

Tickell, A., Peck, J. & Dicken, P. (1995) 'The Fragmented Region: Business, the State and Economic Development in North West England', in Rhodes, M. (ed.), *The Regions and the New Europe: Patterns in Core and Periphery Development*. Manchester: Manchester UP.

Tighe, C. (1994) 'Grants Vital in Tipping the Investment Balance', *Financial Times*, 18 October.

Tighe, C. (1995a) 'Fujitsu in £816 Million Expansion at North East Microchip Plant', *Financial Times*, 9 September.

Tighe, C. (1995b) 'Survey of North East England: A Region Reinvented', *Financial Times*, 13 October.

Tighe, C. (1995c) 'Siemens Woos Top Executive from Fujitsu', *Financial Times*, 4 November.

Tighe, C. (1996a) 'Government Is Accused of Hostility. North-East England – "Issues of the 70s and 80s have largely gone away"', *Financial Times*, 8 February.

Tighe, C. (1996b) 'Nissan Prompted Revival of North-East Fortunes', *Financial Times*, 23 February.

Tödtling, F. (1994) 'The Uneven Landscape of Innovation Poles: Local Embeddedness and Global Networks', in Amin, A. & Thrift, N. (eds), *Globalisation, Institutions, and Regional Development in Europe*. Oxford: OUP.

Tokunaga, S. (1992) 'Japan's FDI-Promoting Systems and Intra-Asian Networks: New Investment and Trade Systems Created by the Borderless Economy', in Tokunaga, S. (ed.), *Japan's Foreign Investment and Asian Economic Interdependence*. Tokyo: University of Tokyo.

Tomaney, J. (1989) 'Workplace Flexibility in the North East', *Northern Economic Review*. 18: 16–29, Autumn.

Tomaney, J. (1990) 'The Reality of Workplace Flexibility', *Capital & Class*, 40: 29–60, Spring.

Tomaney, J. (1994a) 'Alternative Approaches to Restructuring in Traditional Industrial Regions: The Case of the Maritime Sector', *Regional Studies*, 28 (5): 544–9.

Tomaney, J. (1994b) 'A New Paradigm of Work Organisation and Technology?', Centre for Urban and Regional Studies. University of Newcastle Upon Tyne: CURDS Discussion Paper 8a, March.

Tomaney, J. (1995) 'Recent Developments in Irish Industrial Policy', *European Planning Studies*, 3 (1): 99–113.

Turok, I. (1993a) 'Inward Investment and Local Linkages: How Deeply Embedded is "Silicon Glen"?', *Regional Studies*, 27: 401–17.

Turok, I. (1993b) 'Contrasts in Ownership and Development: Local versus Global in "Silicon Glen"', *Urban Studies*, 30 (2): 365–86.

UNCTAD (1993) *World Investment Report: Transnational Corporations and Integrated International Production*. New York: United Nations.

UNCTAD (1994) *World Investment Report: Transnational Corporations; Employment and the Workplace*. New York: United Nations.

UNCTAD (1995a) *World Investment Report: Transnational Corporations and Competitiveness*. New York: United Nations.

UNCTAD (1995b) 'World Investment Report 1995: Transnational Corporations and Competitiveness', *Transnational Corporations*, 4 (3): 101–65, December.

UNCTAD (1996) *World Investment Report: Investment, Trade, and International Policy Arrangements*. New York: United Nations.

UNCTAD (1997) *World Investment Report*. New York: United Nations.

UNCTAD (1998) *World Investment Report: Trends and Determinants*. New York: United Nations.

UNCTAD (1999) *World Investment Report*. New York: United Nations.

Valery, N. (1992) 'Survey of Britain: In the Tracks of Nissan – Foreign Firms are Making Britain a Big Manufacturer Again', *The Economist*, 24 October.

Varaldo, R. & Ferrucci, L. (1996) 'The Evolutionary Nature of the Firm Within Industrial Districts', *European Planning Studies*, 4 (1): 27–34.

Venables, A.J. (1995) 'Economic Integration and the Location of Firms', *American Economic Review, Papers and Proceedings*, 85: 296–300.

Vernon, R. (1966) 'International Investment and International Trade in the Product Cycle', *Quarterly Journal of Economics*, 80 (2): 190–207.

Vernon, R. (1979) The Product Cycle Hypothesis in a New International Environment', *Oxford Bulletin of Economics and Statistics*, 41 (4): 255–67.

Vernon, R. (1993) 'Sovereignty at Bay: Twenty Years After', in Eden, L. & Potter, E.H. (eds), *Multinationals in the Global Political Economy*. New York: St. Martin's Press.

Vet, J. de (1993) 'Globalisation and Local and Regional Competitiveness', *STI Review*, 13: 89–127.

Vickery, G. (1996) 'Globalisation in the Computer Industry', in OECD, *Globalisation of Industry: Overview and Sector Reports*. Paris: OECD.

Wade, R. (1996) 'Globalisation and Its Limits: Reports of the Death of the National Economy are Greatly Exaggerated', in Berger, S. & Dore, R. (eds), *National Diversity and Global Competition*. Cornell UP.

Wagstyl, S. (1996a) 'UK Company News: Siemens Plans IT Acquisitions in UK', *Financial Times*, 13 June.

Wagstyl, S. (1996b) 'Nissan Considers Building New Model in Britain', *Financial Times*, 2 July.

Wagstyl, S. (1997) '150-Year-Old Start-Up That's Just Got Going: Siemens Chief Says the Engineering Company Is Only Just Starting To Exploit Its Potential', *Financial Times*, 11 April.

Walker, W. (1993) 'National Innovation Systems: Britain', in Nelson, R.R. (ed.), *National Systems of Innovation: A Comparative Analysis*. Oxford: OUP.

Wall Street Journal (1998) 'Costa Rica's Sales Pitch Lures High-Tech Giants Like Intel and Microsoft', 2 April.

Walton, R.E., Cutcher-Gershenfeld, J.E. & McKersie, R.B. (1994) *Strategic Negotiations: A Theory of Change in Labour–Management Relations*. Boston, MA: Harvard Business School Press.

WDA (2000) *Promoting Prosperity: WDA Corporate Plan 2000–2003*. Welsh Development Agency, Wales.

Weiermair, K. (1991) 'The Japanisation of European Industry', in Amin, A. & Dietrich, M. (eds), *Towards a New Europe?: Structural Change in the European Economy*. Aldershot: Edward Elgar.

Weiss, S.E. (1990) 'The Long Path to the IBM–Mexico Agreement: An Analysis of the Microcomputer Investment Negotiations. 1983–1986', *Journal of International Business Studies*, 21: 565–96, Autumn.

Wells Jr, L.T. (1998) 'Multinationals and the Developing Countries', *Journal of International Business Studies*, 29 (1): 101–14, 1st quarter.

Wells, L.T. and Wint, A.G. (1991) 'Facilitating Foreign Investment: Government Institutions to Screen, Monitor, and Service Investment from Abroad', *Foreign Investment Advisory Service*, Occasional Paper2. Washington, DC, The World Bank.

Wengenroth, U. (1997) 'Germany: Competition Abroad – Cooperation at Home, 1870–1990', in Chandler Jr, A.D., Amatori, F. & Hikino, T. (eds), *Big Business and the Wealth of Nations*. Cambridge: CUP.

Wendt, A. (1987) 'The Agent-Structure Problem in International Relations Theory', *International Organisation*, 41 (3): 335–70, Summer.

Westney, D.E. (1993) 'Institutionalisation Theory and the Multinational Corporation', in Ghoshal, S. & Westney, D.E. (eds), *Organisation Theory and the Multinational Corporation*. Basingstoke: Macmillan.

Wheeler, D. & Mody, A. (1992) 'International Investment Location Decisions: The Case of US Firms', *Journal of International Economics*, 33: 57–76.

Wickens, P. (1987) *The Road to Nissan: Flexibility, Quality, Teamwork*. Basingstoke: MacMillan.

Wighton, D. (1997) 'CBI Hints Support for Labour Policy', *Financial Times*, 19 March.

Wilkins, M. (1974) *The Maturing of Multinational Enterprise*. Cambridge, Mass: Harvard University Press.

Wilks, S. & Wright, M. (1987) 'Conclusion: Comparing Government–Industry Relations: States, Sectors, and Networks', in Wilks, S. & Wright, M. (eds), *Comparative Government–Industry Relations: Western Europe, the United States, and Japan*. Oxford: Clarendon.

Williamson, O.E. (1975) *Markets and Hierarchies: Analysis and Antitrust Implications*. New York: The Free Press.

Wilson, S. (1998) International Trade Manager. Northern Development Company (Export Mission). Private Interview, July.

Wint, A.G. (1993) 'Promoting Transnational Investment: Organising to Service Approved Investors', *Transnational Corporations*, 2 (1): 71–90, February.

WMRDA (1998) *West Midlands RDA Newsletter*. Birmingham: West Midlands Regional Development Agency, November.

Womack, J., Jones, D. & Roos, D. (1990) *The Machine that Changed the World*. Oxford: Maxwell Macmillan.

Woolcock, S. (1996) 'Competition among Forms of Corporate Governance in the European Community: The Case of Britain', in Berger, S. & Dore, R. (eds), *National Diversity and Global Competition*. Cornell UP.

Woolcock, S. & Wallace, H. (1985) 'European Community Regulation and National Enterprise', in Hayward, J. (ed.), *Industrial Enterprise and European Integration: From National Champions to International Champions in Western Europe*. Oxford. OUP.

Woolcock, S., Hodges, M. & Schreiber, K. (1991) *Britain, Germany and 1992: The Limits of Deregulation*. London: Pinter (Chatham House Papers).

World Bank (2000a) *World Development Report*.
World Bank (2000b) *World Development Indicators*.
Yeung, H. W-C. (1996) 'Attracting Foreign Investment? The Role of Investment Incentives in the ASEAN Operations Transnational Corporations', *The Pacific Review*, 9 (4): 505–29.
Yoffie, D.B. (1993) 'Foreign Direct Investment in Semiconductors', in Froot, K.A. (ed.), *Foreign Direct Investment*. London: University of Chicago Press.
Young, S., Hood, N. & Wilson, A. (1994) 'Targeting Policy as a Competitive Strategy for European Inward Investment Agencies', *European Urban and Regional Studies*, 1 (2): 143–59.
Yutaka, N. (1998) 'Japanese-Style Industrial Relations in Historical Perspective', in Harukiyo, H. & Hook, G.D. (eds), *Japanese Business Management: Restructuring for Low Growth and Globalisation*. London: Routledge.

Index